Fashioning Old and New

SEUH

18

STUDIES IN EUROPEAN URBAN HISTORY (1100–1800)

Fashioning Old and New

Changing Consumer Preferences in Europe (Seventeenth–Nineteenth Centuries)

Bruno Blondé, Natacha Coquery,
Jon Stobart and Ilja Van Damme (eds.)

BREPOLS

Cover illustration: Buying second-hand in Antwerp, end of the nineteenth century

Source: Private collection Janssens, Berchem

D/2009/0095/17
ISBN 978-2-503-52878-6
Printed in the E.U. on acid-free paper

Table of Contents

Editorial Preface

This volume originated from a session organised by Bruno Blondé, Natacha Coquery and Jon Stobart at the Eight International Conference on Urban History in Stockholm, 2006. Hence the editors would like to thank the board of the European Association of Urban Historians for granting them the possibility to organise the major session. The session's chief aim was to describe the relationship between the buying and selling of 'new' and 'old' goods in the seventeenth-nineteenth centuries. In line with the general approach of the conference –'Urban Europe in Comparative Perspective'– a comparative perspective was envisaged with contributions varying in thematic approaches as well as chronological and geographical scope. Although the majority of papers were presented at the Stockholm-conference, some contributions were recruited afterwards to improve the homogeneity of this present volume.

Thanks are due to the editorial board of the Brepols-Series 'Studies in European Urban History', and especially to the series editor, Marc Boone (Ghent University) for accepting this volume into the series. Additional funding for the publication of this volume was provided by the University of Antwerp and the project 'City and Society in the Low Countries, 1200–1800: space, knowledge, social capital' (Interuniversity Attraction Poles Programme – Belgian State – Federal Public Planning Service, PPS Science Policy).

Bruno Blondé, Natacha Coquery, Jon Stobart
and Ilja Van Damme
Antwerp, October 22nd 2008

CHAPTER 1

Fashioning Old and New or Moulding the Material Culture of Europe (Late Seventeenth–Early Nineteenth Centuries)

Bruno Blondé and Ilja Van Damme[1] – University of Antwerp, Centre for Urban History, Belgium

1.1 Changing Consumer Preferences: an Introduction

Few authors would deny the key importance of culture in understanding consumer behaviour. However, classical economic analysis, as is well known, has major problems in dealing with historical and cultural contingent categories such as 'fashion', 'taste' and 'consumer preferences' (Berg, 2001: 521–525). Standard consumer theory reduces the problem of consumer choice to a constrained maximization of utility: taste is discarded as something left unexplained after economic modelling has filtered out the effects of relative price changes, income development, social inequality, and other calculable factors (Ranchetti, 1998: 21–45). By contrast, in historical studies 'taste' and 'consumer preferences' have always played a major role. Changes in consumers' taste were even at the hearth of the 'industrious revolution' thesis, as it is comprehensively forwarded by Jan De Vries (2008) – to name just one influential example. Indeed, the early modern era is now largely recognized as a period in which consumer preferences fundamentally altered, without necessarily being triggered by patterns of economic growth or income redistribution (for instance Brewer and Porter, 1993; Schuurman, De Vries and Van der Woude, 1997). Hence the importance of complementing economic analysis with historical studies that try to grasp the ways in which people moulded and appropriated changing material cultures.

The general pattern of consumer changes occurring in the time frame 1650–1850 are largely known, and will be repeatedly recalled in the present volume (among others by Barnett, chapter 6; and Blondé, chapter 5). To summarize: at least from the end of the seventeenth century onwards, the 'commodity bundles' of households started to alter and diversify. Imported and exotic products, such as tobacco, sugar, chocolate, coffee, tea and the so-called *chinoiseries* played a major role in this process (see also Coquery, chapter 8). They quickly spread through urban and, later, rural societies in England and on the Continent alike (Van Damme, chapter 7). Their appropriation and use in daily consumer patterns created novel, derivative products like pipes, coffee kettles and tea sets. Moreover, local producers and

1 Ilja Van Damme is a Postdoctoral Fellow of the Fund for Scientific Research – Flanders (FWO-Vlaanderen). We whish to thank our co-editors, Natacha Coquery and Jon Stobart, for their insightful comments on this chapter.

retailers stimulated this evolution by an intensive process of import substitution and product innovation (Van der Wee, 1988: 307–381; Styles, 1993 and 2000; Berg, 1998, 2002 and 2004; and Crask, 1999). A whole series of product and process innovations contributed to a 'new' material culture, with 'new luxuries' that developed a different set of characteristics compared to the 'old luxuries' (De Vries, 2003: 41–56; Roche, 1989 and 1997; Weatherill, 1988). Durability, ostentation and intrinsic value declined in importance relative to the use of new and less durable materials. Cheapness, design, pleasurably uses and accessibility became overriding criteria (Clifford, 1999: 147–168). Ever larger quantities of textile and household objects were marketed in increasingly different styles, colours and formats. Snuffboxes, watches and toys, for instance, testify to this pleasurable proliferation of 'gadgets' in daily consumer practices (Fennetaux, chapter 2; and Dequidt, chapter 3). But this product proliferation contributed to an early modern kind of 'consumer choice-stress' as well (Blondé and Van Damme, 2007). The number of alternatives open to consumers enlarged considerably: chairs could be made from wood, rush bottomed, furnished with leather, or upholstered with cloth. Wigs were worn *en bonnet*, *à bourse*, or *à cadogan*, just as books diversified into *in-folio*, *in-quarto*, *in-douze*, large and small, square shaped or rectangular, from the highest to the lowest quality (Kwass, 2006: 646–647). Consumption was solidly entwined with an individual expression of the self, constructed through a myriad variability of consumer goods. Because of the rising circulation of objects, the materiality of the world – and the relationship between people and things themselves – became conceptualized and food for discussion (Berg, 2003). The idea of signifying respectability, comfort, economic utility and even social progress through the act of spending did much to legitimize the material vices of the human 'beehive' (Crowley, 2001; Smith, 2002; Kwass, 2003). Fashion was central to the changes in the period under scrutiny. Although fashion changes were obviously not new, their quickening pace and growing pervasiveness significantly altered material culture (Ribereiro, 1991: 329–345). Last but not least: thanks to the cheapness of their materiality, the 'new luxuries' spread far beyond the households of urban middle-rank consumers and contributed decisively to a blurring of social boundaries.

The present volume takes these changes in the material culture to heart. The articles originate from a session organised by Bruno Blondé, Natacha Coquery and Jon Stobart at the 2006 Stockholm conference of the European Association of Urban Historians. The session's chief aim was not to describe the changing production, distribution and retail patterns that shaped, accompanied or resulted from the consumer transformations described above. Accounting for the overriding *consumer culture* in this period would probably be too ambitious an enterprise. Moreover, there are already several influential monographs that try to tackle the interplay between culture, society and economics on a grand scale. Such studies tend to explore the relationship between consumption and individual or group identities, often framed in terms of gender or respectability (for instance Vickery, 1998; and Carter, 2002). They concentrate on the development of material cultures, the meaning of goods, and their links with cultural and social changes (Smith, 2002; Berg, 2005; Cohen, 2005). Whilst these volumes present compelling arguments, they focus primarily on new goods and changing fashions as the driving force behind consumption and the construction of social identities. None addresses as such the consumption of second-hand goods or the motivations to buy 'used' goods – let alone the interplay between 'new' and 'old'. Only Beverly Lemire (1991b and 1997) does this in a sustained way, but here evidence and arguments are 'limited' to clothing only. This book seeks to address these caveats by presenting new comparative research across north-western Europe, focusing on France, England and the Southern Netherlands in particular. Our aim is to explore practices and mentalities on the supply, demand and distribution sides of society which influenced the changing consumer preferences towards 'new' and 'old' objects from the end of the seventeenth century onwards. As such, new empirical evidence on early modern production, consumption and retailing will be presented, and some basic characteristics of the early-modern interplay between the production, consumption and exchange of new and old goods will be analysed.

1.2 Novelty, Give Us Novelty!

Nowadays, a continuing 'cry for the new', it is said, drives consumerism (Campbell, 1992; Slater, 1997). People are producing and buying new goods in ever larger quantities. As soon as old products show the slightest sign of wear, human wants switch to new desires: a new car, the 'latest' computer, 'novel' furniture, or clothes that are perceived *à la mode*. Mirroring these carefree practices are the typical problems associated with our 'affluent' and 'throwaway-society' (Strasser, 1999). Once perceived as worn-out, the same cars, computers, furniture and clothes are confined to the rubbish bin too often, without even reclaiming valuable components of the product. At best some materials are 'downcycled' in a degraded form or use, without any marketing potential or even ecological bonus (McDonough and Braungart, 2002). The motivations behind this 'neophiliac behaviour' are complex and have been subject to sociological analysis from the days of Thorstein Veblen and Georg Simmel to the recent writings of Jean Baudrillard, Colin Campbell and Grant McCracken (Veblen, 1970; Simmel, 1957: 541–549; Baudrillard, 1970; Campbell, 1987; McCracken, 1988). But historically too, this novelty-driven consumerism can be analyzed as a contingent process, changing the way we produce, distribute and consume material objects.

Deciphering how these altering consumer preferences were changing and, in a dialectical process, changed our practices and mental constructs towards 'old' and 'new' goods is the central focus of this book. Fondness for novelties was certainly a watershed in what McKendrick, Brewer and Plumb have dubbed, in polemic terms, 'the birth of a consumer society' (McKendrick, Brewer and Plumb, 1982). In the wake of this debate crucial insights were gained in the evolution of our present-day acquisitive consumerism in Western Europe (Schama, 1987; Weatherhill, 1988; Shammas, 1990; Goldthwaite, 1993; Brewer and Porter, 1993; Roche, 1997). In the late seventeenth and eighteenth centuries the quest for novelties enhanced a 'tyranny of fashion'. In fact, it was the folly of fashion that heavily affected production, trade and the consumer habits of an ever greater number of people. Silverware was recast in new and fashionable designs, as were earthenware, furniture, wall-hangings, paintings, and other widespread household possessions. Peddlers, fashion dealers, and the mushrooming 'à la mode' shops, sold fashionable 'populuxe': items wedged between popular necessities and aristocratic luxuries (Fairchilds, 1993; Kwass, 2006: 640). Relativly affordable toiletries and portable accessories came within reach of the middling sort, hence the rapid success of wigs, handkerchiefs, fans, watches, canes, umbrellas, toys, snuffboxes, and so on. Appealing to men and women, a bouquet of colourful laces, ribbons, and other haberdasheries adorned eighteenth-century clothing, which in itself underwent striking transformations. Decoration, colour and cut were ever more rapidly adjusted to the latest fashion, while mixed or lighter fabrics – especially the initially imported cottons – rose in popularity (Lemire, 1991b). Consumer preferences were moulded by, amongst other things, fashion magazines, such as the *Journal du Goût, The Lady's Magazine, Cabinet des Modes, Magasin des Modes Nouvelles Françaises et Anglaises,* which appeared simultaneously in France and England, soon followed by Italy, and the German and Dutch speaking parts of Europe (Ribereiro, 1991). As such, geographical differences in material culture, which had previously differentiated one region from another, and towns from the countryside, began to evaporate due to the French, and after 1760 English, inspired fashion changes (see also Van Damme, chapter 7). In some sense the fashion system imbued the pan-European consumer taste with a new sense of uniformity and harmony (Boucher, 1987: 252–253). Socially as well, the disappearance of the age-old sumptuary laws and material similarities between the middling and upper tiers of society gave rise to comments on the mixing of the hierarchical ladder (Hunt, 1996: 357).

1.3 Old Is Out?

All these changes crystallized in the late seventeenth and eighteenth centuries, out of an already well commercialized and highly urbanized European economy. But the nascent tandem of neophiliac and fashion-driven behaviour triggered still other alterations in the material culture. In 1734 a Ghent poet, Jacobus Hije, noted, not without irony, the questionable taste of his fellow citizens: 'Look at the grace of those badly made rags that are followed by everybody: those are the newest fashions' (cited in Braekman, 2002: 65). And several years later, in 1759, no less a person than Adam Smith commented in a similar vein: swift fashion cycles were held responsible for the fact that English furniture and clothing were made no longer 'of very durable materials' (cited in Berg and Clifford, 1999: 10; Edwards, chapter 4). Yielding to the 'tyranny' of newness and fashion, changes in production techniques and the use of less costly basic materials (such as cotton or porcelain) brought fourth a material culture made out of lighter, more breakable and less durable products (Nenadic, 1994; Blondé and Van Damme, forthcoming).

Unfortunately, we still know far too little about secondary market practices, akin to the economies of scarcity of early-modern times (see, however, Woodward, 1985 and 1998; Reith, 2003). Only recently has the history of consumption become interested in the so-called 'alternative' or 'creative' forms of consumption, including the study of second-hand markets. With the writings of Beverly Lemire, a crucial link was made between the burgeoning studies of consumption and the use of second-hand goods in the past (Lemire, 1988, 1991a and b, 1997). Lemire's research demonstrated an important but neglected aspect of pre-industrial demand. The 'birth of a consumer society' was grounded not only in the appearance of new products and new industries; a similar drive manifested itself in the handling, buying and selling of second-hand goods. Use and re-use, adaptation and recycling of 'old' goods generated significant economic, social and cultural dynamics (see Fontaine, 2008). It provided employment, precluded the unnecessary waste of expensive and durable materials, and provisioned different social groups with otherwise unaffordable quality goods, 'novelty' and 'fashion' (Lemire, 2005: 30).

One major aim of this volume is to question the long-term evolution of these secondary markets. From the perspective of the supply side, it is often stated that use and reuse of older products is only economically efficient in societies with an abundance of low wage labour and a scarcity of high-priced resources (see Fox, 1957; Benjamin and Kormendi, 1974; and Scitovsky, 1994). Nowadays, at least in Western societies, the slackening commercial exploitation of 'used' goods and materials is all too obvious: flea markets, swap meets, garage sales, outlet stores and retro shops are only viable as social and cultural constructs (Gregson and Crewe, 2003).[2] Increasing mass-production and technological change has made second-hand markets quasi obsolete, with the exception of some specialized products (such as cars, books, arts and antiques). Only in the so-called 'developing nations' does second-hand exchange remain a complex and booming business (Hansen, 2000).

But exactly when and how did this evolution came about? And did the quest for novelties and fashionable products fundamentally affect consumer attitudes towards older products? The basic assumption goes as follows. Old products had to be replaced more often since their new and fashionable assets were more easily worn out: the ephemeral became attractive and sustained product-durability was made subordinate to style (Lipovetsky, 1987; Campbell, 1992). Wherever purchasing power allowed, household standards started to alter, with consumers aspiring to clean, healthy, and tasteful living (Crowley, 1999). According to Daniel Roche this evolution fostered a growing heap of discarded goods and an intensification of second-hand exchange and consumption (Roche, 1998: 222–223; see also Verlet, 1958: 28). Precisely newness and fashion made the pristine life of products shorter, thus injecting a larger quantity of secondary products in the economic cycle at a quickening pace. Products, eventually depreciated for the home market, could be transported to faraway places and start a new life all over again (see Berg, 2001: 546–552). However, Stena Nenadic rightly points out how *ceteris paribus* evolutions might have seriously crippled the existence of secondary markets in the long run (Nenadic, 1994: 134; Blondé and Van Damme, 2007: 85). In the end, second-hand products no longer had any substantial market value left, unwanted and unneeded by a socially widening base. Some products were even no longer recyclable because of the use of basic materials without any 'hoarding value' (Nijboer, 2005 and 2007).

It is tempting to sketch the balance between 'old' and 'new' in the eighteenth and nineteenth century in a schematic way (see Figure 1.1.). As the eighteenth century progressed the cry for newness and novelty may have indeed fundamentally affected the balance between 'new' and 'old' goods. 'Old goods' were increasingly pushed to the periphery of the consumer pattern. What counted was maintaining appearances, which – in the context of the time – implied being dressed according to the latest fashion (Styles, 1994; Styles and Vickery, 2006). Even second-hand carriages were advertised as 'fashionable', after being upholstered in an up-to-date manner (Stobart, chapter 9). The process cannot be traced easily, since almost all commercial circuits engaged in the selling of both 'new' and 'second-hand' objects (Van Damme, 2006; and various chapters in this book). But, for obvious reasons, the second-hand guilds and auctions were especially affected by the craze for novelties. Whereas the secondary markets were complex venues for polite shopping in

2 Most recently, the Internet has created, with the success of *eBay*, yet another culturally significant locus of second-hand exchange (see Wagner, 2006: 15).

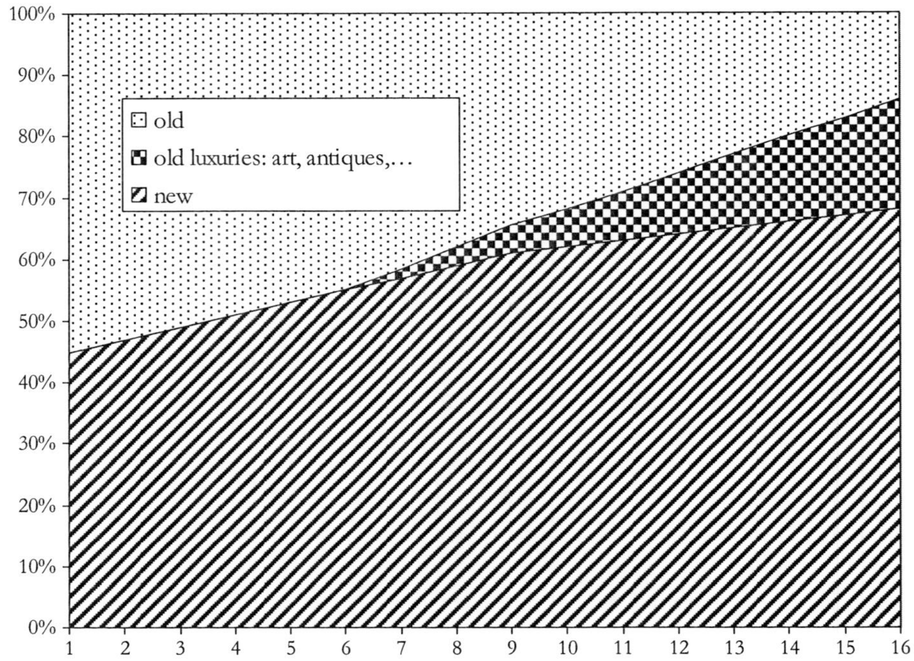

Figure 1.1. Schematic model of the evolution of second-hand exchange and consumption (X-axis representing years; Y-axis representing volumes exchanged and consumed in percentages)

the sixteenth and seventeenth centuries, they were now increasingly considered as inferior, 'lower end' commercial circuits. In nineteenth-century Sweden wealthy customers gradually withdrew from auctions, while landless and poorer people increasingly showed up (Lilja, Murhem, Ulväng, chapter 12). This tendency eventually gave rise of a series of specialized and more respectable auctions, where luxurious and valuable second-hand stuff were sold separate from the majority of worn-out pots and pans (Lilja, Murhem, Ulväng, chapter 12). Lyna and Guichard describe meticulously how spatially and culturally specialized auctions developed into autonomous, independent commercial settings ruled by sociability, respectability, connoisseurship, and civilized manners but also by money (Lyna, chapter 11; Guichard, chapter 13). Whereas affluent seventeenth-century citizens of Antwerp sold and bought costly paintings on the Friday Market, their successors in the Age of Enlightenment preferred the respectable auctions at the 'Kolveniershof'. In Paris the 'hôtel des ventes' served similar cultural aspirations. Sales catalogues increasingly turned into tools for 'expertise, pleasure and fantasy' (Guichard, chapter 13).

In the end 'old' grew so scarce that it derived value again from this scarcity. Interestingly, this marginalization of 'old objects' added value to goods with history and patina (Charpy, chapter 14; Edwards, chapter 4; McCracken, 1988). It is difficult to pinpoint an exact chronology in this respect, but already at the end of the eighteenth century toys were associated with sentiment and memory rather than with novelty (Fennetaux, chapter 2). In furniture as well, 'old things' gained in interest at some point in the late eighteenth century (Edwards, chapter 4). By redecorating their houses with remains from the past and, tellingly, from the provinces, nineteenth-century bourgeois Parisians bought themselves history, respectability, gentility. As early as the 1830s, Parisian second-hand shops were pushed away to poorer wards or suburban areas, while antiquaries settled in fashionable districts. Even at that time, luxurious 'old' was fashionable. Yet although Paris remained unrivalled as a fashion-maker (Gillet, chapter 10), it was the provinces that supplied the capital with history, authenticity and memory (Charpy, chapter 14). Some caveats are in place, though, since the sources most studied until now – newspaper advertisements and auction catalogues – provide a skewed view by primarily targeting a rich clientele. Indeed, the larger part of formerly important secondary markets continued to be marginalised in value terms (Lemire, 1988; Nenadic, 1994). Notable, for instance, is the evolution of the initially corporate organised old-cloth sellers: rich and respected during the early modern times, they evolved into mere rag, old iron and bone collectors in the nineteenth century (Ginsburg, 1980; Du Mortier, 1991; Steffens, 1997).

1.4 Fashioning Old and New

Most of the chapters in this volume fit into the outline described above. Historical developments, however, were always more stratified and diversified according to chronology and region studied; change never followed straightforward, linear paths. Firstly, the boundaries between markets for 'new' and 'old' products were never that clear. In the eighteenth century 'old' and 'new' often peacefully coexisted. Furthermore, both 'markets' cooperated intensely. Retailers advertised 'new' and 'old' for sale simultaneously (Stobart, chapter 9), though very often the price range of 'old' objects floated far below the prices paid for 'new equivalents' (Fennetaux, chapter 2; Dequidt, chapter 3). Price and product diversity was an important publicity marker for eighteenth-century shopkeepers – a way of appealing to different segments of the market (Stobart, chapter 9; and Gillet, chapter 10). Moreover, by offering the service of taking in second-hand objects from wealthy customers, retailers simultaneously enhanced both a fashion-driven consumer model for the wealth-off and a secondary market model for the less affluent customers – though here as well boundaries were never as sharp as phrased (Coquery, 2004: 68–69; Edwards, chapter 4). Retailers simultaneously offered novelties and advise about fashion to those who could afford it, while also keeping second-hand goods in stock to satisfy more modest consumer expectations (Verley, 1997; Gillet, chapter 10). Second-hand goods often equalled luxuries and high quality products, since some shopkeepers even specialised in barter of fashionable luxuries with noble households with insufficient cash at their disposal (Coquery, 2004).

On a more material level as well, the boundaries between 'new' and 'old' were never clear. Shopkeepers and second-hand sellers, for instance, specialised in repairing or even upgrading old-fashioned or worn-out objects (Dequidt, chapter 3; Gillet, chapter 10). On the first of June 1790, for instance, the local *Gazette* of Antwerp advertised the selling of 'a fine bedstead of green cloth, upholstered after the newest taste of two years ago' (SBA, nr. 568713, *GvA*).[3] Here presumably an old object was advertised that had turned into a fashionable item again (see also Figure 1.2.). Watchmakers also did their best to repair old watches and make

3 *'Een schoonen groenen stoffen imperiael, over 2 jaer nieuw gemaekt na de nieuwste smaek'.*

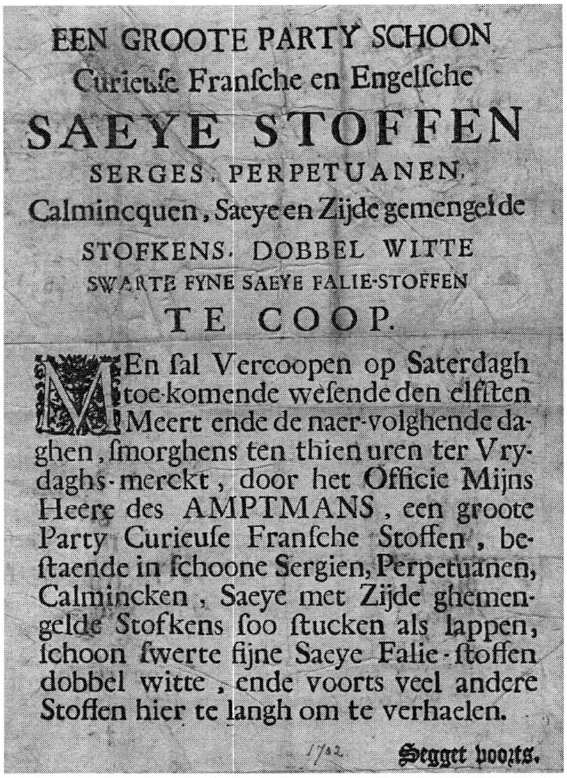

EEN GROOTE PARTY SCHOON
Curieuſe Franſche en Engelſche
SAEYE STOFFEN
SERGES, PERPETUANEN,
Calmincquen, Saeye en Zijde gemengelde
STOFKENS. DOBBEL WITTE
SWARTE FYNE SAEYE FALIE-STOFFEN
TE COOP.

MEn ſal Vercoopen op Saterdagh toe-komende weſende den elfſten Meert ende de naer-volghende daghen, ſmorghens ten thien uren ter Vrydaghs-merckt, door het Officie Mijns Heere des AMPTMANS, een groote Party Curieuſe Franſche Stoffen, beſtaende in ſchoone Sergien, Perpetuanen, Calmincken, Saeye met Zijde ghemengelde Stofkens ſoo ſtucken als lappen, ſchoon ſwerte fijne Saeye Falie-ſtoffen dobbel witte, ende voorts veel andere Stoffen hier te langh om te verhaelen.

Segget voorts.

Figure 1.2. 'Affiche' of a public sale of fashionable textiles on the Friday Market, the most important commercial place in Antwerp for handling second-hand products

Source: *Collectie Internationaal Instituut voor Sociale Geschiedenis*, Amsterdam (we wish to thank Dries Lyna for pointing this out).

them look new again. Conversely, in the nineteenth century a whole industry of fake 'old' developed (Charpy, chapter 14). Shopkeepers sold new and old items, engaged in repairing goods, bartered and sometimes rented out and they did so with an increasing amount of diverse products. As a result, shops remained places where not only a wide variety of commodities but also people of different social ranks could mingle.

Needless to say, the boundaries between consumers of 'new' and 'old' can not be drawn firmly. The historical study of recycling is opening innovative perspectives that reach beyond a consumerism solely defined by modern self-centred acquisitiveness (Trentmann, 2004: 377–401). As Dequidt argues in chapter 3, some objects were loaded with emotional value and in these cases 'ageing' went hand in hand with adding value (see also Barnett, chapter 6). Indeed, people and things have life-histories of their own, dominated by use and re-use, frequency of purchase, disposal and dispersal, gifts, storage and lending, pawning and circulation, renewal or changes in one's lifestyle (Douglas and Isherwood, 1979: 114–127; also see Matchette, 2006). Studying the retentiveness of people towards 'older' products is one way of grasping the 'biographies of things', and, more broadly, placing the history of consumption in an essential social and cultural perspective (Kopytoff, 1986; Miller, 1995). Recently ennobled Antwerp citizens in the eighteenth century borrowed from symbolic systems in which 'old luxuries' played a dominant role, although, in general, they relied heavily upon the 'new luxuries' of the time (Blondé, chapter 5). The Antwerp noblemen studied here were, undoubtedly, forerunners of modernity and novelty. At the same time they also played upon 'patina' and 'luxury' to acquire social status. In doing so they invested both in 'old luxuries' and 'novel toys'.

The separate logics of 'old' and 'new' luxuries could easily converge in one product category. Owning silverware, for instance, clearly served the centuries-old purposes of ostentation and value storage. It did not prevent silver from continuously being melted down and reformed according to the latest fashion (Blondé, chapter 5; Stobart, chapter 9). Toyshops, although specialising in the quintessential eighteenth-century novelties, also acted as pawnbrokers buying old plate and silver (Fennetaux, chapter 2). In a comparable way, Antwerp bourgeois households participated in a *tour à la mode*, a fashionable promenade with richly decorated coaches. While the showing of one's rank with horses and carriages was already a well-established ritual, the quick replacements of carriage-upholstering and embellishments were enhanced by rapidly changing fashion cycles.

Material culture, of course, is about more than acquiring or owning. The mere ownership of toys did not distinguish the owner: status was marked by the way in which they were deployed. It did not suffice to own an elaborate snuffbox; it needed to be handled with an elegant performance (Fennetaux, chapter 2). Similarly, watches were supposed to be worn in the right manner (Dequidt, chapter 3). In her contribution to this volume Amy Barnett surpasses well-known quantified histories of consumer innovation to see how goods functioned spatially and culturally within the houses and households of eighteenth-century Norwich (Barnett, chapter 6). While the exchange value of chinaware was modest, its social value – carefully constructed in rituals of domestic sociability – was much higher.

These and similar observations tend to qualify the preliminary conclusions that can be drawn from the contributions of this book. In the centuries under scrutiny here, 'new' and 'old' were subject to rapidly changing cultural constructions. The interplay between first-hand and secondary markets was extremely complex. Yet a major lesson to be drawn from these papers is that 'history matters'. People studying secondary markets run the risk of dealing with auctions, barter, pawning, and other vital social and economic practices as an *histoire immobile.* In doing so they tend to over-emphasize aspects of continuity. In reality, nothing is less true. The economic and cultural balances between 'new' and 'old' were both highly stratified and complex, but they were continuously shifting as well. And, to end where this introduction started, it was primarily a cultural process, a process of fashioning 'old' and 'new' that accounts for this historical evolution.

Bibliography

Primary Sources

Published sources

Stadsbibliotheek Antwerpen (SBA), nr. 568713, *Gazette van Antwerpen* (*GvA*), 1790.

Literature

Baudrillard, J. (1970) *La société de consommation*, Paris.

Benjamin, D.K. and Kormendi, R.C. (1974) 'The interrelationship between markets for new and used durable goods', *Journal of Law and Economics*, 17, 381–401.

Berg, M. (1998) 'Product innovation in core consumer industries in eighteenth-century Britain', Berg, M. and Bruland, K. (eds.), *Technological revolutions in Europe: historical perspectives*, Cheltenam, 138–157.

Berg, M. (1999) 'New commodities, luxuries and their consumers in eighteenth-century England', Berg, M. and Clifford, H. (eds.), *Consumers and luxury. Consumer culture in Europe 1650–1850*, Manchester, 63–83.

Berg, M. (2001) 'French fancy and cool Brittania: the fashion markets of Early Modern Europe', Cavaciocchi, S. (ed.), *Fiere e mercati nella integrazione della economie Europee secc. XIII–XWVIII*, Prato, 519–556.

Berg, M. (2002) 'From imitation to invention: creating commodities in eighteenth-century Britain', *Economic History Review*, 55, 1–30.

Berg, M. (2003) 'Asian luxuries and the making of the European consumer revolution', Berg, M. and Eger, E. (eds.), *Luxury in the eighteenth century. Debates, desires and delectable goods*, Hampshire and New York, 228–244.

Berg, M. (2004) 'In pursuit of luxury: global history and British consumer goods in the eighteenth century', *Past & Present*, 182, 85–142.

Berg, M. (2005) *Luxury and pleasure in eighteenth-century Britain*, Oxford.

Berg, M. and Clifford, H. (eds.) (1999) *Consumers and luxury. Consumer culture in Europe 1650–1850*, Manchester.

Blondé, B. and Van Damme, I. (2007) 'Een crisis als uitdaging? Kleinhandelsevoluties en verbruiksveranderingen te Antwerpen (ca. 1648-ca. 1748)', *Tijdschrift voor Sociale en Economische Geschiedenis*, 4 (2007), 61–88.

Blondé, B. and Van Damme, I. (forthcoming) 'Retail growth and consumer changes in a declining urban economy: Antwerp (1650–1750)'.

Boucher, F. (1987) *20,000 years of fashion. The history of costume and personal adornment*, New York.

Braekman, W.L. (2002) *Leven en werk van de Gentse rederijker Jacobus Hije (1667–1749)*, Brussel.

Brewer, J. and Porter, R. (eds.) (1993) *Consumption and the world of goods*, London and New York.

Campbell, C. (1987) *The romantic ethic and the spirit of consumerism*, Oxford.

Campbell, C. (1992) 'The desire for the new. Its nature and social location as presented in theories of fashion and modern consumerism', Silverstone, R. and Hirsch, E. (eds.), *Consuming technologies: media and information in domestic spaces*, London, 48–64.

Carter, P. (2002) *Men and the emergence of polite society*, Harlow.

Cipolla, C. (1976) *Before the industrial revolution: European society and economy, 1000–1700*, London.

Clifford, H. (1999) 'A commerce with things: the value of precious metalwork in Early Modern England', Berg, M. and Clifford, H. (eds.), *Consumers and luxury. Consumer culture in Europe 1650–1850*, Manchester, 147–168.

Coquery, N. (2004) 'The language of Success. Marketing and Distributing Semi-luxury Goods in Eigtheenth-century Paris', *Journal of Design History*, Special Issue: *Disseminating Design: The French Connection*, 17, 68–69.

Cohen, D. (2005) *Household Goods*, Yale.

Craske, M. (1999) 'Plan and control: design and the competition spirit in early and mid-eighteenth century England', *Journal of Design History*, 12, 187–216.

Crowley, J.E. (1999) 'The sensibility of comfort', *American Historical Review*, 104, 749–782.

Crowley, J.E. (2001) *The Invention of comfort: sensibilities and design in Early Modern Britain and Early America*, Baltimore.

De Vries, J. (2003) 'Luxury in the Dutch Golden Age in theory and practice', Berg, M. and Eger, E. (eds.), *Luxury in the Eighteenth Century. Debates, Desires and Delectable Goods*, Hampshire and New York, 41–56.

De Vries, J. (2008) *The Industrious Revolution. Consumer behavior and the household economy, 1650 to the present*, Cambridge.

Du Mortier, B.M. (1991) 'Tweedehandskleding in de zeventiende eeuw', *Textielhistorische Bijdragen*, 31, 39–59.

Douglas, M. and Isherwood, B. (1979), *The world of goods: towards an anthropology of consumption*, New York.

Fairchilds, C. (1993) 'The production and marketing of populuxe goods in eighteenth-century Paris', Brewer, J. and Porter, R. (eds.), *Consumption and the world of goods*, London and New York, 228–248.

Fontaine, L. (2003) 'The Circulation of Luxury Goods in Eighteenth-Century Paris: Social Redistribution and an Alternative Currency', Berg, M. and Eger, E. (eds.), *Luxury in the Eighteenth Century. Debates, Desires and Delectable Goods*, Hampshire and New York, 89–102.

Fontaine, L. (ed.) (2008) *Alternative Exchanges. Second-Hand Circulations from the Sixteenth Century to The Present*, Oxford and New York.

Fox, A.H. (1957) 'A theory of second-hand markets', *Economia*, 24, 99–115.

Ginsburg, M. (1980) 'Rag to riches: the second-hand clothes trade 1700–1978', C*ostume*, 14, 121–135.

Glorieux, G. (2002) *À l'Enseigne de Gersaint. Edme-François Gersaint, marchand d'art sur le pont Notre-Dame (1694–1750)*, Seyssel.

Goldthwaite, R.A. (1993) *Wealth and the demand for art in Italy 1300–1600*, Baltimore.

Gregson, N. and Crewe, L. (2003) *Second-hand cultures*, Oxford and New York.

Hansen, K.T. (2000) *Salaula. The world of secondhand clothing and Zambia*, Chicago and London.

Hunt, A. (1996) *Governance of the consuming passions. A history of sumptuary law*, London and New York.

Kopytoff, I. (1986) 'The cultural biography of things: commodification as a process', Appadurai, A. (ed.), *The social life of things*, Cambridge, 64–94.

Kwass, M. (2003) 'Ordering the world of goods: consumer revolution and the classification of objects in eighteenth-century France', *Representations*, 82, 87–116.

Kwass, M. (2006) 'Big Hair: a Wig history of consumption in eighteenth-century France', *American Historical Review*, 111, 631–659.

Lemire, B. (1988) 'Consumerism in preindustrial and early industrial England: the trade in second-hand clothes', *Journal of British Studies*, 27, 1–24.

Lemire, B. (1991a) 'Peddling fashion: salesmen, pawnbrokers, taylors, thieves and the second-hand clothes trade in England, c. 1700–1800', *Textile History*, 1, 22, 67–82.

Lemire, B. (1991b) *Fashion's favourite: the cotton trade and the consumer in Britain, 1660–1800*, Oxford.

Lemire, B. (1997) *Dress, culture and commerce: the English clothing trade before the factory 1660–1800*, Basingstoke.

Lemire, B. (2005) 'Shifting currency: the culture and economy of the second hand trade in England, c. 1600–1850', Palmer, A. and Clark, H. (eds.), *Old clothes, new looks: second hand fashion*, Oxford and New York, 29–48.

Lipovetsky, G. (1987) *L'empire de l'éphémère. La mode et son destin dans les sociétés modernes*, Paris.

Matchette, A. (2006) 'To have and have not: the disposal of household furnishings in Florence', *Renaissance Studies*, 20, 701–716.

McDonough, W. and Braungart, M. (2002) *Cradle to cradle: remaking the way we make things*, New York.

McKendrick, N., Brewer, J. and Plumb, J.H. (1982), *The birth of a consumer society. The commercialization of eighteenth-century England*, London.

McCracken, G. (1988) *Culture and consumption. New approaches to the symbolic character of consumer goods and activities*, Bloomington and Indianapolis.

Miller, D. (ed.) (1995) *Acknowledging consumption. A review of new studies*, London and New York.

Nenadic, S. (1994) 'Middle-rank consumers and domestic culture in Edinburgh and Glasgow 1720–1840', *Past & Present*, 145, 122–156.

Nenadic, S. (1999) 'Romanticism and the urge to consume in the first half of the nineteenth century', Berg, M. and Clifford, H. (eds.), *Consumers and luxury. Consumer culture in Europe 1650–1850*, Manchester, 208–227.

Nijboer, H. (2005) 'Fashion and the Early Modern consumer evolution. A theoretical exploration and some evidence from seventeenth-century Leeuwarden', Blondé, B., Briot, E., Coquery, N. and Van Aert, L. (eds.), *Retailers and consumer changes in Early Modern Europe. England, France, Italy and the Low Countries*, Tours, 21–36.

Nijboer, H. (2007) *De fatsoenering van het bestaan. Consumptie in Leeuwarden tijdens de Gouden Eeuw*, Groningen.

Ranchetti, F. (1998) 'Choice without utility? Some reflections on the loose foundations of standard consumer theory', Bianchi, M. (ed.), *The active consumer. Novelty and surprise in consumer choice*, London and New York, 21–45.

Reith, R. (2003) 'Recycling im späten Mittelalter und der frühen Neuzeit – eine Materialsammlung', *Frühneuzeit-Info*, 14, 47–65.

Ribereiro, A. (1991) 'Fashion in the eighteenth century: some Anglo-French comparisons', *Textile History*, 22, 329–345.

Roche, D. (1989) *La culture des apparences. Une histoire du vêtement XVIIe–XVIIIe siècle*, Paris.

Roche, D. (1997) *Histoire des choses banales. Naissance de la consommation XVIIe–XIXe siècle*, Paris.

Roche, D. (1998) *Le peuple de Paris. Essai sur la culture populaire au XVIIIe siècle*, Paris [1981].

Schama, S. (1987) *The embarrassment of riches: an interpretation of Dutch culture in the Golden age*, New York.

Schuurman, A., De Vries, J. and Van der Woude, A. (eds.) (1997) *Aards geluk. De Nederlanders en hun spullen van 1550 tot 1850*, Amsterdam.

Scitovsky, T. (1994) 'Towards a theory of second-hand markets', *Kyklos*, 47, 33–52.

Shammas, C. (1990) *The pre-industrial consumer in England and America*, Oxford.

Simmel, G. (1957) 'Fashion', *American Journal of Sociology*, 62, 541–549.

Slater, D. (1997) *Consumer culture and modernity*, Cambridge.

Smith, W.D. (2002) *Consumption and the making of respectability, 1600–1800*, New York and London.

Steffens, S. (1997) 'Des chiffoniers et fripiers belges entre 1800 et 1914', *International Paper History*, 7, 17–23.

Styles, J. (1993) 'Manufacturing, consumption and design in eighteenth-century England', Brewer, J. and Porter, R. (eds.), *Consumption and the world of goods*, London and New York, 527–554.

Styles, J. (1994) 'Clothing the North: The Supply of Non-élite Clothing in the Eigtheenth-Century North of England', *Textile History*, 25, 139–166.

Styles, J. (2000) 'Product innovation in early Modern London', *Past & Present*, 168, 124–169.

Styles, J. and Vickery, A. eds. (2006) *Gender, Taste, and Material Culture in Britain and North America, 1700–1830*, New Haven.

Strasser, S. (1999) *Waste and want: a social history of trash*, New York.

Trentmann, F. (2004) 'Beyond consumerism: new historical perspectives on consumption', *Journal of Contemporary History*, 39 (2004), 377–401.

Van Damme, I. (2006) 'Changing consumer preferences and evolutions in retailing. Buying and selling consumer durables in Antwerp (c. 1648-c. 1748)', Blondé, B., Stabel, P., Stobart, J. and Van Damme, I. (eds.), *Buyers and sellers. Retail circuits and practices in Medieval and Early Modern Europe*, Turnhout.

Van der Wee, H. (1988) 'Industrial dynamics and the process of urbanization and de-urbanization in the Low Countries from the Late Middle Ages to the eighteenth century. A synthesis', Van der Wee, H. (ed.), *The rise and decline of urban industries in Italy and in the Low Countries (late Middle Ages-Early Modern times)*, Leuven, 307–381.

Veblen, T. (1970) *The theory of the leisure class: an economic study of institutions*, London [1899].

Verlet, P. (1985) 'Le commerce des objets d'art et les marchands merciers à Paris au XVIIIe siècle', *Annales. Economies. Sociétés. Civilisations*, 13, 10–29.

Verley, P. (1987) *L'échelle du monde. Essai sur l'industrialisation de l'Occident*, Paris.

Vickery, A. (1998) *The gentleman's daughter*, Yale.

Wagner, C.G. (2006) 'The new "secondhand" market. The next new thing you buy may be old', *The Futurist*, march-april, 15.

Weatherill, L. (1988) *Consumer behaviour and material culture in Britain 1660–1760*, London.

Woodward, D. (1985) '"Swords into ploughshares": recycling in pre-industrial England', *The Economic History Review*, 38, 175–191.

Woodward, D. (1998) 'Straw, bracken and the Wicklow whale: the exploitation of natural resources in England since 1500', *Past & Present*, 159, 43–76.

PART I

Producing

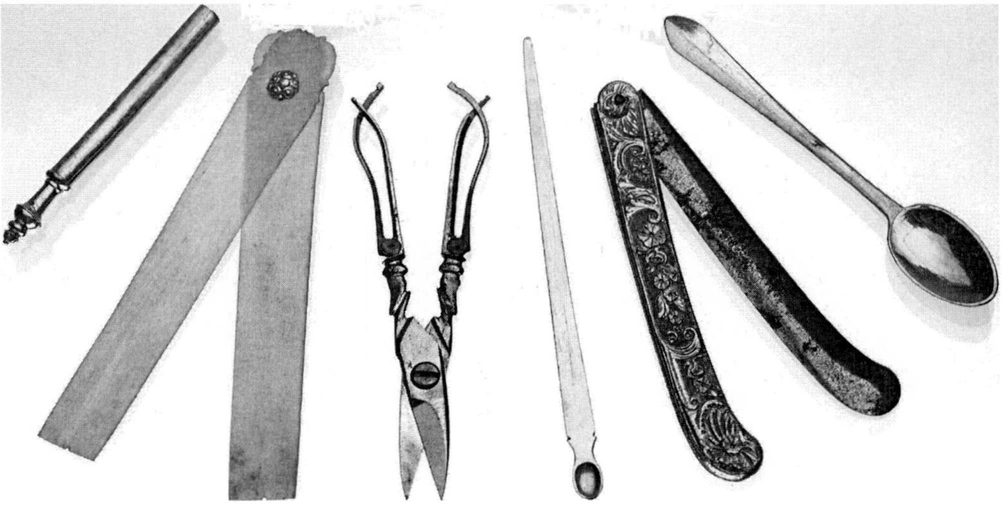

CHAPTER 2

Toying with Novelty: Toys, Consumption and Novelty in Eighteenth-Century Britain

Ariane Fennetaux[1] – Université Paris-Diderot, Paris 7, France

2.1 Introduction

In eighteenth-century discourses, the word toy referred not only to children's playthings or games but also, and more generally, to such fashionable luxury or semi-luxury objects as chatelaines,[2] etuis,[3] watch cases, scent-bottles, snuffboxes, cane heads and sword hilts. The tremendous fashion for such objects and the prevalence of the word toy in contemporary discourse point to their importance in the cultural landscape of eighteenth-century Britain: toys were at the core of several key aspects of the advent of the country's so-called 'consumer revolution' and offer insight into the role played by novelty in this phenomenon (McKendrick, Brewer and Plumb, 1982). Indeed, toys were sold by shops that epitomized the transformations of commerce and the appearance of a new consumer culture based on pleasure, taste, and entertainment; they were products of technological innovations and new manufacturing processes and were themselves novelties whose appeal rested on constantly new shapes and forms. Although toys allow us to grasp something of the crucial role of novelty in the advent of consumerism, they also highlight some of its complexities. Consumption often implied old and new being inter-related rather than opposed, as the commerce for toys will illustrate, while polemical discourses on luxury show that transformations brought about by consumption were not embraced unquestionably, but elicited ambivalent reactions in a country grappling with a series of economic, industrial and cultural changes. Adopting a multidisciplinary approach, this chapter will look at toys and their representations as means to explore the complex role of novelty in the advent of consumer culture in eighteenth-century Britain.

First, the trade for toys will be shown to be emblematic of the emergence of a new consumer culture based on the shop as a place of tasteful entertainment. Yet if toyshops were at the forefront of innovative selling techniques developed in new shops, they were also central to the economy of pawning and second-hand goods that was

1 I would like to thank LARCA, the research centre of the Department of English Studies of the Université Denis Diderot (Paris 7), for kindly providing a grant to help towards the illustrations of this article.

2 'A chatelaine is an ornamental appendage worn by ladies at their waist, supposed to represent the bunch of keys, etc. of a mediæval châtelaine: it consists of a number of short chains attached to the girdle or belt, etc., bearing articles of household use and ornament, as keys, corkscrew, scissors, penknife, pin-cushion, thimble-case, watch, etc., according to taste', (Oxford English Dictionary).

3 An etui or etwee is 'a small case, usually ornamental, for small articles, as bodkins, needles, toothpicks, etc' (OED). The term etui is usually used by curators to refer to such small portable cases to differentiate them from the non portable 'nécessaires'.

central to the emergence of consumerism. Next, the paper will turn to toys themselves and show the importance of novelty in defining these objects – whether because of the innovative materials from which they were made, the new industrial production patterns according to which they were manufactured, or their constant search for innovative design. As such, toys were a fitting embodiment of the transformations that the country was undergoing and became a discursive trope used to deride contemporary luxury or what was seen as a futile craving for ever newer and more useless possessions. Lastly, the success of these objects, most of which were portable, will be studied in the context of the emergence of a new urban lifestyle defined by increasing individual mobility in a city that had become the stage for the performance of taste and politeness. This coincided with the emergence of new criteria for social distinction brought about by increased consumption, which focused on body deportment and elegant gestures at a time when the mere possession of the object had ceased to constitute a reliable sign of social superiority. Of course, this association between toys and the performance of taste was not without its own paradoxes.

2.2 Toyshops: Between Innovation and Tradition

Eighteenth-century Britain witnessed the advent of new retail practices based on the shop – a separate place dedicated to retail from which the messy process of production had been expelled to make room for the more elegant practices involved in the new activity of 'shopping' (Stobart, 1998; Walsh, 1993, 1995a and b, 2001). This went along the appearance of innovative retail strategies, which tended to blur the line between consumption and entertainment. Toys, made by a variety of different craftsmen including jewellers, metalworkers, ivory workers and *japanners*, and sold in toyshops that were often seen as places of entertainment, curiosity and politeness, offer a particularly good illustration of the transformation of retail practices in eighteenth-century Britain.

In his book *A Description of the Trades* published in 1747, R. Campbell defined toy dealers as 'the sellers of or dealers in toys, (not the makers of them) not only of all sorts for the diversion of children (...) but [of] an exceeding variety of curiosities in gold, silver and steel, precious stones, shells, etc . . . whose business is not only clean and genteel, but touches much on taste, and the polite' (Campbell, 1747: 210). As underlined by this quotation, toy dealers sold toys but did not make them. Breaking from the traditional organization of guilds that linked production and retail, the toy trade thus epitomized the emergence of the shop as an independent space where taste and elegance prevailed, in a similar fashion to French *Marchands-Merciers* in eighteenth-century Paris (Sargentson, 1996 and 1998).

Whilst toy-making was located in the new industrial centres of the Midlands, it was in London that the most fashionable toyshops could be found. Almost entirely rebuilt after the Great Fire of 1666, eighteenth-century London appeared as a strikingly modern metropolis: its streets were large and arranged systematically, paved and lined with many shops that were admired by visitors for their window displays. From César de Saussure in the 1720s to Sophie von la Roche in the 1780s and Henry Meister in 1799, European visitors to the capital were unanimously struck by the elegance of London's streets and shops (Saussure, 1995: 22; von la Roche, 1933: 86–87; Meister, 1799: 16–17). Along with theatres and the pleasure gardens of Vauxhall and Ranelagh, shops were integral to fashionable sociability in the capital and took part in the urban renaissance of England during the early modern period (Borsay, 1989). According to contemporary sources, the splendour of toymen was particularly remarkable. As early as 1726, when Daniel Defoe wrote against the excessive expense involved in fitting out new shops, he chose the example of toy dealers: 'It is a modern custom and wholly unknown to our ancestors (. . .) to have tradesmen lay out two thirds of their fortune in fitting up their shops. By fitting up I do not mean furnishing their shops with ware and goods to sell; (. . .) but in painting and gilding, fine shelves, shutters, boxes, glass doors, sashes and the like, in which they tell us now, 'tis is a small matter to lay out two or three hundred pounds, nay five hundred pounds to fit up a pastry's cook's or a toy shop' (Defoe, 1726–7: 312–313).

Inventories confirm the luxury of toyshops which were fitted with mahogany counters, glass shelves running along the shop walls, chests of drawers lined with velvet where small metallic objects could be elegantly displayed, and elaborate glass cases where watches and chatelaines could be suspended whilst a mirror enabled clients to see their backs (Walsh, 1993, 1995a: 97–99; and 1995b: 160–169).

Some London toyshops were so famous that they became part of the sights foreigners came to see when visiting the capital. Fashionable toy dealers had tradecards printed in several languages — English, French and sometimes German — thus highlighting their claim to the patronage of the European elite (Heal Collection, Heal 67–39 or 67–75). The most famous toyshop was undoubtedly that of Daniel Chenevix, and later of his widow; it was repeatedly mentioned in contemporary correspondences and novels as one of the landmarks of the capital (see Fielding, 1987: 314). Horace Walpole took the Marquis de Rinuncini to see Chenevix's shop when the latter visited London — he wrote to Horace Mann on 15 September 1746 that: 'I stayed literally an entire week with him, carried him to see palaces and Richmond Gardens and Park and Chenevix's shop' (Walpole, 1983: vol. XIX, 308). It was to Chenevix's shop that the Princesse de Craon wanted to go on her visit to London: 'the Princess pleases herself already with the hopes of having at least half Chenevix's shop, *et tant de petites commodités d'Angleterre*' (Walpole, 1983: vol. XX, 23–24).

Toy dealers often cultivated the link between their business and fashionable entertainment by turning their shops into venues for exhibitions. An advertisement published in 1750 invites 'the curious' to come and view a series of miniature pieces of work at a toyshop in the Haymarket amongst which are a miniature chain, a toy chaise and a miniature set of instruments (John Johnson Collection: Waxworks 3.41). James Cox, a high-profile jeweller, mounted several exhibitions of his work for which he issued tickets and catalogues (Cox, 1772). The curios that could be admired at toymens' shops – such as surprising *faux-montres* whose lids revealed portraits in miniature, musical boxes and automatons or delicate sets containing several dozen miniature instruments – sometimes turned the shops into amusing museums, blurring the line between entertainment and commerce. The link between toydealers and fashionable entertainment is nicely illustrated by the successful play *The Toy Shop*, first produced in 1735 and subsequently performed and republished throughout the eighteenth century. It features three characters who decide to visit a famous toyman as a form of entertainment: 'I dare say you will be much diverted', the character who suggests the expedition tells his companions at the beginning of the play (Dodsley, 1775: 8).

Figure 2.1. Frontispiece of Robert Dodsley, 1775

Source: *The Toy Shop, to Which are Added Epistles and Poems on Several Occasions. A New Edition*, London. © British Library Board. All Rights Reserved, 1606/1819

The frontispiece to the 1775 edition shows the interior of the toyman's shop with its counter and large display cases (Figure 2.1.). The three smartly-dressed friends are represented having a polite conversation with the toy dealer; their dress and postures foreground taste and fashionability. Such literary and pictorial representations bear witness to the way, in the course of the century, toyshops became a byword for the refined taste and politeness associated with new consumption spaces.

Yet if toyshops were at the forefront of the developments that affected retail, they were also central to the economy of resale and second hand. Toy dealers often acted as pawnbrokers who bought old plate and silver and sold second-hand snuffboxes and buckles. According to his tradecard, a London toyman called Morris sold 'all sorts of enamel work in snuff boxes, watches and chains, toothpick cases, trinkets and gold work (. . .) [and] every kind of false stone work set in the newest patterns' whilst offering 'the utmost value (. . .) for any quantity of second-hand jewels, plate, watches etc . . .' (Heal Collection, Heal 67–284). Serving as pawnbrokers and second-hand outlets, toyshops were therefore not only dedicated to the new forms of commerce but also carried on more traditional forms of retail. As Beverly Lemire has shown with the trade in textiles and clothing, second hand and pawning provided those who would not otherwise have had access to material goods with the possibility of consumption and trained them into the habit of renewing their possessions more rapidly, even if those were not always themselves new *per se* (Lemire, 1991a, b, and c; 1994; 1997). In a similar manner, toy dealers played a crucial part in allowing people to acclimate to a quicker turnover of objects like buckles, watchcases, snuffboxes and sword hilts. As such, toyshops can be seen as sites where the new and the old intersected, enabling the middle-classes to have access to objects that had become associated with fashion and novelty.

2.3 Novelty, Fashion and the Luxury Debate

Beyond the varied shapes, sizes and materials of the objects sold by toy dealers, the objects referred to as toys were often characterized by novelty. Toyshops sold snuffboxes, toothbrushes and coffee grinders, for instance, which were related to relatively recent cultural practices. They also sold a wide range of technological innovations, including umbrellas, fountain pens and small optical instruments, like reading and opera glasses. The novelty of toys also lay in the materials from which they were made. Chatelaines or etuis made in pinchbeck (a copper and zinc alloy invented by Christopher Pinchbeck in the first half of the century – Figure 2.2.), snuff boxes made in *papier mâché* or Sheffield Plate (a new plating technique designed by Thomas Boulsover in 1742), cut-steel buttons and buckles, paste jewellery or China scent-bottles (Figure 2.3.): the objects sold by toydealers used all the new materials developed in the course of the century.

In terms of production, toys were also associated with innovation. The transformations prompted by mechanisation or the division of labour affected the toy industry rather earlier than they did other fields, as stamping and rolling, and the sub-division of tasks, were common practice in the making of toys quite early in the century. In 1766, ten years before Adam Smith's famous description of a pin factory where efficiency is improved by the division of labour, Lord Shelburne gave an account of his visit to the manufacturer John Taylor, a Birmingham toymaker, which reads as an encomium to industrial modernity and progress: 'they do buttons, buckles and toys and everything in the hardware way by stamping machines which were before obliged to be performed by human labour. Another thing quickly followed, instead of employing the same hand to finish a button or any other thing, they subdivided it into as many different hands as possible' (Fitzmaurice, 1912: vol. II, 404; Berg, 2005: 174). The same division of labour can be gathered from the autobiographical memoirs of James Bisset, a *japanner* in the Birmingham toy industry at the end of the eighteenth century, who tells about the impressive amount of snuffboxes he decorated in a week 'painting upwards of twenty gross of snuffboxes in a week with roses, anemones and various coloured flowers with three tints to every flower and three to every leaf' (Berg, 2005: 161).

Finally, the innumerable pattern books for snuffboxes and watchcases produced throughout the century by goldsmiths and toymen show that innovative design was at the heart of the attraction of these objects. Toy makers were expected to present new designs and ideas constantly. The author of *A Description of All Trades Digested in Alphabetical Order* published in 1747 describes snuffbox makers in those terms: 'these artists (. . .) not

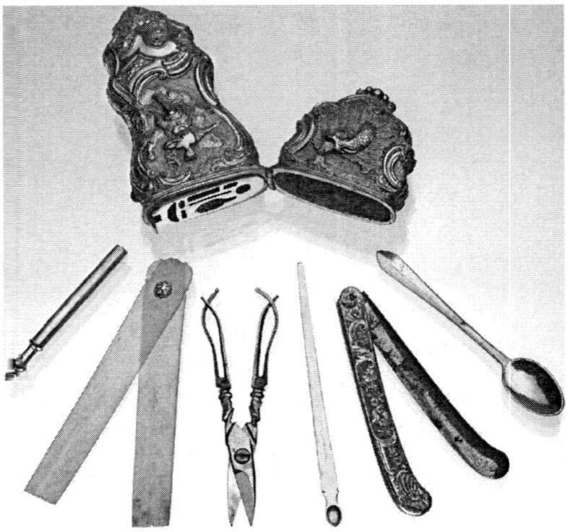

FIGURE 2.2. Etui cast with classical figures in high relief, c. 1750

SOURCE: Museum of London, inv: MoL 62. 121/116

FIGURE 2.3. Charles Gouyn, ('Girl on a Swing Factory'), China scent-bottle, c. 1750

SOURCE: Museum of London, inv: MoL A. 9902

only (...) invent a very great variety of fashions but also (...) bring them to surprising degrees of beautiful workmanship in all manner of metals, stones, shells, etc. [and] are continually striving to improve and vary them, in order to strike the taste of the curious' (Anon., 1747: 195). Matthew Boulton, whose archives in Birmingham contain a huge number of designs for chatelaines, buckles, buttons and watchcases, is undoubtedly one of the most famous examples of the spirit of innovation which governed the toy trade (Birmingham Central Library, City Archives, Matthew Boulton Papers. On Boulton see Robinson, 1963; Jones, 1973; McKendrick, Brewer and Plumb, 1982; Berg, 2005:167–8, 173–9).

Novelty was all the more important as it often determined the price of the object, rather than its intrinsic value. Indeed, thanks in particular to the new metal alloys (such as pinchbeck or Sheffield plate), the value of some toys did not depend less on their material than on their fashionability (Clifford, 1999: 147–170). A snuffbox containing just over one pence worth of gold could be sold for over 18 shillings, provided it was new and caught the public's fancy (Berg, 2005: 167). In this respect, the metal toys produced in the second half of the century encapsulated the very phenomenon of fashion, since their prices were determined not by how much they were worth but by the fluctuating and elusive added value of novelty and taste. As a result, toy dealers were often portrayed as arbiters of elegance and taste, deciding what was in or out of fashion by constantly offering new models of snuffboxes or shoe buckles. An article published in *The Tatler* thus mocks the capacity of the prominent toy dealers of the capital to dictate fashion. The article warns that Charles Lily, one of the city's leading toymen, is about to issue a new snuff box 'which will be the only in fashion till after Easter'. The satirist adds that: 'The Gentlemen that gave fifty pounds for the box set with diamonds may shew it till Sunday night (...) but not after that time there being one published on Monday which will cost fourscore guineas' (Steele, 1987: vol. II, 313–4).

Because of their constant search for novelty, toys were often regarded as an emblem of modern consumerism and luxury. Not only did these costly objects frequently have little resale value, but they were often unnecessary objects and were even frequently denounced as perfectly useless. The Earl of Chesterfield thus warned his son against buying these trinkets: 'a fool cannot withstand the charms of a toy shop; snuff boxes, watches, heads of canes (...) are his destruction' (Chesterfield, 1774: vol. I, 387). He urged moderation: 'Have one handsome snuff-box (if you take snuff) and one handsome sword, but then no more very pretty and very useless things' (Chesterfield, 1774: vol. II, 53). This idea that toys were costly, useless gadgets came to play a prominent role in contemporary discourses, in which toys were invariably seen as symbols of luxury and vanity. In the *Theory of Moral Sentiments* Adam Smith derided the modern habit of his contemporaries of walking about equipped with all sorts of useless 'conveniencies' [sic]: 'How many people ruin themselves by laying out money on trinkets of frivolous utility? What pleases these lovers of toys is not so much the utility as the aptness of the machines which are fitted to promote it. All their pockets are stuffed with little conveniencies [sic]. They contrive new pockets, unknown in the clothes of other people, in order to carry a great number. They walk about loaded with a multitude of baubles, in weight and sometimes in value not inferior to an ordinary Jews' box, some of which may sometimes be of some little use, but all of which might at all times be very well spared, and of which the whole utility is certainly not worth the fatigue of bearing the burden' (Smith, 2002: 211).

Although Adam Smith highlights the superfluous nature of toys, in *The Wealth of Nations* he underlined the role of these trinkets in the economic transformations of the country, stating that it was because the elites had traded their titles 'for trinkets and baubles fitter to be the playthings of children than the serious pursuits of men' that 'a revolution of the greatest importance to the public happiness', meaning the birth of consumerism and the development of Britain's industry, could have occurred (Smith, 1997: 514–515). As trifling as they might appear, or rather precisely because they were associated with vanity and luxury, toys played a fundamental role in the economic and industrial development of the country. Birmingham, nicknamed by some 'the toyshop capital of the world', underwent extraordinary economic and demographic growth over the course of the century due in large part to the production of these small objects (Bisset, 1799: 32). Toys were a perfect illustration of Bernard de Mandeville's analysis of luxury whereby private vices led to public benefits (Mandeville, 1924). Toys provided a fitting embodiment of these changes so that the recurring use of toys in contemporary discourses on luxury and consumption can be read as a manifestation of Britain's ambivalence towards the economic transformations brought about by consumption, as a discursive trope enabling the British to come to terms with their country's recent changes.

Adam Smith's quote about the vanity of the 'lovers of toys' also highlights that many objects sold by toy dealers were meant to be carried along when the person was out and about. Toys are indeed emblematic of the advent of a distinctively urban lifestyle, one characterized by individual mobility as well as of new strategies of distinction in a context of consumption being made accessible to a growing section of society.

2.4 Toys, Mobility and the New Strategies of Distinction

The objects sold by toy dealers were accessories that took part directly or indirectly in the polite practices linked to urban sociability. Offering tobacco, writing letters and notes, eating at an inn with one's portable cutlery set, jotting down social engagements in one's pocket book, and making and keeping appointments thanks to one's watch: many of the objects sold by toy dealers were at the heart of the practices of urban sociability and politeness, whilst making for an individual who was mobile and independent.

This was emblematic of the new ways in which social and cultural superiority could be displayed. Beyond the actual uses to which these items were put, portable objects played a central role in individuals' performance of politeness and fashion. 'People where they are not known, are generally honoured according to their clothes and other accoutrements they have about them', Mandeville observed in the *Fable of the Bees* (Mandeville, 1924: 127–128). In the 'gathering of strangers' which eighteenth-century London had become, clothes and accessories gave people their identities (Sennett, 1974: 47). In the *Female Spectator* (1745), Eliza Haywood underlines the importance to elegance of portable knickknacks and of knowing how to handle these accessories tastefully: 'The snuff-box and smelling bottle are pretty trinkets in a lady's pocket and are frequently necessary to supply a pause in conversation, and on some other occasions; but whatever virtues they are possessed of, they are all lost by a too constant and familiar use, and nothing can (...) render one more ridiculous in company than to have either of them perpetually in one's hand' (Haywood, 1745: vol. 2, 104). An advertisement published in *The Spectator* announced that Charles Lily, the toy dealer mentioned earlier, organised classes to teach people how to hold their snuffboxes and take them gracefully out of their pockets to offer tobacco: 'The exercise of the snuff box according to the most fashionable airs and motions (...) will be taught (...) at Charles Lillie's (...) and attendance given for the benefit of the young merchants about the Exchange for two hours everyday at noon, except Saturdays, at a toyshop near Garraway's coffee house. There will be likewise taught the ceremony of the snuff box, or rules for offering snuff to a stranger, a friend, or a mistress, according to the degrees of familiarity or distance; with an explanation of the surly pinch and the gestures proper to each of them' (Addison, 1965: vol. II, 297).

Although this advertisement must be understood as a joke, it nonetheless points to the social importance of body deportment and gestures in the display of taste and refinement. In the wake of Mimi Hellmann's analysis of furniture, minute portable objects can therefore be seen as crucial props in the performance of the elegant deportment that had become the benchmark of social and cultural superiority (Hellmann, 1999: 415–445; see Figures 2.4. and 2.5.). At a time when consumption had been made available to a growing section of society, the mere ownership of an object had ceased to be a socially

Figure 2.4. L. P. Boitard, after Bartholomew Dandridge 'To Offer or Receive', c. 1737

Source: plate 11 in François Nivelon (1737) *The Rudiments of Genteel Behaviour*, London. © British Library Board. All Rights Reserved, 1812 a. 28.

Figure 2.5. John Russell, *Portrait of Mrs Shurlock*, 1801. Pastel on paper laid down on canvas (61 × 45,4cm)

Source: Metropolitan Museum of Art New York, gift of Olive Shurlock Sjölander, 1975 (inv:1975.217.2).

Figure 2.6. Niklaus Wilhelm von Heideloff, 'Afternoon Dress' (detail)

Source: *The Gallery of Fashion*, plate 120, Nov. 1796. Victoria and Albert Museum, National Art Library.

discriminating criterion: distinction shifted from the possession of the object to its elegant performance. The arrival on the social stage of consumption of new protagonists, such as those merchants invited to take snuffbox-handling classes by Lily's advertisement, called for new, more subtle criteria for distinction than mere ownership, especially at a time when the use of imitative materials such as pinchbeck or Sheffield plate was making the reading of the signs of conspicuous consumption less certain (Veblen, 1994). The proliferation of portable accessories whose diminutive size rendered them difficult to handle can thus be seen as a result of the cultural and social changes brought about by consumerism. The smaller and the more delicate these objects were, the trickier their manipulation and the more elegant and graceful the gestures involved in using them had to be.

Taking out one's watch and flicking it open, handling an exquisitely small scent-bottle, or screwing and unscrewing the different parts of a writing set allowed one to display the elegance of his gestures – or, on the contrary, exposed his clumsiness – thus demonstrating a person's cultural and social standing. Objects like the watch, the snuffbox or the pocketbook, which the individual brought with him as he went about town, all played their parts in fashioning social and cultural identities. These portable accessories thus multiplied the range of props available for the performance of elegance and taste whilst widening the stage on which it could take place.

This shift from possession to performance came to a climax at the end of the century, when traditional social markers were most blurred. Yet, with the fashion for sentimentality, this also corresponded to a time when the very objects used in the performance of taste became associated with memory rather than novelty. Sentimental jewellery or miniatures of loved ones were set in lockets or snuffboxes and these objects became part of the paraphernalia of the sentimental man or woman (see Figure 2.6.). The new codes of conduct, which gave primary importance to deportment and elegant gestures for distinguishing between social ranks, were then used to handle sentimental lockets or snuffboxes, thus demonstrating yet again the complexity of the notion of novelty in trying to understand consumption in eighteenth-century Britain.

2.5 Conclusion

Looking at the relationships between toys and novelty at the various levels of commerce and production as well as the cultural practices involved in their use has allowed a more nuanced understanding of the role of the new in the transformations of consumption in eighteenth-century Britain. Far from being an unequivocal equivalent or embodiment of novelty, toys are a good illustration of the ways in which old and new combined and sometimes conflicted to bring about transformations in consumption. Although toyshops were in the vanguard of new retail spaces and practices, they were also places where cutting-edge selling techniques intersected with more traditional ones such as pawning and second hand. In the same way, because toys were associated with novelty, they became a polemical trope used to discuss issues such as luxury and the excesses of fashion, and captured the period's ambivalence towards the economic changes it was undergoing. Moreover, in their relationship to cultural transformations, toys enable us to see novelty in more complex ways. As portable objects that were carried on one's person, toys are characteristic of the advent of increased personal mobility as well as of the appearance of new distinctive cultural codes, whilst the vogue for sentimentality at the end of the century made for toys that were associated with sentiment and memory, rather than the new.

Finally, I would like to return to the term 'toy' itself. Not only does it capture the ambiguity of objects denounced as useless rattles; it also points to another meaning of the word. The verb 'to toy' with can mean literally to play with something but also, in a more figurative use of the word, to think about, to contemplate — as in 'to toy with an idea'. Toys which, as we have seen, were props to be toyed with, handled, and manipulated can therefore be seen as playing a role in the individual's appropriation of novelty in the form of new cultural practices based on sociability and the new codes of conduct that emerged in the wake of enlarged consumption. More generally, I would like to suggest that, as a figure repeatedly used in contemporary discourses – and precisely because they occupied a strange place between old and new – toys played a role in helping the British come to terms with novelty in the form of the economic and industrial as well as social and cultural transformations the country was undergoing at the time.

Bibliography

Primary Sources

Unpublished sources

Bodleian Library, Oxford
John Johnson Collection of Printed Ephemera
British Museum, Department of Prints and Drawings
Heal Collection of Tradecards

Birmingham Central Library, City Archives
Matthew Boulton Papers

Published sources

Addison, J. and Steele R. (1965) *The Spectator* (1711–1712), Bond, D. F. (ed.), 5 vols., Oxford.
Anon. (1747) *A general description of all trades digested in alphabetical order*, London.
Bisset, J. (1799) *A poetic survey round Birmingham, with a brief description of the different curiosities and manufactories of the place. Intended as a guide to strangers. Accompanied by a magnificient directory*, Birmingham.
Campbell, R. (1747) *The London tradesman. Being a compendious view of all the trades, professions, arts, both liberal and mechanic now practised*, London.
Chesterfield, Philippe Dormer Stanhope, Earl of (1774) *Letters written by the late right honourable Philip Dormer Stanhope, Earl of Chesterfield to his son, Philip Stanhope*, 2 vols., London.
Cox, J. (1772) *A descriptive catalogue of the several superb and magnificent pieces of mechanism and jewellery exhibited in the Museum at Spring Gardens, Charing Cross, London*, London.
Defoe, D. (1726–1727) *The complete English tradesman*, 2 vols., London.
Dodsley, R. (1775) *The toy shop, To which are added epistles and poems on several occasions. A new edition*, London.
Fielding, H. (1987) *Amelia* (1751), Harmondsworth.
Haywood, E. (1745) *The Female Spectator*, 4 vols., London.
Fitzmaurice, Lord (1912) *Life of William Earl of Shelburne*, 2 vols., London.
Mandeville, B. de (1924) *The fable of the bees, or private vices, publick benefits* (1714), Kaye, F.B. (ed.), 2 vols., Oxford.
Meister, H. (1799) *Letters written during a residence in England*, London.
Saussure, C. de (1995) *A foreign view of England in 1725–1729: The letters of Monsieur César de Saussure to his family*, van Muyden, M. (ed.), London.
Smith, A. (1997) *The wealth of nations* (1776), Harmondsworth.
Smith, A. (2002) *The theory of moral sentiment* (1759), Haasonssen, K. (ed.), Cambridge.
Steele, R. (1987) *The Tatler* (1709–1711), Bond, D. F. (ed.), 3 vols., Oxford.
von la Roche, S. (1933) *Sophie in London. The diary of Sophie von la Roche* (1786), C. Williams (ed.), London.
Walpole, H. (1983) *Correspondence*, Lewis, W. S. (ed.), 48 vols., London and New Haven.

Literature

Berg, M. (2005) *Luxury and pleasure in eighteenth-century Britain*, Oxford.
Borsay, P. (1989) *The English urban renaissance: culture and society in the provincial town, 1660–1770*, Oxford.
Clifford, H. (1999) 'A commerce with things: the value of precious metalwork in early modern England', Berg, M. and Clifford, H. (eds.), *Consumers and luxury. Consumer culture in Europe 1650–1850*, Manchester, 147–170.
Hellman, M. (1999) 'Furniture, sociability and the work of leisure in eighteenth-century France', *Eighteenth-Century Studies*, 32:4, 415–445.
Jones, E. L. (1973) 'The fashion manipulators, consumer tastes and British industries, 1660–1800', Cain, L. P. and Uselding, P. J. (eds.), *Business enterprise and economic change*, Ohio, 198–226.
Lemire, B. (1991a) *Fashion's favourite: the cotton trade and the consumer in Britain, 1660–1800*, Oxford.
Lemire, B. (1991b) '"A good stock of cloaths": the changing market for cotton clothing in Britain 1750–1800', *Textile History*, 22:2, 311–328.

Lemire, B. (1991c) 'Peddling fashion: salesmen, pawnbrokers, taylors, thieves and the second-hand clothes trade in England, c.1700–1800', *Textile History*, 22:1, 67–82.

Lemire, B. (1994) 'Redressing the history of the clothing trade in England. Ready-made clothing, guilds, and women workers 1650–1800', *Dress*, 21, 61–74.

Lemire, B. (1997) *Dress, Culture and Commerce. The English clothing trade before the factory, 1660–1800*, London.

McKendrick, N., Brewer, J. and Plumb, J.H. (1982) *The birth of a consumer society. The commercialisation of eighteenth-century England*, London.

Robinson, D. E. (1963) 'Eighteenth-century commerce and fashion: Matthew Boulton's marketing techniques', *Economic History Review*, 16, 39–60.

Sargentson, C. (1996) *Merchants and luxury markets: the marchands merciers of eighteenth-century Paris*, London and Malibu.

Sargentson, C. (1998) 'The manufacture and marketing of luxury goods: the marchands merciers of late 17th and 18th century Paris', Fox, R. and Turner, A. (eds.), *Luxury trades and consumerism in Ancien Régime Paris. Studies in the history of the skilled workforce*, Aldershot, 99–137.

Sennett, R. (1974) *The fall of the public man*, New York.

Stobart, J. (1998) 'Shopping streets as social space: leisure, consumerism and improvement in an eighteenth-century county town', *Urban History*, 25:1, 3–21.

Veblen, T. (1994) *The theory of the leisure class* (1899), Harmondsworth.

Walsh, C. (1993) 'Shop design and the display of goods in the eighteenth century', MA thesis V&A/RCA London.

Walsh, C. (1995a) 'The design of London goldsmith's shops in the early eighteenth century', Mitchell, D. (ed.), *Goldsmiths, silversmiths and bankers: innovation and the transfer of skill 1550–1750*, Stroud, 96–112.

Walsh, C. (1995b) 'Shop design and the display of goods in eighteenth-century London', *Journal of Design History*, 8:3, 157–176.

Walsh, C. (2001) 'Shopping in Early Modern London, c.1660–1800', Ph.D. thesis, European University Institute, Florence.

CHAPTER 3

WATCH AND CLOCK OWNERSHIP IN PARIS, 1750–1850

Marie-Agnès Dequidt – Université de Paris XII, France

3.1 Introduction

The years 1750–1850 correspond to the age in which the modern consciousness of time took hold, asking for more and more synchronisation. This consciousness was paralleled by increasing production of watches and clocks, and French horology reached what is usually called its 'golden age'. After being successful in the seventeenth century, the industry had declined. This was partly because many watchmakers, being Protestants, had to leave France at the time of the *Révocation de l'Edit de Nantes* (the royal act forbidding Protestantism in France in 1685) and partly because of a lack of interest and stimulation. London and Geneva, the other two main horology centres, benefited from this situation and led the market at the turn of the eighteenth century. In France, new 'heroic' figures of horology such as Julien Le Roy and his sons, together with the implementation of a brand new manufactory in Versailles in 1718, were not enough to stimulate the production at the beginning of the century: indeed, the manufactory had to close after just two years of existence. However, it was a first step towards the revival of French watch making which started in the middle of the century. At that time, Paris housed the greatest names of horology, including men like Louis Abraham Breguet, Ferdinand and Louis Berthoud, Jean Antoine Lépine, and Antide Janvier. The interest that both Louis XV and Louis XVI showed in mechanical arts and watch making is probably not unrelated to its development. But the mechanical arts were of wider interest, and promoting French watch and clock making was in line with the ideas developed in Diderot's *Encyclopedie*, for which Berthoud himself wrote the articles *Horloge* (Clock), *Horloger* (watch maker) and *Horlogerie* (watch making).

But who owned watches and clocks? How, and from whom, did these people acquire such goods? Was it only brand new items or also old ones which excited interest? These are the questions which concern me in this chapter. Addressing them will help us understand if the motivations were so different from those of our time: an age when a new watch can be bought by a low-paid worker for half a day's salary, whilst the firm Breguet spends the equivalent of almost 100 years' salary of the same worker to buy an original Abraham-Louis Breguet watch for its museum. This buying back of the history of the brand is quite fashionable in the early twenty-first century. What was it like two centuries ago?

Figure 3.1. Julien Le Roy (Tours 1636 – Paris 1759), King's watchmaker in 1739: *L'innocence protégée par la justice*

Source: Petit Palais, Musée des Beaux-Arts de la Ville de Paris, Tuck donation, OTUCK00246.

3.2 A Complex Market

To understand the flow of watches and clocks, I propose to analyse the various actors involved: makers, sellers and various categories of buyers. But before entering into details, it seems important to draw a general picture of the Parisian watch and clock market. The watchmaker was both a producer and seller of watches and clocks to individuals. He also sold to retailers such as jewellers, upholsterers or haberdashers or even to second-hand clothes dealers who, in turn, sold to individuals. This indirectly enlarged the watchmaker's customer base by giving access to new layers of the population. Sometimes, however, the retailer entered into competition with the watchmaker, creating conflict and tensions between the two. Watchmakers complained that retailers tended to lower prices by not taking care of the quality of what they sold, describing the retailers' trade as being 'as huge as absurd', as a King's watchmaker put it (Béliard, 1767: 4).[1] The problem lasted through the whole period and another King's watchmaker mentioned watches sold by tailors, shoemakers, joiners and even seminarists in 1832.[2] This did not, however, prevent the watchmaker himself from buying from a retailer or from another watchmaker, to supplement his own offer. For example, the jeweller Aubourg

1 'Le commerce aussi immense qu'absurde que font de l'horlogerie les Marchands, les Bijoutiers, les Tapissiers, les Fripiers'. The King's watchmakers were appointed by the King. There were four of them working in turns during three months. They were in charge of winding up royal watches and clocks, and generally maintaining them.

2 French national archives (Archives nationales, later noted A.N.), F^{12} 2464, Hahn watchmaker, 1833: 'les pacotilles de la Suisse et de Genève sont en montre de toutes parts; on les voit vendues par des tailleurs, Cordonniers, menuisiers, séminaristes, coureurs des marchands Genevois'.

sold, directly or indirectly, close to 2,000 watches between 1774 and 1781. For 712 of these watches, the occupation of the buyer is identified, and this shows that watchmakers bought 145 watches, or 20 per cent of the sales (Coquery, 2006: 547–551 and annexes 54–6 and 55).

The Parisian watchmaker also had to deal with competition from Geneva and Neufchatel County watchmakers selling to retailers through dealers or travelling salesmen. Once again, the Parisian watchmaker also bought from these competitors, whilst at the same time complaining about the low prices they offered. In reality, despite the added costs of tolls and transportation, Geneva and Neufchatel products remained competitive thanks partly to a high division of work, which allowed lower wages to be paid to less skilled workers, and partly to a gold standard less strict than that in France (where the standard had to be 20 Carats with a stamp to justify it, compared to the generally used 18 Carats for Geneva). The previously mentioned Beliard speaks, as early as 1767, of 'the introduction of an immense quantity of horrible foreign horology, from Geneva and from Switzerland as well, finished or to be finished by Merchants, and sometimes the watchmakers themselves' (Beliard, 1767: 3).[3] This trend increased throughout the eighteenth and into the nineteenth century. Indeed, the archives are full of such indications. A report dated 1839 (probably inflating the figures) indicates that Geneva annually exported more than 800,000 watches and Switzerland twice as many. It quotes another report dated 1800 showing that Geneva made and sold 250,000 watches. A document dated 1830 states that each year 60,000 watches were imported from Geneva to France, about half simple watches and half repeating watches (A.N., F^{12} 2462).[4]

It is more difficult to estimate the production of Paris, as there were no big manufacturers but instead a large number of small shops. However, the production figures of the most famous Parisians workshops suggest that it was modest at best. For instance, Le Roy's workshop produced 150–200 watches per annum during the years 1840, down from as many as 400 pieces in 1786, whilst the Breguet workshop produced between 60 and 200 watches per annum between 1780 and 1823, with low production years corresponding to the French Revolution and the Napoleonic wars (Le Roy, 1840: 1–7; Breguet, 1997: 110–150). Since around 200 to 300 watchmakers are established with shops and workshops, we can estimate an annual production of roughly 20,000 to 30,000 watches in Paris.

We must note here that watch making was a highly technical job and required knowledge that could only be obtained through a long training. In the eighteenth century, watch making was an activity regulated by the guilds.[5] For instance, to be allowed to open a shop in Paris and mark watches with his own name, a watchmaker had be either the son of a Parisian Master watchmaker or to have gone through an apprenticeship with a Parisian

3 'L'introduction d'une quantité immense de méchante horlogerie étrangère, tant de Genêve que de Suisse, établie ou prête à établir par des Marchands, & quelquefois par les Horlogers eux-mêmes'.

4 A repeating watch is a watch that strikes the hour when a button is pressed.

5 Most Parisian craftsmen were working within guilds dictating all kinds of rules: the type of objects to be produced in terms of size, weight and quality, but also the education and recruitment of members, or who could be employed. They also checked that other guilds did not interfere by making or selling objects under their own control. In the seventeenth century and eighteenth century up to 1776, almost 150 such guilds ruled the work in Paris. In 1776, their number was reduced to 50. At their head stood two to four *Jurés* elected among Masters of the craft. The *Jurés* could visit the workshops at any time to check whether the workers obeyed the rules. Generally, to reach Mastery one had to be the son of a Master or go through apprenticeship. The only way to escape from the guild's control was to live and work in what were called privileged areas, such as the neighbourhood of *Saint-Germain-des-Prés* (centre of Paris, left bank) or *faubourg Saint-Antoine* (east of Paris).

FIGURE 3.2. Julien Le Roy (Tours 1636 – Paris 1759), King's watchmaker in 1739: *Le Bouquet*

SOURCE: Petit Palais, Musée des Beaux-Arts de la Ville de Paris, Tuck donation, OTUCK00271.

Master. Apprentices had to be less than 20 years old when they started. Their training lasted for eight years (along with goldsmiths, the longest in Paris) during which time the young man lived in his Master's home.[6] Although guilds disappeared with the French Revolution in 1791 along with their disciplinary organisation (the d'Allarde decree being reinforced by the Le Chapelier Law), the training principles remained roughly identical in the early nineteenth century. Rules were no longer dictated by the guild, but the government sent the best pupils from the *Ecoles des Arts et Métiers* (Arts and Crafts Schools) to famous watchmakers to learn the professional skills required. Whilst there, conditions for a handful of students (Lenoir had two in 1806, Berthoud had four in 1810 and Perrelet six in 1832 and 1838) closely resembled those experienced by earlier apprentices. When they started, they had to be between 14 and 18 years old, able to read and write, and able to know at least rough calculation, geometry and drawing elements as well as wheel and file usage. Their training lasted between four and six years, during which time they lived with their master (A.N., F^{12} 2452). With so few newcomers on the Parisian watch making market, the production of the French Jura (close to Neufchatel county and Geneva) began to overtake that of Paris. The Jura had started with only small pieces (such as unfinished movements, called movement-blank or *ebauche*) in the mid eighteenth century, but its development was so rapid that Parisian production became increasingly dedicated to luxury items.

6 In reality, 29 per cent of Masters were sons of Masters, 24 per cent came from apprenticeship (one fourth of the apprentices reached Mastery) and 47 per cent (almost half) received the title through royal dispensation. This allowed an openness of the guild which does not appear in the statutes.

This brief overview has covered only the market for new watches. A full view requires adding other elements: the second-hand market, gift, inheritance, barter and theft. This is summarised in the diagram below.

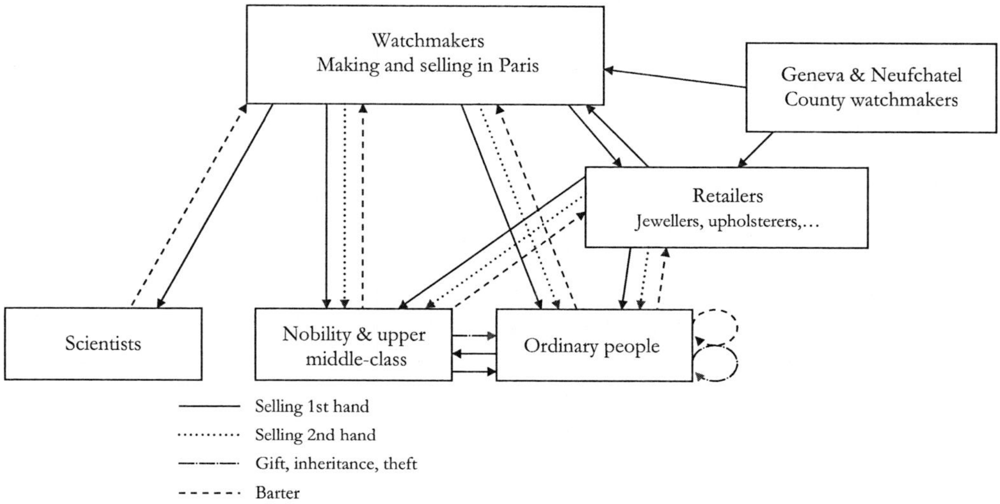

If watchmakers faced competition in selling and even in producing watches, they were alone in servicing and repairing watches and clocks: those produced by themselves and those made by other Parisian watchmakers or coming from abroad. This is why the description of their day to day activities involves such tasks as filling (holes), changing (watch glasses, springs, chains), filing (wheels), cleaning (movements, cases), adjusting, correcting (frictions), dressing and winding. These tasks could only be done by watchmakers, making these craftsmen crucial not only in making new items but also to the continued life of watches and clocks.

Turning from producers to consumers, we must consider what the user was looking for when acquiring a watch or clock. One key interest group was the growing body of professional and amateur scientists; another comprised those who bought watches for their decorative rather than their practical qualities. Here I discuss these in turn.

3.3 Scientists' Interest

In the mid eighteenth century, watches and clocks reached an impressive precision. However, precision was not for everyone, and watchmakers divided their craft into two categories: on one hand precision watch making (including chronometry, astronomic and marine horology) and precision watches; on the other hand, civil watch making. The first branch was dedicated to scientists and aimed primarily at measuring time flow with almost perfect consistency. Reading the hour was thus little more than means of checking the accumulation of minutes and seconds (Havard, ca 1895: 7).

Watches and clocks were technological items from two perspectives. First, they used the latest and most skilled techniques; second, they were used by other sciences as tools. In both cases, they attracted the attention of all types of scientists. As the *Encyclopédie Méthodique* noted, horology required knowledge of mathematics for calculating the relative

Figure 3.3. Jean Romilly (Genève 1714 – Paris 1796) *La Musique*, from C. Van Loo, engraved by Etienne Fessard in 1756

Source: Petit Palais, Musée des Beaux-Arts de la Ville de Paris, Tuck donation, OTUCK00260.

number of revolutions of the various wheels and shafts contained in a watch or clock; of geometry for calculating the bend of gear teeth; of physics and mechanics for working out the strengths to apply on the various parts; of fluid mechanics for the friction of the various parts between themselves with the air, and of metallurgy to understand the influence of heat on expansion. The watchmakers' involvement in practical research appears also through the numerous patents that they filed and through the presence of the most famous amongst them in the Science Academy: Ferdinand Berthoud (1795) and Abraham-Louis Breguet (1816).

At the same time, many sciences used the help of watches and clocks as precision instruments. In this case, the instruments were bought directly from the watchmaker and were always brand new in order to benefit from the latest technical developments. All sciences related to movement were involved: instrument making, astronomy, cartography and navigation. The last of these had been stimulating research in precision instrumentation because of political and economic imperatives, as the big maritime nations desperately sought to resolve the 'longitude problem': that is, determining the longitudinal position of a ship. This was accomplished by comparing noon on board (by measuring the position of the sun) and the local time of the port of departure given by a clock. Longitude was then easily calculated since one hour in time corresponds to 15° of longitude. The clock being used had to be extremely precise, as a difference of one second corresponds to an error in determining the ship's position of more than 460 metres at the equator.

However, the scientific market was not a large one. If we take the example of marine clocks, King Louis XV ordered four of them per year from 1772 for the Royal Navy from Ferdinand Berthoud, who, though he was not the only French watchmaker able to

FIGURE 3.4. Jean Baptiste Albert Baillon (?- Paris 1772), Queen's watchmaker in 1751, *Le Don perfide*

SOURCE: Petit Palais, Musée des Beaux-Arts de la Ville de Paris, Tuck donation, OTUCK00255.

build them, managed to attract all the Navy orders. In 1782, Louis XVI bought 16 marine clocks. In 1832, the Navy owned a total of 143 marine clocks: 44 from Berthoud, 29 from Breguet and 70 from Motel (Marguet, 1917: 204). The total Parisian production before 1815 is estimated at around 200 pieces and it was another twenty-five years before the merchant navy started using marine clocks (Landes, 1987: 272; Chapuis, 1999: 82). Clocks for astronomers were also only a few, and were held mainly in observatories.

Although precision was not broadly available for everybody, in the early nineteenth century fashions coming from England – namely, horse and boat races – expanded demand beyond the scientific realm. Although old in their conception, races changed markedly in the way that they were appreciated. First, competitors were often so closely matched that a measuring instrument needed to be more precise than the eye. Second, the aim was no longer simply to know who arrived first in a race, but to be able to compare two races by recording the time results. Such trends, of course, were largely restricted to the rich upper middle-class who could afford the leisure time and the most recent chronometers (Landes, 1983: 201; Vigarello, 1995: 199–201).

3.4 Jewels and the Like

Highly technical objects can be nice to look at – and time-pieces usually were, all the more so because they were often decorated. However, the pieces acquired by the nobility in the eighteenth century and the upper middle-class in the nineteenth century were primarily decorative and only secondarily technical instruments. Watches were decorated with enamel painting and made of precious metal, whilst clock cases were of precious or inlaid wood. On the technical side, they may be fitted with a movement that has many so-called *complications* – calculation of the phase of moon, indication of the day, the month, the zodiac and so on. Generally speaking, the decoration cost up to two or three times the price of the movement (Béliard, 1767: 7). Watches were thus thought of as jewels, and clocks were the ornament of the living place. The latter were found in every main room of important houses. The Duke of Chevreuse, in his château de Chevreuse, had clocks in the guards room, the canopy room, the assembly room, the Duke's bedroom, a natural history closet, the small library, a transit room, the large library, the Duchess's assembly room (two) and in her canopy room. Nine clocks adorned the Château de Dampierre (A.N., Minutier Central, XCII 743). At the end of the century, Louis Sébastien Mercier, the great observer of Parisian ways of life, complained in his *Tableau de Paris* that every fireplace in every house held a clock (Mercier, 1994: 1517). He exaggerated, of course, but perhaps not by much.

Watchmakers' customers give an idea of who bought 'civil' watches. Abraham-Louis Breguet was known as the greatest French watchmaker. Amongst his customers appear Queen Marie-Antoinette, the Dukes of Lauzun, La Rochefoucault, Talleyrand, Noailles and Praslin; later there was Napoleon's family (buying close to a hundred pieces, among which were 34 watches and clocks for Caroline Murat, queen of Naples), as well as marshals and generals (Cardinal, 1997: 11). At this end of the market, even the less expensive watches cost the equivalent of a workman's annual wage. Breguet called them *subscription watches* and produced around 1,500 of them in small series of twelve to twenty. They were based on the same pattern and the customer had to make a down payment when ordering. A little earlier, Lenoir father and son owned a shop called *A la repetition d'Angleterre* ('the English repeater'). Their customers were all high ranking individuals, including the Duchesse de Villeroy (with three watches and fifteen clocks in two castles); the Duke of Gramont; the Princess of Armagnac; the earls of la Marck, Bentheim, Chabot, Husson de Bonnac, Fumel, Montigny and Boufflers; the marquises of Bissy and Saint Sulpice and the marquess of Ségur.[7]

For these persons, watches were conceived as jewels and were prized for both their artistic merit and their monetary value. As such, they were part of 'Les presents du roi', that is, gifts made by the King to emissaries from other countries as a friendship pledge or after the signing of an important commercial agreement. This tradition was kept by Napoleon, mainly for ambassadors from Alger, Tunis, Constantinople and Mascate (Maze-Sensier, 1893: 142–160). In 1811, Breguet asked the favour to be the provider of such goods (A.N., F^{12} 2462). Rich watches were also a traditional element of the bride basket for important weddings. Marie-Antoinette had 51 of them in her basket, which were distributed amongst the guests (Franklin, 1987: 389).

Watches offered as presents were new and mostly bought directly from the watchmaker who produced them. However, other watches had different origins. The 1786 inventory of the watchmaker Jacques Thomas Bréant shows a wide range of watches, clocks and other small objects held in his shop in the Palais Royal (then a high place of luxury trade). Of the 81 watches described, 21 bore his own name, 33 showed no name and 27 were signed by another watchmaker (among whom were the very famous Le Roy, Romilly, Robin and Lépine). These 81 watches amounted to 21,284 livres, of which 6,762 livres (32 per cent) was

7 Archives of Seine district, (Archives de Paris, later noted ADP), DE1 Papiers 13, Papiers Lenoir.

FIGURE 3.5. François Pierre Gaston Jolly (Master in 1781) *Colin et Colinette*, Paris, c. 1780

SOURCE: Petit Palais, Musée des Beaux-Arts de la Ville de Paris, Tuck donation, OTUCK00266.

for watches signed by another watchmaker and 1,262 livres (6 per cent) for nine second-hand watches (ADP, D^4B6, 58-3727). We see here one of many examples of a watchmaker buying new watches from other watchmakers, selling both new and old items. Moreover, there was little apparent awkwardness in selling second-hand watches alongside new ones. The second-hand market allowed consumers to buy luxury items at a lower price, although, if bought from a famous watchmaker, a second-hand piece would be restored to look almost like a new one. The key difference was in price, a point illustrated by another example. At the death of his wife, Henri François Verneaux, at some point leader of the watchmakers corporation, held 30 new watches in his shop, ranging in price from 780 livres (for a gold repeating watch with enamel painting) to 192 livres (for a simple gold watch with enamel painting). He also had eight second-hand watches from 180 livres (gold) down to 90 livres for two watches, one silver and one copper. Even comparing gold to gold, the price difference is substantial.

There were other ways of acquiring watches and clocks which lay outside the traditional buy retail circuit, beyond the watchmaker's or any form of shop. First, watches were transmitted through legacy. Many wills included bequests of watches; perhaps as a posthumous reward to a servant for a lifetime service, or to a young member of the family who nursed or took care of the testator, or (most commonly) for all kinds of services rendered during the life of the testator. Through this process, people who would not have had enough money to buy a new watch could receive an old one. The monetary value of the watch was largely taken into account, but transmission through bequest also represents a token of memory. The object is then loaded with emotional value. Such was the case when Napoleon bequeathed to his son his two watches along with locks of his hair and that of the empress, but it was just as true for any father who bequeathed his watch to his son (Maze-Sensier, 1893: 359–365).

Second, barter was a process that was used even by important people, who perhaps preferred it over simply selling back their unwanted time-pieces. Two examples taken from many others can be found in Lenoir's papers. We see that the watchmaker exchanged with the Duchess of Villeroy a ringing clock four feet high designed by himself against 264 livres entering into their account and with the Duke of Gramont a ringing clock also designed by himself for 300 livres. In both cases, no sales were entered in the book (ADP, DE1 Papiers 13, Lenoir).[8] Such practices were linked to the fact that clocks and watches, as objects of decoration, were subject to fashion: they might be replaced, therefore, at a point when they were thought unfashionable, at least by people who could afford such frequent renewals of their personal and domestic decoration.

Another characteristic of watches was that, in the eighteenth century, they were worn in pairs, hanging from the belt – a fashion which held sway in Paris as in England (Franklin, 1987; McKendrick, Brewer and Plumb, 1982: 75). As such, they showed the economic and social importance of the owner, as well as signalling his awareness of fashion (Lemire, 1997: 5). This way of wearing watches was copied by servants who attempted to imitate their master with one or if possible two watches worn over their clothes (Mercier, 1994: 408). Such practices extended the importance of the watch well beyond its primary functioning of indicating the time.[9]

3.5 Mr Jones' Watch and Clock

Beyond nobility and the upper middle class, the account books of many watchmakers show a wide variety of customers. In Jean Gabriel Imbert's book (1780–1784), we find a knight, a priest, three gilders, a jewellery maker and a locksmith, as well as a tailor, a baker, four wine merchants, a draper, a stove-maker, a harquebusier, a butcher, two upholsterers, a cafe owner and Madame de Montesson's cook. In 1789, Lapret's customers numbered a turner, locksmith, abbot, baker, builder, merchant, sculptor, clerk, cafe owner, wig-maker, surgeon, servant, grocer, soldier, deliveryman, carpenter, joiner, priest and physician (ADP D^{5}B6 2606; D^{5}B6 5246).

At this stage, it is important to differentiate luxury items from common watches. If a coloured gold watch or a watch ornamented with guilloche cost about one year's salary, a plain gold watch was half this price. Of course, any additional technical feature (such as moon indications or repeater mechanism) or any addition of precious stones or enamel drawing dramatically increased the prices. A silver watch was one-quarter the price of a gold watch and was worth about the same as 50 litres of wine, and a copper watch was half the price again. In the early nineteenth century, prices fell and second-hand silver watches could be bought for 20 francs (when a very simple wooden table cost 10 francs and a chest of drawers 50 francs).[10] Later, in 1848, the inventory of a watchmaker shows two types of

8 'Pris en troc une Pendulle sonnante a quatre pieds et sa consolle de notre façon pour la somme de deux cent soixante et quatre livres'.

9 'Enfin, un laquais *du dernier ton* porte deux montres comme son maître; et cette insigne folie ne scandalise plus qu'un misanthrope'.

10 The French currency was the *livre tournois* up to the Revolution, a livre (4.5g of silver) holding 20 sols, each sol holding 12 deniers. In 1795–1796, the franc (holding 100 centimes) replaced the livre but kept the same value (after some turbulence).

Figure 3.6. Jean Antoine Lépine (Challex 1720- Paris 1814), *Suzanne et les vieillards*, from J.M. Wien, c. 1780

Source: Petit Palais, Musée des Beaux-Arts de la Ville de Paris, Tuck donation, OTUCK00236.

items: on the one hand, silver watches for 25 francs and gold watches for 80 francs (a dining table and four chairs were auctioned for 42 francs in the same inventory); and on the other hand, luxury items including a blue enamel watch with a chain for 200 francs (ADP D^{11}U3, 2674-42, 1807; D^{11}U3 7231-110, 1848).

Generally speaking, watches spread throughout this period and reached all layers of society. After 1750, 40 per cent of all homes in Paris (that is, far more than just the elite) had at least one clock and, in 1790, 70 per cent of servants' inventories and 32 per cent of wage-earners' inventories included at least one watch (Pardailhé-Galabrun, 1988: 396; Roche, 1998: 302). Rates of ownership steadily increased as everyday life became more and more governed by time: in factories and with public transport, for example. As early as 1764, a travelling guide indicated departure and arrival times by the half hour or even 15 minutes (Michel et Desnos, quoted by Studeny, 1995: 76). In 1788 times were given to the minute and in 1854 the omnibus was so regular and punctual that it was said that it could be used to set the clocks (Dutens quoted by Studeny, 1995: 77; Frémy quoted by Studeny, 1995: 117).

Literature brings another view since the characters in novels and plays tend to own more and more watches and clocks, especially in Paris. For instance, Balzac mentions nine watches and six clocks in *Les Illusions perdues*, as well as nine watches and eight clocks in *Le Père Goriot*, Dumas mentions 7 watches and 11 clocks in *Les Trois mousquetaires*, and Sue 19 clocks in *Les Mystères de Paris*. The various characters tend to check the hour more and more, by looking at their watches or a clock. Only occasionally are these objects mentioned because of their monetary or decorative value. It is interesting to note that these nineteenth-century characters belonged to the middle-class and were not necessarily very rich people. By this time, business was the driving force in society, prompting a quickening pace in the movement of everyday life (Studeny, 1995).

However, once again, owning a watch did not necessarily mean that it has been bought. Transmission through barter, inheritance or gift was as important for common watches as it was for expensive ones. For example, a watchmaker's account book includes a butcher buying a wall clock with coloured ribbons, with the account being settled in meat; a baker exchanging a movement against a clock and the rest in money, and a gold watch being exchanged for an English gold watch and money. Another watchmaker noted in his books that he bartered one watch for cloth for woollen shirts and another for 32 pairs of stockings; he exchanged four silver watches for cloth and towels needed for the house and another for a hazelnut suit and garments for the children (ADP, D^5B6 2606, D^5B6 3255).[11]

Such exchanges involved new watches, but old and used examples also retained a value that was generally recognised. Indeed, watches and clocks were virtually never discarded. Inventories show that they were not only kept but also evaluated – even if that value was very small. They were also itemised separately rather than being cast into the generic category of goods 'not worthy of description'. For instance, in 1772 we find an old English watch signed, with the hour hand only, valued at 24 livres with a knife, and another described as in a very bad state, or again an ancient clock without a name valued at 12 livres (A.N., Minutier Central, XXVII 385, XCI 1097).

To complete the picture, we must not forget that common watches were also frequently stolen, as numerous policemen's reports show. Examples include a silver watch with a steel chain, silver key and seal stolen from a servant; a silver watch stolen from a tailor, and two gold watches stolen from a king's officer (A.N., Y 13 969 A, 3 March 1776, Y 11 578, 6 June 1761, Y 9 480, 30 June 1777). Mercier comments on these thefts: 'Rogues find the way of catching your attention on a specific object or getting you into trouble or having you move so as to make their manoeuvre easy; and the robber, skilful and subtle, has already pinched your snuffbox, your watch, your purse' (Mercier, 1994: 91).[12] Later on, between 1815 and 1870, watches represented 27.7 per cent of the objects stolen at night in Paris, the thieves being attracted by watches because they were small (and therefore easy to steal and hide), valuable and easy to sell (Delattre, 2000: 705).

3.6 Conclusion

By the mid eighteenth century, the search for precision started to bear wonderful results and scientists finally had the tools they needed. However, this precision was not yet largely available or useful in day-to-day life: a King's watchmaker even created what he called a polycameric clock, that is, a single central movement distributed in several ('poly'-) rooms (-'camera') on several dials, explaining that there was no other way to have the same hour displayed in all rooms and in the gardens of a house (*Encyclopédie Méthodique*, 1784: 282).

11 'Vendu en trocq une montre sur le pied de deux cent livre contre de la toile pour des chemises de drap (. . .) trocqué (. . .) une Montre de paris de 9 louis contre trente deux paires de bas de soye (. . .) trocqué quattre montre dargent à un marchand de toile et serviette pour les besoins de la Maison sur le pied de deux cent cinquante six livres (. . .) Livré au tailleur une montre de Prince sur le pied de cent soixante huit livre pour un habit noisette et ouvrage pour les enfan soldé avec cette piece'.

12 '[les filous] trouvent le moyen, ou de fixer votre attention sur un objet, ou de vous susciter un embarras, ou de vous imprimer un mouvement favorable à leur coup de main; et le voleur adroit et subtil a déjà pincé votre tabatière, votre montre, votre bourse'.

FIGURE 3.7. Jacob Mardochée dit Jacob Petit (Paris 1796-Paris 1868), *Pendule au Mamelouk*, c. 1845

SOURCE: Petit Palais, Musée des Beaux-Arts de la Ville de Paris, Tuck donation, ODU01740.

Generally speaking, the market was quite complex. On the supply side, Parisian production was increasingly challenged by that of Geneva and Neufchatel County. On the demand side, different customers had very different requirements, from the greatest precision (desired by scientists and later by sportsmen) to the highest luxury (wanted by the wealthy to display their social position) and down to cheaper time-pieces (for simple people who wanted to know the hour). But even this categorisation is too simple. If two markets can be differentiated quite easily in economic terms (luxury and commonness) and related to the essential structure of society (Verley, 1985: 132), they tend to hide other circulations, including barter, second hand, gift, inheritance or theft, which blurred the picture of ownership. Moreover, watches and clocks presented more than an economic or a social value often found with new objects. They also bore an emotional value that reinforced the power of old items – especially when given as post-mortem gifts.

BIBLIOGRAPHY

Primary Sources

Unpublished sources

Archives Nationales de France
Série F12, Commerce et Industrie: F^{12} 2452, F^{12} 2462, F^{12} 2464

Serie Y, Châtelet de Paris: Y 13 969A, Y 11 578, Y 9 480
Minutier Central des Notaires: XCII 743, XXVII 385, XCI 1097
Archives du Département de Seine (Archives de Paris)
Archives privées, papiers de familles: DE1 Papiers 13, Papiers Lenoir
Archives judiciaires, Livres de comptes des commerçants faillis: D5B6, 2606; D5B6, 5246; D5B6, 3255
Archives judiciaires, Faillites commerciales, dossiers de procedure: D4B6, 58-3727
Tribunal de commerce de la Seine, Faillites et liquidations judiciaires: D11U3, 2674-42; D11U3, 7231-110

Published sources

Béliard, F. (1767) *Réflexions sur l'horlogerie en général, et sur les Horlogers du Roi en particulier*, Paris.
Diderot, D., d'Alembert, J. Le Rond (1751–1765) *Encyclopédie ou dictionnaire raisonné des sciences, des arts et des métiers*, Paris.
Encylopédie méthodique (1784) 3rd book: 'Arts et Métiers Mécaniques', Paris.
Le Roy, Ch.-L. (1840) *Rapport sur l'horlogerie de Paris*, Paris.
Mercier, L.-S. (1994) *Tableau de Paris* [1783/1788], Paris.

Literature

Breguet, E. (1997) *Abraham-Louis Breguet: horloger depuis 1775: vie et postérité d'Abraham-Louis Breguet, 1747–1823*, Paris.
Cardinal, C. (ed.) (1997) *Abraham-Louis Breguet (1747–1823): l'art de mesurer le temps*, La Chaux-de-Fonds.
Chapuis, O. (1999) *A la mer comme au ciel – Beautemps-Beaupré & la naissance de l'hydrographie moderne (1700–1850)*, Paris.
Coquery, N. (2006) *La boutique à Paris au XVIIIe siècle*, typed HDR thesis.
Delattre, S. (2000) *Les Douze heures noires – La nuit à Paris au XIXe siècle*, Paris.
Franklin, A. (1987) *Dictionnaire historique des arts, métiers et professions exercés dans Paris depuis le XIIIe siècle* [Paris 1905–1906], Marseille.
Havard, H. (ca 1895) *L'horlogerie*, Paris.
Landes, D. S. (1987) [*Revolution in time, clocks and the making of the Modern World*, 1983]/ *L'heure qu'il est, les horloges, la mesure du temps et la formation du monde moderne*, Paris.
Lemire, B. (1997) *Dress, Culture and Commerce – the English Clothing Trade before the Factory, 1660–1800*, London.
Marguet, F.-Ph. (1917) *Histoire de la longitude à la mer au XVIIIe siècle en France*, Paris.
Maze-Sensier, A. (1893) *Les fournisseurs de Napoléon et des deux impératrices*, Paris.
McKendrick, N., Brewer, J. and Plumb, J.H. (1982) *The Birth of a consumer society. The commercialisation of eighteenth-century England*, London.
Pardailhé-Galabrun, A. (1988) *La naissance de l'intime – 3000 foyers Parisiens – XVIIe–XVIIIe siècles*, Paris.
Roche, D. (1998) *Le peuple de Paris. Essai sur la culture populaire au XVIIIe siècle*, Paris [1981].
Studeny, C. (1995) *L'invention de la vitesse, France, XVIIIe–XIXe siècles*, Paris.
Verley, P. (1985) *La révolution industrielle, 1760–1870*, Paris.
Vigarello, G. (1995) 'Le temps du sport', Corbin, A. (ed.), *L'avènement des loisirs – 1850–1960*, Paris.

Illustrations

The pictures are all taken in the Petit Palais, Musée des Beaux-Arts de la Ville de Paris. The watches belong to the Tuck donation.

CHAPTER 4

Perspectives on the Retailing and Acquisition of New and Old Furniture in England, 1700–1850

Clive Edwards – Loughborough University, School of Art and Design, United Kingdom

'Whosoever shall be minded to buy any goods that London doth offer (...) or shall desire to have their wants supplied with any kind of household stuff at first or second-hand (...) they may have their choice either by parcels as they have need: or the full furniture of a house from executors, or from such as have occasion to give up housekeeping (...)' (Harleian *Miscellany*, c. 1589: 549)

4.1 Introduction

Any analysis of the sale and use of furniture must be prepared for ambiguities and contradictions, as the factors involved are not based simply on rationality or desire, economic or taste motives, but are also dependent upon other factors such as the nature of the consumer, the supply and demand for the furnishings at any one time, but perhaps above all, the culturally constructed environment in which they are produced and purchased.

To make sense of these and other factors, a methodology of enquiry that considers cultural contexts in relation to house furnishings is therefore helpful. Both new and second-hand purchases denote a particular range of behaviours, practices, modes of discourse, words, ideas, values, goals, institutions and material objects. The words and images that 'underlie consciousness' are revealing as the language used conveys the meanings. In this case it is the connotation of new and fashionable or second hand, antique or just old. It is of course not a simple either or, as old furniture can be very fashionable in some quarters, when defined as antiques or works of art for example. What determines these contexts are the behavioural habits, fashions, and accepted ways of buying and using material objects. (Consumption practices are one pattern.) These habits are explained and legitimated through organised institutions such as the church, government and businesses, as well as social classes, professions and families.

In this chapter, I will also follow the line that the creation and constitution of identities is an important part of the consumption of both new and used furnishings and one of the major arbiters in this process are the suppliers of these goods. Therefore a proportion of this essay considers the choices of retail outlets available and the type of customers they served over the period. In addition to these contexts there is the matter of the 'category of shopper' that should be considered. A number of attempts have been made to categorise shoppers (Falk and Campbell, 1997), but here I am suggesting four major categories of shoppers: the economic (who considered price), the personalising (who captured difference), the respectable (who captured value), and the hybrid (who variously used all three dependent upon circumstances).

Culturally Mediated Decisions or Choices – The use of goods, whether old or new, to express oneself is well known. A number of approaches to understanding how culture mediates these decisions have been put forward in recent years. Looking at other people's goods is one way of making decisions about what to purchase, but this is not straightforward. For example, Colin Campbell has suggested that the theory of emulation, which simply uses purchasing power to attain status, should be questioned. In addition, the trickle-down phenomenon does not necessarily indicate a motive of emulation: that is, the facility to copy does not mean that this is the reason – perhaps there is an actual desire for goods for their own sake (Campbell, 1993). Clearly then, there can co-exist examples of consumption as imitation or copying, emulation which is trying to equal or even excel, as well as attempts at personal or group distinction. Glennie has usefully pointed out that many consumers were adaptors, not mere adopters 'to be counted among the creators of consensual cultures' (Glennie, 1995: 169). Hence most homes will have a selection of new and used furniture.

Although fashionable new goods would often appear to be more appealing, the twin attractions of second-hand goods appear to be that they often represented quality and usefulness, and retained some resale value, as well as the more pragmatic issue of simply being available and affordable. This apparent willingness to include second-hand goods in an interior may appear to negate the argument about goods 'going together' but it is likely that second-hand goods were often used in non-public rooms or in homes that were not aspirational. Indeed, as Nenadic points out, the second-hand purchases were often acquired because of their functional value rather than their status value (Nenadic, 1994). On the other hand when a taste for the antique comes to the fore, the demand for such goods rises and a market develops for copies or reproductions that often attempt to imitate used goods.

Fashion and Taste – Although it seems that forms of self-consciousness – in the sense that individuals were knowingly able to express themselves – were well established by the eighteenth century, there were also 'standardised' systems of social communications. Thus ordinary people adopted, and then adapted to their own various special needs, a system of courtly behaviour borrowed ultimately from a protocol developed in France and disseminated through Amsterdam and London to provincial England and the colonies. Standardised architectural spaces equipped with fashionable furnishings became universally recognized settings for social performances that were governed by internationally accepted rules of etiquette (Carson, Hoffman and Albert, 1994: 523).

For many social groups, the importance of entertainment and the social round, and the subsequent display of oneself and one's home, meant that fashion had a major role to play in the maintenance of self-image. Although the fashion system was particularly influential in matters of personal dress and adornment, furniture was also affected by the changes fashion demanded. Adam Smith noted that clothes were out of date within a year, and furniture fashions were superseded every five or six years. Defoe, the astute observer of his time, wrote that 'the fashions alter now in the more durable kind of things, such as Furniture of houses, Equipages, Coaches, nay even of Houses themselves'. This meant that: 'This must needs give a new turn to the trade, and that of course gives new methods and new measures to the Manufacturers, obliges them to a continual study of novelty, and to rack their inventions for new fashions, introduces new customs, and even gives a turn to Trade it self' (Defoe, 1727, Part 2: 6).

In terms of the home, the example of the chintz craze showed how 'novel' goods were purchased as much for the 'sign-value' as for the 'use-value'; a fact that retailers were very well aware of. Defoe had noticed this particular demand early in the century. In 1708 he wrote *in A Review of the State of the British Nation*: '[chintz] crept into our houses, our closets and bedchambers, curtains, cushions chairs, and at last beds themselves, were nothing but calicoes and Indian stuffs, and in short everything that used to be made of wool or silk relating to the dress of the women or the furniture of our house, was supplied by the Indian trade' (Defoe, 1708: 602).

One hundred years later, in its advice to new entrants to the furniture trade, a guide expressed the same sentiments: 'In a business where change and caprice rule with unbounded sway-in that the fashion of today may become obsolete tomorrow-an inventive genius and discriminating judgment are certainly essential qualifications' (Stokes, 1829: 4).

Demand for particular goods was also derived from other changes in furnishings. These included developments in polite social habits – for example, tea drinking, social entertaining, reading, and writing – which meant that practical, functional forms of furniture were required. Another demand came from people who desired objects for their own intrinsic worth: the polished surfaces with dramatically coloured and grained veneers, rare timbers from the Indies, and contrasting inlays of wood and metals all excited the visual appetite, as well as satisfying other egotistical demands. When goods were desired but were financially out of reach, it was often possible to purchase substitutes or simulations (Berg, 1999). These ideas reflect the analysis of the economist, Adam Smith, in his *Lectures on Jurisprudence* where he points out that desirability in goods was based on four factors: colour, form, variety or rarity, and imitation (Berg and Clifford, 1999: 8). The goods in furniture shops could meet these desires in all aspects of the fashionable interior.

Self-Consciousness and Difference – The growth of eighteenth century consumption has sometimes been explained by contemporary commentators in terms of emulation. Again, the observant Daniel Defoe thought that 'the poorest citizens strive to live like the rich, the rich like the gentry, the gentry like the nobility and the nobility striving to outshine one another, [it was] no wonder that all the sumptuary trades increase' (Defoe, 1727, Part 2: 167). Another contemporary writer, N. Forster (1767), was also aware of the change in demand, seemingly brought about by fashionable emulation: 'In England, the several ranks of men slide into each other almost imperceptibly, and a spirit of equality runs through every part of their constitution. Hence arises a strong emulation in all the several stations and conditions to vie with each other (. . .). In such a state as this, fashion must have uncontrolled sway. And a fashionable luxury must spread through it like a contagion' (McKendrick, 1982:11).

In spite of these comments, our analyses of the reasons for consumption are now much less clear-cut than these contemporary writers. Consumption processes might in fact indicate a number of differing messages. These could include the desire to establish a status difference, a particular community distinction or an individual identity. The last of these was particularly so in towns, where spending on furnishings was part of the process of establishing one's family, especially if others in the town had little knowledge of your background. Contrary to this, the well-established rural family often had little need to demonstrate their position in a hierarchy. As the concept of status already existed and was acknowledged, conspicuous consumption of fashions and furnishings may well have been tempered by this awareness. In the case of poorer homes, it is often an internal status that is declared through goods which is not in itself comparative or emulative. Consumption of objects is as much about maintaining and consolidating status and standing, as it is about embracing novelty (Pennell, 1999: 559). Therefore, the goods that people either bought or ignored, according to their preferences and finances, helped in the process of defining or redefining a group identity.

Despite the practical purchasing decisions identified above, what were the other motives or intentions of the consumer? When consequences are recognized as objects, the analysis of intention can be useful. In other words, we can try to use furniture objects (amongst others) to assist in interpreting eighteenth-century consumer ambitions. Campbell suggests that the key to this understanding is recognition of particular personal characters: the individuals' desires to express ideals in themselves (Campbell, 1993). In the case of furniture and interiors, the selection of particular merchandise directly relates to this. Not only do interiors and their furnishings tell others about the occupants, but they also remind the owners of themselves and their position. Whilst this remains the case, the home will inevitably be bound up with individual self-concepts.

The accepted symbolic meanings of objects as 'codes' were intended to establish both differentiation from others and integration within a particular strata of society (Douglas, 1992). The former was aimed at separating the owner and emphasizing his/her individuality and thus creating distinction. In the latter, the object symbolically expressed the integration of the owner into a context that was both narrow (the building) and broad (the social stratum) (Csikszentmihalyi and Halton, 1981: 38–9). Therefore, one of the most valuable symbolic functions of goods, and especially of furnishings, was 'making visible and stable the categories of culture' (Douglas and Isherwood, 1980: 59). This process was not lost on contemporaries. Thomas Sheraton clearly demonstrated this when giving advice to upholsterers (retailers) upon their role: 'When any gentleman is so vain and ambitious as to order the furnishings of his house in a style superior to his fortune and rank, it will be prudent in an upholsterer, by some gentle hints to direct his choice to a more moderate plan'. In addition, Sheraton noted that even 'in furnishing a good house for a person of rank, it requires some taste and judgment, that each apartment may have such pieces as is most agreeable to the appropriate use of the room' (Sheraton, 1803: 215). So, the retailer not only had to make sure that the standard of furnishing was congruous with a social level, but also that the particular schemes were suitable for specific room types.

This reliance upon the retailer is not surprising since many people had little or no experience of purchasing stylish house furnishings on a regular basis. This service was to be one of the reasons why the upholsterer, later the retail furnisher, aimed to be a professional arbiter of domestic taste for the 'personalising shoppers' and later for the 'respectable shoppers' requiring value. The hybrid shoppers used a range of outlets as appropriate, and the 'economic shoppers' relied on local suppliers but with little requirement for advice or service. Of course there were a number of other types of outlet in addition to the retail furnisher.

4.2 Selection of Outlet for Purchase – New or Second Hand?

The range of sources for acquiring furniture was quite wide and most of the categories well known to modern readers were available in the eighteenth century. Shops, of course, the bespoke craftsmen-makers, agents, auctions, single sales, markets, fairs lotteries, and even smuggling, were common. The particular location of urban sites of selling signal particular approaches to the purchase of both new and second hand. For purchasers wanting to personalise through capturing difference, auctions and the antique and curio dealers were appropriate; for a different personalising experience, bespoke products made by well-known cabinet makers or upholsterers afforded a tasteful solution. For those seeking the economic, who considered price through a demand for value or through necessity, there was a variety of local producers of new goods and brokers' shops. For those seeking respectability, the cabinet-makers and upholsterers were able to supply new goods (and sometimes second-hand) and auctions were in business to provide second-hand (and sometimes new) goods. These changed over time as circumstances altered.

During the eighteenth century, the production and distribution of furniture had developed into a reasonably complex set of interconnected business types that were organized on a number of levels. These included the working masters or journeymen producing furniture in their own workshops for sale to wholesalers or retailers; the integrated manufacturing firms operating from extensive premises (including showrooms), combining a variety of skilled workmen and selling direct to clients; craftsmen-shopkeepers working from their own premises both making and selling, and the furniture retailers with showrooms that sold bought-in goods. The latter three types sometimes operated appraising, auctioneering, and second-hand departments as well. The diversity of customers ranged from the full furnishing of wealthy country estates to one-off sales of new or second-hand items.

At the beginning of the nineteenth century, the structure of the retail furnishing trade was still influenced by the activities of the previous century. This included the continuing separation of workshops from showrooms, the craftsman-shopkeeper selling from his workshop, the large enterprises selling exclusive furnishings with a very high level of individual attention and service, and the retail-only establishments that were increasingly meeting the demands of the growing middle and artisan classes. However, in the following one hundred years wide-ranging changes would also occur, with the development of the department store, the change of some drapers' businesses into complete house furnishers, the growth of the specialist concept stores, and the slow development of multiple shops. The growth of the market for new furniture means that the easy disposal of second-hand and unwanted goods had a twofold influence on the market. Firstly, it made space for the new and fashionable goods in the homes of those who could afford them. Secondly, for those who could not afford new, it gave them access to furniture that when new they could only aspire to.

The opportunity to buy used, second-hand or antique furniture from auctions or house sales – or sometimes from sales of bankrupt stocks – continued to be a useful outlet for some people. In some cases, the brokers' shops developed into dealers in curiosities and knick-knacks and eventually became antique shops dealing with a more exclusive clientele, whilst the true brokers operated at various levels in the market. The continued existence of brokers and second-hand dealers demonstrated both a continuing supply and demand for part-used furniture and furnishings.

Nenadic suggests that this abundance of second-hand goods was built on 'business failure, death, and high levels of middle rank movement between towns and cities [which] all ensured a vast supply of high value second-hand household good, particularly in urban areas' (Nenadic, 1994: 130). She goes further to argue that second-hand purchases were not only a pragmatic decision but were also based on supply problems. In terms of furniture, Nenadic suggests that particularly in non-London sites, timber shortages, the high cost of new materials, and small production facilities all encouraged 'recycling in the middle ranks'. This probably reflects a situation where demand outstripped supply for a while. Nenadic also argues that in the eighteenth century, well-made furniture from selected timbers was an asset that could be realised into cash and represent a form of saving. This explains the propensity of many retailers and cabinet-makers to offer appraising services that valued the goods either for their own purchase and subsequent sale or as a guide to others.

The measure of the usefulness of second-hand goods was found in their function, quality and patina rather than necessarily in their style. Pragmatic decisions were the order of the day. Sara Pennell makes reference to Edward Belson, a journeyman distiller, who, in 1710, furnished the bedroom for his new wife with the latest printed-paper hangings and fashionable fabrics for the bed hangings, but she then notes that the bedstead and bed were purchased second hand (Pennell, 1999: 560). The probable logic here is that whilst the hangings of the bed were on view, the bed and bedsteads were hidden behind the fabric façade.

It has been shown above that people who wanted to furnish their homes had a variety of routes to choose from, dependent upon their income and inclination. Mrs Purefoy wrote about her purchases for mundane items of furniture from a local auction, whereas she usually sent orders to London for special or particular items, thus indicating the use of a range of supply sources (Eland, 1931: 110). The status of goods, whether new or second hand, is often directly related to the nature of the outlet it came from. The division of the market between, cabinet-makers and upholsterers, retailers, furniture-dealers or brokers and auctioneers confirm a tentative hierarchy of furniture supply that was reflected in the locations of business, although there were many cross-overs.

Cabinet-Makers, Upholsterers and Retailers – Eighteenth-century trade cards for furnishing businesses often have the words 'makes and sells' in 'the newest fashions' or 'new and old' types of 'household goods bought sold and appraised' often 'at reasonable rates'. Although this ephemeral evidence is not perfect by any means, it gives a flavour of the range of possibilities that were offered to those who wanted to buy furnishings.

The involvement of cabinet-makers and upholsterers, who were often representative of the better end of the trade in the appraisal and supply of second-hand furniture, was probably as much to do with providing a service to clients as to a direct business proposition. When supplying new goods, old goods had to be disposed of or even part-exchanged, so a stock might be built up by default. The role of appraiser was a crucial one and was naturally taken up by many furniture retailers as an adjunct to their business. Retail trade cards confirm this, Wilkinson and Sons' business in Cheapside c. 1779, for example, advertising that: 'Estates, stock in trade, and all sorts of household furniture appraised, bought and sold by commission' (Heal, 1953). Their role as appraisers was also ambivalent since, in the mid-eighteenth century at least, 'they are obliged to take the goods if it is insisted on, at their own appraisement' (Campbell, 1747:175).

On the other hand, there is evidence of simple trading. In 1760, George Browning, an upholsterer, appraiser and auctioneer noted on his trade card: 'Ready money given for all manner of household goods' (Heal, 1953). George Reynolds, a cabinet-maker, appraiser and undertaker of Soho Square, recorded in 1765 on his trade card that 'estates and all sorts of household furniture bought or sold by commission in town or country'. Another example is the c.1768–86 trade card of Thomas Moore of Whitechapel in London which reveals the range of services commonly offered by many eighteenth-century furniture retailers. He was an upholsterer, cabinetmaker and broker who: 'Makes up in the Newest and Genteelest Taste Four Poster Bedsteads w Drapery & other Furniture. Desk and Bookcases, Chairs, Soffas, Tables, Glasses, Venetian and Spring Blinds &c. Household Goods Bought sold and Appraised. Variety of Paper Hangings. Funerals equipped'. Throughout the nineteenth century, there was a gradual shift in the nature of the cabinet maker/upholsterers business that manifested itself in an increasing division between those firms that concentrated on production, those that focused more on direct retailing, and others that kept a foot on both camps. Indeed as the market grew and became more segmented during the nineteenth century, the divisions became clearer.

In 1875 the trade journal *Furniture Gazette* explored the contemporary situation through a very informative article. It gives a clear overview of the developments of the range of furnishing outlets in London. The first group were the most prestigious: 'First we have the high class houses, represented by such firms as those of Gillows, Morant, Dowbiggin &c., whose reputation is such for the superiority of their productions that it is not necessary for them to make any display whatsoever'. These firms were superior manufacturers who supplied the upper-class carriage trade from both London and county addresses. Some of these firms had been established in the eighteenth century and continued the trade in bespoke work made on the premises. They offered the utmost degree of service across the whole of the home furnishing needs of families and in many cases served across generations.

The journal next identified those 'firms famous for the production of articles of high artistic order, of whom Jackson and Graham are a fair representative house. Their windows are never crowded with goods, but exhibit frequently one article only, rarely more than two or three, but these are always distinguished for some rare excellence of design or colouring'. These relatively new suppliers worked for customers who were interested in expressing difference, but in a more contemporary taste. Again this was a relatively small market segment that particularly flourished in the second half of the nineteenth century. These firms catered for a clientele who were influenced by commentators such as Charles Eastlake and William Morris.

Thirdly the journal identified a class of shops that 'deal only in old furniture which realises high prices leaving a goodly residuum of profit (. . .) their windows look as if they had migrated thither from the South Kensington Museum'. These we would recognise as 'antique dealers' today, although they were often known as brokers at that time. Clearly they were of interest to the 'personalising shopper', as tastes in some quarters moved towards using curiosities and bric-a-brac in domestic interiors. Whilst initially this taste was rather limited in its appeal to collectors and those imbued with a spirit of romanticism, there was a gradual growth in interest in furnishing with antiques that reached its height towards the end of the nineteenth century.

The article then went on to identify the major retail outlets that were part of the development of large stores that were 'represented by such firms as Shoolbred and Co. Marshall and Snelgrove and Maple, [who] make magnificent displays, in their large well-arranged windows of resplendent carpets, rich curtains fabrics, and inlaid cabinet work'. Although these stores did have workshops, sometimes quite extensive ones, they were mainly in the business of retailing. They appealed to the 'respectable shoppers' – the middle classes – because the stores tried to develop a reputation for value and service that satisfied the customers' egotistical needs. These types of stores developed in many urban centres, and were instrumental in serving the needs of the rising and growing middling classes.

Fifthly there was a 'class [of shop who] makes good displays of useful ordinary goods judiciously ticketed with a view of attracting by price more than by pattern or texture. The houses of Meeking, Tarn, Oetzmann, Whiteley and Venebales are representative of this class'. These stores were attractive to the 'economic shopper'. An interesting example is the bazaar that was similar to a department store. In 1841 Charles Knight writing in a guide to London commented upon the Pantechnicon in Belgrave Square that: 'Another department is for the sale of furniture, and consists of several long rooms or galleries filled with pianofortes, tables, chairs, sideboards, chests of drawers, bedsteads, carpets, and all the varied range of household furniture, each article, as in the former case, being ticketed with its selling price' (Knight, 1841–4). The distinctions between this group and the one above are probably a matter of degrees of service and range of stock.

Finally, 'there is the sixth and very numerous class [of shop] who depend solely upon ticketing and startling announcements [where the goods are] shovelled in piles' into the windows. This store type probably developed from brokers businesses and became suppliers to the 'economic shoppers' who had limited funds or required little in the way of service.

Brokers and Dealers – The term broker or dealer covers a very wide range of supplier types and includes the sale of new and/or second-hand goods. Depending on a range of circumstances, brokers might be large enterprises with extensive warehouses, small one man or woman operations working from a domestic address, or simply an offshoot of another business type. For example, street directories show 'poulterer and furniture broker', 'publican and furniture broker', and so on.

In eighteenth-century London, there was a Brokers Row near Moorfields. It was to here that on 18 April 1768 Lady Mary Coke 'went from the carpet manufactory [Moorfields] to a place called Brokers Row, where I bought several things: my coach was almost filled' (Wainwright, 1989: 34). That this was a respectable shopping location is demonstrated by the insurance value of £800 for the house in Brokers Row of one Samuel Swain, an upholsterer and broker (Wainwright, 1989: 34). However, this particular shopping area apparently suffered a decline. By 1817, Johnston's *London Directory* listed Brokers Row as having twenty-eight premises housing ten brokers and appraisers, two furniture-brokers and six upholders/cabinet-makers. 'A description of the area in the 1820s would appear to confirm the second-hand bias of the businesses: When I remember

Moorfields first [it had] line of shops without fronts, occupied chiefly by dealers in old furniture, to the east and north. Most of these shops were covered in by screens of canvas or rough boards, so as to form an apology for a piazza (. . .) a broken down four poster or a rickety tent bed might be secured at almost any price (. . .) a tall stiff upright easy chair, without a bottom; a cupboard with one shelf left of three, and with half a door; here a black oak chest groaning to be scraped (. . .)' (Aleph, 1864: 35).

An analysis of the London trade directories shows an interesting trend. In 1820 there were only two brokers listed. By 1833 this number had risen to 632, by 1854 there was a drop to 567 and by 1890 a further drop to 390. Allowing for probably incorrect listing in 1820, there is a clear rise in numbers followed by an equally clear decline as the century progressed. It is also likely that many furniture brokers who were at the bottom end of the market would not have been included in trade directories. Shaw and Tipper suggest that agents for the directories did not venture into courts to collect information resulting in the down-market traders escaping inclusion (Shaw and Tipper, 1989: 22).

Although there was a growth of interest in 'old things' from the later eighteenth century, it is difficult to pinpoint the development of specialist antique dealers. It seems that some brokers developed the trade into specifically antiques or curiosities to meet a small but growing demand for such items. There was a growing number of these traders in London, but less so elsewhere. They adopted the title of antique dealer in the early nineteenth century and were often concentrated in particular parts of town. Clive Wainwright has shown how Wardour Street in Soho, London developed into a centre of antique shops and traders. In 1817 there were no brokers but thirteen cabinet-makers or upholsterers. In 1838 there were nine brokers and twelve cabinet-makers/upholsterers. By 1850 this number had increased to twenty-three 'brokers' and twenty-four cabinet-maker/upholsterers (Wainwright, 1989). The distinction between brokers and antique dealers is difficult to establish, as the naming might be misleading. The trade directories only list seven antique furniture dealers in 1833, sixteen in 1854 and forty-seven by 1890; so clearly the term broker could cover antique dealers as well.

The prevalence of women dealing in second-hand clothes was repeated to some extent in the second-hand furniture trade, particularly at the lowest end of the business. In London, by the 1830s, evidence from the street directories shows a Broker's Alley, off Drury Lane, with twelve premises occupied by brokers; four of them run by women. That these were small-scale enterprises is indicated by several of them sharing premises with other furniture brokers. However, another reason for the presence of female furniture brokers was that widows who took over their husbands' cabinet-making and/or upholstering businesses were not always in a position to continue the trade in the same way so became dealers rather than makers (Kirkham, 1995).

In 1836 Charles Dickens drew attention to the distinctions between brokers of new and second-hand furniture in his *Sketches by Boz,* which gave descriptions of the two classes of shops either of which his readers would recognise: 'Perhaps when we make use of the term 'Brokers' shops', the minds of our readers will at once picture large handsome warehouses, exhibiting a long perspective of French polished dining tables, rosewood chiffoniers, and mahogany wash-hand stands, with an occasional vista of a four poster bed and hangings (. . .). Perhaps they will imagine that we mean an humble class of second-hand furniture repositories. Their imagination will then naturally lead them to that street at the back of Long Acre, which is composed almost entirely of broker shops: where you walk through groves of deceitful, showy looking furniture' (Chapter 21). He continues with an acerbic comment on the quality of the goods likely to be found there: 'The goods here are adapted to the taste, or rather to the means, of cheap purchasers. There are some of the most beautiful LOOKING Pembroke tables that were ever beheld: the wood as green as the trees in the Park, and the leaves almost as certain to fall off in the course of a year'. The moves of the more sophisticated dealers to distance themselves from the taint of the broker's image seem understandable in the light of these comments.

Auctions – Auctions were another site of potential purchase that sold both new and second-hand goods. People from all levels of society sold up their furniture and belongings (or had it seized by creditors) for a variety of reasons. The best-documented examples are auctions of house contents, advertisements for which were regularly carried in newspapers in the form of a list of goods for sale. Sometimes reasons for the sale were given: the death of the householder was the most common, but others included bankruptcy. Whilst goods sold in an auction room had no provenance or guarantee of their quality, the sale of house contents often made a feature of the owner's name and gave the name of the house. Indeed, the sale often took place on the premises. Holding the auction at the house had the benefit of sending a clear message to the prospective buyer: it gave an indication of the relative value of the goods and their authenticity, and perhaps this was particularly important when the sale was for a member of the gentry.

In relation to the issue of taste transfer and goods acquisition, Katherine Grier has pointed out how public contact with the auctioning of household furniture 'on the premises' of the vendor, provided a chance to see the goods 'in situ' as well as to have an opportunity to purchase them. She cites a passage from 'A Bargain: Is a Penny saved Twopence Got?' published in 1854 in *Gleason's Pictorial Drawing Room Companion* which explains how tasteful objects filter down the social scale through the function of the auctioneer and the second-hand market. Commenting on the swarms of viewers: 'That's it, you see. Mr Allen said (. . .) that's the way so many people of moderate means have their house so handsomely furnished. A man of taste like Lyons [the vendor] or yourself, collects books, and pictures and furniture, to be dispersed eventually after this fashion [i.e. by auction]. The next owner 'declines housekeeping' [sells] in turn, and things being a little more tarnished by removal and use, are purchased a shade cheaper by a class a grade lower in the scale, and so *decencus averni*' (Grier, 1988: 25).

Although purchases were often made because of their functional rather than their status value, the more specialised case of antiques and collectibles provided other motives for purchase of used goods. As with all sales outlets there was a range of types and qualities. The image of auctioneers and appraisers was apparently rather different to furniture brokers and might suggest a more desirable form of consumption (Wall, 1997). However, contemporary accounts suggest that there was a wide range of outlets, some of very dubious character.

Auctions were also a common way of disposing of stock, particularly in the event of a death or bankruptcy. A famous example was conducted on 17 March 1766, when the *Public Advertiser* published details of an auction sale planned to realize the assets of the partnership of Chippendale and Rannie. Amongst the items listed in the advertisement were: 'A great variety of fine mahogany and tulip wood cabinets, desks, and bookcases, cloaths presses, double chests of drawers, commodes, buroes, fine library, writing, card, dining and other tables (. . .) fine pattern chairs and sundry other pieces of curious cabinet work' (Wills, 1969: 14). Since the eighteenth century, auctioneers had also sold new furniture, and it was still annoying retailers in the nineteenth. In the *Hampshire Telegraph* of 10 March 1817, the following advertisement appeared: 'To be sold by Auction by Mr. Garnett at his auction room, Queen Street [Portsea], on Friday 14th March 1817, – About twenty sets of handsome drawing room and other painted chairs, twelve bedsteads, feather beds, tea trays, six copper coal scuttles, twelve sets of fire irons, dining and Pembroke tables, two slipper baths (. . .).' (Stabler, 1991: 101). Two weeks later, the newspaper included an advertisement for the sale of a cabinet-maker's stock that made the following point: 'When the public are satisfied that the goods are really of the late Mr. Eastman's manufacture, any further comment on them will be unnecessary: and the failure of the several attempts lately made to sell large quantities of cheap London made goods by Auction, in this neighbourhood, leads him to conclude that the attention of the public is not diverted from this opportunity of purchasing at a cheap rate (. . .)' (Stabler, 1991: 101).

Of course, traditional retailers were very disparaging of auction sales as they detracted from the sale of new goods. Indeed the 'legitimate' trade elsewhere also took exception to auctions. One correspondent to the *Edinburgh Evening Courant* wrote in March 1788: 'Tradesmen and shopkeepers complain much at this time of dullness in business, and want of employment (. . .) [a reason for this is] their customers going to sales and roups [auctions] with the ready money they ought to pay their debts with. It is notorious that at some late sales of furniture, higher prices were given than the articles cost a dozen years ago' (Pryke, 1989: 55).

Books and periodicals gave advice on purchasing from auctions. For example, in 1829, readers of *The Home Book* were told that if they thought that a house could be furnished 'in a superior style, at a very modest expense' by going to auctions, they should know that: 'A young person is in great danger of being drawn on, by the artful dealers who attend such sales, to continue bidding for an article which pleases the fancy, till at last it becomes his property at a price far beyond that for which it might be purchased of a regular tradesman' (Lady, 1829: 107). The author concedes that good-quality articles might be obtained in this way, but that the homemakers would need a friend with some experience to advise them. George Augustus Sala, writing in 1850, observed that in his opinion auction sales were 'the Bohemianism of commerce [because] there always enters into the deed of selling something wild, something picturesque, and something exciting' (Sala, 1859:172). Clearly a friend to moderate the excitement might have been a good thing.

Magazines also warned about new goods. For example, in 1838, *The Magazine of Domestic Economy* advised homemakers that the use of veneers and unseasoned wood by unscrupulous manufacturers led to materials splitting and it was best, they advised, to purchase items 'which had been sometime on sale; because the chances are that the union of the two woods will be thoroughly effected'. It would appear that the acquisition of second-hand furniture made out of solid timber posed less of a risk than purchase of new. This is clearly demonstrated by the experience of James Hopkinson, a cabinet-maker in Liverpool who commented, in his diary in 1851, on purchasing goods at an auction. He wanted to fill his showroom and did not have sufficient items that he had made, so he went to an auction and bought what he thought were second-hand, good quality pieces, only to find that they were new, slop-made goods. The furniture had been darkened to look old and the auction room was poorly lit. He had difficulty reselling the furniture (Goodman, 1968: 36). It is important to note that in this instance Hopkinson had been fooled by the bad practises of the auction room, but that he had expected to find a ready market for the good quality second-hand furniture that he thought he was buying.

Whereas the apparent up-market status of some auction houses and the information given in homemaking literature suggests a middle-class market for at least some of the second-hand furniture in circulation throughout the period, as the nineteenth century progressed, the range of auction rooms was very wide and catered for all classes of the furniture purchasing public.

4.3 Acceptance and Use

Returning to the four major categories of shopper – the economic, the personalising, the respectable, and the hybrid – and linking these to the notion that the constitution of identities is an important part of the consumption of both new and second-hand furnishings, we can begin to see how these goods were acquired. As it was the importance of objects and their cultural meanings, as opposed to the idea of simple materiality, people were less likely to make a distinction between first and second cycle purchases – they were simply means of getting goods that were desirable for whatever reason. For the economic shopper, price and value were important; for the personalising shopper, difference was valued, and for the respectable, value was important but so were the associative qualities that the goods brought with them. These may have been related either to 'newness' or 'the antique'. *The Magazine of Domestic Economy* recommended homemakers to purchase the best furniture that they could afford partly because such goods would fetch a reasonable price if resold (September 1840: 65). So, good quality furniture was seen as an investment that would hold its value reasonably well because it was perceived to be desirable within the second-hand market.

For most of the period under review, an underlying assumption was that there was a search for a degree of respectability evidenced in part through home furnishings. Woodruff Smith has argued that 'respectability' arose out of a bourgeois appropriation of a range of contexts to create a new ideal based on gentility, luxury, virtue. Respectable families therefore purchased goods for comfort, status and convenience as well as any connotations the goods might have (Smith, 2002). For most home-makers, whatever their level of income, there was the possibility of purchasing goods that tried to reflect this.

Evidence of the actual process of buying is notoriously difficult to find. Locating evidence for the motives for the purchase of goods is particularly elusive. However, it seems probable that the 'hybrid shopper' type was the most widespread category, as people probably had various and variable spending patterns according to their age, circumstance and purse. A variety of purchasing methods is well illustrated in the example of Parson Woodforde of Norfolk, who records a number of purchases over a period in the late eighteenth century. These reveal that he bought second-hand goods from a cabinet-maker, made a purchase at a house sale, and also used part exchange. On 12 January 1788, for example, he discussed the delivery of a sofa from 'my upholsterer Mr Horth'. On

13 November 1789 he recorded that he had 'bought this day of William Hart, cabinet-makers on Hog Hill Norwich, 2 large second-hand double flapped mohogany (sic) tables also one second-hand mohogany dressing table with drawers also one new mohogany wash stand for all which paid 4.14.6d'. A year later, on 2 April 1793, Woodforde attended the sale of goods of Mrs Michelthwaite where he bid for 'a very handsome mahogany sideboard, a very good and large Wilton carpet and a mahogany cellaret', the first two of which he successfully purchased. The next day he noted that 'we brought home the carpet that I bought, and gave orders to Sudbury my upholsterer to send home my sideboard by 2 men'. Six months later, he again employed Sudbury to supply new tables. The upholsterers 'took my two large tables and smaller one in part of exchange for the others and he is to allow me for the three, only £2.18.0d' (Beresford, 1929: 148–51).

Changes in shopping practices in urban areas were clear by the early nineteenth century. In 1833 a question from the Select Committee on Manufactures, Commerce and Shipping asked one witness: 'Does not the increase of that practice [fixed price ticketing] arise from an entire change in the mode of carrying on the retail business, that is, that it has now become more casual and less dependant upon regular constant customers to particular shops than it used to be formerly?' (Benson and Shaw, 1992: 32). The witness replied in the affirmative and suggested that it had only occurred in the last ten to fifteen years. This seems to indicate a change from particular retailers of new goods relying on a few regular customers to those new entrants serving a wide range of passing customers. In terms of the second-hand market, Stana Nenadic, suggests the customer base had also changed: 'By the second decade of the nineteenth century, it was much less likely that middle-rank men and women would own either furniture or clothing that had previously belonged outside their family, and it was much more likely that working people would be able to purchase second-hand goods that had once belonged to the relatively wealthy' (Nenadic, 1994: 129).

Prior to the 1850s, respectable room designs had a tendency to be based on a planned and unified décor, supplied by a retailer or architect. In lesser homes, a retailer might provide parlour furniture, whereas upstairs was furnished with goods from brokers or auctions. From around 1850 to 1880, comfort was encouraged as rooms developed particular functions, and required appropriate furnishings. By then, the choice of supplier had increased dramatically. Apart for the hierarchy of furniture suppliers already mentioned, the department store began to supply appropriate goods, and mail order firms began to encroach on the cheaper end of the market. From the 1880s an interest in *bric-a-brac*, 'accessorisation' and individual expression encouraged the growth of a species of broker at one level and 'antique dealers' at another. The fashionable second-hand, this time labelled as 'antique', returned to favour.

4.4 Conclusion

The culture of consumption that revolves round the sequence of selling, buying, using, disposing and subsequent re-selling of possessions has been reflected in this article and the life cycles of the goods it discusses. Objects acquire a life history, which may represent a rise or a decline in fortunes that is somewhat dependent upon how they fit into the wider cycle of consumption. To this end, I have considered the status of both new and second-hand furniture and shown how the nature of the site of sale – whether upholsterer, broker or auctioneer – makes a great difference to the image of acquiring various goods, both new or used.

The examples suggest that people reacted in various ways to the issue of the second-hand and that this was based very much on one's position in society. For the poorer groups, purchasing 'part used' furniture was a necessity brought out of financial pressures, and while to some extent this was also true for middle-class groups it was, more importantly, an opportunity to buy into an image of quality and success which might be reflected in patina of age and rank, expressed in the better quality furniture sold. The distinctions between categories of culture can also be seen in the differences between 'old' and 'new' wealth. In the case of old wealth (gentry and nobility), McCracken (1988) has posited the idea of 'patina' as a representation of status prior to and after the eighteenth century. He goes on to suggest that, during the eighteenth century, the fashion system took over and status was to be found in new things rather than old. This in turn encouraged regular changes in styles enabling distinctions to be continually made. These choices reflected the various cultural values placed by differing groups upon the comparative value of second-hand furniture, but also reflected the limits on choice imposed by financial circumstances. The problem of a mis-match between supply and demand began to fall away by the beginning of the nineteenth century as improvements in production and retailing started to meet the growing demand, so that the distinctions between 'new' and 'second hand' became related to identify choice and affordability. In any event it seems clear that the market for the sale and acquisition of new or old furniture was fully catered for.

Bibliography

Primary Sources

Published sources

Aleph, W.H. (1864) *London scenes and London people*, London.
Anon. (1870) *Cassel's household guide*, London.
Campbell, R. (1747) *London tradesmen*, Newton Abbot.
Defoe, D. (1708) *A review of the State of the British Nation*, London.
Defoe, D. (1727) *The complete English tradesman*, Part 2, London.
Knight, C. (1841–4) *Knight's London*, London.
Lady, A. (1829) *The home book*, London.
Loudon, J. C. (1839) *An encyclopedia of cottage, farm and villa architecture and furniture*, revised edition, London.
Magazine of Domestic Economy, (May 1838), London.
Oetzmann, J. (c. 1871) *Hints on house furnishing and decoration*, London.
Sala, G.A. (1859) *Twice round the clock*, London.
Stokes, J. (1829) *The complete cabinet maker and upholsterer's guide*, London.
Thomson, J. and Smith, A. (1877) *Street life in London*, London.

Literature

Adburgham, A. (1979) *Shops and shopping 1800–1914*, London.
Benson, J. and Shaw, G. (1992) *The evolution of retail systems 1800–1914*, Leicester.
Beresford, J. (ed.) (1929) *The diary of a country Parson*, Oxford.

Berg, M. (1999) 'New Commodities, luxuries and their consumers in eighteenth century England', Berg, M. and Clifford, H. (eds.), *Consumers and luxury: Consumer culture in Europe 1650–1850*, Manchester, 63–83.

Campbell, C. (1993) 'Understanding traditional and modern patterns of consumption in eighteenth century England: a character action approach', Brewer, J. and Porter, R. (eds.), *Consumption and the world of goods*, London, 40–57.

Carson, C., Hoffman, R. and Albert, P. (eds.) (1994) *Of consuming interests: the style of life in the eighteenth century*, Charlottesville.

Csikszentmihalyi, M. and Rochberg-Halton, E. (1981) *The meaning of things, domestic symbols and the self*, New York.

Douglas, M. (1992) 'Why do people want goods?', Hargreaves-Heap, S. and Ross, A. (eds.), *Understanding the enterprise culture: Themes in the work of Mary Douglas*, Edinburgh.

Douglas, M. and Isherwood, B. (1980) *The world of goods, Towards an anthropology of consumption*, Harmondsworth.

Edwards, R. and Jourdain, M. (1955) *Georgian cabinet makers*, London.

Eland, G. (ed) (1931) *Purefoy letters*, London.

Falk, P. and Campbell, C. (1997) *The shopping experience*, London.

Glennie, P. (1995) 'Consumption within historical studies', Miller, D. (ed.), *Acknowledging consumption*, London, 164–203.

Goodman, J. (ed.) (1968) *Victorian cabinet maker: the Memoirs of James Hopkinson 1819–1894*, London.

Gregson, N. and Crewe, L. (2003) *Second-hand cultures*, Oxford.

Grier, K. (1988) *Culture and comfort: people, parlors and upholstery 1850–1930*, New York.

Heal, A. (1953) *The London furniture makers from the Restoration to the Victorian era, 1660–1840*, London.

Hopkinson, J. (1968) *Victorian cabinet maker, memoirs of James Hopkinson 1819–1894*, New York.

Kirkham, P. (1995) '"If you have no sons": Furniture-making in Britain', Attfield, J. and Kirkham, P. (eds.), *A View from the interior: women and design*, London.

McKendrick, N., Brewer, J. and Plumb, J. (1982) *Birth of a consumer society*, Bloomington.

McQuoid, P. (1905) *Age of walnut*, London.

Muthesius, S. (1988) 'Aspects of the antique in Britain 1870–1910', *Art History*, 11:2, 231–254.

McCracken, G. (1988) *Culture and consumption*, Bloomington.

Nenadic, S. (1994) 'Middle rank consumers and domestic culture in Edinburgh and Glasgow 1720–1840', *Past & Present*, 145, 122–156.

Pennell, S. (1999) 'Consumption and consumerism in Early Modern England', *The Historical Journal*, 42:2, 549–564.

Pryke, S. (1989) 'A Study of the Edinburgh furnishing trade taken from contemporary press notices 1708–1790', *Regional Furniture*, 3, 52–67.

Shaw, G. and Tipper, A. (1989) *British directories: A bibliography and guide to directories published in England and Wales 1850–1950 and Scotland 1773–1950*, London.

Sheraton, T. (1803) *The Cabinet Dictionary*, London.

Smith, W. D. (2002) *Consumption and the making of respectability 1600–1800*, New York.

Stabler, J, (1991) 'English newspaper advertisements as a source of furniture history', *Regional Furniture*, V, 93–102.

Stobart, J. (2006) 'Clothes, cabinet and carriages second hand dealing in eighteenth century England', Blondé, B., Stabel, P., Stobart, J. and Van Damme, I. (eds.), *Buyers and Sellers. Retail circuits and practices in Medieval and Early Modern Europe*, Turnhout.

Symonds, R. and Whinnery, B. (1962) *Victorian Furniture*, London.

Wainwright, C. (1989) The *Romantic Interior*, New Haven.
Wall, C. (1997) 'The English Auction: Narratives of Dismantlings', *Eighteenth Century Studies*, 31:1, 1–25.
Wills, G. (1969) *English furniture 1760–1900*, London.

PART II

CONSUMING

CHAPTER 5

Conflicting Consumption Models? The Symbolic Meaning of Possessions and Consumption amongst the Antwerp Nobility at the End of the Eighteenth Century

Bruno Blondé[1] – University of Antwerp, Centre for Urban History, Belgium

5.1 Introduction

The history of consumption as an historic sub-discipline is long past its infancy (Brewer and Porter, 1993). Research into the daily life and consumption habits of specific social groups in the Southern Netherlands, however, remains under-developed and, despite the more favourable source situation, the same is broadly true of research into the nobility (De Vlieger-De Wilde, 2003). Thanks to the excellent research work carried out by Karel Degryse we possess good field knowledge of the fortunes and lifestyles of several households belonging to the Antwerp elite (Degryse, 1974, 1977, 1980, 1982, 1985a, 1985b; Coppens and Degryse, 1994; Coppens, 2002). In this historiography the process of aristocratisation of the city on the Scheldt after 1585 forms a leitmotif (Janssens, 1998a; Duerloo, 1991: 107). Gradually excluded from opportunities for commercial expansion and profits, growing numbers of wealthy men opted for the life of ease, although their heart was not always in it. Established merchant families sought alliances with patrician families, bought castles and country houses and built up art collections – in short, they assumed the lifestyle of the nobility (Soly, 1993: 43; Timmermans, 2002). As early as the seventeenth century the 'noble' lifestyle began to leave its mark on the daily culture of the urban elites. In painting, for example, genres such as hunting scenes and portraits in particular were considered to be levers to the construction of a noble identity (Balis, 1991; Van der Stighelen, 1991:143). Yet a large scale investigation on wealth conducted by Degryse reveals that, in the eighteenth century, all-in-all, the top Antwerp families had a fairly modest lifestyle. In comparison with the Brussels nobility, most of whose family trees contained more high officials, members of the Antwerp nobility generally give a more frugal, mercantile impression. This is confirmed by certain measurable parameters, such as the number of servants in their employ (Figure 5.1.) (Blondé, 1999: 94–98). In 1755, despite the incomplete nature of the census, Brussels not only contained many more families of independent means, but also a striking number of households with very

1 I would like to thank Luc Duerloo, Koen De Vlieger-De Wilde, and Jon Stobart for their help and valuable suggestions to earlier versions of this text.

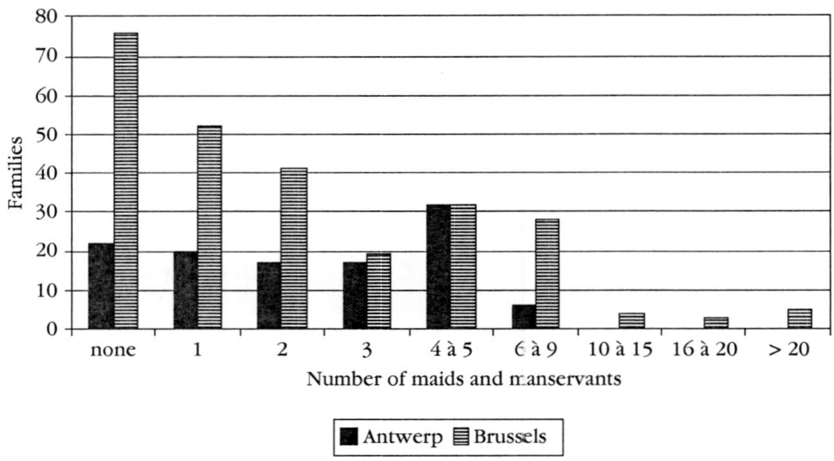

FIGURE 5.1. Domestic staff employed by families of independent means with a man at the head of the family, Antwerp and Brussels, 1755

SOURCE: Algemeen Rijksarchief Brussel (ARA), *Fiscaal Officie Brabant*, nrs. 388–405; *Staten van Brabant*, Cartons 409–410; Stadsarchief Antwerpen (SAA), *Privilegiekamer* (*Pk*), nrs. 2561–2564.

extensive staffs.[2] When compared with them, even the richest families in Antwerp lived far more modestly. In Antwerp, families of independent means employing more than four servants formed an exception; none employed more than ten maids and menservants.

The example of servants sets the tone of this contribution. It is not concerned with the process of aristocratisation in all its legal and social complexity. In the following pages I would like to raise some questions about the social and cultural impact of the process of aristocratisation on consumption in Antwerp. In spite of the frugal reputation of the people of Antwerp can we rightly speak of a specifically 'noble' everyday culture?

5.2 An Explosion of Conspicuous Consumption?

We have already demonstrated in an earlier article on the evolution of horse ownership in the eighteenth century that the aristocratisation of the Antwerp elites may have had a major impact on the consumption of luxury goods (Blondé, 2001). For various reasons horse and carriage ownership can be seen as a classic example of conspicuous consumption in the more narrow sense of the term (Burke, 1993). Riding horses and keeping carriages and coaches was an expensive business. The costs of feeding and looking after the animals were considerable. For certain social groups horses for recreation no doubt formed responsible investment in symbolic capital. They were, after all, the *pars pro toto* of a way of life (Burke, 1987: 139). Together with an impressive mansion, a country estate and a retinue of well-dressed maids and manservants, the possession of a horse and carriage was one of the most discussed ingredients in a *train de vie* through which real or

2 Our processing of this census only deals with families with a male at their head.

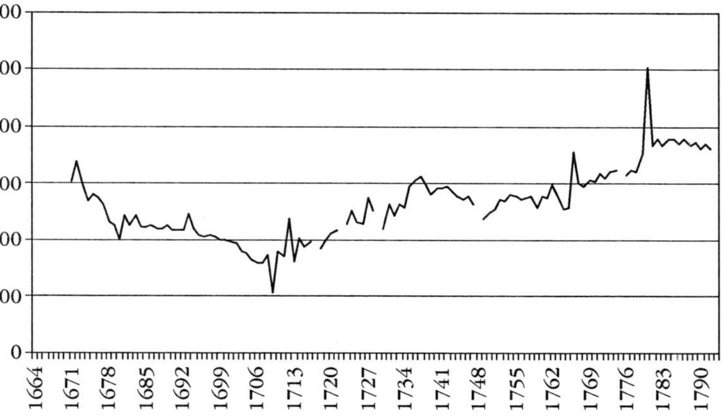

FIGURE 5.2. Revenue from horse tax in Antwerp, c. 1670–1790

SOURCE: Blondé, 2001.

aspiring notables assumed the requisite style (Janssens, 1998b: 235–238; Degryse, 1980: 469–470 and 1982: 114). With the help of data about horse ownership in Antwerp it is possible to make a realistic estimate of the demand for luxury goods and thus the process of aristocratisation. Figure 5.2. charts the revenue from the annual horse tax. For a number of fiscal and source-technical reasons the figure only indicates the general trends of the ownership of luxury horses.

The course of the graph roughly corresponds to our view of the economic climate of the city in this period. During the second half of the seventeenth century the Antwerp market for luxury goods was hit by export problems. The drop in demand resulting from the loss of purchasing power of the Antwerp elites may then have played a part in the economic crisis (Thijs, 1993: 112). It is not surprising that, in this respect, the first decade of the eighteenth century was a disastrous one. Consequently, several horse owners were forced to dispose of their animals. On the other hand, during the first half of the eighteenth century, the luxury goods market went through a period of steady growth, in spite of the deep economic crisis and strong de-industrialisation. Between 1693 and 1709 the population of Antwerp fell from about 77,000 to an estimated 70,000 (Klep, 1981: 352). By 1755 Antwerp had barely 48,600 inhabitants (Blondé, 1999: 255). Although all authors agree that de-industrialisation caused considerable damage during the first half of the eighteenth century, the demand for luxury goods remained firm – at least judging from the patterns of horse ownership. Various factors may help to explain this paradox. In the first place, the shrinking economic horizon obliged a large number of Antwerp merchants to retire from business, often against their aspiration. In this respect Jacomo de Pret wrote in 1730 about 'rentiers que nous devenons tous, faute de commerce' (Degryse, 1985b: 320). Several families tried to get themselves included in the ranks of the nobility, and they displayed the lifestyle that was expected of them there.[3] On the other hand we must not

3 The abrupt climb in the horse-tax curve during this period was the result of an agreement with the brewing trade, not of a sudden increase in horse ownership

FIGURE 5.3. Alexander II Casteels, Detail from the 'Paardenmarkt', c. 1750

SOURCE: Ghent University Library.

forget that, particularly from the second decade of the eighteenth century, important new paved roads were constructed, making the ownership of horses and vehicles *relatively* attractive as an 'investment' (Baillieul, 1973). During the first half of the eighteenth century there was a considerable increase in *interurban traffic* in particular, and passenger travel was probably a driving force behind this (Blondé, 1999: 203). Some authors emphasise on the other hand that the strong de-urbanisation in the first half of the eighteenth century was perhaps coupled to an increase in individual incomes in the towns of Brabant (Van der Wee, 1988: 365). The great majority of horse owners in the middle of the eighteenth century had a 'noble' title, although the term may be somewhat exaggerated for a nobility that was generally of recent origin. The growth continued through the second half of the eighteenth century, in both absolute and relative terms. While the urban population only increased by about 11 percent between 1755 and 1784, and road traffic in the Antwerp region grew by 'only' 26 percent, the revenue from the horse tax rose by 36 percent (Figure 5.2.).

The strong desire for luxury goods landed some families in financial problems. Several scions of prominent Antwerp families were made wards of court in the last decade of the eighteenth century because their profligate ways endangered their fortunes and their honour (Degryse, 1985b: 641–654; Blondé, 2001: 498; Soly, 2001: 126–131). The increase in conspicuous consumption, moreover, forms a glaring contrast with the grinding poverty in which the lower social groups in Antwerp lived in the second half of the eighteenth century (Blondé, 1996). Furthermore, some authors suggest that (changes in) consumption patterns largely contributed to a widening of the socio-cultural rift (Muchembled, 1990: 174). Hugo Soly, for example, pointed out that the rapid changes in fashion in the eighteenth century – many and more varied materials, clothes, jewellery and decorations – enlarged the possibilities for social differentiation (Soly, 1991: 42; Soly, 1988; Blondé and Greefs, 2001). The gap between rich and poor was not only widened by an ever-increasing material culture but also by the use of the French language, more civilised manners and a growing tendency towards spatial segregation. A visit to the theatre became socially selective, for example, and even the space inside the theatre was increasingly protected by higher prices and subscriptions (Thijs, 1990: 161–168). In the public forum the carriage parade referred to earlier also formed an almost physical boundary between the 'happy few' and the bulk of the Antwerp population. In what follows, we shall examine some of these elite households to see the extent to which this stereotypical view of the Antwerp nobility in the late eighteenth century corresponds to reality.

5.3 'Noble' Living Patterns

The approach we are following here is intentionally explorative and descriptive. In our research into the material culture we have only a handful of descriptions of the household effects of noble households dating from the late eighteenth century. That sample is certainly too small a base from which to draw any firm conclusions. Within the nobility the differences formed by origin, rank, income and social network guarantee that every household is by definition almost only representative of itself (De Vries, 1993). Nonetheless, a first survey reveals patterns that perhaps indicate a group-regulated everyday culture, as we will try to demonstrate.

Maximilien-Frédéric-Ernest, Prince of Salm-Salm and Duke of Hoogstraten (who died in 1773), is the first nobleman we shall visit (Spaepen, 1993). For a variety of reasons the notarial description of the contents of the Court of Hoogstraten gives only a partial picture of the material culture of this nobleman and his household. In the first place it is evident that a number of objects are missing – for example, there was no inventory drawn up of the clothing. Moreover and even more importantly, the duke owned other houses, among them the castle of Hoogstraten, which escape from our eye (Lauwerijs, 1979). Yet the Duke conforms in every respect to the archetype of the great noble. The (incomplete) description of his property reveals that his mansion had no fewer than 36 rooms.[4] Maximilian of Salm-Salm moreover proves the rule that, in the course of the early modern period, an increasingly dramatic functional specialisation and differentiation of the living quarters was taking place (Sarti, 2002: 138–139). The appearance of separate bedchambers and the introduction of antechambers was entirely in keeping with the process of increasing privacy. The presence of more than twenty so called 'gambling tables' and candelabra designed especially for gaming, as well as countless comfortable armchairs and sofas, shows that a number of rooms were aimed at providing a sociable atmosphere and comfort (Van den Berg, 1985). The Duke of Hoogstraten was in many ways a man of his times: the colours and furnishings of the rooms were balanced, there were practically no religious symbols (apart from one silver

4 SAA, *Not. Prot.*, 186, acte 1: 'bureau, chambre du Prince, l'antichambre, grande salle enhaut, garderobe du Prince enhaut, chambre bleue, chambre verde, garde robe, antichambre, garde-meubles, autre garde-meubles, chambre des domestiques, chambre du cuisinier, chambre du jeune prince, chambre sur la cuisine, chambre des deux princes ainés, chambre des domestiques en bas, chambre à manger en bas, chambre verde, chambre rouge, chambre de Mme. la Princesse, garde robe de Mme. la Princesse, antichambre, office, chambre du Maî tre d'hotel, une seconde chambre, chambre de la servante, la forge, la lingerie, les écuries, chambre sur le devant, chambre suivante, cuisine, office, cave'.

holy water stoup), and few paintings (Baetens and Blondé, 1991: 70). Just ten pictures, all of them portraits, adorned the walls of the *chambre du Prince* and the *grande salle enhaut*. There was even one work in the *garde-meubles*, a room that no doubt served as storage space. Yet the duke was also attached to tradition. Tapestries (at that time rather dated) hung in his mansion, there was no trace of wallpaper and the chairs round the table in the diningroom were leather. In contrast, Maximilian was entirely in fashion when it came to table subtleties and dining culture. Coffee and tea were already relatively 'democratised', as were coffee and tea services, but the silver chocolate jugs seem to indicate a drinking culture that was only available to the very rich (Blondé and Greefs, 2001: 217–219). Beltens, a notary in Antwerp, counted that the duke owned six brown horses at the time of his death. And his magnificent fleet of two berlins, two coupés, one barouche, two cabriolets and one cart, many of them upholstered in velvet, moquette or morocco leather, was very impressive. Unlike the majority of the elite, Maximilian did not live on one of the city's great arterial roads where it was easier to manoeuvre with a coach and six. In 1766 one thing and another caused a serious conflict between the prince and his neighbours, the church wardens of St. Andrew's: some of the churchyard fencing made it difficult for him to drive his carriage inside quickly. The prince's concerns about being able to park easily form a sharp contrast with the social profile of the neighbourhood in which he moved. The Sint-Andriesstraat was located in the centre of the Sint-Andries district, traditionally one of the poorer neighbourhoods of the city. This one, briefly-described event seems to confirm the picture depicted above of a distressing social polarisation.

Almost everything in the house of the Prince of Salm-Salm – from family coats of arms to real arms; horses, coaches, countless maids' rooms and manservants' rooms – exudes the atmosphere of a splendid noble household. Yet in many respects the prince was atypical of the Antwerp nobility (compare Coppens and Degryse, 1994: 197). In the following analysis we shall see how matters stood with four other noblemen of Antwerp, inventories of whose properties were put into a database and whom we then compared to the rest of the inhabitants of Antwerp. The four are Franciscus Ignatius Gansacker esq., who died in 1774 (SAA, *Not. Prot.*, 712; Janssens and Duerloo, 1992b: 134–135); the lord of Vroylande, Johannes Antonius du Bois esq., who died in 1779 (SAA, *Not. Prot.*, 189; Janssens and Duerloo, 1992a: 309–310); Petrus Josephus Herry esq., who was placed under legal restraint because of his financial mismanagement (SAA, *Not. Prot.*, 784; Janssens and Duerloo, 1992b: 341); and Catharina Louisa Guyot esq. (SAA, *Not. Prot.*, 4744; Janssens and Duerloo, 1992b: 254). In rank and chronology of ennoblement the four families are representative of the young nobility of Antwerp which Degryse had in mind when he formulated his hypothesis about the mentality and consumption habits of this elite. This is evident, for example, from the presence of domestic servants. In her will dated 1 July 1774 Catharina Guyot left an annuity of 100 *gulden courant* each to her manservant and two maids. This was on the binding condition that they were still in her service at the time of her death. Originally it referred to Peeter Van Ael, Elisabeth Janssens and Joanna Mombaers, but a codicil dated 5 August 1776 also mentions Martinus de Visser, current servant, in addition to the two trusted female servants (SAA, *Not. Prot.*, 4744). Gansacker too kept three servants and the 1755 census showed that Jozef du Bois kept as many as six. In his testament of 4 August 1774 the former left 6000 *gulden courant* to *syn meyssen* (his servant) Theresia De Gottal, widow of Peter Cuvilier. In addition, Theresia was to receive a diamond ring, the furniture in her room and the entire supply of wood, coal, peat, butter, beer and wine in the home of the deceased. To Josephus Cuvilier, his manservant, Gansacker left a golden pocket watch and case, silver shoe and trouser buckles, six undershirts, twelve shirts as well as a single legacy of 200 guilders cash and 25 double sovereigns. He also bequeathed 25 double sovereigns to Catharina Cuvilier, the sister of this servant, but from the wording of the will it seems unlikely that she was then in service as a maid. To his coachman, Joannes Gijbels, Gansacker left his walking stick with a golden top, 100 fl. cash and 25 double sovereigns. In addition to this the servants were allowed to keep their livery even if they had not fully 'earned' this by the day of his death. Indeed, to the servants' clothing a great economic as well as symbolic value was attached (SAA, *Not. Prot.*, 712, Testament of 4 August 1774; De Vlieger-De Wilde, 2003: 56–57; Coppens, 2002: 191).

The domestic staff available to the lord of Vroylande clearly shows him to be one of the wealthier figures in the series of noblemen studied. This is also confirmed by the number of horses he owned. The probate inventory reveals that he kept seven horses inside the town walls, an extremely high number by Antwerp standards. Indeed, fiscal sources show that in 1785 there was just one household with eight horses, one with seven and four with six (SAA, *R*, 222). Of the Herry family we only know with any certainty that they employed a coachman (Blondé, 2001: 499). Out of the four families studied it seems that only Catarina Guyot did not use her own coach in the period preceding her death, although this does not mean that she would not have used the services of a hired coachman. Herry traveled about in a green painted coupé coach with four mirrors and upholstered in yellow moquette. He also had at his disposal a green-painted, four-wheeled gig with four mirrors, upholstered in flowered green velvet. Gansacker appears to have had only one coupé, upholstered in red velvet with matching cushions and three mirrors. Finally, du Bois had two fine English sprung coaches and one 'ordinary' sprung coach, one English coupé and one ordinary coupé, two gigs and two rigged snow sledges. All of them lived on the most respectable and prestigious residential streets of eighteenth-century Antwerp: the Prinsstraat, the Huidevettersstraat, the Lange Nieuwstraat and the Vuil(nis)straat.[5] We do not have the space here to describe in detail the magnificence of their houses. In every case our noble testators shared the Prince of Salm-Salm's preference for a radically functional specialisation of the living space. The Gansacker and Herry families, for example, had a 'make up' room, and the *Groote Robijn*, the great house of Jozef du Bois, contained several *cabinets* (closets). Moreover, all four houses had a salon, a dining room and also passages, which contributed greatly to privacy within the home even if they were not made for that particular purpose (Sarti, 2002: 143).

In theory it was in the interests of these newly ennobled families that their households and material culture were enhanced by a patina glow of history (McCracken, 1988; De Vlieger-De Wilde, 2003: 119–121). Without any doubt the coat of arms was one of the principal providers of this. Very precise descriptions of family coats of arms or insignia were

5 In the Lange Nieuwstraat, in 1755, of all male heads of family 4.4 percent referred to themselves as of independent means (with domestic servants), in the Vuilstraat that percentage is nearly 9 percent, for the Huidevettersstraat 11 percent, and for the Prinsstraat 18.5 percent. Only the Vuilstraat had a truly 'mixed profile', for a number of poor families lived there at that time! The Lange Nieuwstraat, because it extended right to the outskirts of the town, had a less respectable standing, so that in 1834 the street as a whole was not considered to have a particularly high cadastral revenue, even though buildings in some parts of it clearly could be counted among the most prestigious in the city (Vandermeersch, 1991: 64).

FIGURES 5.4.–5.5. 'De Grooten Robijn', Lange Nieuwstraat, designed by J.P. Van Baurscheit, c. 1740

SOURCE: Museum Vleeshuis, Antwerp (design) and City Archive, Antwerp (picture).

found in all four households studied (Pietri, 2001: 434; De Vlieger-De Wilde, 2003: 109; Duerloo, 1991). Silver objects in particular lent themselves for this purpose. The spinster Catarina Guyot had a rich and varied collection in which the coats of arms of diverse prominent families were engraved. Among others a milk jug, mustard pot, pepper pot, four candlesticks and a dozen knives and forks bore the Bollaert family arms. The teapot, snuff box and seal carried the arms of the Guyot family. The arms of other families were also found in her collection. In the house of the family du Bois, a travelling trunk and some six chairs, among other objects, were finished with satin and embroidered coats of arms. Most eye-catching, however, were the arms of the du Bois and Van Colen families, which were supported by a wild man and a wild woman on the balcony of the *Groote Robijn* (Baudouin, 1994: 279).[6] *Esquire* Petrus Ignatius Gansacker was clearly satisfied with a silver seal ring embossed with the family arms. And, finally, Petrus Josephus Herry had his insignia embossed on twelve silver knives and forks. No doubt the family crest was found more often than the inventories lead us to suppose. The blazon often adorned chimney-pieces and fire backs, tapestries and porcelain, glasses and bottles, handkerchiefs and coverings, although no mention of all this was made by the notary. Very typical, for example, were the

6 Joan Anthoni du Bois was married first to Theresia Joanna Josepha Van Colen; becoming a widower, he then married Dymphna Della Faille (SAA, *Not. Prot.*, 189).

coats of arms that the nobility had placed 'front stage'. In the household accounts of Van De Werve, for example, Degryse and Coppens found payments to painters who painted armorial bearings on his carriages (Coppens and Degryse, 1994: 69–70). Briefly, coats of arms displayed the lineage of a family and its membership of the second estate. It cannot be chance that no mention of such coats of arms is made amongst rich but non-noble families.

It is clear that portrait galleries, which in theory could serve the same purposes, by 1780 no longer played a large part in the construction of the identity of the group studied (De Vlieger-De Wilde, 2003: 110–111; Wijsenbeek, 1996: 122–124). There is no doubt that this is entirely connected to the somehow atypical waning popularity of large painting collections in Antwerp elite households in general (Blondé, 2002a). Unfortunately, for this reason several pictures were not referred to in detail in the notarial inventories. Happily, among the members of the nobility whom we studied this 'information damage' could have been worse: we do not know the subject matter of only about 36 percent of their paintings. For the paintings for which we do know the subject matter, the following 'clusters' can be seen: almost 20 percent of the paintings were landscapes and seascapes, religious themes count for a remarkably high 23 percent, but the biggest category is still formed by the portraits, which together account for some 42 percent of the paintings described. Apart from a few less important categories, the portraits not described in detail account for about 12 percent. The main cluster is then found in the portraits of family members (20.3 percent) and the so-called family portraits (6.7 percent) (Wijsenbeek, 1996: 123). Three of the four noble families possessed a portrait of a family group or a portrait of a family member (perhaps by then deceased) (Pietri, 2001: 435–437; Sarti, 2002: 128).

In non-noble households, portraits in general, and family groups in particular, no longer had an important role by that time. The data in Table 5.1. refer to between 80 and 100 inventories from the notarial archives of Antwerp for each period. These inventories were put into a database and then divided into 'social categories' numbered from I to VI, according to the number of rooms counted in the property.[7] In the categories II and III the total absence of (family) portraits in 1780 is particularly striking and is very different from the situation one hundred years earlier. In the seventeenth century the possession of personal portraits was seen as an important element in buttressing the status of the better families (Baetens and Blondé, 1994: 536; Van der Stighelen, 1991: 143). By the late eighteenth century, just a few non-noble testators stand out as far as the ownership of family portraits is concerned. Coincidence or not, two of them were captains in the civic militia (SAA, *Not. Prot.*, 3984, Johannes Baptista van den Grijn; and SAA, *Not. Prot.*, 3240, P.H. De Rumallo). It seems that, in the matter of portrait ownership, the nobility developed a distinctive consumer pattern, inspired by a specific set of values. In the case of Catarina

7 Unlike other 'inventory researchers' we were not fortunate enough to have external classification criteria at our disposal such as, for example, the tax on burials that was used by Wijsenbeek, 1987: 31. The grouping of inventories according to 'taste-groups' as Wijsenbeek herself suggests was not the best alternative for this research, because – in the long term – 'taste' is highly susceptible to change (Wijsenbeek, 1994). Testators who lived in just one room – a heterogeneous group varying from rich annuity holders to poor people – were placed in Category I. Category II contains houses with 2 or 3 rooms; category III contains houses with from 4 to 7 rooms; category IV includes houses with between 8 and 11 rooms, and category V houses of 12 to 15 rooms. Above 16 rooms an inventory falls into category VI. The correctness of using the size of the house to represent the particular circumstance of the testator is in no way inconsistent with the history of the Antwerp property market after 1585. House rents remained remarkably stable in this period (Scholliers, 1962; Scholliers, 1965)

Table 5.1. Presence of portraits and family portraits bequeathed to family members, based on four random samples of notarial inventories (%)

Social category	1630 n = 105	1680 n = 86	1730 n = 93	1780 n = 75
I	9.1	0	0	7.4
II	0	0	9.1	[0]
III	8.7	8.1	12.5	0
IV	19.3	25	10.5	14.3
V	57.9	54	35.7	[33.3]
VI	[100]	100	71.3	83.3

Guyot, who outlived many members of her family, it is particularly noticeable how many family portraits had probably been inherited from previously deceased family members.

Noblemen and urban elites often preserved their archives with the utmost care, thus making their family history palpable. Inventories contain interminable lists of marriage settlements, divorces and the division of property, wills and lists of chattels, often of long-deceased members of the family (De Vlieger-De Wilde, 2003: 113). Moreover, the genealogy of some specific objects was often very dear to them, though the question remains to what extent this is a typical phenomenon for gentlemen and -women (Dibbits, 1996). *Esquire* du Bois, for instance, left his eldest daughter the house known as the *Schoonselhof* and its entire contents, as well as two paintings by Rubens coming from the Van Colen family (*voortcomende uit de familie Van Colen*) (SAA, *Not. Prot.*, 189, acte nr. 11, Testament 21 mei 1779). Indeed, of his seven children *Jonkvrouw* Ludovica du Bois was the only surviving one from his first marriage to Theresia Van Colen. Du Bois attached a marked importance to the destination of his furniture after his death – far more so than the other noble testators. His eldest son, Charles Josephus Marie du Bois esq. inherited not only his large house (*grooten woonhuyse*) but also the furniture from the large salon, the dining room and the parlour (*meubelen van de grooten salette de eetkamer en de voorkamer*). In this way he immediately defined what were in his eyes the most prestigious rooms.

The exclusiveness of the nobility is similarly expressed through the possession of hunting rifles and knives. These articles were found in all the blue-blooded households of about 1780. In only two non-noble inventories is there any reference to an object directly connected to hunting. Only Johannes du Bois seems to have had a gun collection of any significance, and it is probably no coincidence that in his will he made it perfectly clear what should happen to it. He wills all the weapons such as guns, canons, pistols, daggers, hunting knives, sabres etc. (*allen de waepenen soo fusiken, canons, pistolen, als degens, jachtmessen, sabeles ende andere wapenen*) to his two sons. (SAA, *Not. Prot.*, 189, acte nr. 11, Testament 21 mei 1779). Maximilian of Salm-Salm also had a fine collection of weapons. In the Court of Hoogstraten in Antwerp there were 18 rifles and carbines and 13 pistols, but his largest weapon collection the Duke kept at the castle at Hoogstraten (Pietri, 2001: 426–427; De Vlieger-De Wilde, 2003: 109; Duerloo, 1985: 91–93). Numerous exceptions existed, though, to the noble prerogative of carrying weapons. In three of the four noble households, for example, we found a dagger – an essential part of the representation of

Table 5.2. Presence of hunting scenes in Antwerp households, based on four random samples of notarial inventories (%)

<table>
<tr><th>Social category</th><th>1630</th><th>1680</th><th>1730</th><th>1780</th></tr>
<tr><td>IV</td><td>3.2</td><td>0</td><td>0</td><td>7.0</td></tr>
<tr><td>V</td><td rowspan="2">5.3</td><td>18.8</td><td>7.1</td><td rowspan="2">22.0</td></tr>
<tr><td>VI</td><td>60.0</td><td>28.6</td></tr>
</table>

nobility – but a dagger also appears in another inventory in category VI, and also in three inventories in categories I and IV. Moreover, while paintings of hunting scenes were clearly elite possessions, it is difficult to draw a fixed line: hunting scenes were by no means the prerogative of the nobility.

In addition to attending balls and visiting the theatre or the opera, gambling in private houses was a typical feature of the lifestyle of the leisured class in the eighteenth century (Van den Berg, 1985: 166–169). This picture is confirmed in the current, modest survey. Gaming tables were found in three of the four noble households, but in only two of the wealthy non-noble testators. Half a century earlier, around 1730, we find only a single similar gaming table in just one household from category IV. Catharina Guyot owned six such tables, two of which were covered with red moquette. The du Bois family outdid them all, possessing no fewer than fourteen gaming tables. Ten of them stood with two red-flowered screens and eight similarly-covered armchairs and a stove in a ground-floor room whose walls were covered in the same material. It appears that even the arrangement and furnishings of the rooms in the du Bois house were attuned to sociability at home.

5.4 Conflicting Consumer Models?

Although the information available at present does not allow us to draw cast-iron conclusions, everything seems to indicate that the late-eighteenth-century nobility studied here were not only rich, but that they also had their particular group culture (Schuurman, 1989: 13–14). Coats of arms, portraits and elements of the hunting and gaming culture are clear material evidence of this. Certainly when these strategic features are combined together the inventories of the nobility set them apart, not only in respect of material riches (obviously) but also in respect of the lifestyle. This is also confirmed by their ownership of horses. Not only were vast majority of those owning recreational horse members of the nobility; in proportion to the number of their domestic servants and in comparison with the merchants, in 1755 members of the nobility spent far more on maintaining a stable (Blondé, 2001: 508). In this way these observations link perfectly to the picture evoked above of social and cultural polarisation in the age of enlightenment.

Yet the idea of a society in which the growing gulf between rich and poor was articulated in language use, forms of social intercourse (Deceulaer, 2002: 221–225) and material culture, clashes with the evidence of a burgeoning 'consumption society' in the early modern period and more especially during the Enlightenment (Brewer and Porter, 1993). From the seventeenth century, according to several authors, large middle groups in English society had access to a more varied consumption culture (Earle, 1989). There are some very good reasons for believing that this was also happening outside England and more specifi-

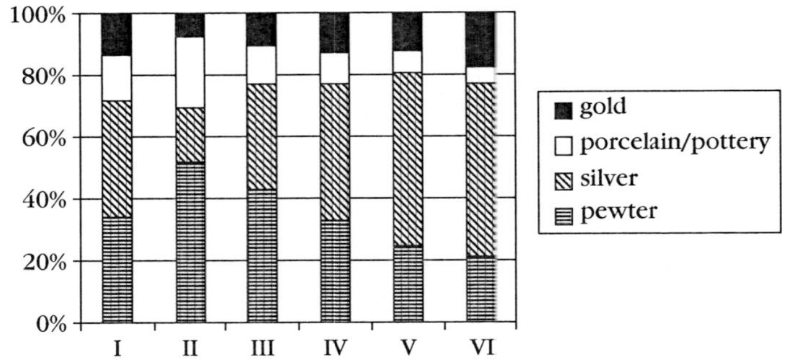

FIGURE 5.6. Relative composition of the database for inventories, according to materials and social category, 1680

cally in Antwerp as well (Blondé, 2002b). As the eighteenth century progressed a more varied material culture could be seen in more and more modest households. This apparent material wealth was made possible by a number of underlying structural changes. In the seventeenth and eighteenth centuries there was a growing use of cheaper materials. Spanish leather chairs gave way to chairs with wooden, rush or material seats. The wall coverings of gold leather and tapestries were replaced by wallpaper or textiles. The entire material culture thus became less expensive and at the same time less durable: as the price of clothing decreased so did the durability. At table this evolution translated into the rise of porcelain and other ceramics, at the expense of pewter and silver objects. The 'transience' of the eighteenth-century material culture made it at the same time more sensitive to fashion. Colours, forms, material and design were all burned up more quickly than before.

Unfortunately for us, the Antwerp inventories did not include any estimates of the value of the goods, so that for the time being it is only possible to indicate these structural changes with extreme caution. Figures 5.6. and 5.7. show the relative share of gold, copper, silver, porcelain and pottery objects for each inventory category. The precise numbers of objects were not counted. Instead the number of different descriptions of objects (records) in the inventories database was counted. A reference to twelve silver knives is given as much weight as a buckle, a saltcellar or a washbasin, but also as much as a porcelain dinner service of more than 100 pieces that is not further described. It is thus not necessary to stress that a single gold or silver object can represent a far greater value than dozens of other items. And in time even comparisons with similar objects fall short. Eighteenth-century silver saltcellars – to use the same example – were generally smaller and more homely, intended less to impress fellow-diners than to serve a functional purpose (Baudouin et al, 1988: 105). The increasing variety and assortment of goods in the eighteenth century leaves an ever-growing and more varied trail of object descriptions in our databank of inventoried goods, while for porcelain services, for example, precisely the opposite tendency can be observed. Such services were often dealt with in a very brief description, such as 'a porcelain set of 24 pieces'. Moreover, the chance that similar glass or porcelain services disappeared from the household – through breakage, for example – is not inconceivable. It is less likely to happen in the case of objects made of reusable or costly metals: even broken objects kept their potential to be melted down again or recycled (Woodward, 1985). For all of these reasons the figures below can give no more than a rough impression of the relative composition of the inventories.

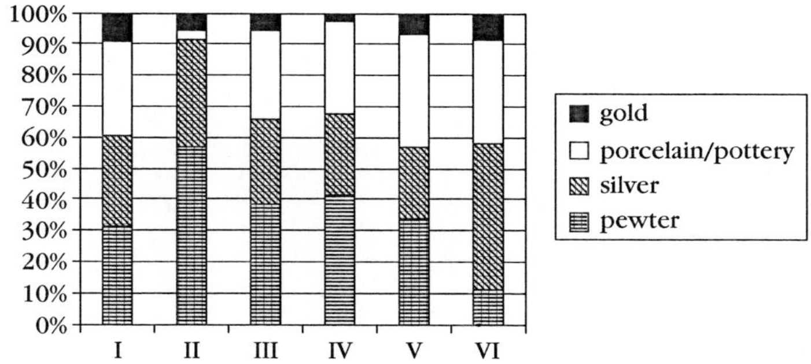

Figure 5.7. Relative composition of the database for inventories, according to materials and social category, 1780

When the inventories from the period around 1680 are compared with those of about a century later, one main tendency springs to the eye. Except in one social category the relative share of porcelain, glassware and pottery objects gained ground at the expense of silver in particular. Gold objects in almost every group undergo a relative regression. The same is true of silver and pewter objects, albeit to varying degrees. We have shown how the supply of increasingly cheap substitute materials ensured a strong spread of what were previously relatively exclusive luxury consumer goods. The spreading use of the individual plate and the table manners it brought with it were, for example, served by the democratisation of the materials and price of plates (Blondé, 2002b: 311). At the eighteenth century table, it became increasingly cheaper to be rich, especially because a large number of the dinner services – however modest some of them were – clearly fulfilled a decorative or ostentatious function. The master mason Petrus Corebloem, for example, who died in 1777, displayed a tea rack on his mantel piece with tea cups and a set that the notary or clerk described as old or even damaged (SAA, *Not. Prot.*, 814; Sarti, 2002: 126–128). Daniel Roche pointed out that the popularity of the new materials laid the foundation for a true consumption mentality (Roche, 1993: 574). It was in established social milieus that porcelain was seen as a way of satisfying new needs, such as curiosity and the constant urge for new stimulants and sensations. Was this then true of the Antwerp nobility too?

In the inventories in category VI pewter loses greatly but silver stands firm. This proves to be even truer when we take the absolute numbers into account: in 1730 the average testator in category VI possessed some 15 assorted silver objects, and by 1780 that had increased to almost 60 items. Closer examination shows that it was the noble households that were primarily responsible for this. The two non-noble households in category VI had a silver collection containing an average of 13.5 objects, while in the four noble households no fewer than an average of 71.5 silver items were counted. Yet the interiors of their houses are similarly characterised by a relative explosion in the use of porcelain and glassware that became so popular in the eighteenth century: on average more than 40 descriptions of this type of object as opposed to less than ten at the beginning of the century. The glass cabinets of the four noble households overflowed with coffee, tea and chocolate services, salad bowls, sugar basins and soup tureens. However fleeting, perishable and vulnerable the porcelain services were was emphasised by the fact that many of these services were described under a general term such as 'set of porcelain', or, conversely,

FIGURE 5.8. Silver coffee pot, Johannes Josephus II Hennekin (1738–1739)

SOURCE: Zilvermuseum Sterckxhof, Deurne.

were catalogued as mere 'junk'. As far as table services are concerned, we see the same tendencies in noble circles. In the households of the nobility, tradition and modernity clearly went hand in hand. On the one hand, new members of the nobility did not waste any opportunity in moving with the times; on the other hand, they held on tightly – even more so than other inhabitants of Antwerp – to the traditional elements of consumption (compare Pietri, 2001: 424–425; Sarti, 2002: 128; Fairchilds, 1994: 58).

5.5 Conclusions?

Compared to the traditional elite of Brussels, the Antwerp noblemen led a more modest lifestyle. However, their mercantile background did not prevent them from developing a distinct group culture. Karel Degryse has already pointed out the endogamous nature of this social environment, which also developed its own unique social and cultural circuits (Degryse, 1995: 38). This group culture was probably enhanced by the growing tendency towards privacy and the segmentation of public life and the public space.[8]

8 Greefs (1990: 197–200), however, also points to the existence of several societies where members of the nobility and great merchants mixed with each other.

Figure 5.9–5.10. 's-Gravenwezel castle

Source: Axel Vervoort.

Further research is needed to show how far the late-eighteenth-century climate of consumption was influenced by the process of aristocratisation. But the dazzling theatre life, horse ownership and the spectacular cases of extravagant noble offspring suggest in every respect that the traditionally frugal elites of Antwerp were charmed by the conspicuous consumption of the late Enlightenment.

In so doing they developed a kind of a hybrid consumer pattern, mixing traditional and novel models of consumption. To a far larger extent than the Antwerp middle groups, who (by choice or out of necessity) followed the path of a new kind of consumption pattern, the four noblemen whom we placed under the microscope, seem to have moved with the greatest of ease between paths of modernisation and tradition. One final example may help to illustrate this point. Shortly after 1728, Melchior Van Susteren *Lord of 's-Gravenwezel* contacted the famous Antwerp architect, Jan Peter van Baurscheit the younger, in order to get his 's-Gravenwezel castle rebuilt according to the latest fashion. The latter drew up plans, but also advised his client to safeguard the feudal characteristics of this magnificent building. In the following years the castle was indeed renovated, but with its outdated tower prominently figuring as an eye-catcher and referring to the historical lordship of its owner (Breedveldt Boer, 2003: 238).

At first sight there was no question of 'conflicting consumption models'. But the question about the precise meaning of consumption by the nobility and the processes of appropriation coupled to it, has barely been touched upon in this contribution (Blondé, 2003). Precisely because members of the nobility were often very conscious of their possessions and purchases, and carefully saved the paperwork relating to them, a closer study of their material world would offer invaluable insights into their lifeworlds and identities, and into the broader development of consumer society.

Bibliography

Primary Sources

Unpublished sources

Algemeen Rijksarchief Brussel (ARA), *Fiscaal Officie Brabant*, nrs. 388–405; *Staten van Brabant*, Cartons 409–410.

Stadsarchief Antwerpen (SAA), *Notariaat Protocollen (Not. Prot.)*, 186, 189, 712, 814, 3240, 3984, 4744; *Privilegiekamer (Pk)*, nrs. 2561–2564; *Rekenkamer (R)*, 222.

Literature

Baetens, R. and Blondé, B. (1991) 'Wonen in de stad: aspecten van de stedelijke wooncultuur', Van der Stock, J. (ed.), *Stad in Vlaanderen. Cultuur en Maatschappij, 1477–1787*, Brussel, 59–70.

Baetens, R. and Blondé, B. (1994) 'A la recherche de l'identité sociale et de la culture matérielle de la bourgeoisie anversoise aux temps modernes', *Histoire, Economie et Société*, 13, 531–541.

Balis, A. (1991) 'De nieuwe genres en het burgerlijk mecenaat', Van der Stock, J. (ed.), *Stad in Vlaanderen. Cultuur en maatschappij, 1477–1787*, Brussel, 248–249.

Baillieul, B. (1973) 'De steenwegaanleg rond Antwerpen tijdens het Oostenrijks bewind (1715–1794)', *Bijdragen tot de Geschiedenis*, 56, 102–134.

Baudouin, F. (1994) *Jan Peter van Baurscheit de jonge, architect, 1699–1768*, *Lira Elegans*, 4, 1–383.

Baudouin, P., Colman, P. and Goethals, D. (1988) *Edelsmeedkunst in België. Profaan zilver XVIde-XVIIde-XVIIIde eeuw*, Tielt.

Blondé, B. (1996) 'Economische groei en armoede in de pruikentijd. Het voorbeeld van de Brabantse steden, 1750–1780', Reyns, C. (ed.), *Werkgelegenheid en inkomen. Referaten colloquium 30 jaar UFSIA*, Antwerpen, 343–358.

Blondé, B. (1999) *Een economie met verschillende snelheden. Ongelijkheden in de opbouw en de ontwikkeling van het Brabantse stedelijke netwerk (ca.1750–ca.1790)*, Brussel.

Blondé, B. (2001) 'Indicatoren van het luxeverbruik? Paardenbezit en conspicuous consumption te Antwerpen (zeventiende-achttiende eeuw)', *Bijdragen tot de Geschiedenis*, 84, 4, 497–512.

Blondé, B. (2002a) 'Art and economy in seventeenth- and eighteenth-century Antwerp. A view from the demand side', Cavaciocchi, S. (ed.), *Economia e Arte secc. XIII–XVIII*, Prato, 379–391.

Blondé, B. (2002b) 'Tableware and changing consumer patterns. Dynamics of material culture in Antwerp, 17th-18th centuries', Veeckman, J. (ed.), *Majolica and Glass. From Italy to Antwerp and beyond. The transfer of technology in the 16th-early 17th century*, Antwerp, 295–311.

Blondé, B. (2003) 'Toe-eigening en de taal der dingen. Vraag- en uitroeptekens bij een stimulerend cultuurhistorisch concept in het onderzoek naar de materiële cultuur', *Volkskunde*, 104, 159–174.

Blondé, B. and Greefs, H. (2001) 'Werk aan de winkel. De Antwerpse meerseniers: aspecten van de kleinhandel en het verbruik in de 17de en 18de eeuw', *Bijdragen tot de Geschiedenis*, 84, 1–3, 203–225.

Breedveldt Boer, I.M. (2003) *Tekenen en vasseren: Het bedrijf van Jan Peter van Baurscheit (1699–1768) en de architectuur in het tweede kwart van de achttiende eeuw*, Utrecht.

Brewer, J. and Porter, R. (eds.) (1993) *Consumption and the world of goods*, London.

Burke, P. (1987) 'Conspicuous consumption in seventeenth-century Italy', Burke, P., *The historical anthropology of early modern Italy. Essays on perception and communication*, Cambridge, 132–149.

Burke, P. (1993) 'Res et verba: conspicuous consumption in the early modern world', Brewer, J. and Porter, R. (eds.), *Consumption and the world of goods*, London, 148–161.

Coppens, H. and Degryse, K. (1994) 'Levenswijze en consumptiepatroon van een Antwerps adellijk gezin. De huishoudboeken van Charles Bernard van de Werve de Vorselaer (1764–1786)', *Een kompas met vele streken. Studies over Antwerpen, scheepvaart en archivistiek aangeboden aan dr. Gustaaf Asaert ter gelegenheid van zijn 65ste verjaardag* (Archiefkunde, 5), Antwerpen, 52–73.

Coppens, H. (2002) 'Het uitgavenpatroon van een laat-achttiende-eeuwse Antwerpse familie aan de hand van de huishoudboeken (1764–1786) van Karel-Bernard van de Werve de Vorselaer', *Provinciale Commissie voor Geschiedenis en Volkskunde. Jaarboek 2000–2001*, Antwerpen, 186–197.

Deceulaer, H. (2002) 'De glans van de eenvoud. Kleding, mode en textiel in de eeuw van de Verlichting', *Provinciale commissie voor geschiedenis en volkskunde. Jaarboek 2000–2001*, 12, 221–225.

Degryse, K. (1974) 'Sociale ongelijkwaardigheid te Antwerpen in 1747', *Bijdragen tot de Geschiedenis*, 57, 126–145.

Degryse, K. (1977) 'Fortuin en sociaal prestige. Enkele beschouwingen over het "verraad van de burgerij" tijdens het Ancien Régime', *Tijdschrift voor Sociale Geschiedenis*, 3, 283–298.

Degryse, K. (1980) 'Stadsadel en stadsbestuur te Antwerpen in de 18e eeuw. Een sociaal-economische benadering', *Tijdschrift voor Geschiedenis*, 93, 466–482.

Degryse, K. (1982) 'Ridder Gaspar Joseph van Horne (1688–1748). Antwerps stadssecretaris, schepen en rentenier. Een socio-economische benadering van een loopbaan in stadsdienst', *Bijdragen tot de Geschiedenis*, 65, 109–126.

Degryse, K. (1985a) 'De Antwerpse adel in de 18de eeuw', Verbesselt, J. et al (eds.), *De adel in het hertogdom Brabant*, Brussel, 133–141.

Degryse, K. (1985b) *De Antwerpse fortuinen. Kapitaalaccumulatie, -investering en -rendement te Antwerpen in de 18de eeuw*, (RUG, non-published doctoral thesis), Ghent.

Degryse, K. (1995) 'The Aristocratization of the Antwerp Mercantile Elite (17th–18th Century)', Lesger, C. & Noordegraaf, L. (eds.), *Entrepreneurs and entrepreneurship in Early Modern Times. Merchants and Industrialists within the Orbit of the Dutch Staple Market*, Den Haag, 35–40.

De Vlieger-De Wilde, K. (2003) *Adellijke levensstijl. Dienstpersoneel, consumptie en materiële leefwereld van Jan van Brouchoven en Maria Livina de Beer, graaf en gravin van Bergeyck (ca. 1685–1740)*, (K.U.L., non-published Master thesis), Leuven.

De Vries, J. (1993) 'Between purchasing power and the world of goods: understanding the household economy in early modern Europe', Brewer, J. and Porter, R. (eds.), *Consumption and the world of goods*, London, 85–133.

Dibbits, H. (1996) 'Between society and family values: the linen cupboard in early-modern households', Schuurman, A. and Spierenburg, P. (eds.), *Private Domain, Public Inquiry: families and life-styles in the Netherlands and Europe, 1550 to present*, Hilversum, 125–145.

Dibbits, H. (2001) *Vertrouwd bezit. Materiële cultuur in Doesburg en Maassluis, 1650–1800*, Nijmegen.

Duerloo, L. (1991) *Privilegies uitbeelden. De Zuidnederlandse wapenkoningen en wapenkunde in de eeuw der verlichting*, Brussel.

Duerloo, L. (1985) '"Seer groote ongeregeltheden . . .aengaende de titulen". Evaluatie van de rol en het belang van het heraldisch proces', Verbesselt, J. et al (eds.), *De adel in het hertogdom Brabant*, Brussel, 89–110.

Earle, P. (1989) *The making of the English middle class: business, society and family life in London, 1660–1730*, London.

Fairchilds, C. (1994) 'Determinants of consumption patterns in eighteenth-century France', Schuurman, A.J. and Walsh, L.S. (eds.), *Material culture: consumption, life-style, standard of living, 1500–1900*, Milan, 55–67.

Greefs, H. (1990) *Kooplieden te Antwerpen tijdens de overgang van de 18de naar de 19de eeuw: een socio-economische en socio-culturele benadering*, (University of Ghent, unpublished Master-thesis), Gent.

Janssens, P. and Duerloo, L. (1992a) *Armorial de la noblesse Belge du XVe au XXe siècle, A-E*, Brussel.

Janssens, P. and Duerloo, L. (1992b) *Armorial de la noblesse Belge du XVe au XXe siècle, F-M*, Brussel.

Janssens, P. (1998a) *De evolutie van de Belgische adel sinds de late middeleeuwen*, Brussel.

Janssens, P. (1998b) 'Le niveau de consommation et l'endettement de la noblesse aux Pays-Bas espagnols et autrichiens', *"Proeve 't al, 't is prysselyck". Verbruik in Europese steden (13de-18de eeuw). Liber Amicorum Raymond van Uytven. Bijdragen tot de Geschiedenis*, 81, 235–238.

Klep, P. (1981) *Bevolking en arbeid in transformatie. Een onderzoek naar de ontwikkelingen in Brabant, 1700–1900*, Nijmegen.

Lauwerijs, J. (1979) 'Het kasteel van Hoogstraten', *Hoogstratens Oudheidkundige Kring*, 12–33.

McCracken, G. (1988) *Culture and consumption. New approaches to the symbolic character of consumer goods and activities*, Bloomington.

McKendrick, N., Brewer, J. and Plumb, J.H. (1982) *The birth of a consumer society: the commercialisation of eighteenth-century England*, London.

Muchembled, R. (1990) *Société et mentalités dans la France moderne, XVIe–XVIIIe siècle*, Paris.

Pietri, V. (2001) *Famille et noblesse en Provence orientale de la fin du XVIIe siècle à la veille de la Révolution* (Université de Nice, Thèse de doctorat nouveau régime en Histoire), Nice.

Roche, D. (1993) *La France des Lumières*, Paris.

Sarti, R. (2002) *Europe at home: family and material culture, 1500–1800*, New Haven.

Scholliers, E. (1962) 'Un indice du loyer: les loyers anversois de 1500 à 1873', *Studi in onori di Amintore Fanfani*, 5, Milaan, 593–617.

Scholliers, E. (1965) 'Prijzen en lonen te Antwerpen en in het Antwerpse (16de–19de eeuw)', Verlinden, C. (ed.), *Dokumenten voor de geschiedenis van prijzen en lonen in Vlaanderen en Brabant*, 2, *(XIVde–XIXde eeuw)*, Brugge, 641–1056.

Schuurman, A.J. (1989) *Materiële cultuur en levensstijl. Een onderzoek naar de taal der dingen op het Nederlandse platteland in de 19e eeuw: de Zaanstreek, Oost-Groningen, Oost-Brabant*, Utrecht.

Soly, H. (1988) 'Social aspects of structural changes in the urban industries of eighteenth-century Brabant and Flanders', Van der Wee, H. (ed.), *The rise and decline of urban industries in Italy and in the Low Countries (Late Middle Ages-Early Modern Times)*, Leuven, 241–260.

Soly, H. (1991) 'Economische en sociaal-culturele structuren: continuïteit en verandering', Van der Stock, J. (ed.), *Stad in Vlaanderen. Cultuur en Maatschappij, 1477–1787*, Brussel, 31–44.

Soly, H. (1993) 'Social Relations in Antwerp in the Sixteenth and Seventeenth Centuries', Van der Stock, J. (ed.), *Antwerp. Story of a Metropolis, 16th–17th century*, Ghent, 37–47.

Soly, H. (2001) 'Probleemjongeren in Brabantse en Vlaamse steden, zestiende-achttiende eeuw', Lis, C. and Soly, H. (eds.), *Tussen dader en slachtoffer. Jongeren en criminaliteit in historisch perspectief*, Brussel, 126–131.

Spaepen, B. (1993) *Wooncultuur in de achttiende eeuw: Maximiliaan van Salm-Salm, 1732–1773* (UFSIA, Oefening Tweede Kandidatuur Geschiedenis, 1992–1993).

Thijs, A.K.L. (1990) *Van geuzenstad tot katholiek bolwerk. Maatschappelijke betekenis van de Kerk in contrareformatorisch Antwerpen*, Turnhout.

Thijs, A.K.L. (1993) 'Antwerp's luxury industries: the pursuit of profit and artistic sensitivity', Van der Stock, J. (ed.), *Antwerp, story of a metropolis, 16th–17th century*, Ghent, 105–114.

Timmermans, B. (2002) 'The seventeenth-century Antwerp elite and status honour. The presentation of self and the manipulation of social perception', Van Houdt, T. et al (eds.), *On the edge of truth and honesty. Principles and strategies of fraud and deceit in the early modern period. Intersections*, 2, 149–165.

Van den Berg, M. (1985) 'De adel in de 18de eeuw: een "leisure class"?', Verbesselt, J. et al (eds.), *De adel in het hertogdom Brabant*, Brussel, 143–183.

Vandermeersch, P., Blondé, B. and Marynissen, R. (1991) 'Typologie sociale du parc de logements à Anvers basée sur le cadastre de 1834', Baetens, R. and Blondé, B. (eds.), *Nouvelles approches concernant la culture de l'habitat*, Turnhout,

Van der Stighelen, K. (1991) 'Burgers en hun portretten', Van der Stock, J. (ed.), *Stad in Vlaanderen. Cultuur en Maatschappij, 1477–1787*, Brussel, 141–156.

Van der Wee, H. (1988) 'Industrial dynamics and the process of urbanization and de-urbanization in the Low Countries from the late middle ages to the eighteenth century. A synthesis', Van der Wee, H. (ed.), *The rise and decline of urban industries in Italy and the Low Countries (late middle ages-early modern times)*, Leuven, 307–381.

Wijsenbeek, Th. (1987) *Achter de gevels van Delft. Bezit en bestaan van rijk en arm in een periode van achteruitgang (1700–1800)*, Hilversum.

Wijsenbeek, Th. (1994) 'A matter of taste. Lifestyle in Holland in the seventeenth and eighteenth century', Schuurman, A.J. and Walsh, L.S. (eds.), *Material culture: consumption, life-style, standard of living, 1500–1900*, Milan, 43–54.

Wijsenbeek, Th. (1996) 'Noblesse oblige. Material Culture of the Nobility in Holland', Schuurman, A. and Spierenburg, P. (eds.), *Private Domain, Public Inquiry. Families and Life-styles in the Netherlands and Europe, 1550 to Present*, Hilversum, 112–124.

Woodward, D. (1985) 'Swords into ploughshares: recycling in pre-industrial England', *The Economic History Review*, 38, 175–191.

CHAPTER 6

In with the New: Novel Goods in Domestic Provincial England, c. 1700–1790

Amy Barnett – University of Northampton, United Kingdom

6.1 Introduction

The question of what makes a house into a home is central to attempts to understand the nature of material culture and its relationship to domestic life. Scholars of British material culture have tended to concentrate their efforts on quantitative research in order to trace the emergence and use of novel and luxury items during the seventeenth and eighteenth centuries. Lorna Weatherill's ground breaking national study of probate inventories undertaken in the late 1980s set the benchmark for subsequent regional and local studies, which followed a now predictable numerical analysis (Weatherill, 1988). The general picture created by her study was one of a distinct alteration in the type and number of goods appraised, between 1675 and 1725. Overton et al's comparison of Kent and Cornish inventories highlighted the regional differences thrown up by Weatherill's study, and Estabrook's discussions regarding the region around Bristol, exposed localised differences between urban and rural communities (Overton et al, 2004; Estabrook, 1998). These, and other studies, confirm Weatherill's conclusion that, regional differences notwithstanding, there appeared to be a shift in consumption patterns away from wealth-retaining goods and towards a material culture marked by less durable, cheaper goods which in later years was increasingly influenced by fashion, (see for example, Beckett and Smith, 2000; Shammas, 1990). These developments were also seen across Europe (Clifford, 1999; Nijboer, 2005; Sarti, 2002).

According to Maxine Berg, novelty was as much about innovative production and material use as it was function and decoration (Berg, 1999: 63–85). Novel goods, with a greater emphasis on style and decoration, the use of new materials (for example, mahogany and porcelain), and changes in production processes both fuelled and responded to the demand for semi-luxury goods from a growing middling class (Berg, 1999; Crowley, 2001; Edwards, 2006; Overton et al, 2004). The desire for these new things, including clocks, mirrors, china and glassware, window curtains, toys, trinkets, pictures and goods relating to leisure time, was not born out of a need to emulate the social elite as Veblen supposes, nor were people purchasing goods that would previously have been produced at home. Rather, these objects were integral to the negotiation of changes in the wider socio-cultural context and were utilised as a means of negotiating social position, identity and space within a relatively fluid cultural framework (Grieg, 2006; Herman, 2006).

Utilising data from a survey of around two hundred probate inventories, this chapter is able: firstly to place Norwich within the framework outlined by the studies above; and secondly to build on previous investigations by extending our knowledge of ownership into the latter part of the eighteenth century. While discussing very briefly the numerical analysis of the inventory data in section one, this chapter argues that a more qualitative use of the inventories is better able to highlight the rich nuances in eighteenth century domestic home making – nuances which often remain hidden by numerical analyses. The second section will therefore argue that, in interpreting the data recorded by appraisers as whole rooms and groups of objects, a more fluid understanding of the boundaries between particular types of space within the home is required, particularly if we are to understand the meaning of space and identity as reflected in the novel goods found in Norwich homes.

6.2 The Numbers: Ownership of Material Goods in Norwich

Quantitative analysis of 201 Norwich city probate inventories between 1674 and 1791, concurs with the findings of the above mentioned surveys and is comparable with the national figures for the earlier period, 1674–1720 (see Table 6.1.). During this period, Norwich citizens displayed similar levels of ownership to those recorded nationally by Weatherill, although, in the case of silverware, the levels are more readily comparable with those in London (Weatherill, 1988: 26). There was a clear increase within Norwich of the items suggested (in other studies) as indicative of the transformation of domestic material culture, with particularly strong increases in china, silverware, hot drinks utensils and pictures.

Weatherill's survey stops in 1725, just as such growth appears to be taking hold (see Table 6.2.) and therefore the Norwich data is able to build on the Weatherill's survey, extending our understanding of domestic material culture by some seventy years (1720 to 1791). Such an extension encompasses the changes seen in the ownership of different goods and also provides evidence that these changes were neither short lived nor confined to particular social strata. Newer items were increasingly prevalent in Norwich inventories (Figure 6.1.), with the growth in ownership of chinaware, window curtains, pictures, knives and forks, and decorative items such as bird cages being especially notable. Moreover, these changes affected households of all types, suggesting that decorative (and pleasurable) objects were both more popular and increasingly within the reach of the less well off. Innovative production techniques, partly as a means of copying imported goods for the domestic market, were creating opportunities for the people of Norwich to furnish their homes with more references to fashion and with less emphasis on intrinsic value. By the end of the century, most items that were part of the 'novel' goods range at the beginning of the century were commonplace within a large percentage of homes (Table 6.2.).

The converse of this spread of novel goods was often a decline in the importance of older style goods (Overton et al, 2004). Indeed, from the late seventeenth century the Norwich inventories do show relatively fewer pieces of traditional furniture and linen, with silver and pewter (where itemised) often valued by weight. However, initially in richer households and later more generally, there is evidence that two apparently distinct types of material culture – new and old – were being accessed and utilised concurrently (see for example the extensive inventory of Sarah Bocking in 1674, Norfolk Record Office [NRO], ANW 23/3/188).

Table 6.1. Comparison of material objects found in Norwich, Nottingham and Kent inventories, with Weatherill's national survey

Location/Date	Pewter	Earthen-ware	Silver/gold	Hot drinks	Books	China	Delft	Looking glass	Window curtains	Knives/forks	Pictures	Clock
National[1] 1675–1725	93%	73%	23%	4%	19%	4%	–	33%	13%	4%	13%	19%
Norwich 1673–1719	65%	30%	45%	4%	30%	1%	2%	58%	20%	3%	27%	10%
Nottingham[2] 1688–1720	62%	13%	28%	–	20%	4%	–	48%	–	–	23%	16%
Kent[3] 1690–1719	95%	–	–	4%	25%	–	–	36%	16%	5%	6%	41%

Table 6.2. The appearance of objects in Norwich City inventories between 1673–1791

Date	Total Number of Inventories	Pewter %	Earthen-Ware %	Silver/gold %	Hot drinks %	Books %	China %	Delft %	Looking glass %	Window curtains %	Knives/Forks %	Pictures %	Clock %	Birdcage %	Leisure %
1673–1699	37	76	40	51	3	40	0	0	43	19	0	24	8	3	0
1700–1719	56	57	23	41	5	23	2	3	68	21	5	28	11	0	2
1720–1739	57	49	37	46	24	19	12	26	72	25	21	46	19	12	9
1740–1759	30	50	40	40	47	27	37	10	77	43	20	40	13	13	7
1760–1791	20	55	35	60	95	15	50	25	70	45	40	50	45	15	10

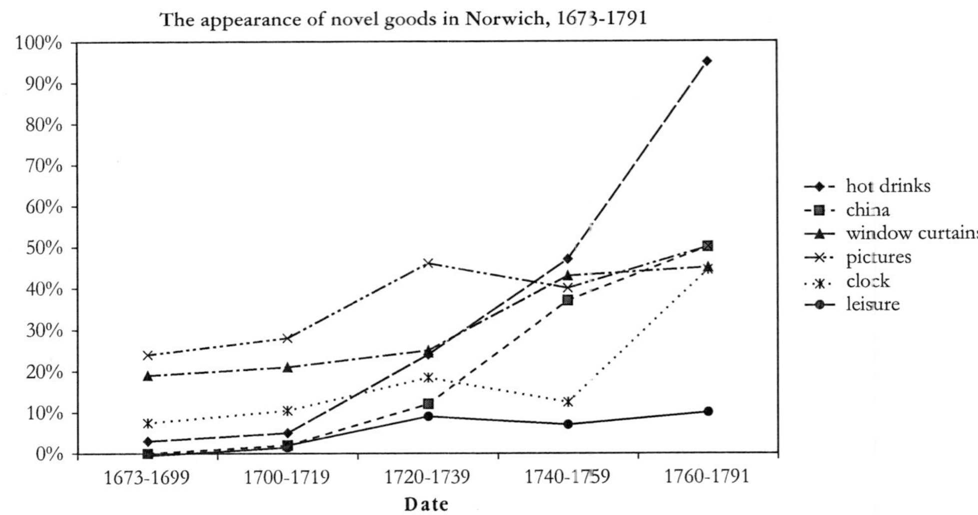

Figure 6.1. The appearance of novel goods in Norwich

How did these two types of material culture interact? Were the newer items placed in public areas as part of new interpretations of what signifies status, or wealth, or success? And were the less fashionable goods, relegated to private spaces? These questions, and others, will be addressed in the following section, which utilises a more qualitative approach towards the inventories, looking more closely at groups of objects, and the rooms in which they were located, in an effort to understand the complexities of domestic space, and to rebuild an eighteenth-century context for these 'novel' goods.

6.3 The Context: Locating Novel Goods in Domestic Spaces

From the inventories, we can see that there was a distinct shift in domestic material culture during the eighteenth century, but the inventories can also give us clues about the domestic scene and the use of space. Indeed, thanks to many appraisers who made a note of the location of these items within the home, they can throw light on how owners viewed, placed and valued their possessions. This is of great interest, particularly when considering the wealth retention motivations of consumers or the importance such material groupings might have as status indicators. If, as Veblen suggests, people actively and publicly displayed items of status and wealth (non-essential and expensive goods), we might suppose that these newer items would appear in particular domestic spaces such as the parlour – or at least be able to conceive of predictable domestic locations where such items might appear (Veblen, 1899). Andersson's recent study of a local group of the Swedish elite shows that the public spaces within their homes were considerably more richly appointed than were the private areas. This, she argues, was a conscious strategy for maintaining social position (Andersson, 2006).

Norwich, however, did not follow this pattern; instead the inventories highlighted the decorative nature of many chambers and the obvious care with which some private spaces were created. The survey results indicate that the distinctive separation of space on the grounds of monetary value or display is not as clear as might have been expected, with items of value appearing in all rooms of the house and more decorative items appearing in bed chambers as well as 'public' areas. For example, clocks were found most often in kitchens and window curtains appeared in chambers more often than parlours. During the period after about 1720, this separation is blurred further still by the multiple appearance of some items (such as mirrors – see below). Not only were goods appearing in more inventories, therefore, owners often had more than one of something; novel goods were fast becoming the norm.

However, too narrow a view of value – one relating to a purely financial interpretation – prevents the consideration of objects as retainers of cultural and social meaning, of knowledge and identity. Social scientists have long discussed the importance of goods in the creation of social identities, in maintaining family and social group cohesion, as coded messages to those 'in the know', and in forming the indicators of social boundaries and acceptance. Rather than talking of status, this discourse focuses on symbolism and communication through all things material: the creation of visual messages (Baudrillard, 1996; Douglas and Isherwood, 1978; see also Berger and Luckman, 1966).

Since these various messages require an audience of some kind, it might be worth utilising Goffman's notion of front and back stages of social interaction existing, in this case, within the spatial boundaries of the home (Goffman, 1959). Indeed, Weatherill's analysis of material culture draws on this premise, now more usually described as a distinction between public and private space (Weatherill, 1988). In recent years, this has been extended further to look at the presence of different types of public (within a defined space), multiple publics or indeed the creation of gendered spaces (Kross, 1999; Nenadic, 1994). The introduction, therefore, of goods displaying novelty, innovation and fashion both enabled the articulation of these varying types of space and began to extend the idea of status symbol beyond the limitations of intrinsic value, and towards the more complex arena of socio-symbolic value and the negotiation of taste (Berg, 2005: 205–206).

The negotiation of space, in these terms, was not lost on the inhabitants of Norwich and Norfolk. In 1771, the mirrors of Felbrigg Hall in Norfolk were appraised and sketched, giving both their location and dimensions. They were found in the dressing rooms, bed chambers and eating parlour, and their decorative nature was as important as their physical dimensions (Figure 6.2.). Such objects were at once practical and decorative, and were no doubt part of an elaborate display of taste and wealth. James Woodforde, in 1783, remarked on the size of a mirror in the home of Charles Townshend, an MP, 'which was the finest and largest I ever saw, cost at second hand £150.0.0' (Beresford, 1967: 210). The ownership of looking glasses in Norwich peaked between the years 1740 and 1759 (see again Table 6.2.), although their presence was noticeable from as early as 1674. Between 1720 and 1791, the period covered here, 68 percent of mirrors were located in bed chambers, and only 13 percent in parlours. Even the most modest households could boast a mirror, though far less impressive than the mirror noted by Woodforde or indeed the quantity of those at Felbrigg Hall (see Crowley, 2001). In 1720 for example, Michael Mason died leaving only £7 worth of moveable goods, located in three rooms, but he still had a mirror in his chamber. This mirror was noticeable within a sparsely populated room as the only non-essential means of decoration. It was not grouped within a larger decorative collection of material goods and probably served as a functional addition to the room, increasing the effects of light and presenting an opportunity for personal grooming.

However, next to the pewter (which was also in this room), the mirror might have been a statement of his awareness of the socio-symbolic realm, and of wider cultural expectations (NRO, ANW 23/14/36).

Sixteen years later, Mary Delitate left four mirrors as part of her moveable estate, appraised at £97 8s. These were located in the kitchen, little parlour, little parlour chamber and the kitchen chamber. Again, the contextualisation of the mirrors within the material groupings that occurred in each of these rooms, suggests that looking glasses were both functional and indicative of an attention to notions of taste and comfort, both of which were relatively new assimilations to the cultural framework of provincial England (Edwards, 2006). In the kitchen, for example, the mirror is listed alongside the more usual cooking utensils and furniture, whilst in the bedchamber the looking glass appears with window curtains and pictures. The little parlour however, is an example of the contrast, found in this study, between formal and other rooms with a greater emphasis on intimacy. The little parlour contained: 'Stove, fender and board, a brass catch, a brass sconce, a marble table, a looking glass, 2 small tables, 6 chairs, window curtains and hangings, window cushions and screens, a brass sconce, 2 pictures and a small parcel of goods' (NRO, ANW 23/22A/22). The great parlour, on the other hand, housed the delft ware and glassware, together with an oval table and chairs; but lacked the small detail of the little parlour and, although nine pictures and window curtains featured in this room. Moreover, the dining table enforced a singular formality over the space; unlike the two small tables which allow separation, movement and spatial fluidity in the little parlour. But this does not mean that the lesser space was wholly private or indeed that the formal great parlour was entirely public in its use. Again a strict adherence to static notions of distinct spaces within the home, on the basis of conspicuous display, is unhelpful in determining the use or meaning of domestic arenas.

Andersson suggests that there is a need for a third type of space, one that she describes as semi-public, reserved for a more intimate public of family and friends. This implies that Goffman's distinction of front and back stages do not address the true nature of household usage. This is, of course, useful in enabling a more complex view of how people used and populated their domestic environment, but Andersson's results are limited by linking décor with degrees of intimacy. The more expensively decorated rooms were those with a public function and, as the intimacy of the area increased, the decorative nature and monetary value of the space decreased (Andersson, 2006). In Norwich, decorative items, such as pictures, prints and maps, showed a steady increase between 1720 and 1791. Their distribution within homes was not as clear-cut as Andersson's results might lead us to expect, with a relatively even distribution between parlours (or living spaces) and chambers (those with beds). Kitchens, halls and garrets also housed pictures, but only in a minority of cases. In 1736 Phyllis Stanton, a widow leaving moveable goods valued at just £12, had pictures in three of her five rooms. In the parlour chamber, two prints were appraised and, in the parlour itself, five pictures and four prints were listed in addition to a corner cupboard, chairs and stools, window curtains and six pieces of earthenware. In the less formal kitchen chamber, 'a bed . . . window curtains.. [fireside goods], a chest of drawers, a table, a looking glass, six chairs, sixteen small glazed prints and a chest' (NRO, ANW 23/22/9). The goods, as a collective, were responsible for defining space. The bedchamber was used for social engagement (chairs) and had a decorative interior, unlike the rooms that were described in the study of Swedish elites. In contrast to the highly decorated public rooms which were dressed with wallpaper, tapestry hangings and cloths, these 'private' rooms were 'sparsely furnished, figuratively as well as literally, containing beds and tables of a more ordinary kind' (Andersson, 2006: 31; se also Overton et al, 2004: 132–134).

Window curtains too are decorative and practical, although they appeared in less than half of the inventories in the latter part of the sample, so their presence in any house could well be seen as an indicator of social status and of fashionable associations. In only one example was the fabric used for window curtains noted, those in the dining room of William Money (died 1770) being made of chintz (NRO, ANW 23/26/35). From the sample, however, most window curtains were found in chambers, well away from the public areas of the home. We have already seen that this separation is simplistic and it is not really surprising that window curtains appear in semi-public and private spaces, alongside other newer goods. Here, their colour and pattern was on display as much as the objects hung on the walls or arranged around the room. As well as their decorative nature, window curtains had more practical purposes such as minimising draughts or keeping in the warmth – neither being functions primarily related to the assessments made by visitors. However, in assisting other objects within the room to create a decorative space – one that was, moreover, comfortable and warm – they maintained a level of intimacy conducive to smaller gatherings and made all the right kinds of suggestions to social knowledge in a more subtle way than those visitors restricted to more formal areas.

These details, often lost when probate inventories are discussed in quantitative terms (see Berg, 2005: 199), are useful in illustrating the conscious creation of domestic space – a premeditated spatial construction that is confirmed in other sources such as correspondence, diaries and journals. In letters to her brother-in-law in 1707, Mary Knyvett asks for his assistance in the purchase of a clock and appeared to have considered where she would place such an imposing item prior to the request: '(. . .) and a pendulum clock I would have and thinke to sit it in the Great Parlour' (NRO, KNY 912). Nearly a month later she sent a further letter: 'Deare Brother, Yesterday the clock came home and we have this day fix't it in our Great Parlour it's a mighty ornament to the room and hope it will goe very well' (NRO, KNY 913). According to a letter sent in the following July her initial thoughts about the clock, and its appeal in the parlour, were justified: 'I must not forgitt to thank you for the kindness you did us in buying our clock it's reckoned very well worth the money and goes very well and is a mighty ornament in our parlour' (NRO, KNY 914). There appears little doubt that the £12 which Mary Knyvett paid for the clock was money well spent; her pleasure at its addition to the space is obvious.

Mary Knyvett must have considered the implications the addition of the clock in her parlour would have on space as well as her pocket, but there would have been implications too for how other people would receive such a 'mighty ornament'. Taste was something that, whilst incredibly difficult to define, was a large factor in the social life of the home and its inhabitants. Objects were often seen as the material articulation of taste and the right kind of material culture had to be constructed in order to create the right impression within social groupings, either to maintain those groupings or create links with others, particularly through marriage. Relationships in the eighteenth century were increasingly subject to a social vigour, one that reflected familial reputation and individual accomplishments, alongside wealth; appearances really did matter (Berg, 2005: 241; Bourdieu, 1994; Gell, 1986: 136; Smith, 2002).

The rise in fashionable associations across the tea table – as illustrated by the astounding growth in the numbers of hot drinks utensils seen in Norwich (see Tables 6.1. and 6.2.) – were linked to a domestic sociability as the platform by which people displayed not only their moral worth, through their manners and self control, but also their social knowledge, wealth and cultural capital (Bourdieu, 1994). Household and individual identity was created by this type of social interaction. Gender, family ties, social relationships and hierarchies were all affirmed by the consumption of specific types of objects whose meaning was part of a symbolic language shared by others (Breen, 1993; Gell, 1986; Smith, 2002; Styles and Vickery, 2006: 1–36). People were concerned with keeping up to date with fashion, but were aware that being 'too showey' was unacceptable (Vickery, 2006). Social knowledge was paramount and a lack of acquaintance with the rules was reflected in one's material accessories; self and social awareness were as much on display over the tea table as the china teapots and silver sugar tongs (Berg, 2005: 230). Such presentation must have been more than adequate at Felbrigg Hall where an inventory of china in 1771, 'some of it very old fine', included some 12 different tea pots, with 9 stands for them, 105 plates of differing sorts, 83 tart pans, 2 complete sets of tea china, each with 6 coffee cups, and 22 other tea cups, including 8 small, old, octagon, blue and white cups (NRO, WKC 6/460, 464x4). The household was obviously well prepared for every sort of social interaction.

Parson Woodforde is well known for his tea taking and social visits, and the diary of Mary Hardy shows that visits enabled links to be formed within communities and between families (Beresford, 1967; Hardy, 1968). These relationships were maintained by repeated interaction and social knowledge was transferred through visits to other people's homes (Grieg, 2006). This was as important in Norfolk as elsewhere in England and Ann Fellowes' notebook, listing an enormous number of visits to pay and receive between 1778 and 1799, is evidence of how seriously this was taken. Each accepted visit was carefully crossed out and a return visit added to the list of those to pay (NRO, FEL 619; see also Whyman, 2002: 87–109).

It is important to note that tea taking – together with visiting and sociability – was central to the cultural imperatives of the day and that women, in presiding over a ritual which included both men and women, were able to exert a controlling influence which they were prevented from doing elsewhere. Women, literate in the visual language of material culture, would have manipulated their setting to the best social effects, perhaps regardless of the limitations of space.

Domestic sociability, therefore, had an effect on the recorded items in the inventories too (see hot drinks and china in Tables 6.1. and 6.2.; Berry, 2005). The majority of goods associated with the consumption of tea – tea tables, trays, cups and saucers, tea pots, spoons, boards, chests – were found in parlours, but these items were also present in chambers. The division of goods in this case appears not to be on the grounds of public or private spaces or indeed of formality and intimacy, but rather by function and practicality. Objects associated with the preparation of hot drinks (including coffee and chocolate as well as tea) were found in kitchens and pantries, whilst parlours or best chambers appear to be the rooms in which these hot drinks were taken. The parlour of Thomas Bell, a baker, (c. 1738), is one of a few examples of collections of china and glassware within the survey, but is the only one appraised 'upon the tea table', where there were '2 Burntin china tea pots and saucers, a ditto sugar dish, a basin, 8 cups and saucers'. The glassware was located in the corner cupboard with some other bits of china, but 'Upon the chimney piece' were '2 enamelled chocolate pots, 12 tea cups, ditto Burntin basins, 6 ditto coffee pots, 3 ditto tea cups and other china there' (NRO, ANW 23/22A/44).

The tea table is linked to the notion that certain goods, and domains, can be gendered in some way. Bernard Herman suggests that 'tea tables [are] associated with behaviors that we tend to categorize as more feminine, more refined, and more intimate' (Herman, 2006). The tea table became the seat of female domestic power in a world more generally controlled by men: a place where material goods could be manipulated to serve a myriad of purposes. It is possible to assume that the goods themselves – the tables, tea pots, cups and saucers, and so on – were themselves considered feminine (Smith, 2002: 171–187; see also Dahn, 2001). But it is a big leap to assume that the rooms in which these utensils were found were the dedicated personal space of women. Indeed, other areas noted as female include the closet where women were able to create a private or intimate space over which they had some control. In 1797 Louisa Gurney, a teenager at the time, noted that, following a walk 'instead of going in after tea we thought it would be snugger to go and write our journals, so here we are now in Elizabeth's suite closet as snug and as happy as possible' (NRO, MC 1593/1).

Nenadic argues that, as part of a separation of gendered spheres, the dining room became the domestic alternative to the (male) coffee house: a safer, more controlled arena in which men discussed external (that is, non domestic) affairs and created their own rituals (Nenadic, 1994; Smith, 2002: 139–169; see also Kross, 1999). Other sociable activities in the home, like card playing or gambling, could also be linked to the spaces away from feminine dominance, but they did not exclude women in the same way that after dinner separation apparently did. In January 1777, Mrs Leathes wrote to her parents Mr and Mrs Reading, apologising for not sending a note with the turkey sent for Christmas, by saying: 'and having only an hour notice found it impossible to leave the Card table where I was engag'd with a good deal of company'. This illustrates the fact that card games were a diversion enjoyed by both men and women. Later she writes that: '[once] called to dinner & there is no stirring out of the Parlour afterwards except into the Drawing Room where tea coffe and cards are the evenings amusement till nine o clock. After that supper and cheerful conversation engage us till Eleven when we all retire to our different apartments' (NRO, BOL 2/27/3). However, the movement from one space to another – from the dining room to the drawing room – suggests that, where house size permitted, different rooms were associated with different kinds of activity. Each room was populated with different groups of material goods, yet entertained the *same* company, supporting the idea that boundaries between spaces were fluid and related to more than just a notion of different levels of public access or, indeed, of gendered spaces.

There were ten examples of 'games' in the probate inventories surveyed, from 1722 onwards, and all of them were owned by men. These included such things as, card tables, a 'massassippa board and ball', Gammon tables, gaming tables. There are too few examples of such leisure activities to recognise any patterns, but domestic diversions were not only found in the records of the rich, with occupations ranging from a weaver to a gentleman. The Card table of Jeremiah Bottomly (died 1722) appeared in the parlour chamber and it is not clear whether this room was used for lodgers or for himself (NRO, ANW 23/16/50). It shared its space with window curtains, a looking glass, six prints, six black chairs, two enamelled and five brass candlesticks, and a bed. The only table in the room was the card table. Mr Bottomly was an alehouse keeper and it is possible that the card table was the feature of a gentleman's room within the establishment and therefore that the presence of such a table was necessary. Richard Clark's 'Massassippa board and ball' were in the sparsely furnished 'little chamber', alongside a bed, a forme, and a table (1730, NRO ANW 23/19/44), highlighting the social heterogeneity of gaming. And in 1771, Isaac Spratt had a card table as part of his dining room furniture, which included, 'a painting of game, seven chairs, a settee, a jamb glass, a card table, a wilton carpet, an India cabinet (...) a small round table, a tea kettle stand, window curtains and two chests' (NRO, DN/INV 81B/11). This latter example illustrates a collection of goods with a masculine edge in a space seen as increasingly male oriented (see Nenadic, 1994). It also demonstrates a connection with outdoor pursuits and an expanding empire being displayed alongside the status items, such as the carpet – significant enough for its makers to be noted.

Gendered spaces, however, were not limited in their creation by specific objects or groups of objects. A personal and emotional connection to objects allowed women, in particular, to bypass social constraints by stamping a strong personal identity and an emotional ownership on particular things. Berg argues, through the analysis of the bequests in wills that women were concerned with creating and maintaining links with family and friends across generations, through the goods they left to their loved ones, very much more so than men. Women were more likely to bequeath china, linen and items of clothing (which were altered and spruced up with fashionable trimmings), whose value was emotional as well as financial. Women, therefore, created their own property transfer, often to other women, through passing on goods whose value is related to an emotional investment (Berg, 2005: 239–241). Value, therefore, becomes more complex.

From another angle, this ownership of material goods – with monetary, emotional or social value – is linked to Bourdieu's notion of 'cultural capital', the construction and communication of which allowed people enhance their life-chances. Social accomplishments, such as knowledge, musical ability and artistic appreciation, run alongside an informed attitude which allows for success within the higher echelons of society. Material goods necessary to establish such cultural achievement (for instance books and musical or scientific instruments), as well as those objects demonstrating a knowledge of taste, fashion and social affiliation, are present in the home in order to equip new generations with the cultural capital they need to succeed and to provide the household with a reputation of cultural and social achievement (Bourdieu, 1994; see also Andersson, 2006: 37–42). In the eighteenth century cultural achievement was linked closely to gentility and a lack of accomplishment reflected badly on ones character. On the other hand, the acquisition of appropriate cultural attributes and material objects helped to ensure social acceptance and good reputation. The diaries of both Parson Woodeforde and Mary Hardy include references to such matters. In the former, the parson comments in 1787 that 'Miss Mary Donne is a very genteel, pretty young Lady and very agreeable with a most pleasing Voice abt 21 yrs' (Beresford, 1967: 313); Mary Hardy tries, and eventually succeeds, in enrolling her children with a dance master, in order for her children to learn an important social skill (Hardy, 1968).

Books and musical instruments might be examples of objects projecting a level of cultural attainment, not necessarily linked to the ownership of other material goods. Books saw an increased prevalence in the early part of the sample, but their appearance in inventories was not as widespread as in other areas of the country. Gattuso's recent article on book ownership in Norfolk highlights the difficulties in gauging the spread of book use through probate inventories (Gattuso, 2006). In most inventories, books were collected together at the end of the list simply as 'a parcel of books', giving a value for the lot without noting numbers or locations. For example, we have John Bosely (died 1739) whose musical instruments and books were valued together (NRO, DN/INV 80D/13) and Reverend Stukely's 'parcel of old books' valued in 1729 at just £1 (NRO, ANW 23/19/12). Occasionally, greater detail was included, such as 'a family bible, Practicall Goonistry, and other old books' (W. Robbins, died 1738, NRO ANW 23/22A/69), or '6 volumes of ye magazines, 2 large volumes of Humfres Anotations, A bible, a common prayer book, and other old books' (O. Barlow, died 1740, NRO ANW 23/23/24).

These inventories allow insight into reading matter, but the location of the books was not noted often enough to detect any clear patterns or norms. Gattuso's study, which uses probate inventories to trace the location of books within Norfolk households from the mid-sixteenth century until the early eighteenth century, suggests that location was dependent on whether books were used for household administration or for leisure. In the former case, books would be stored in easily accessible areas, such as the kitchen or the hall; in the latter, books were found in parlours, chambers and studies (Gatusso, 2006: 79). In Norwich itself, twenty-seven inventories included books within a particular room: the kitchen and the chamber were each noted on eleven occasions, the study and the parlour twice, and the wash-house only once. From the point of view of a differentiation of book use, the results suggest an even spread between leisure and administrative functions, but such analysis needs to include a note on the number of rooms available for use. However, if we take into consideration the flexible use of the semi-public spaces or the well turned out chambers, as mentioned above, the presence of books here seems to fit a more general pattern of display. Whilst books might have implied cultural achievement to a variety of publics on the one hand, they were also a source of private leisure.

6.4 Conclusion

In conclusion, the Norwich inventories provide data and findings comparable with studies for the period including that of Weatherill (c. 1675–1725). With the benefit of inventory data available to 1791, it is clear that the trend for increased volumes of newer, novel, goods continued until the end of the century. Items associated with domestic sociability were present in an increasing proportion of the sample from mid-century, whilst items of soft furnishings, cushions and other decorative items also continued to rise. However, the above discussion has highlighted two further points. The first is that, despite their imperfections as a source, probate inventories enable us to recreate a context for the goods listed. This provides a deeper understanding of material and cultural life, beyond the rather flat impression given by numbers alone. The second is that ideas about the use and meaning of space in the eighteenth century domestic environment must be more flexible than the polarisation of public and private spaces or indeed the notion of definitively gendered spaces. Like today, the use of space was affected by its availability and by the type of functions it had to perform. The clear benefit of utilising a case study approach when looking at probate inventories is in the creation of a context which allows us to assess the

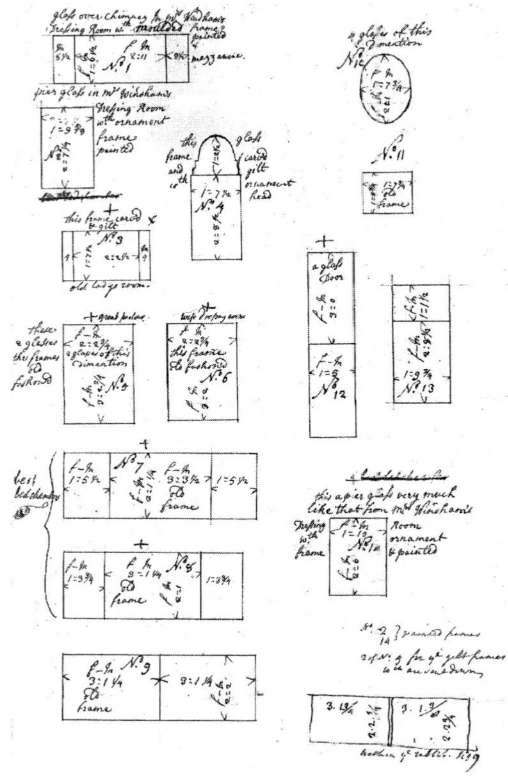

FIGURE 6.2. An inventory of mirrors, Felbrigg Hall, Norfolk, 1771

SOURCE: reproduced by permission of the Norfolk Record Office, (WKC 6/460, 464 × 4).

material culture of a room in its entirety and perhaps gain a better idea of the people who populated these spaces. If a useful separation is required at all it might be worth looking at the distinctions between living and utility, formality and intimacy, decoration and function or consumption and preparation, rather than simply public and private (front and back). Or perhaps we should view room use on a public/private sliding scale, with very few spaces being wholly one or the other.

Within this fuller context, it is possible to trace the arrival of novel and semi-luxury goods, as outlined above and increasingly discussed in recent years. These newer goods, accessed and utilised alongside traditional goods, became valued as much for their decorative and social aspects as their intrinsic value. In the case of china, social value seemed to be of much higher than their exchange value. Such items, often found together in defined spaces, fulfilled a practical function and were markers for transmitting and understanding social messages, signals that were heightened by their collective nature (see Douglas and Isherwood, 1978). These goods were used to negotiate the changing cultural landscape, to maintain and affirm familial and social ties, and to give expression to the visual language of culture which became increasingly important as the century wore on.

Bibliography

Primary Sources

Unpublished sources

Norfolk Record Office, Norwich
ANW 23/3/188
ANW 23/14/36
ANW 23/16/50
ANW 23/19/12
ANW 23/19/44
ANW 23/22/9
ANW 23/22A/22
ANW 23/22A/44
ANW 23/22A/69
ANW 23/23/24
ANW 23/26/35
BOL2/27/3
DN/INV 80D/13
DN/INV 81B/11
FEL 619
KNY 912
KNY 913
KNY 914
MC 1593/1
WKC 6/460,464X4

Published sources

Beresford, J. (ed.) (1967) *The diary of a country parson – James Woodforde*, London.
Hardy, M. (1968) *Mary Hardy's diary*, Norwich.

Literature

Andersson, G. (2006) 'A mirror of oneself: Possessions and the manifestation of status among a local Swedish elite, 1650–1770', *Cultural and Social History*, 3, 21–44.
Baudrillard, J. (1996) *The system of objects*, London (Trans. James Benedict).
Beckett, J. and Smith, C. (2000) 'Urban renaissance and consumer revolution in Nottingham, 1660–1760', *Urban History*, 27, 31–50.
Berg, M. (1999) 'New commodities, luxuries and their consumers in eighteenth century England', Berg, M. and Clifford, H. (eds.), *Consumers and luxury. Consumer culture in Europe 1650–1850*, Manchester, 63–85.
Berg, M. (2005) *Luxury and pleasure in eighteenth century Britain*, Oxford.
Berger, P. and Luckman, T. (1966) *The social construction of reality. A treatise in the sociology of knowledge*, New York.
Berry, H. (2005) 'Women, consumption & taste', Barker, H. and Chalus, E. (eds.), *Women's history: Britain 1700–1850. An introduction*, Abingdon.
Bourdieu, P. (1994) *Distinction: A critique of the social judgement of taste*, London.

Breen, T. H. (1993) 'The meanings of things: interpreting the consumer economy in the eighteenth century', Brewer, J. and Porter, R. (eds.), *Consumption and the world of goods*, London.

Clifford, H. (1999) 'A commerce with things: the value of precious metalwork in Early Modern England', Berg, M. and Clifford, H. (eds.), *Consumers and luxury. Consumer culture in Europe 1650–1850*, Manchester, 147–168.

Crowley, J. E. (2001) *The Invention of comfort. Sensibilities & design in Early Modern Britain and Early America*, Baltimore.

Dahn, J. (2001) 'Mrs Delany and ceramics in the objectspace', *Interpreting Ceramics*, 1, at *www.uwic.ac.uk/icrc/issue001/delany/delany.htm*.

Douglas, M. and Isherwood, B. (1978) *The world of goods: towards an anthropology of consumption*, Hammondsworth.

Edwards, C. (2006) *Turning houses into homes*, Aldershot.

Estabrook, C. B. (1998) *Urbane and rustic England. Cultural ties and social spheres in the provinces 1660–1780*, Manchester.

Gattuso, S. (2006) 'Did they own books? Book-ownership revealed in Norfolk probate inventories', *Norfolk Archaeology*, XLV, 74–85.

Gell, A. (1986) 'Newcomers to the world of goods: the Muria Gonds', Appadurai, A. (ed.), *The social life of things. Commodities in cultural perspective*, Cambridge.

Goffman, E. (1959) *The presentation of the self in everyday life*, London.

Grieg, H. (2006) 'Leading the fashion: The Material Culture of London's *Beau Monde*', Styles, J. and Vickery, A. (eds.), *Gender, taste and material culture in Britain and North America 1700–1830*, New Haven and London, 293–314.

Herman, B. L. (2006) 'Tabletop conversations: material culture and everyday life in the eighteenth century atlantic world', Styles, J. and Vickery, A. (eds.), *Gender, Taste and Material Culture in Britain and North America 1700–1830*, New Haven and London, 37–60.

Kross, J. (1999) 'Mansions, men, women and the creation of multiple publics in eighteenth century British North America', *Journal of Social History*, 33, 385–408.

Nenadic, S. (1994) 'Middle rank consumers and domestic culture in Edinburgh and Glasgow, 1720–1840', *Past & Present*, 145, 122–156.

Nijboer, H. (2005) 'Fashion and early modern consumer evolution. A theoretical exploration and some evidence from seventeenth century Leeuwarden', Blondé, B., Briot, E., Coquery, N. and Van Aert, L. (eds.), *Retailers and consumer changes in Early Modern Europe, England, France, Italy and the Low Countries*, Tours, 21–36.

Overton, M., Whittle, J., Dean, D. and Hann, A. (2004) *Production and consumption in English households, 1660–1760*, London.

Sarti, R. (2002) *Europe at Home. Family and material culture, 1500–1800*, New Haven.

Shammas, C. (1990) *The pre-industrial consumer in England and America*, Oxford.

Smith, S.D. (1996) 'Accounting for taste: British coffee consumption in historical perspective', *Interdisciplinary History*, XXVII, 2, 183–214.

Smith, W.D. (2002) *Consumption and the making of respectability, 1600–1800*, London.

Styles, J. and Vickery, A. (eds.), *Gender, taste and material culture in Britain and North America 1700–1830*, New Haven and London.

Veblen, T. (1899) *The theory of the leisure class*, New York.

Vickery, A. (2006) '"Neat and not too showey" words and wallpaper in Regency England', Styles, J. and Vickery, A. (eds.), *Gender, taste and material culture in Britain and North America 1700–1830*, New Haven and London, 201–222.

Weatherill, L. (1988) *Consumer behaviour and material culture in Britain, 1660–1760*, London.

Whyman, S.E. (2002) *Sociability and power in Late Stuart England. The cultural world of the Verneys, 1660–1720*, Oxford.

PART III

Retailing

CHAPTER 7

The Lure of the New: Urban Retailing in the Surroundings of Antwerp (Late Seventeenth-Early Eighteenth Centuries)

Ilja Van Damme[1] – University of Antwerp, Centre for Urban History, Belgium

7.1 Any Demand on the Countryside? An Introduction

It is a curious thing. Although the old and impressive city walls of the European landscape did not withstand the onslaught of industrialisation and modernisation, they remain a reality to be reckoned with. This is less true physically than in the minds of historians, especially those studying the period before the nineteenth century. They contributed to an historiographical bias which has urban and agrarian historians occupying separate worlds. The use of different sources, different methodologies and a lack of dialogue has created a situation in which the relations between town and countryside are considered 'one of the key historical problems' (De Vries, 1999: 121). So far, relations between town and countryside have been studied by looking at migration flows, and property and labour differences between urban and rural dwellers (Stabel, 1996: 1–27). The proto-industrialisation debate in particular has widened our knowledge of 'industrial villages', the actions of urban entrepreneurs on the countryside, putting out and *Kauf*-systems, and the interconnections between urban and rural investments (Van der Wee, 1988; Ogilvie and Cerman, 1996). However, much remains to be done regarding demand-side and distribution issues, especially for the Southern Netherlands (Deceulaer, 2001: 218; Thoen, 2001: 145–146).

These kinds of problems were pioneered independently from each other in the seventies by Hans Medick and Jan De Vries respectively (Medick, 1976: 291–315; De Vries, 1975: 205–266). Both formulated very different answers to basically the same question: can the countryside provide a significant stimulus for consumption? In their sweeping account of 'industrialization before industrialization', Kriedte, Medick and Schlumbohm answered this question only marginally, in line with the overall tenets of their model. In general they agreed that the needs of peasant households were essentially focused towards physical subsistence. Since only a small proportion of their total output passed through the market, the peasant household consumed very little from urban retailers and producers. Furthermore, the standards of living of agrarian wage earners were simply too low to make a substantial contribution to trade or industry. If a survival or target income was reached, patterns of daily

1 Postdoctoral Fellow of the Fund for Scientific Research – Flanders (FWO-Vlaanderen). I would like to thank all the people of the Centre for Urban History who gave good advice and made useful comments on this chapter.

consumption became embedded in a so-called 'plebeian culture' (as opposed to a 'bourgeois culture'). Thus peasant demand was leisure and pleasure oriented, working less rather than buying more. Rural inhabitants indulged in excessive meals and festivities or, as market opportunities were 'forced upon them', bought only 'superfluous luxuries' like coffee, tea, fashionable clothing or jewellery (Kriedte, Medick and Schlumbohm, 1981: 64–73). Essentially this was a degrading process, leading to further proletarianisation and misery in the countryside (see Ogilvie and Cerman, 1996a: 2–5).

De Vries, on the contrary, detected a creative rural force, capable of stimulating production and trade. He rejected the vision of a 'conservative homosociologicus peasant; the market insensitive, immutable, unpersuadable peasant; the kin-bound, cast-bound, contented peasant'; a peasant suspicious of the market and eager to keep the market 'at arm's length' (De Vries, 2001: 71; De Vries, 1976: 176–182). De Vries labelled the transition he noticed in the late seventeenth and eighteenth centuries an 'industrious revolution' (De Vries, 1993: 107–121; De Vries, 1994: 249–270). During this process, agrarian households came to intensify their market labour and/or production and (thus) were able to increase their demand for market-supplied goods and services. The introduction of new, seductive and fashionable goods created the incentives for the rural population to commercialise and work even harder than in the past (De Vries, 1976: 181). Thus, as a recent publication wittily remarks, 'it appears as though Weber's work ethic was driven by consumption rather than by religious conviction' (Overton et al, 2004: 6).

The idea of an 'industrious revolution' is still much in need of empirical testing (De Vries, 2003: 49–66; and 2008). Effective methods to measure the labour strategies of rural families have to be designed (Engelen et al, 2004: 123–135) and consumer historians are only beginning to uncover the material motivations of agrarian households (for instance Soly, 1988; Kamermans, 1999; Overton et al, 2004). Lorna Scammell (formerly Weatherill) also underlined the importance of retailing as a necessary condition for rustic consumerism of some sort (Scammell, 2000: 48). In rural regions with burgeoning commercial outlets and existing economic exchange with neighbouring towns, the new production and consumer habits were integrated much more easily into daily life. Retailers seem to have acted as crucial 'middlemen', mediating between the pastoral surroundings and an urban setting in which fashionable and desired products were made and imported.

Unsurprisingly, then, the debate about rural changes in consumption (and broader cultural) practices and attitudes remains highly active (Ogilvie and Cerman, 1996b: 235–237). For the Southern Netherlands, Erik Thoen recently stressed that 'It is hard to detect any creative force from the countryside which might stimulate production or trade' (Thoen, 2001: 146). In his extensive analysis of the 'Flemish' countryside, Thoen signalled the enduring existence of survival strategies and the disturbing impact of surplus extraction on the general standards of living of the peasants. His pessimistic viewpoint, however, stands in sharp contrast with more optimistic interpretations, which reject any clear-cut impoverishment of the rural dwellings (for instance Vandenbroeke, 1996: 102–117; Klep, 1988: 261–286). In the light of this debate, the question remains open: was the countryside capable of fostering significant demand or not?

This chapter aims to tackle this intriguing and broad question by offering a survey of the retail infrastructure of the Antwerp hinterland in the 'long eighteenth century'. However, in doing so, I hope to provide some insights into the role of rural demand around the city. Undoubtedly, the setting under study is quite specific. Firstly, the countryside comprising the immediate hinterland of Antwerp was remarkably integrated into the urban economy. Since the late Middle Ages a strong transportation system had linked the surroundings to the city (Blondé, 1999). As a gateway and port town, Antwerp lay in a transitory area between northern and southern Brabant, two distinctive demographic and agricultural zones (Limberger, 2001c: 161–166). In the northern as in the southern part of Brabant agrarian activity was based on cultivation of grain and livestock breeding, but there were important differences in the intensity of agriculture. To the south of Antwerp (much like Flanders), a large number of small plots characterised a very densely settled rural area. Yet this labour-intensive and market-oriented farming often proved insufficient to guarantee economic reproduction. Hence, we see the appearance of non-agrarian sectors, oriented towards Antwerp, such as brick ovens around Rupel and peat cutting in nearby Duffel (Limberger, 2001b: 158–173). Furthermore, settlements to the south of Antwerp profited from the important inland trade routes leading to Mechlin and Brussels. Due to the low fertility of the sandy soil, the north of Antwerp was thinly populated. Yet in the sixteenth century these marginal areas became dominated by large lease-farms in the hands of wealthy Antwerp citizens, providing a good environment for intensive husbandry (Limberger, 2001c: 168–175).

The symbiotic relationship between Antwerp and its hinterland triggered parallel conjunctures in town and countryside. The strong upsurge of Antwerp, for instance, at the beginning of the seventeenth century (following the severe economic crisis after 1585) was at least partially the result of a revived countryside (Klep, 1990: 105). From the end of the seventeenth century onwards – the period under study in this chapter – both Antwerp and its surroundings were again on similar tracks. It has been agreed that the agrarian sector outside the former metropolis underwent a steep decline from the 1670s onwards (Van der Wee, 1993: 62–63). Enduring warfare at the end of the seventeenth century stopped any long-term process of rural industrialisation (Limberger, 2001a: 39–62; Limberger, forthcoming) with the result that the rural population only started to grow again around the middle of the eighteenth century (Billen, 1987: 96 and 102). The city itself witnessed a process of decline and crisis, of de-industrialisation and de-urbanisation from the end of the seventeenth century onwards (Van Damme, 2003: 6–39; Blondé and Van Damme, 2003: 392–394). Yet, at the same time, a wider, colourful and more diverse material culture was taking shape in Antwerp homes (Blondé, 2002: 295–311; Blondé, 2005: 37–52). New, exotic, and fashionable goods were imported more frequently from France and overseas, and familiar commodities came in ever larger quantities and variations in quality, shape and material (Van Damme, 2004: 187–203; Van Damme, 2007). The findings of recent probate inventory research indicate the existence of social groups wealthy enough to place Antwerp alongside Amsterdam, London, Paris, and other important early modern consumer cities.

The Antwerp countryside likewise showed remarkable changes in this period of decline and crisis. As I show in the first section of this chapter, retail activity as a whole intensified in this period: rural markets, peddlers, and even fully-fledged country shops were all booming. Qualitative sources reveal yet another aspect of this unexpected growth in rural distribution. As early as the late Middle Ages urban/corporate protests against industrial activities (such as cloth weaving and beer brewing) in the hinterland of Antwerp were common (Bousse, 1975: 139–150; De Nave, 1989: 59–93; Limberger, forthcoming). However, pre-industrial cities were in no position to effectively exercise their longstanding market and manufacture monopolies within the immediate surroundings (the so-called urban *banlieu*). Non-agrarian production flourished on the countryside because of a relative lack of urban and corporate control and taxation. Without paying for it properly, surrounding areas profited from so-called *economies of agglomeration*: external advantages common to a densely populated and urbanised environment such as Antwerp (Blondé, 1999: 122). The proximity of Antwerp investors, commercial infrastructure and demand, amongst other things, were vital in this respect. It is little wonder that civic authorities and artisans tried to contain non-agrarian production in the nearby hamlets like Borgerhout.

However, after 1648 urban cries and complaints about 'unfair' competition from the countryside multiplied. In addition, not only productive but also distributive activities gave rise to complaints. These protests have usually been explained as a passive or protectionist response to the growing problems of the Antwerp guilds from the end of the seventeenth century onwards (Prims, 1945: 27–28). Seen against the backdrop of consumer changes, the enduring dynamic of the countryside and the parallel urban reactions can be interpreted in a very different way. In the second section of this chapter, I seek to explain how after 1648 the urban struggle against the hinterland took on the character of an aggressive, expansionist drive to serve a growing group of potential buyers *outside* the city walls. As will become clear in analysing the auction activities of the urban guild of second-hand dealers (*oudekleerkopers*), Antwerp retailers actively looked for consumers in the countryside in the late seventeenth and early eighteenth centuries. This was not new, of course, but it probably became more important as rural demand for novel and fashionable products grew during the course of the eighteenth century. Indeed, if we accept that the rural population increased its demand for market-supplied goods and services, the growth of retail circuits in the countryside becomes more comprehensible.

Causality in this chapter will therefore be sought in the interactions of retailers and consumers (see also De Vries, 2003: 65). Emerging rural motivations for consuming novelty and fashion – the lure of the new – spurred increasing commercial activity, whilst rural purchasing power made villagers important potential shoppers. At the same time, the actions of all kinds of retailers were altering consumption opportunities. Increasing rural distribution facilitated typical consumer problems such as shopping time, exchange and liquidity (credit). By bringing urban goods to rural homes, more and more agrarian consumers absorbed an urban-based consumer pattern. Rising retail activity in the countryside unlocked consumer passions previously unheard of, whilst retailers opened up geographical and social groups which were susceptible to adding more and different goods to their homes. I argue that rural demand around Antwerp not only existed after 1648 but that it also triggered significant economic changes, precisely in a classic period of downturn and crisis.

7.2 Retailing in the Surroundings of Antwerp

It is well known how, on weekly market days in the seventeenth and eighteenth centuries, the city of Antwerp swarmed with countryside producers and consumers. On Wednesday, Friday or Saturday, depending on the products on sale, country folk could sell their vegetables, fruits, eggs, milk, bread and other commodities freely at certain specific areas in town (Baetens, 1989: 169–202). These commercial high days were crucial in provisioning citizens with food (cereals, vegetables, meat), construction materials (such as wood and bricks) and fuel (for instance wood and peat) (Van Uytven, 1983: 75–116; Stabel, 1996: 2). However, this inflow from the surroundings sometimes incurred the wrath of the mercers' gild (*meerseniers*), the most important corporate group of retailers, which formally organised and controlled all distribution activity in the city (Van Aert and Van Damme, 2005: 143–151). Complaints were issued about the sale of durable products (which was allowed under strict conditions only on Fridays) and about rural peddlers who were found wheeling and dealing in backstreets or at times *wesend geen marktdagen*, 'being no market days' (SAA, *Pk*, nr. 925 (M): city ordinance dated 26 February 1722, f. 265v–266). Nevertheless, city-based shopkeepers of all sorts most certainly welcomed the commercial frenzy on Friday, as is attested by the business practices of eighteenth-century sellers of ironware and pottery. As can be read in judicial documents, shopkeepers packed the approaching roads to the markets with heaps of goods, hoping to lure the swollen streams of passers-by (SAA, *Pk*, nr. 1449: *policiekamer*, f. 23–25r). This 'retailing in the streets' likely attracted many a farmer, buying city products in return for the earnings he had just made.

However, it is often forgotten that country dwellers had other, probably cheaper opportunities to buy attractive and alluring consumer durables. Diverse commercial circuits – markets, peddlers, and shops – operated outside the city walls, all providing rural households with a chance of by-passing the nearby town. It is likely that these retail outlets were also more in tune with the specificity of rural demand. The growth of retail activity in the Antwerp hinterland from 1648 onwards may have produced a situation in which agrarian households had the chance to ignore the city altogether, infringing on the market monopolies of the city. In this way, Antwerp became less obligatory as a central place for buying new and fashionable items – a process which unquestionably posed serious problems for certain retailers in the city. In response, some forged networks of dependency or co-operation with the commercial actors in the countryside (sometimes profitable for both), or went head-on with the surroundings in an attempt to reclaim their former customers – which could lead to an effective trade war (Fontaine, 1996: 42; Steegen, 2006: 271–278). In any case, the Antwerp mercers' guild made use of an existing body of urban legislation to try to abolish distribution on the countryside altogether – complaints to which I will return later.

Did rural consumers profit from this increasing commercialism? Certainly, many more goods (including new and fashionable ones) were made available on more occasions and in more locations, and credit facilities proliferated (Lambrecht, 2003: 237–261). Annual rural fairs were a first cornerstone, fundamentally imbedded in the overall retail infrastructure of the countryside (Alexander, 1970: 29; Plattner, 1989: 171). The opinion that such markets faded away with the dawn of country shops is no longer accepted (Phillips, 1992: 63; Denecke and Shaw, 1992: 76–86). In England, for instance, Chartres calculated on the basis of *almanacs* that the number of markets in the countryside was actually rising: around 1750 there were 7 per cent more markets than a hundred years before (Chartres, 1977: 48). It is possible to make a comparable calculation for the Southern Netherlands on the basis of the same sources. Almanacs appeared frequently in big cities like Antwerp and Ghent from at least the end of the sixteenth century and were crammed with practical information (Mortier, 1981: 27–28; Moens, 1983: 203–273). Clearly aimed at a commercially active audience, all kind of useful details were provided about weights, measures, the currency of coins, the hours when postal and transportation services departed, and a list with all annual fairs in the surrounding areas.[2] An almanac of 1678 made its use and accuracy for all market travellers very explicit, by stating: 'Thou who frequent Markets/ Have here what thou desire: All the Markets of the year/ Collected with trouble and much labour'.[3]

The almanacs of Ghent and Antwerp show trends to each other and reflect the findings of earlier research for England. In essence, the number of annual fairs and horse markets in almanacs of the area of Ghent and Antwerp rose significantly over the course of a hundred years (Table 7.1.). Importantly, this growth was not merely a product of the increasing accuracy or completeness in the sources (although this does account for some of the increase noted); it reflects real expansion in rural marketing. The appearance, for instance, of annual fairs in such backwaters as the 'Campine' area or *Kempen*, northeast of Antwerp, is striking to note. These were novel, eighteenth-century markets, appearing in new areas, and indicative of the spread of commercialism to even the lesser populated parts of the countryside to the north of Antwerp (Limberger, 2001c: 162–164).

However, an effective growth of countryside markets tells us nothing about their importance for rural dwellers. Indeed, it is sometimes assumed that, in this period, annual fairs especially were rapidly losing their economic significance (Clapham, 1967, vl. 2: 297; Van Houtte, 1977: 92). They became social events, places 'characterised by *drolls* and *poppit* shows' (Chartres, 1977: 49). Such comments must be qualified in more than one way. Usually they reflect upon the demise of international fairs, visited by tradesmen from throughout the world, such as the famous Brabantine fairs of Antwerp and Bergen-op-Zoom at the end of the fifteenth century. In all aspects, eighteenth-century fairs were more regionally or even locally centred, and often very specialised, for instance in the selling of cattle or horses. However, they also remained important retail places, attracting peddlers with all kind of products or facilitating the settlement of country shops (Michielsen, 1938: 43). For rural households, again, this evolution had significant advantages: more products for sale, more opportunities to buy and less time wasted going to and

Table 7.1. Annual fairs and horse markets in almanacs of the area of Ghent and Antwerp in the late seventeenth and late eighteenth centuries

Almanacs Ghent	1680	1780	Percentage increase
Number of markets	99	159	61%
Almanacs Antwerp	**1691**	**1783**	**Percentage increase**
Number of markets	164	283	73%

Source: Mortier, 1981: 297–300; and Moens, 1983: 240–250.

2 In principle only annual fairs and horse markets were mentioned in almanacs. In practice, however, such lists also included other types of markets (see Michielsen, 1938: 51).

3 '*Gy die Merten frequenteert/ Hier hebt gy recht naer u begeert: De Merten vn het gansch iaer/ Vergaert met kost en moeyten swaer*' (Cited in: Mortier, 1981: 103).

from town. According to Scholliers and Vandenbroeke certain parts of Flanders had more than fifty market days a week at the end of the eighteenth century. Each market was jammed against another; consequently a consumer needed less than an hour on foot to reach the closest market (Scholliers and Vandenbroeke, 1979: 259). The spread and increasing density of rural markets unlocked even the least commercial parts of the Southern Netherlands.

Rural fairs were not the only aspect of a vital and intensifying commercial activity in Antwerp's hinterland. Other commercial circuits cashed in on the widening rural demand. Peddling was a well-known strategy to provision thinly populated regions. As early as 1622 an Antwerp publication defined a peddler as 'a trader whose credit is better known in the inns of the villages, than in the Antwerp Bourse' (Versteegen, 1622: 106–107).[4] Yet peddling seems to have intensified from the end of the seventeenth century onwards. Certainly, the Antwerp ordinances claiming actions against peddlers grew remarkably: all such legal measures concerning the peddling of durable consumables were situated in the years 1642–1743.[5] These findings correlate neatly with earlier results for the Southern Netherlands, England, and France. Everywhere, the eighteenth-century countryside experienced a peddler boom (Deceulaer, 2006: 171–198; Fontaine, 1996: 41–43; Spufford, 1984). However, because of the lack of any 'hard evidence' concerning their actual numbers, the perceived rise of peddling might again be seen as a product of the sources. This rings true for the Southern Netherlands where, especially in the late eighteenth century, the burgeoning measures taken by the central authorities against vagrants, beggars and smugglers led to a growing visibility of peddling in general (Lenders, 1992: 198–203; Winter, 2004: 267–268). And yet the growing presence of peddlers in the Antwerp city ordinances from the middle of the seventeenth century onwards was not accompanied by a drastic change in economic regime or moral policy. Complaints about 'strangers' (*vrempdelinghen*) within the city walls or 'unfair competition' on the countryside had existed for ages, primarily motivated by economic concerns. And harsh, morally inspired actions to remove beggars of all kinds had been common since the sixteenth century (Lis and Soly, 1979: 82–96). Nevertheless, Antwerp peddling complaints proliferated, clearly reflecting a changing socio-economic reality on the countryside. So, what was happening in there?

Again a pessimistic and an optimistic interpretation can be weighed against each other. On one hand, growing poverty and unemployment can be held responsible for this 'peddler boom'. Thus, the previously mentioned processes of rural and urban stagnation led to widespread marginalisation. Peddling became a useful survival strategy to weather the hard times or supplement household earnings. Enduring warfare on the Brabantine countryside at the end of the seventeenth and the beginning of the

4 '*Eenen coopman wiens credit beter bekent is inde herberghe op de dorpen dan op de borsse van Antwerpen*'.

5 According to my own calculations, based on Génard, 1864, 1865 and 1934. More precisely, of all 122 Antwerp ordinances concerning the retailing of durable consumables in the period 1489–1794, all eight city ordinances concerning the peddling of consumer durables by *vrempdelinghe*, people outside the corporate and urban structures, were situated in the years 1642–1743. These counts do not include any recurrences of the same ordinance, and exclude all ordinances referring to peddling by *voddeliden*, *uytdraegsters*, *corfsters* and the like. Such retailers were a fundamental part of the urban retail circuits.

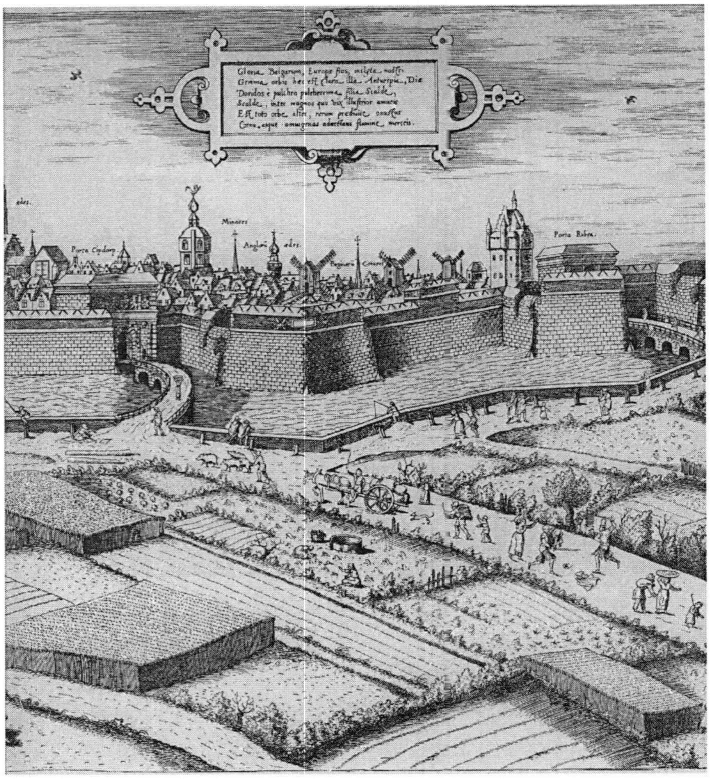

FIGURE 7.1. A peddler coming from the countryside entering the Antwerp Kipdorppoort, c. 1557

SOURCE: Frans Huys, *Bibliothèque National*, Paris.

eighteenth centuries certainly condemned some people to a wandering existence. On the other hand, peddling in the Antwerp hinterland might also have grown in response to a widening demand for market-supplied goods in rural homes. Instead of going to the city, agrarian households could realise their desire for new and attractive products each time a peddler stopped at their dwellings. Margaret Spufford was one of the first authors to suggest that petty chapmen were responsible for the rising 'standard of comfort amongst the occupants of the humbler cottage' (Spufford, 1984: 3). Laurence Fontaine also attests how peddlers were instrumental in providing large social groups with 'populuxe' items: fashionable and cheap products, sold at better prices than elsewhere (Fontaine, 1996: 183–201). Peddlers were not necessarily paltry figures, but regular traders imbedded in strong credit and dependency networks that surpassed city walls and state borders.

In the Southern Netherlands, what little evidence we have regarding the peddler's pack reveals a broad assortment of small and cheap – and sometimes new and fashionable – items: mirrors, snuffboxes, watches, fans, jewellery, bottles of perfume, soap, glasses, textiles, tea tableware, books and so on (Deceulaer, 2006: 194–195). When the peddler Duciel Bourgeoin visited the annual fair of Sint-Niklaas in 1764 (in the *Waasland*, near

Antwerp) he was carrying 'all kinds of jewellery, fancy-articles, ironmongery, nice things, clothings and textiles of gold and silver imported from France'.[6] Within the city walls of Antwerp, peddlers were accused of handling, amongst others, periwigs, cottons, new clothing and imported hand gloves (SAA, *Pk*, nr. 924 (L): city ordinance dated 16 October 1685, f. 40v; SAA, *Pk*, nr. 925 (M): city ordinance dated 21 January 1722, f. 265; and SAA, *GA*, nr. 4259: city ordinance of 1730). Clearly these kinds of products underline the much neglected role of peddlers in appealing to the lure of novelty and fashion consciousness among widening social groups. The goods handled also indicate that peddlers were not exactly a needy bunch. Although little is known about the networks in which they operated, peddlers were arguably organised on a more regular basis and possibly co-operated with suppliers and tradesmen in the city. I will return to this in the second section of this chapter.

Rural fairs and peddling at rural homes were not new activities, although the intensification of both commercial circuits marked something of a fresh start. In general, Antwerp's hinterland became more and more 'contaminated' by the city in the eighteenth century: it evolved into a kind of urban suburb with a strong professional differentiation (Van Uytven, 1972: 180; Vermoesen, forthcoming). In 1702 almost every village around Antwerp included an alehouse keeper, a tailor, a shoemaker, a carpenter and a shop. In the more densely populated areas a baker and a brewer could also be found, sometimes even a thatcher, bricklayer, cooper and physician. These were basic, non-agrarian occupations whose goods and services were widely available in the countryside immediately around Antwerp (Leenders, 1983: 176–183 and annexes IV–VII). The city remained the only place to purchase the more specialised products of skilled artisans and professionals, such as cabinet-makers or skilled blacksmiths (Blondé, 1999: 45). Nevertheless, at the end of the eighteenth century, more occupations were active in the countryside and they were more equally distributed (De Rammelaere, 1959: 223–243; Leenders, 1983: 167–228).

Of all these trades, rural shops were naturally the most significant in the distribution of new and fashionable consumer goods. According to Mui and Mui, the multitude of petty shops in the English countryside were 'a necessary concomitant of the many changes occurring in the social and economic life of the country' (Mui and Mui, 1989: 148). Carole Shammas has also underlined how rural shops became an important commercial circuit in the eighteenth century, complementary with market and peddling activity (Shammas, 1990: 158). The same seems to apply for the Antwerp hinterland. Here, rural shops were already in place in 52 per cent of all villages at the beginning of the eighteenth century; this figure which rose steadily and reached 82 per cent in 1796 (Leenders, 1983: 179 and annexe VII). At the same time, the number of shops per 1000 inhabitants more than doubled: from a density of 2.2 in 1702 to 4.9 in 1796 (Leenders, 1983: 176, 179 and annexe I–III, VII). Without a doubt, shops became a common aspect of most of the

6 *Marchandises de bijouterie, mercerie, quincaillerie, jolités, nippes et étoffes d'or et d'argent qu'il a tiré de France.* See Algemeen Rijksarchief Brussel (ARA), *Raad van Financiën* (*RvF*), nr. 7581: colporteurs, 1765, 'mess. les tresoriers generals, conseillers et commis de domaines et finances de sa Mjt'. For other examples of stuff being peddled in the Southern Netherlands, see ARA, *RvF*, nrs. 7579–7581.

rural communities in the Southern Netherlands in the course of the eighteenth century (Billen, 1987: 117).[7]

Not much is known about the products that these rural shopkeepers sold or about their suppliers. It has been suggested that country shops were instrumental in commercialising new imported groceries on the countryside, such as tobacco, tea, coffee, chocolate, sugar and so on (Shammas, 1990: 258–260). Indeed, shopkeepers of the Maastricht area (at the border of the Southern Netherlands) sold these products widely to country folk (Steegen, 2006: 271–278). Antwerp country shops were less specialised. Durable products of low value (buttons, pins, ribbons, pots and pans, and so on) were sold next to old and new groceries, such as salt and occasionally tobacco or snuff (Van Uytven, 1972: 185; Leenders, 1983: 179). However, more research is needed to understand how rural shops fit into the global retail infrastructure of the Antwerp countryside. It is clear, though, that all commercial circuits in the countryside were surprisingly active and growing from the middle of the seventeenth century onwards, possibly in response to rising rural demand for market-supplied goods. How did the corporately organised retailers in the nearby city of Antwerp respond to these evolutions?

7.3 A Breach in the Wall: the Struggle for Consumers

The Antwerp guilds had a long history of complaining and agitating against non-agrarian activities on the countryside. These grievances became louder in the second half of the seventeenth century, culminating in a royal ordinance, dated 10 November 1685 (Prims, 1936: 225–231; Dickschen, 1993: 199–211), which aimed to drastically curtail all occupations that were not strictly necessary 'for the maintenance of the agricultural activities'.[8] Theoretically this meant the removal of industrial plants (like beer brewing facilities) and the clipping of 'surplus' occupations. Every village around Antwerp was henceforth allowed to have only one carpenter, one shoemaker, two bakers, one tailor, and so on. For some professions, such as the joiners, it was even forbidden to settle in the countryside (SAA, *GA*, nr. 4016: *Register der stadt Antwerpen nopende de buyten neringen*). In practice, however, the clock was not turned back so easily. Effective control of the Antwerp hinterland was hard to enforce and simply stopped in the recurrent periods of warfare (between 1688–1697 and 1700–1715). An inquiry in the years 1717–1718 plainly stated: 'how in the same villages and hamlets [around Antwerp] all trades were active again' (SAA, *GA*, nr. 4011: *Carel bijder gratie godts*, dated 24 January 1718). Even more people than before were working in the non-agrarian sector. During the years of agricultural depression and crisis, the Antwerp hinterland had developed an increasing specialised and differentiated occupational structure.

The city guilds again proposed measures to be taken (Van Damme, 2006: 512–516). However, there were notable differences from the outcries at the end of the seventeenth century. In those days, the anger of the urban corporations was directed at industrial activities like beer brewing and the cheap manufacturing of shoes, textiles and

7 Unpublished data from the PhD-research of Thijs Lambrecht (University of Ghent) and Reinoud Vermoesen (University of Antwerp) confirm these findings.

8 SAA, *GA*, nr. 4012: *Coincklijck Placcaet* van 10 november 1685: '(...) *tot onderhoudinghe vande lantbouwerije*'.

hats, which were produced mainly for the urban market. From 1718 onwards the urban retailers also asked for the oppression of an apparently sprawling rural distribution system. The country shops in particular were an aggravation to the mercers' guild, which wanted to eradicate commercial outlets on the basis of the royal ordinance of November 1685.[9] Corporate and urban rhetoric reveals this striking change, suggesting that countryside dwellers were not only diligent producers but had become valuable consumers as well. Under these circumstances, fighting against rural producers and retailers became a struggle for control over rural demand. Whereas previously the city was the only place to buy new and fashionable products, the proliferation of retail outlets on the countryside made this less evident. Moreover, rural retailing could even attract urban consumers. In 1738, for instance, trouser and hosier makers complained about rural shops, 'in the villages close to the city gates', which were successfully selling to citizens similar products at lower prices.[10]

As mentioned, growing rural retailing and demand could trigger different reactions from urban actors. Not much is known about the networks of dependency and co-operation between, on one hand, city-based suppliers/traders and, on the other, agrarian shopkeepers and peddlers. It seems plausible that urban and rural distribution was organised along parallel lines, resembling the more widely studied proto-industrialisation networks (Van der Wee, 1988: 301–381; Vandenbroeke, 1996: 102–117). In this way, a kind of 'merchant-distributor' could have acted in manner similar to the famous 'merchant-entrepreneurs', supplying countryside shopkeepers and peddlers with new, attractive goods. However, hard evidence regarding such practices is missing, although urban complaints hint at their existence. In 1729, for instance, it was attested how strange peddlers came 'to the doors of city shops', apparently settling affairs with Antwerp shopkeepers.[11] In the countryside of Luxemburg, it was attested how 'pedlars are part of the shopkeepers' staff; the goods [peddlers carry around] are supplied in the shops'.[12] Thus, by subcontracting peddlers, city-based tradesmen could regain some of the countryside customers they would otherwise have lost by dealing only within the city walls.

Officially, such networks were deemed 'little honourable' and hardly tolerated by the mercers' guild and the city authorities.[13] It only deepened the commercial competition between town and countryside. Furthermore, setting up rural shops or subcontracting peddlers was a practice that only wealthy merchants with an abundance of stock could afford. Therefore, recurrent complaints kept urging for containment or abolition of rural retailing (Van Den Nieuwenhof, 1997: 142–144; OCMW-AA, *GH*, R, nr. 38: *resolutieboek meerseniers*, f. 500v°, 22 August 1763). But in light of the relative impotence of legislation, other strategies were also possible. Rather than fighting an uphill battle to 'force' rural consumers back to the city, urban retailers themselves could actively tap into

9 For instance Rijksarchief Anderlecht (RABA), *Processen Raad van Brabant* (*PRvB*), Ambachten en naties, nr. 568: *Joannes Van Thuijst, suppliant, teghens die dekens van den hoofdambacht vande meersche binnen de stadt Antwerpen, rescribenten* (1756).

10 SAA, *GA*, nr. 4007: *Consistentie van de ambachten, neiringen, ende fabriquen soo ende gelijck de selve binnen de stadt Antwerpen sigh bevinden in de maendt augustus 1738.*

11 SAA, *Pk*, nr. 926 (N), f. 19: city ordinance dated 17 November 1729: '*aen de deuren van de winckeliers*'.

12 ARA, *RvF*, nr. 7578 (colportage): '*Que ces porte-panniers sont leurs domestiques, que ce sont des marchandises tirées de leurs boutiques*'.

13 SAA, *GA*, nr. 4012: *Van wegens de laeckenbereijders ende laekenvercoopers der steden van Antwerpen ende Herentals* (dated: 23 August 1652).

the rising demand outside the city walls. If we accept that there was a proliferation of rural buyers during the course of the seventeenth and eighteenth centuries, the effort of leaving the confines of the city certainly become a worthwhile business strategy. Although, as before, figures are lacking, this hypothesis is in line with the evidence presented so far.

At least one Antwerp corporation of retailers – the second-hand dealers or *oudekleerkopers* – is known to have tried to cash in on rural consumption. The importance of rural demand for the *oudekleerkopers* of Ghent and Brussels has already been attested (Deceulaer, 2002: 452–464). In Antwerp too, the second-hand dealers were renowned for selling used clothing and the like at rural dwellings from the sixteenth century onwards (Deceulaer, 2001: 225). Discussion remains about how rising retail competition and changing consumer preferences affected the overall evolution of this trade in used and 'old' goods (Deceulaer, 2002: 446–451; Van Damme, 2006 215–216; Blondé and Van Damme, 2007: 83–86). However, the Antwerp second-hand dealers had an important additional service to offer to the rural households: they held the privilege on public auctions. This monopoly was originally urban oriented, but the growing number of rural customers prompted second-hand dealers to organise auctions in the countryside too. Apparently, they did so with some success: in 1769 the mercers' guilds of Brussels and Antwerp held a special meeting 'to prohibit selling days and auctioning in the countryside, which is very harmful for the shops in the cities'.[14] Urban shopkeepers saw their 'natural' control over the hinterland being infringed by yet another commercial circuit. Part of the success of rural auctions was due to the wide range of products for sale (including new and fashionable ones) and attractive prices. According to the contemporary trade manual of Jacques Savary, buying at auctions yielded a ten per cent saving compared to shop goods: 'plus de dix pour cent de bon marché' (Savary, 1749, vl. 1: 111).

Sadly, the Antwerp archives of the *oudekleerkopers* do not contain private accounts or annotated 'selling books' (*coopboecken*), which could give a better picture of products, prices and buyers (Van Damme, 2007). Yet a peculiar lawsuit around the middle of the eighteenth century offers information on some of these aspects, precisely regarding auctions that occurred 'in several places and villages outside the city of Antwerp' between October 1694 and August 1747.[15] It would lead us too far astray to elaborate on the exact events that led to the compilation of these judicial documents. However, it should be noted that the second-hand dealers gathered this information to justify their auction activity on the countryside, which was disputed by the authorities of *'t Kiel*, a hamlet close to Antwerp.[16] According to introductory statements made about these archives, the content was taken from the now lost *coopboecken*. Although comparison with the original sources is no longer possible, these annexes were nevertheless considered authentic during the time of the lawsuit. The so-called 'selling books' held an

14 OCMW-AA, *GH*, R, nr. 88: *resolutieboek meerseniers*, f. 517v° (11 May 1768): '*verbieden de coopdagen en het loven op het plattelant, het welck is tot groot naerdeel van de winckels in de vaste steden*'; see also f. 519v° (12 and 15 April 1769) and f. 524v° (21 September 1771).

15 See SAA, *Pk*, nr. 1283: *Replique met voldoeninghe voor die dekens ende ouderlingen van het oude cleercoopersambacht binnen Antwerpen supplianten teghens die drossaerdt ende schepenen der heerlijckheyt van 't Kiel*, annex 4, 5 and 6 (dated: 10 December 1761): '*op verscheyde plaetsen ende dorpen buyten de stadt Antwerpen*'.

16 See SAA, *GA*, nr. 4277–78; SAA, *Pk*, nr. 1283; and Rijksarchief Anderlecht (RABA), *Processen Raad van Brabant* (*PRvB*), Ambachten en Naties, nr. 604.

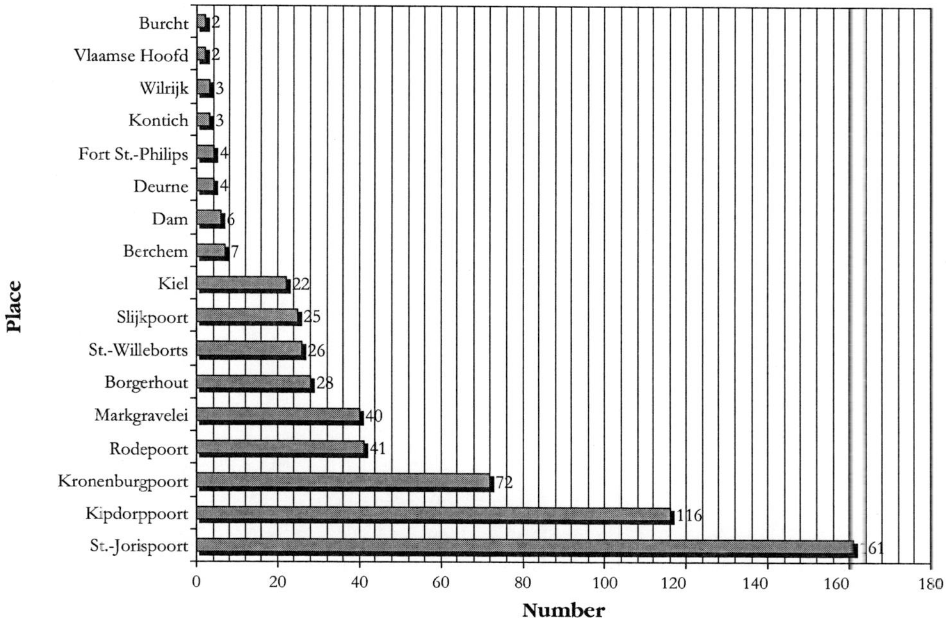

FIGURE 7.2. Frequency of public auctions in the surroundings of Antwerp, by geographical description, 1694–1747 (n = 588)

SOURCE: SAA, *Pk*, nr. 1283: *replique met voldoeninghe*, annexes 4, 5 and 6.

official character during the seventeenth and eighteenth centuries: the 'official criers' (*gesworen roepers*) – who organised the functioning of public auctions together with the 'official appraisers' (*gesworen schatters*) and their respective clerks (*gesworen schrijvers* or *clerken*) – had a legal duty to note each auction that took place inside or outside Antwerp. Excerpts from these 'selling books' appear regularly in lawsuits concerning the *oudekleerkopers*, like the one analyzed here. Because a value tax on all auctioned goods existed in Antwerp, it was almost certainly in the interest of the official criers not to record every auction or to falsify the content (or value) of the goods for sale. In this peculiar case, however, it does not seem likely that these documents distorted reality, as the purpose of the lawsuit was to prove the thriving activities of the second-hand dealers in Antwerp's hinterland. The figures are by no means a complete record of rural auctions, but they provide a reliable sample of some of the public auctions that were held in the countryside during the first half of the eighteenth century.

The first graph and adjoining map represent 95 per cent (or 562 of a total of 588) of the auctions between 1694–1747 mentioned in the judicial annexes, plotted by geographical location (Figure 7.2. and Map 7.1.). The remaining 5 per cent were not represented because the location was stated only once, was sometimes unclear or was not reported at all. The most popular places to organise public auctions were clearly 'outside' (*buyten*) the city gates, with almost 70.5 per cent of all auctions in the Antwerp countryside being situated in the proximity of the five city gates (*Slijkpoort*, *Rodepoort*, *Kipdorppoort*, *St.-Jorispoort*, *Kronenburgpoort*) or on the approaching roads to these

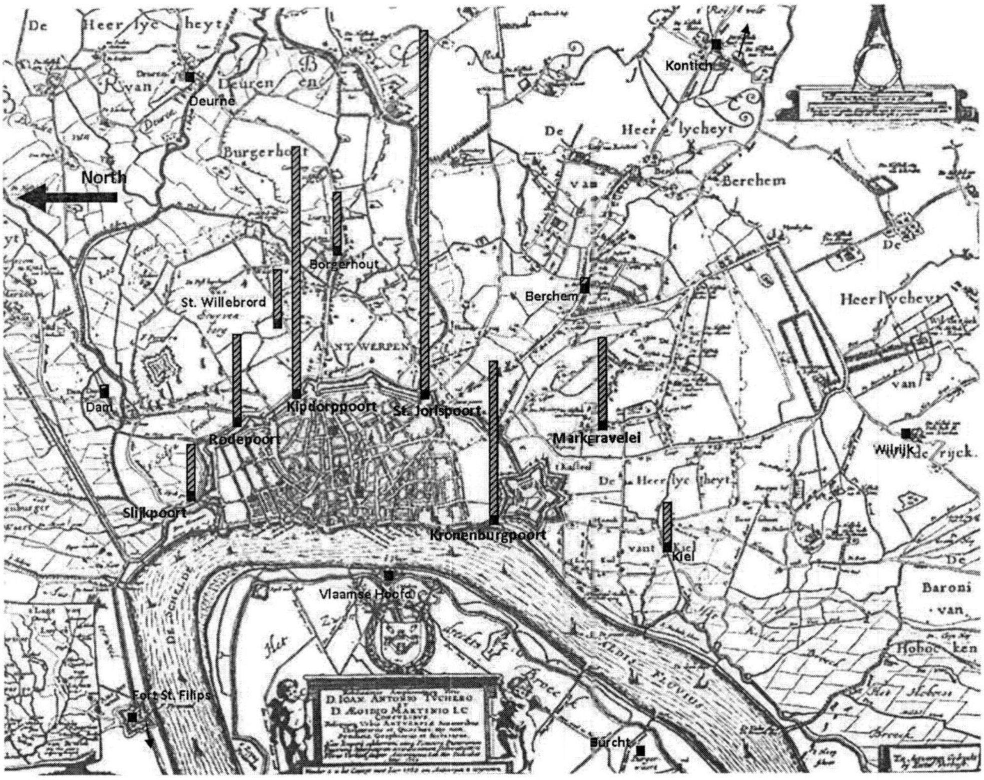

MAP 7.1. Frequency of public auctions in the surroundings of Antwerp, by geographical description, 1694–1747 (n = 588)

SOURCE: SAA, *Pk*, nr. 1283: *replique met voldoeninghe*, annexes 4, 5 and 6.

gates.[17] Especially striking is the frequency with which the south-east *Kipdorp* and *St.-Joris* gates appear: these were on popular roads with dense traffic. Apparently the *oudekleerkopers* sought out crowded places to secure a maximum attendance at the auctions from city and country dwellers alike. The same logic was at work in populous villages and hamlets such as *Borgerhout, St.-Willebrord* and *'t Kiel*. At the end of the sixteenth century the area around the *Markgravelei* already harboured many urban consumers, who were wealthy enough to build *villas rustica* there (Baetens, 1991: 166). Besides the presence of potential buyers, the second-hand dealers had made good contacts with an innkeeper on the *Markgravelei*. His establishment, called *den Assijn*, was ideally placed on the busy road from *Wilrijk* to the *Kronenburgpoort*, and close to *'t Kiel*.[18] Other inns were also used as places to organise public auctions: *den Arend* in *Deurne* or *In den Koninck van Spagnien*, just outside the *Kronenburgpoort*.

17 It is essential to stress the word 'outside' (*buyten*) in the sources. This clearly indicates that the auctions were not confined to the gates alone, but comprised the extended area surrounding or leading to the Antwerp city gates.

18 SAA, *Pk*, nr. 1283: *Inscriptie met verclaeren van de drossaard en de schepenen van het Kiel tegen het oudekleerkopersambacht van Antwerpen* (dated: 17 December 1731).

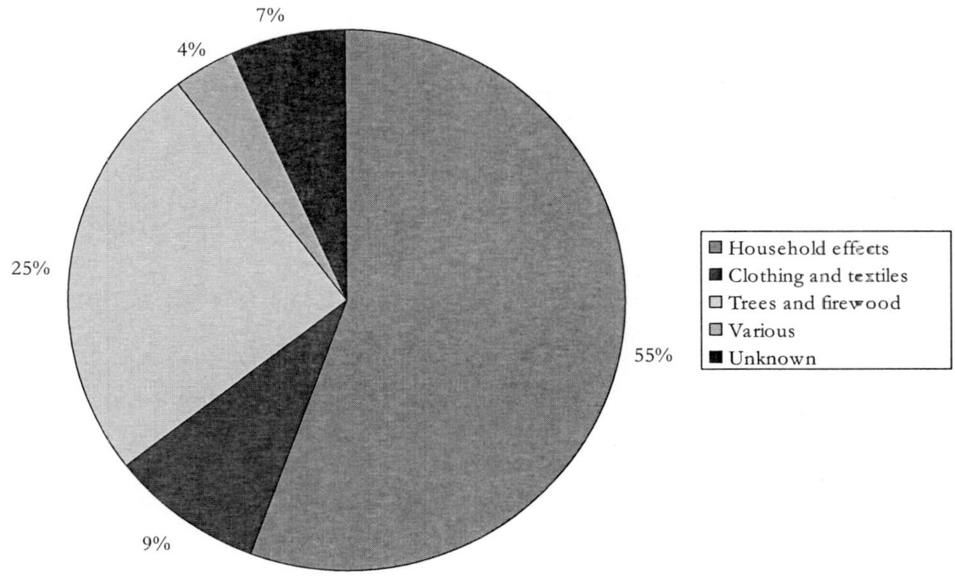

FIGURE 7.3. Public auctions in the surroundings of Antwerp, by product description, 1721–1734 (n = 151)

SOURCE: SAA, *Pk*, nr. 1283: *replique met voldoeninghe*, annexe 4: '*extract uyt sekeren boeck gehouden bij ofte door de thien gesworen clercken van het oude cleercoopersambacht binnen Antwerpen*'.

Turning to the question of products and prices, it is unfortunate that only 26 per cent (or 151 of the total of 588) of all auctions mention goods by name. However, all these specific cases were situated in a fairly short time between the 4th of April 1721 and the 19th of May 1734. Since no other auctions were mentioned in this period, these 151 cases provide a representative sample of the goods offered for sale (Figure 7.3. and Table 7.2.). They also provide an indication of the estimated total value of all offered goods at an auction.

The majority (55 per cent) of the auctions in the Antwerp surroundings between 1721 and 1734 dealt in household effects. This large category comprised different kinds of furniture, including chairs, beds, pots and pans, paintings, jewellery, paintings, and so on. Auctions of this kind undoubtedly facilitated the regular renewal of rural household belongings. The estimated total value of auctions with household effects varied from a meagre 50 guilders on one occasion to a staggering 1000 guilders and more on another. Again, this underlines the range of the products offered for sale at these auctions. Cheap chairs as well as luxurious or fashionable ones; pewter, earthenware or objects made of gold or silver: all could be auctioned, the mix varying from sale to sale. This reinforces the impression that people with very different social backgrounds could participate in these sales, not only as mere spectators of the wealthy few, but sometimes even as active buyers (Van Damme, 2006: 210). Auctions, as processes of commercial recycling and re-use, were thus instrumental in controlling the tensions in household incomes (De Vlieger-De Wilde, 2005: 126–146; Lemire, 2005: 29–48). The increasing demand for market-supplied goods in the countryside was certainly mediated, at least for some part, by these popular commercial circuits.

TABLE 7.2. Price frequency in guilders of the estimated total value of all auctioned goods, by product description, 1721–1734 (n = 151)

Price	Household effects	Clothing and textiles	Trees and firewood	Various	Unknown
≤50gl	8	2	2	1	2
51 ≤ 100gl	3	3	18	–	–
101 ≤ 150gl	11	3	10	–	3
151 ≤ 200gl	11	–	4	2	–
201 ≤ 300gl	11	2	1	2	3
301 ≤ 400gl	11	2	1	–	1
401 ≤ 500gl	11	1	–	–	–
501 ≤ 600gl	6	–	1	–	1
+600gl	8	–	1	–	–
+1000gl	5	–	–	–	–

SOURCE: SAA, *Pk*, nr. 1283: *replique met voldoeninghe*, annexe 4: '*extract uyt sekeren boeck gehouden bij ofte door de thien gesworen clercken van het oude cleercoopersambacht binnen Antwerpen*'.

Clothing and textiles figured in just 9 per cent of auctions between 1721 and 1734. The estimated total value of auctions offering these kinds of products also varied, but never reached more than 500 guilders. It was probably more convenient to sell clothing and even new textiles (like cotton) door to door (Deceulaer, 2001: 225; Lemire, 1991: 67–82). The other product categories, like trees and firewood, and auctions of various products (like real estates, horses, flowers and so on) clearly reflected the rural setting of these sales.[19] Firewood, however, had a special meaning for the city of Antwerp, where it was consumed as construction material and comprised a valuable fuel for industry and house heating. According to the local newspaper, most public auctions of trees and firewood usually took place outside Antwerp and, if not, close to the city walls, where green areas remained (database *Gazette van Antwerpen*). According to Table 7.2. the prices of firewood and trees were quite moderate: the estimated total value of the majority of these selling days being under 100 guilders.

Clearly the *oudekleerkopers* had found a way to tap into rural demand. Between 1694 and 1747 an average of eleven auctions were held each year in the Antwerp hinterland (Figure 7.4.). However, numbers ranged widely – from a minimum of two auctions to a maximum of twenty – making it impossible to plot any significant linear trend. By going to the hinterland and actively seeking out the rural consumers, the Antwerp guild tried to broaden the scope of its business activities. It remains to be seen, however, if the corporation was successful in establishing a structural grip on the countryside in the eighteenth century. The guild of second-hand dealers certainly experienced growing rivalry from local officials, solicitors, notaries and bailiffs, who all

19 A small percentage (7 per cent) of all mentioned auctions between 1721 and 1734 did not report the products for sale, hence the category 'unknown'.

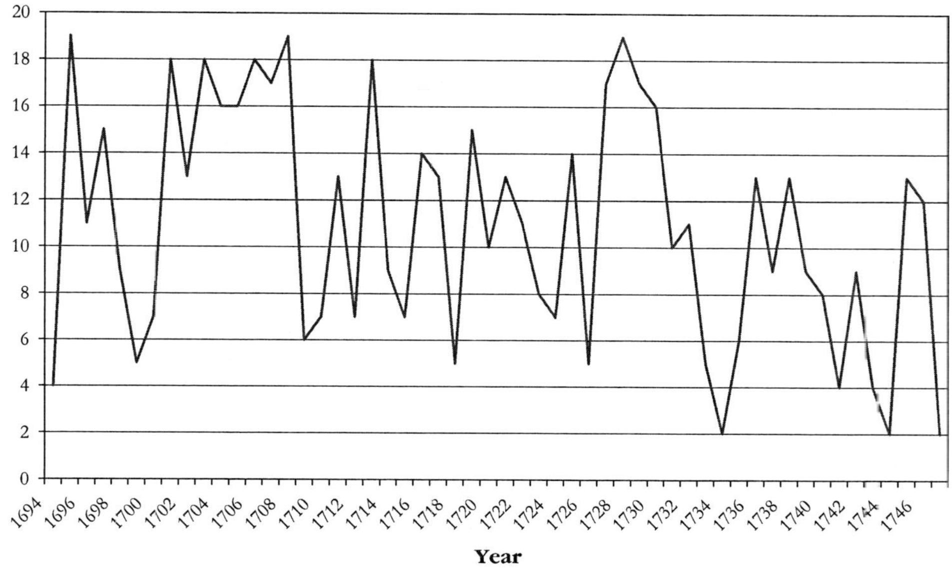

FIGURE 7.4. Yearly frequency of public auctions in the surroundings of Antwerp, 1694–1747 (n = 588)

SOURCE: SAA, *Pk*, nr. 1283: *replique met voldoeninghe*, annexes 4, 5 and 6.

organised public auctions on the countryside on their own (Meulemans, 1957: 191–194; SAA, *Pk*, nr. 792: request from 19 October 1705, f. 116v°–117r°). On 9 November 1762, for instance, the Antwerp guild complained that local auctioneers were very well organised and attracted consumers from within the city walls. In *Dambrugge*, just a fifteen-minute walk outside town, all sorts of goods were 'publicly cried and sold by a local sheriff, assisted by two farmer aldermen'.[20] Printed flyers were handed out in the city, mentioning the day, location and hour of the auction, and promising 'carriages at the city gates that will bring everybody to the destined location and back'.[21]

If rural auctioneers were luring urban consumers away from the city, sometimes harsh measures were taken to discourage the *oudekleerkopers* from coming to the Antwerp surroundings. In *'t Kiel*, in the autumn of 1761, an *oudekleerkoper* was attacked and threatened with shooting by the local sheriff 'and eight or ten armed persons' if he proceeded in organising a sale.[22] This incident eventually gave rise to the legal dispute concerning auction activity on *'t Kiel*, analysed above. Again, this action is best understood if we acknowledge rising rural demand for market-supplied goods. Apparently the

20 SAA, *GA*, nr. 4277: request from the *oudekleerkopers* to the *Raad van Brabant* (dated: 9 November 1762): '*door den meijer van aldaer uter presentie van twee boere schepenen publiquelijck sijn opgeroepen ende vercocht geworden*'.

21 SAA, *GA*, nr. 4277: request from the *oudekleerkopers* to the *Raad van Brabant* (dated: 9 November 1762): '*dat aen de stadtspoorten sullen staen de noodige voituren om een iegelijck naer de gedestinueerde plaetse te brengen ende weder om 't huys te voeren*'.

22 SAA, *GA*, nr. 4278: '*die dekens ende ouderlingen van het oudt cleercoopersambacht binnen Antwerpen suppli̇anten tegens die drossaert ende schepenen der heerlijckheijt van het Kiel geinsinueerde ende rescribenten*' (dated: 2 May 1763).

authorities of the hamlet *'t Kiel* found those auctions lucrative enough to start a dangerous quarrel about it. Rather than allowing the *oudekleerkoopers* to penetrate the countryside, the inhabitants of the village tried to control the diverse retail outlets themselves.

In general, the Antwerp corporation of second-hand dealers experienced increasing difficulties in the eighteenth century (Van Damme, 2006: 215–216). Within the city walls of Antwerp, rising retail competition had an essential part to play. Changing consumer wants and parallel changes in the material culture were probably equally important in the overall evolution of the *oudekleerkopers*. Not only were eighteenth-century products going out of fashion faster than before, they were also made of less durable materials, and thus less easy to be re-used, recycled and re-sold (Blondé and Van Damme, 2007: 83–84; Nenadic, 1994: 134). As prices for novel consumer goods gradually dropped in the eighteenth century, a 'cry for the new' began to dominate consumer wants (Campbell, 2001: 246). These changes certainly affected the commercial auction circuit. Antwerp merchants brought cargos of new goods to the less regulated countryside to be sold publicly 'in the first villages or hamlets outside the town'.[23] Contracting local criers and appraisers became an option, thus bypassing the guild of second-hand dealers altogether.

7.4 Conclusion

Changes in retailing and consumption in the seventeenth and eighteenth centuries were not restricted to the urban environment alone. Although the early-modern city dominates the relevant historical literature (and most of the chapters in this book), this introductory survey has nevertheless tried to demonstrate how similar evolutions in the distribution of old and new goods existed in the immediate surroundings of Antwerp. In the first place, the countryside harboured a retail infrastructure almost as complex and diverse as the nearby town. Notwithstanding the proximity of a highly specialised occupational structure in Antwerp, many retailers and non-agrarian occupations were active in the surrounding hamlets and villages. Markets and fairs were widespread, peddlers visited home after home, auctions or public sales were organised on a regular basis, and at the end of the eighteenth century almost every village had at least one shop.

Indeed, in the sixteenth century, the Antwerp hinterland was already quite commercialised, especially to the south of the city. However, as the growth of shops, peddlers and markets indicates, commercial circuits were not only active but also proliferated from the late seventeenth century onwards. Thus, the Antwerp countryside became part of a broader, European 'urbanisation from below' (Blondé, 1999: 231–247). No longer were big towns like Antwerp essential for the rural consumer. The surroundings became 'contaminated' by the nearby city: they evolved in kinds of urban suburbs with a strong professional differentiation. Agrarian households almost certainly

23 SAA, GA, nr. 4277: request from the *oudekleerkopers* to the *Raad van Brabant* (dated: 9 November 1762): '*ten platten lande in den eersten aengelegen dorpe ofte gehuchte omtrent de cuijpe der selve stadt*'.

profited from this situation. Time could be saved in by-passing the city and more credit facilities were available than ever before. Thus, consumption was facilitated, even in periods of economic recession such as the decades around the beginning of the eighteenth century.

The existence of a severe economic crisis in the Antwerp industry and agrarian sector, starting around the 1670s and lasting at least until the 1720s, prompts another conclusion. Apparently, economic growth was not a necessary precondition for the overall growth in retail activity on the countryside (or the city). Other factors accounted for this increase in commercial outlets (Blondé and Van Damme, 2007: 61–88). This chapter has put forward the changing force of a specific rural demand as a plausible hypothesis. Many an agrarian household became attracted by the new and fashionable goods imported from France and overseas (and soon to be made in the Southern Netherlands itself) (Van Damme, 2004: 187–203). To meet this demand for market-supplied goods, the retail infrastructure had to react accordingly, thus bringing novelty and newness to farmers' homes. The reaction of the urban guilds, backed by the city authorities, was initially in line with the past: laments went hand in hand with legislation, sanctions and judicial tussles. However, controlling a legal framework beyond the confines of the city walls was a task that proved impossible for the corporation and civil officials alike. Trying to control rural demand by setting up distribution networks or spreading business activities beyond the urban environment (as the *oudekleerkopers* did) was probably a more sensible strategy. However, the enduring dynamic in the eighteenth century countryside made a corporate and city-centred economic organisation eventually obsolete. Retailing at the dawn of the nineteenth century gave way to free entrepreneurship in the city and the surroundings alike.

This is a partial explanation, and a hypothetical one at that. The existence of a specific form of rural demand is simply taken as a suitable model to interpret qualitative evidence of rising rural distribution in a time of decline and economic crisis. Rural population, production and incomes were not, for all we know, growing in the late seventeenth and early eighteenth centuries. Significantly, though, the overall level of retail activity certainly was increasing. It is my impression that this cannot be sufficiently explained as a mere survival strategy, a logical response to a harsher economic climate. In this reasoning, retailing becomes a phenomenon of spreading rural poverty and marginalisation, a strategy for increasingly unemployed and impoverished country dwellers. Earlier viewpoints have lingered over similar pessimistic interpretations to analyse the social and economic structures of the 'Flemish' countryside (Thoen, 2001: 102–157). Nevertheless, a specific rural demand not only continued to exist but probably became more significant in the course of the 'long eighteenth century'. Addressing the causes of this is beyond the scope of this chapter. The rural consumer would need to be scrutinised far more thoroughly than has been done hitherto. New research is needed concerning standards of living, credit encroachment and material possessions. Furthermore, we must gain better insight into networks of dependence between the urban and rural economic agents. But denying the countryside any creative force in stimulating trade or production would be a critical underestimation of reality. Only by focusing on the symbiosis between town and countryside will it become possible to analyse changes in rural distribution in a satisfactory way.

Bibliography

Primary Sources

Unpublished sources

Algemeen Rijksarchief Brussel (ARA), *Raad van Financien* (*RvF*), nrs. 7578–7581.
Openbaar Centrum voor Maatschappelijk Welzijn-Archief Antwerpen (OCMW-AA), *Godshuizen* (*GH*), Rekeningen (R), nr. 88.
Rijksarchief Anderlecht (RABA), *Processen Raad van Brabant* (*PRvB*), Ambachten en naties, nr. 568; 604.
Stadsarchief Antwerpen (SAA), *Gilden en Ambachten* (*GA*), nr. 4007; 4011–4012; 4016; 4259; 4277–78; *Privilegiekamer* (*Pk*), nr. 792; 924 (L); 925 (M); 926 (N); 1283; 1449.

Published sources

Savary, J. (1749) *Le parfait négociant ou instruction générale pour ce qui regarde le commerce des marchandises de France & des Pays Etrangers*, 2 vls., Paris.
Versteegen, R. (1622) *Scherp-sinnighe characteren, oft subtiele beschrijvinghe van de proprieteyten ofte eyghendommen van verscheyden persoonen*, Antwerp.

Literature

Alexander, D. (1970) *Retailing in England during the industrial revolution*, London.
Baetens, R. (1989) 'De lokale markten te Antwerpen (16e–18e eeuw)', *Antwerpen in de XVIIde eeuw*, Antwerp, 169–202.
Baetens, R. (1991) 'La "Bellezza" et la "magnificenza": symboles du pouvoir de la villa rustica dans la région anversoise aux temps modernes', Baetens, R. and Blondé, B. (eds.), *Nouvelles approches concernant la culture de l'habitat. New approches to living patterns*, Turnhout, 159–179.
Billen, C. (1987) 'Een ingebeelde landbouwrevolutie?', Hasquin, H. (ed.), *Oostenrijks België. 1713–1794. De Zuidelijke Nederlanden onder de Oostenrijkse Habsburgers*, Brussels, 95–120.
Blondé, B. (1999) *Een economie met verschillende snelheden: ongelijkheden in de opbouw en de ontwikkeling van het Brabantse stedelijke netwerk (ca. 1750-ca. 1790)*, Brussels.
Blondé, B. (2002) 'Tableware and changing consumer patterns. Dynamics of material culture in Antwerp, 17th–18th centuries', Veeckman, J. (ed.) *Majolica and glass. From Italy to Antwerp and beyond. The transfer of technology in the 16th-early 17th century*, Antwerp, 295–311.
Blondé, B. and Van Damme, I. (2003) 'Low Countries: Southern Netherlands between 1585 and 1830', Mokyr, J. (ed.), *The Oxford encyclopedia of economic history*, 3, Oxford, 392–394.
Blondé, B. (2005) 'Cities in decline and the dawn of a consumer society: Antwerp in the 17th–18th centuries', Blondé, B., Briot, E., Coquery, N. and Van Aert, L. (eds.), *Retailers and consumer changes in Early Modern Europe. England, France, Italy and the Low Countries*, Tours, 37–52.
Blondé, B., Stabel, P., Stobart, J. and Van Damme, I. (2006) 'Retail circuits and practices in Medieval and Early Modern Europe: an introduction', Blondé, B., Stabel, P., Stobart, J. and Van Damme, I. (eds.), *Buyers and sellers. Retail circuits and practices in Medieval and Early Modern Europe*, Turnhout, 7–29.
Blondé, B. and Van Damme, I. (2007) 'Een crisis als uitdaging? Kleinhandelsevoluties en verbruiksveranderingen te Antwerpen (ca. 1648-ca. 1748)', *Tijdschrift voor Sociale en Economische Geschiedenis*, 4, 61–88.

Bousse, A. (1975) 'De verhoudingen tussen Antwerpen en het platteland', *Bijdragen tot de geschiedenis*, 58, 139–150.

Campbell, C. (2001) 'The desire for the new. Its nature and social location as presented in theories of fashion and modern consumerism', Miller, D. (ed.), *Consumption. Critical concepts in the social sciences*, 1, London and New York, 246–261.

Chartres, J.A. (1977) *Internal trade in England, 1500–1700*, London.

Clapham, J.H. (1967) *An economic history of Modern Britain*, 2 vols., Cambridge.

Deceulaer, H. (2001) 'Urban artisans and their countryside customers: different interactions between town and hinterland in Antwerp, Brussels and Ghent (18th century)', Blondé, B., Vanhaute, E. and Galand, M. (eds.), *Labour and labour markets between town and countryside (Middle Ages – 19th century)*, Turnhout, 218–235.

Deceulaer, H. (2002) 'Consumptie en distributie van kleding tussen stad en platteland. Drie regionale patronen in de Zuidelijke Nederlanden (zestiende-achttiende eeuw)', *Tijdschrift voor Sociale Geschiedenis*, 28, 239–468.

Deceulaer, H. (2006) 'Dealing with diversity: peddlers in the Southern Netherlands in the eighteenth century', Blondé, B., Stabel, P., Stobart, J. and Van Damme, I. (eds.), *Buyers and sellers. Retail circuits and practices in Medieval and Early Modern Europe*, Turnhout, 171–198.

Denecke, D. and Shaw, G. (1992) 'Traditional retail systems in Germany', Benson, J. and Shaw, G. (eds.), *The Evolution of retail systems, c. 1800–1914*, Leicester, London and New York, 76–86.

de Nave, F. (1989) *Antwerpen, stad en land (1394–1402). De innerlijke vervlechting van stedelijk en landelijk milieu in de late middeleeuwen op basis van het privé-bezit aan gronden en renten en andere soorten van goed* (Unpublished PhD-dissertation, Vrije Universiteit Brussel).

De Rammelaere, C. (1959) 'De beroepsstructuur van de plattelandse bevolking in Zuid-Oost-Vlaanderen gedurende de 18de eeuw', *Tijdschrift voor sociale wetenschappen*, 4, 223–243.

De Vlieger-De Wilde, K. (2005) *Adellijke levensstijl. Dienstpersoneel, consumptie en materiële leefwereld van Jan van Brouchoven en Livina de Beer, graaf en gravin van Bergeyck (ca. 1685–1740)*, Brussels.

De Vries, J. (1975) 'Peasant demand patterns and economic development: Friesland 1550–1750', Parker, W.N. (ed.), *European peasants and their markets. Essays in agrarian history*, Princeton, 205–266.

De Vries, J. (1976) *The economy of Europe in an age of crisis*, Cambridge.

De Vries, J. (1993) 'Between purchasing power and the world of goods: understanding the household economy in Early Modern Europe', Brewer, J. and Porter, R. (eds.), *Consumption and the world of goods*, London and New York, 85–132.

De Vries, J. (1994) 'The industrial and the industrious revolution', *Journal of Economic History*, 54, 249–270.

De Vries, J. (1999) 'Great expectations. Early modern history and the social sciences', *Review: a journal of the Fernand Braudel center for the study of economics, historical systems and civilizations*, 22, 133–140.

De Vries, J. (2001) 'The transition to capitalism in a land without feudalism', Hoppenbrouwers, P. and Van Zanden, J.L. (eds.), *Peasants into farmers. The transformation of rural economy and society in the Low Countries (Middle Ages-19th century) in the light of the Brenner debate*, Turnhout, 67–84.

De Vries, J. (2003) 'The industrious revolution and economic growth, 1650–1830', David, P.A. and Thomas, M. (eds.), *The economic future in historical perspective*, Oxford, 43–71.

De Vries, J. (2008) *The industrious revolution. Consumer behavior and the household economy, 1650 to the present,* Cambridge.

Dickschen, S. (1993) 'De Antwerpse brouwersnatie en de corpsbrouwers in de 17de en 18de eeuw', *Bijdragen tot de geschiedenis*, 76, 199–211.

Engelen, T., Knotter, A., Kok, J. and Paping, R. (2004) 'Labor strategies of families: an introduction', *History of the Family*, 9, 123–135.

Fontaine, L. (1996) *History of pedlars in Europe*, Cornwall.

Génard, P. (1864, 1865, 1934) 'Index der Gebodsboeken (1489–1794)', *Antwerpsch Archievenblad*, first series, 1, 1864, 120–464 and 2, 1865, 1–68; and second series, 9, 1934, 115–157; 186–236 en 241–315.

Kamermans, J.A. (1999) *Materiële cultuur in de Krimpenerwaard in de zeventiende en achttiende eeuw. Ontwikkeling en diversiteit*, Wageningen.

Klep, P.M.M. (1981) *Bevolking en arbeid in transformatie. Een onderzoek naar de ontwikkelingen in Brabant, 1700–1900*, Nijmegen.

Klep, P.M.M. (1988) 'Urban decline in Brabant: the traditionalization of investments and labour (1374–1806)', Van der Wee, H. (ed.), *The rise and decline of urban industries in Italy and in the Low Countries (Late Middle Ages – Early Modern Times)*, Leuven, 261–286.

Klep, P.M.M. (1990) 'Het Brabants stedensysteem en de scheiding der Nederlanden, 1565–1650', *Bijdragen tot de geschiedenis*, 73, 101–129.

Kriedte, P., Medick, H. and Schlumbohm, J. (1981) *Industrialization before industrialization. Rural industry in the genesis of capitalism*, Cambridge.

Lambrecht, T. (2003) 'Reciprocal exchange, credit and cash: agricultural labour markets and local economies in the southern Low Countries during the eighteenth century', *Continuity and Change*, 18, 237–261.

Leenders, G. (1983) 'De beroepsstructuur op het platteland tussen Antwerpen en Brussel (1702–1846)', Craeybeckx, J. and Daelemans, F. (eds.), *Bijdragen tot de geschiedenis van Vlaanderen en Brabant. Sociaal en economisch*, vol. 1, Brussels, 167–228.

Lemire, B. (1991) 'Peddling fashion: salesmen, pawnbrokers, tailors, thieves and the second-hand clothes trade in England, c. 1700–1800', *Textile History*, 22, 67–82.

Lemire, B. (2005) 'Shifting currency: the culture and economy of second-hand trade in England, c. 1600–1850', Palmer, A. and Clark, H. (eds.), *Old clothes, new looks: second hand fashion*, Oxford and New York, 29–48.

Lenders, P. (1992) 'Vrachtvoerders en teuten. Retourmigranten in de oude Brabantse en Luikse Kempen (1500–1920). Zin, opkomst en ondergang van de stroming', *Het Oude Land van Loon*, 47, 167–211.

Limberger, M. (2001a) '"No town in the world provides more advantages": economies of agglomeration and the golden age of Antwerp', O' Brien, P. (ed.), *Urban achievement in early modern Europe. Golden ages in Antwerp, Amsterdam and London*, Cambridge, 39–62.

Limberger, M. (2001b) 'Early forms of proto-industries in the backyard of Antwerp? The Rupel area in the fifteenth and sixteenth centuries', Blondé, B., Vanhaute, E. and Galand, M. (eds.), *Labour and labour markets between town and countryside (Middle Ages -19th century)*, Turnhout, 158–173.

Limberger, M. (2001c) 'Merchant capitalism and the countryside. Antwerp and the west of the duchy of Brabant (XVth–XVIth centuries)', Hoppenbrouwers, P. and Van Zanden, J.L. (eds.), *Peasants into farmers. The transformation of rural economy and society in the Low Countries (Middle Ages-19th century) in the light of the Brenner debate*, Turnhout, 158–178.

Limberger, M. (forthcoming) 'Urban periphery and processes of sub-urbanization in sixteenth-century Antwerp'.

Lis, C and Soly, H. (1979) *Poverty and capitalism in pre-industrial Europe*, Hassocks.

Medick, H. (1976) 'The proto-industrial family economy: the structural function of household and family during the transition from peasant society to industrial capitalism', *Social History*, 1, 291–315.

Meulemans, A. (1957) 'De oude-kleerkopers', *Eigen schoon en de Brabander*, 40, 60–68, 134–142, 185–194, 301–314, 365–375.

Michielsen, A. (1938) *De evolutie van de handelsorganisatie in België sedert het begin van de 18de eeuw*, Turnhout.

Mortier, M. (1981) *Inhoudsanalyse van de Gentse almanakken uit de 16de, 17de en 18de eeuw. Het schetsen van een wereldbeeld* (unpublished MA-dissertation, Rijksuniversiteit Gent).

Moens, K. (1983) *Inhoudsanalyse van de Antwerpse volksalmanakken: 16de-17de-18de eeuw. Schets van een geografische horizon* (unpublished MA-dissertation, Rijksuniversiteit Gent).

Mui, H.C. and Mui, L.H. (1989) *Shops and shopkeeping in eighteenth-century England*, London.

Nenadic, S. (1994) 'Middle-rank consumers and domestic culture in Edinburgh and Glasgow 1720–1840', *Past & Present*, 145, 122–156.

Ogilvie, S.C. (1996) 'Social institutions and proto-industrializtion', Ogilvie, S.C. and Cerman, M. (eds.), *European proto-industrialisation*, Cambridge, 23–37.

Ogilvie, S.C. and Cerman, M. (1996a) 'The theories of proto-industrialization', Ogilvie, S.C. and Cerman, M. (eds.), *European proto-industrialisation*, Cambridge, 1–11.

Ogilvie, S.C. and Cerman, M. (1996b) 'Proto-industrialization, economic development and social change in early modern Europe', Ogilvie, S.C. and Cerman, M. (eds.), *European proto-industrialisation*, Cambridge, 227–239.

Overton, M., Whittle, J., Dean, D. and Hann, A., (2004) *Production and consumption in English households, 1600–1750*, London and New York.

Phillips, M. (1992) 'The evolution of markets and shops in Britain', Benson, J. and Shaw, G. (eds.), *The Evolution of retail systems, c. 1800–1914*, Leicester, London and New York, 53–75.

Plattner, S. (1989) 'Markets and marketplaces', Plattner, S. (ed.), *Economic anthropology*, Stanford, 171–208.

Prims, F. (1936) 'De verbanning der dorpsneringen. 1685. Stedelijk corporatisme', *Antwerpiensia*, 10, 225–231.

Prims, F. (1945) *Het herfsttij van het corporatisme te Antwerpen*, Antwerp and Utrecht.

Scammell, L. (2000) 'Town versus country: the property of everyday consumption in the late seventeenth and early eighteenth centuries', Stobart, J. and Owens, A. (eds.), *Urban fortunes: property and inheritance in town, 1700–1900*, Aldershot, 26–49.

Scholliers, E. and Vandenbroeke, C. (1979) 'Structuren en conjuncturen in de Zuidelijke Nederlanden 1480–1800', Blok, D.P. et al (eds.), *Algemene Geschiedenis der Nederlanden*, vol. 5, Haarlem, 252–310.

Shammas, C. (1990) *The pre-industrial consumer in England and America*, Oxford.

Soly, H. (1988) 'Materiële cultuur te Gent in de 18e eeuw: een terreinverkenning', *Oostvlaamse Zanten*, 63, 3–15.

Spufford, M. (1984) *The great recloathing of rural England. Petty Chapman and their wares in the seventeenth century*, London.

Stabel, P. (1996) 'Town and countryside in the Southern Low Countries in the late 15th-early 19th century. Preliminary reflections upon changing relations in de pre-industrial economy', Ni Néill, R. (ed.), *Town and countryside in Western Europe from 1500–1939*, Leicester, 1–27.

Steegen, E., *Kleinhandel en stedelijke ontwikkeling. Het kramersambacht te Maastricht in de vroeg-moderne tijd,* Hilversum, 2006.

Thoen, E. (2001) 'A "commercial survival economy" in evolution. The Flemish countryside and the transition to capitalism (Middle Ages-19th century)', Hoppenbrouwers, P. and Van Zanden, J.L. (eds.), *Peasants into farmers. The transformation of rural economy and society in the Low Countries (Middle Ages-19th century) in the light of the Brenner debate*, Turnhout, 102–157.

Van Aert, L. and Van Damme, I. (2005) 'Retail dynamics of a city in crisis: the mercer guild in preindustrial Antwerp (c. 1648-c. 1748)', Blondé, B., Briot, E., Coquery, N. and Van Aert, L. (eds.), *Retailers and consumer changes in Early Modern Europe. England, France, Italy and the Low Countries*, Tours, 139–167.

Van Damme, I. (2003) 'Het vertrek van Mercurius. Historiografische en hypothetische verkenningen van het economisch wedervaren van Antwerpen in de tweede helft van de zeventiende eeuw', *NEHA-Jaarboek*, 66, 6–39.

Van Damme, I. (2004) 'Zotte verwaandheid. Over Franse verleiding en Zuid-Nederlands onbehagen, 1650–1750', de Bont, R. and Verschaffel, T. (eds.), *Het verderf van Parijs*, Leuven, 187–203.

Van Damme, I. (2006) 'Changing consumer preferences and evolutions in retailing. Buying and selling consumer durables in Antwerp (c. 1648-c. 1748)', Blondé, B., Stabel, P., Stobart, J. and Van Damme, I. (eds.), *Buyers and sellers. Retail circuits and practices in Medieval and Early Modern Europe*, Turnhout, 199–223.

Van Damme, I. (2007) *Verleiden en verkopen. Antwerpse kleinhandelaars en hun klanten in tijden van crisis (ca. 1648-ca. 1748)*, Amsterdam.

Vandenbroeke, C. (1996) 'Proto-industry in Flanders: a critical review', Ogilvie, S.C. and Cerman, M. (eds.), *European proto-industrialisation*, Cambridge, 102–117.

Van den Nieuwenhof, P. (1997) *Faiseurs de rien, vendeurs de tout: het Brussels meerseniersambacht in de achttiende eeuw* (unpublished MA-dissertation, Vrije Universiteit Brussel).

Van der Wee, H. (ed.) (1988) *The rise and decline of urban industries in Italy and in the Low Countries (Late Middle Ages – Early Modern Times)*, Leuven.

Van der Wee, H. (1993) 'Agricultural development of the Low Countries as revealed by tithe and rent statistics, 1250–1800', Van der Wee, H., *The Low Countries in the Early Modern world*, Cambridge, 47–68.

Van Houtte, J.A. (1977) 'Les foires dans la Belgique ancienne', Van Houtte, J.A., *Essays on medieval and early modern economy and society*, Leuven, 81–107.

Van Uytven, R. (1972) 'Peiling naar de beroepsstructuur op het Brabantse platteland omstreeks 1755', *Bijdragen tot de geschiedenis*, 55, 172–203.

Van Uytven, R. (1983) 'L'approvisionnement des villes de l'Europe occidentale au Moyen Age et aux Temps Modernes', *Flaran: L'approvisionnement des villes de l'Europe occidentale au Moyen Age et aux Temps Modernes*, 5, 75–116.

Vermoesen, R. (forthcoming) 'Gescheiden door de wallen? Commerciële circuits in de stad en op het platteland, 1650–1800'.

Winter, A. (2004), 'Vagrancy as an adaptive strategy: the duchy of Brabant, 1767–1776', *International Review of Social History*, 49, 249–277.

CHAPTER 8

THE SEMI-LUXURY MARKET, SHOPKEEPERS AND SOCIAL DIFFUSION: MARKETING *CHINOISERIES* IN EIGHTEENTH-CENTURY PARIS

Natacha Coquery[1] – University of Nantes, Centre de recherches en histoire internationale et atlantique (CRHIA), France

8.1 Introduction

Involved in both the acceleration of processes of exchanges and the spread of consumption, shops – 'first competitors to markets (. . .). Restricted cells, innumerable, they are another elementary tool of exchanges' (Braudel, 1979: 44) – grew increasingly important in the circulation of goods. Their ability to offer diversity, scope of choice, availability, adaptability, advertising, and credit does much to explain their success (Fowler, 1998: 37–54). Their numbers increased everywhere in Europe: in Paris, London, Madrid, Antwerp and Malta, in Sicily and in Bavaria, in capital cities and in provinces. Shops were a central element in the developing process of consumption: plain or sophisticated, mediocre or luxurious, they offered considerably an ever greater range of products and prices to very diverse consumers (Coquery, 2004: 71–89; Coquery, 2006: 63–77).

In this chapter, I want to examine the role that shopkeepers played in the acceleration of new forms of consumption, focusing in particular on the spread of exotic products. The aim is to understand how innovation, consumption and the 'legibility' of shops are linked. Shopkeepers took advantage of product innovations and the growth of consumption, but at the same time were important in stimulating and shaping demand. The new legibility of the shop phenomenon, maturing in the second half of the eighteenth century, corresponded in part to the development of both shops and consumption: going back to the old idea of a *Bureau d'adresses* (address directory) or almanac, dear to Montaigne's father, shopkeepers tried to make themselves known. This is one aspect of the emergence of advertising.

I shall first discuss the links between luxury, the East and consumption. I shall then turn to the strategies by which products were promoted: advertisements illustrate the importance of novelty and exoticism for both imported products and, more commonly, imitations; but shopkeepers managed at the same time to valorise the old, such as Japanese lacquer which remained a luxury item, scarce and expensive, despite the appearance of numerous imitations.

1 With thanks to Marie-Agnès Dequidt for her translation.

8.2 Luxury, the East and Consumption

Semi-luxury: Where Markets Meet – The semi-luxury market – which, as Maxine Berg has demonstrated, perfectly associated innovation and imitation – was central in spreading goods since it blurred the boundaries between two worlds: luxury and necessity (Berg, 1999: 63–85; 2003: 228–244; 2004: 85–141; 2005; Craske, 1999: 187–216). Semiluxury goods comprised a new form of merchandise, produced by recent industries and spread through various agents from the manufacturer to the street seller. They carried a highly symbolic value, but lost part of their quality. They attracted more and more consumers thanks to their pleasing nature and their price: cotton instead of silk, earthenware instead of porcelain, paste instead of real jewels, and so on. Through their diversity, which seemed unlimited, the new goods answered the demand for differentiation and customisation which was coming from an increasingly diverse range of consumers. This broadening of consumption beyond the urban elites was one of the main factors underpinning the burgeoning of consumption.

The growing consumption of the middle classes and even the upper part of labouring classes is a commonplace (Roche, 1981; 1997; Ferrières, 2004; Styles, 1996: 295–308; 1994: 139–166; 2003: 103–115; Medick, 1982: 84–112). It gave birth to a new material culture, characterised by the escape from basic needs, the increase of the unnecessary, the confusion of signs and conditions, the obsolescence of objects, and what Daniel Roche has called the 'culture of the appearances' (Roche, 1997: 71; 1981: chapters V–VI). Probate inventories show just how common many consumer goods became in the eighteenth century: ceramics, cloth, *Indian* or *Chinese* wall paper, printed calico and watches all appear in a growing proportion of inventories (Roche, 1981; Pardailhé-Galabrun, 1988; De Vries, 1997: 100; Weatherill, 1988; Fairchilds, 1993: 228–248).

The advent of semi-luxuries was related to the quick turnover of objects, to changes in fashion, and to the decrease of prices relative to income (Fine and Leopold, 1990: 155). According to Maxine Berg, middle-class consumers did not buy semi-luxury products because of their lower price, but because they were 'fashion leaders' (Berg, 2005: 6). The success encountered by semi-luxury items came both from their newness, which set fashion, and from their meeting the desire for fancy items, a desire that was felt by more and more consumers, both privileged and not. These new products were not seen as ersatz of aristocratic luxury, aiming as such at popular classes (Lemire, 1990: 256).[2] Rather, consumers were united in showing the same desire for fancy items, luxuries and novelties, although this was expressed differently in different social groups. Emulation enhanced 'keeping up' with fashion, and can thus be considered a key element in the origin of *popular luxury* (Styles, 1994). The evidence of the inventories and the ledgers shows that non-élite consumers too bought fashion clothes, and took pleasure to be elegant (handkerchiefs, stockings, gloves and hats etc.). Each object was emotionally laden anew; reinvented by the one who appropriated it – a phenomenon which was picked up by professionals, such

2 Beverly Lemire uses that phrase *ersatz fashions* in referring to the second hand cloths market: 'An extensive second-hand trade thrived during the pre-industrial and early industrial period as a result of this popular demand, providing ersatz fashions in all manner of clothing to consumers of the middling and labouring ranks alike'.

as Mr Jourdain's tailor, the famous Molière's character: 'I kept you waiting a little, but it is that I am to be dressed to-day like a man of rank, (. . .) I have had this printed calico made for me (. . .). My tailor told me that people of quality are dressed like this in the morning' (Molière, 1962: 404).[3]

The case of printed calico (hereafter *indiennes*), which became widespread, not least amongst the labouring classes, is a typical example. Many young adults from lower orders gave themselves over to the pleasure of being elegantly dressed, with flower-patterned dresses, hats, scarf, kerchiefs, lace boots, watches, batiste and linen (Styles, 1994: 139–166). At the same time, the *indiennes* remained a luxury product that aristocrats looked for in the early 1780s: most of the Duke de Coigny's jackets were made of *Indian cloth*, the Duke de la Trémoille bought *indienne* dressing gowns, and the Princess Kinsky had dresses of *indienne*, Persian cloth, Indian taffeta or cirsaka. *Indienne* was present in every home, as a Parisian upholsterer account books shows. In the Marquis de Trémouville's house, the rooms of the housekeeper and of the servant each contained a bed with an *indienne* canopy (9 and 6 £); the furniture of the meeting room included a sofa, six armchairs (358 £), 4 wing chairs (330 £), six cabriole chairs (230 £), 'all of yellow and white Indian damask'.[4] Further down the social scale, an attorney in Châtelet bought a screen made of six Indian paper sheets (36 £),[5] and a gilder owned *indienne* quilt.[6] The combined desires of both rich and less affluent consumers – an unprecedented uniformity of tastes noted by Chapman and Chassagne (1981: 6) – does much to explain the success of oriental products, particularly of *indiennes*. But why were such products so fascinating to western consumers?

The Taste for the Orient: Fascination, Imitation and Innovation – The technical superiority and the trade success of oriental arts and manufactures have long fascinated economist authors. Some have underlined what the West can learn from the East – most notably Jacques Savary des Bruslons (*Dictionnaire universel de commerce*, 1723–1730) or his British equivalent, Malachy Postlethwayt (*The Universal Dictionary of trade and Commerce*, 1751–1755), but also Montesquieu, David Hume or Adam Smith. All of them considered the social structures, psychological presuppositions and aesthetic values which underlined the growing demand for and spending on new consumption goods (Berg and Clifford, 1999: 5–10). What commentators admired above all were the objects that showed uncommon skill and know-how: the fineness of fabric, the liveliness of colours and the transparency of china: 'Indian painted cloth, (. . .) the value and price of the Indian cloths come from the liveliness, the long-lastingness and the adherence of the colours they are painted with, which is such that, when washed, far

3 'Je vous ai fait un peu attendre, mais c'est que je me fais habiller aujourd'hui comme les gens de qualité (. . .). Je me suis fait faire cette indienne-ci (. . .). Mon tailleur m'a dit que les gens de qualité étaient comme cela le matin (. . .)'.

4 Archives de Paris (Arch. De Paris), D5B6/3451: 'complete bedstead with chassis for a pillar bed 150 etc. making-up of the complete bed 240 covered with an Indian embroidery on white satin fabric, the making of the whole bed being very difficult'. ('bois complet et chassis pour lit à colonne 150 etc. façon du lit complet 240 couvert d'une étoffe en satin fond blanc et broderies des Indes dont l'exécution au total du lit tres difficile').

5 Arch. de Paris, D5B6/3066.

6 Arch. de Paris, D5B6/3066: 'I undid two *indienne* quilt, I reset them, (. . .) I fretted 4 pieces, supplied to do them 3 alders of *indienne* 7'. ('avoir défait deux courtepointes d'indienne, les avoir remises (. . .) avoir fait 4 chantournés, fourni pour les faire 3 aunes d'indienne 7')

from losing their brightness, they are all the more beautiful' (Diderot, d'Alembert, 1966).[7]

As Maxine Berg argues in the British context and Serge Chassagne in the case of *indiennes* in France, the response of manufacturers to the appeal of Asian products was imitation (Chassagne, 1991). However, this was not a slavish imitation, less beautiful or more expensive than the original, but an imitation which created new products. For Adam Smith, imitation was 'a source of wonder' (Berg, 2005: 20). New materials, inventiveness in patterns and modernism combined the art of imitation with the science of invention. With the aim of reducing expensive imports, protectionist policies started a process of innovation and invention which led to new products (cotton fabric and earthenware, for instance) which marked the beginning of the mass production. The European trade policy was particularly restrictive on textiles: there were prohibitions on importing and wearing *indiennes* in France during the years 1686–1759; there was a ban on imports of Indian and Chinese textiles in Spain from 1717, in Britain from 1700, and in Prussia from 1721. Germany, Holland and Switzerland did not have such restrictions, and Neufchatel, Lausanne, Geneva, Basel, Amsterdam, Bremen, Frankfurt and Hamburg became active centres of production. In England, the development of a fabrication process for (coloured) *indiennes* in 1740 was an important stage in the growth of the textile industry. *Indiennes* production – the first industrial product of mass consumption which enjoyed an international market – was the starting point of European industrialisation (Verley, 1997: 160–179; Chapman and Chassagne, 1981; Chassagne, 1991). The result of the creative adaptation facing luxury was, in France as in England, an industrialisation relying on national consumer products, thought as a modern alternative to older Asian or European luxury products. In this process – which led to an unprecedented expansion of consumption – the role played by retailers was crucial: linking producers, wholesalers and consumers.

8.3 Advertising Rhetoric: the Prestige of Novelty and Exoticism

With their awareness of the concerns and tastes of wealthy and less wealthy people, and being experts in advertising, shopkeepers – particularly those operating in luxury and semi-luxury markets, such as the haberdashers in Paris – were central to the diffusion of goods and fashions. Advertisements were emblematic of the trading dynamics. The parallel expansion of printed material and commerce in the eighteenth century prompted an unprecedented development of the commercial press. Newspapers, directories, billboards and trade cards aimed at spreading information intended to be useful to the consumer.

Advertising media, commercial directories, guide books and almanacs surfed on the ideas in the air. Together, they marked the growing impact of shopkeepers and consumption: the shop occupied a growing place in these urban representations, especially in Paris, which was celebrated in the guidebooks of the time as the European fashion capital. Since the sixteenth century, Paris had been one of the main European centres for luxury industries, including goldsmiths, bookbinders, watchmakers and cloth weavers. Indeed, the *indienne* was

7 'TOILE peinte des Indes (. . .) les toiles des Indes tirent leur valeur & leur prix de la vivacité, de la ténacité & de l'adhérence des couleurs dont elles sont peintes, qui est telle, que loin de perdre leur éclat quand on les lave, elles n'en deviennent que plus belles' (art. 'Toile peinte').

a product of Parisian fabrication (Bergeron, 1975: 237–263; Fox and Turner, 1998). With the directory, the shopkeepers had at last a dedicated printed medium in book form in which they could announce their presence in the city and through which they could address consumers, whose good taste they flattered (Coquery, 2004: 73–75). This new legibility of shops corresponded to the growth in trade: it was both an incentive and an answer to the expansion of consumption. The trade directory was a medium intended to highlight trade and commerce: under the pretext of information, it was in reality loaded with advertisements (Sarrazin, 1997: 619–620). It was thus part of a whole set of advertising practices: some, like shop signs, were very old; but most of them were new, directly connected to the development of consumerism: bill headings, trade cards, prospectuses, billboards and newspaper announcements (Feyel, 1995: 438–511; Coquery, 1998: 93–105).

Shopkeepers fully realised the essential nature of this promotional activity because novelties did not necessarily find a ready market. The shift of an object, such as a product of exotic origin, from the status of curiosity to that of common use was by no means automatic. John Styles recalls the failure, in the mid 1700s, of Indian imports of upholstery fabrics (for bed and tables), originally produced for Asian customers. He also notes that even goods produced for the British market were not always easy to sell: in October 1682, the British East India Company ordered 200,000 ready-made cotton shirts and shifts from producers in Madras; in December 1685, 100,000 pieces were piling up unsold in the company warehouses (Styles, 2000: 136–139). British consumers, it seems, remained attached to linen and hemp. Novelties needed to be tamed and made attractive, hence the importance of adapting the product to European tastes and of circulating information between producers, traders and consumers. John Styles uses as an example of successful acclimatization the object turned essential in British homes: the teapot in silver and in porcelain, as originally used in China. It was introduced then adopted in the years 1660–1720 (Styles, 2000: 140–147; Berg, 2003: 228–244).

In a simplistic discourse which kept repeating the same formulas, advertising revealed in its own way the growth and change in consumption as well the in techniques and methods used by the shopkeepers to stimulate customers. Advertisements both conveyed and renewed the infatuation for new products of consumers who were better informed and increasingly numerous. The expression *des Indes* (from *the Indies*) was a recurrent theme in shopkeepers' advertisements without necessarily designating an Indian origin – a point noted in contemporary dictionaries. 'Cloth painted in India'. This name became appellative and referred to all sorts of painted cloths. A fine *indienne*. A dress of *indienne* (*Dictionnaire de l'Académie française*, Paris, J.-B. Coignard, 1762, art. 'Indienne'). The occurrence of the words India or *indiennes* was an index of the trading success and attraction of the product. Some even exhibited it as a sign: *At the Fleet of the Indies (spices, jewels), At the King of the Indies, At the port of the Orient* (haberdashers), *At the Coral of the Indies* (sculptor and *rocaille* maker).

The textiles themselves took several forms, from low to top quality: 'Indies muslin of all qualities';[8] 'sells all sorts of *indiennes*';[9] 'Indies clothes of all sorts and qualities';[10] 'sells all sorts of foreign *Indiennes*';[11] 'a shop of all sorts of silk material.

8 Thomas, 1770: 151, entry of the haberdasher Bail ('Mousselines des Indes de toutes qualités').
9 Thomas, 1770: 152 and 178, entries of the haberdashers Bailly, Benoist, etc. ('vend toutes sortes d'Indiennes').
10 Thomas, 1770: 172, entry of the haberdasher Chandellier frère ('Toiles des Indes de toutes qualités et espèces').
11 Thomas, 1770: 210–211, entries of the haberdashers Martin, Mathié ('vend toutes sortes d'Indiennes étrangères').

Persian cloth. *Indiennes*. All kinds of kerchiefs';[12] 'also a shop of Indies kerchiefs of the rarest qualities';[13] 'a new manufacture of very fine hats made of Indian and Provencal silk'.[14] The headings of the shopkeepers' invoices were identical: the haberdasher Thibault, *The Emperor's* 'shop of French and Indian fabrics; (. . .) Persian, English, Indian, and Jouy Cloths, Cirsaka, Candaris, Muslin embroidered with silk and gold; striped and plain Indian fustian'.[15]

The product was no longer the preserve of the elite, but it still kept an aura of prestige: in 1777, the *Almanach Dauphin* listed eleven 'shopkeepers selling Indian silk material and other precious material'. Most chose to insist on the foreign origin, in order to distinguish themselves from others: 'one of the most famous shops and with one of the best collections of Chinese and Indian material for dresses and furniture';[16] 'a shop with a very good choice of new Chinese embroideries, of very good taste';[17] 'a wholesale and retail shop with foreign silk fabrics, Persian, coloured cloths, *Indiennes* (. . .), Indies cloths for dresses'.[18]

The *Indies* production, as it appeared through the almanacs or the headings of invoices, is far from being limited to textile fabrics: associated with Chinese production, it involved porcelain (faience), fine wood carving, the grocery and drug trade (including tea, sago, carmine), and wall papers. The fine wood worker Vaugeois offers, among a vast number of objects (snuffboxes, wallets, backgammon boards, canes, combs, boxes, *Chinese* ink, coffeepot from *the Levant*, kettle *d'Hollande* . . .), skittles from *Indias* (A.N., T186/52). The association between India and China was related to the vagueness of the designation '*Indies*' (*des Indes*), as the *Encyclopédie* regretted: '[Indies] include four big parts of Asia, that are the Industan, the peninsula this side of the river Ganges, the peninsula beyond the river Ganges, & the isles of the Indies sea, the main being that of Ceylon, Sumatra, Java, Borneo, Celebes, Maldives, Moluccas, to which are usually added Philippines & the Mariana Islands. When the matter is only trade, under the name of East Indies are yet included Tonkin, China, & Japan; but to speak truly, these vast countries, neither Philippines and even less the Marian Islands, should belong to the East Indies, since they extend beyond' (Diderot, d'Alembert, 1966, art. 'Inde').[19]

12 Thomas, 1770: 214, entry of the haberdasher Regnier ('tient Magasin de toutes sortes d'Etoffes de soie. Perses. Indiennes. Mouchoirs de toutes espèces').

13 Thomas, 1770: 154, entry of the haberdasher Le Bas ('tient aussi magasin de Mouchoirs des Indes des qualités les plus rares').

14 Thomas, 1770: 172, entry of the haberdasher Le Conte ('tient (. . .) une nouvelle fabrique de Chapeaux de soie des Indes et de Provence très-beaux').

15 Archives National (A.N.), T186, invoice heading from Thibault, haberdasher, 1780 ('tient Magasin d'Etoffes de France et des Indes; (. . .) Perse, Anglaise, Indienne et Toiles de Jouy; Cirsaka, Candaris, Mousseline brodée en soie et or; Basin des Indes, rayé et uni').

16 *Almanach du Dauphin*, 1777: entry of the haberdasher Boudard, n.p. ('tient un des plus fameux Magasin et des mieux assortis en étoffes de Chine et des Indes pour habits, robes et meubles').

17 *Almanach du Dauphin*, 1777: entry of the haberdasher Dartigalongue, n.p. ('tient Magasin très-bien assorti de nouvelles broderies de la Chine, d'un très-bon gout').

18 A.N., T186, invoice heading from Baudelaire, haberdasher, 1778 ('tient Magasin en gros et en détail, d'Etoffes de soie étrangeres, Perses, Toiles peintes, Indiennes (. . .), Toiles des Indes pour robes').

19 '(Les Indes) comprennent quatre grandes parties de l'Asie, savoir l'Indoustan, la presqu'île en-deçà du Gange, la presqu'île au-delà du Gange, & les îles de la mer des Indes, dont les principales sont celles de Ceylan, de Sumatra, de Java, de Bornéo, les Celebes, les Maldives, les Moluques, auxquelles on joint communément les Philippines & les îles Marianes. Lorsqu'il n'est question que de commerce, on comprend encore sous le nom d'Indes orientales, le Tonquin, la Chine, & le Japon; mais à parler juste, ces vastes pays, ni les Philippines, moins encore les îles Marianes, ne doivent point appartenir aux Indes orientales, puisqu'elles vont au-delà'.

Consumers were conscious of the luxury of the new products, which was equated – in their eyes – with refinement, good manners and civility: owning them was a mark of taste (Berg, 1999: 66). Novelty and variety competed with quality, which is why the less expensive semi-luxury items were just as attractive as their luxurious equivalent: they addressed as much, if not better, the increasing desire for fashion and fancy (Clifford, 1999a: 164–165; Clifford, 1999b: 241–255; Styles, 2000: 124–169; Hilaire-Pérez, 2000: 290–295). Shopkeepers certainly appear to have felt that signs and meanings were getting blurred. Less than on clear distinction, commercial success depended on the ability to play with the diversity of objects and qualities. Several craftsmen boasted of their imitation skills: 'Paints all sorts of silk material, in an indelible way, and applies gold and silver with art, in the Peking style';[20] '*Kerchiefs of fast red thread,* Indies style, from Mr *Maraud's* factory (. . .)';[21] 'Manufacturer of Paper for Hangings (. . .) imitating watered Damask, Peking, Perse, *Indiennes,* Gros de Tours, and all possible kinds of fabrics in the newest designs, a large collection of Chinese paper with brush made pictures and flowers is also available'.[22]

In contrast, some shopkeepers insisted on selling genuine stuff: 'sells (. . .) Genuine Perse from Indies and from England in pieces';[23] 'a Shop with true Indies Papers of all sizes, with Landscapes, Figures, Flowers and Birds to adorn Desert trays, Cabinets, Dessus de porte, Screens, fits them with neatest attention on chassis'.[24]

8.4 The Emphasis of the *Old*: the Japanese Lacquer

The taste for *chinoiseries* and objects from Japan illustrates the interaction between style and economy, where *old* came into play. Porcelain and lacquered goods incorporated an enormous volume of novelties and inventions spawned by the growing fashion for anything *Chinese,* but they also included goods that were valuable because of their scarcity and age. The historian Th. Wolvesperges examines the trading circuits and their agents, the craftsmen, the techniques and inventions, the evolutions of taste (Wolvesperges, 1998). Lacquer was more and more appreciated and became a collectors' item in the middle of the eighteenth century. The first pieces had arrived in Paris 150 years earlier, but imports remained modest for a long time. With porcelains – widely imported and thus less expensive – Chinese products were more numerous on European markets. Lacquer therefore represented a marginal market, less profitable than the markets for silk, tea or porcelain. In the last third of the seventeenth century, high prices and mediocre quality of Japanese lacquer intended for export, forced trading companies to stop purchasing them. However, since Europeans liked to adorn the wainscots of their 'Chinese' living-rooms with lacquer, the companies turned to the Chinese market which offered more moderate prices.

20 *Almanach du Dauphin,* 1777: entry of the lady painter Mlle Hébert, n.p. ('peint toutes sortes d'étoffes de soie, d'une manière indélébile, et y applique avec art l'or et l'argent, à l'imitation des Pékin').

21 *Notices des dix premières années de l'Almanach sous verre,* 1779: note 12, col. 69 ('Mouchoirs de fil rouge bon teint, façon des Indes, de la fabrique du sieur Maraud').

22 A.N., T166 ('Marchand Fabricant de Papier pour Tenture (. . .) imitant les Damas Moires, Pekin, Perses, Indiennes, Gros-de-tours, et toutes les Etoffes possibles dans les desseins les plus nouveaux, l'on trouve aussi un grand assortiment de Papier Chinois à figures, et à fleurs fait aux pinceaux').

23 A.N., T186 ('vend vraies Perses des Indes et Anglaises en pieces').

24 A.N., T220/5-7 ('tient Magasin des véritables Papiers des Indes de toutes grandeurs, à Paysages, à Figures, Fleurs et Oiseaux pour garnir les plateaux de Desserts, les Cabinets, dessus de Portes, Paravents et Ecrans, les accommode de la derniere propreté sur les chassis').

The development of the trade in lacquered furniture in the eighteenth century was related to its change in status: while some pieces became collectors' items, others were recycled. As a result, unfashionable pieces (including cabinets, coffers and screens) were dismantled to retrieve the finest panels of lacquer which were then incorporated into more fashionable furniture (such as chests, desks and secretaries), or sold as collectors' items. The idea of cutting into pieces precious Japanese or Chinese coffers to adorn furniture in the rocaille taste was a ruinous folly, the initiative of which came from important Parisian haberdasher merchants like Gersaint, Lazare Duvaux, as well as Hébert, Darnault, Julliot, Poirier and Daguerre (Glorieux, 2002: 276).

Early on, European shopkeepers had made a distinction between old Japanese lacquer, which was expensive and scarce, and the new lacquer, necessarily Chinese, which was cheap and of mediocre quality. William Dampnier wrote in 1697 that Japanese lacquer-work 'is appreciated as being the best in the world'. A few years later, the shopkeeper Lorenz Lange added that 'the best varnished furniture comes from Japan and are smuggled in China' (Wolvesperges, 1998). Amongst all the *chinoiseries* which became semi-luxury or even everyday items in the eighteenth century, Japanese lacquer remained a luxury traded in a privileged market both in terms of consumers (the court, aristocracy and rich collectors) and craftsmen and dealers (including the most important haberdashers, cabinetmakers and glazers of the capital). In 1745, Gersaint added in one of his sales catalogues: 'Lacquer is still a sort of curiosity little known and hence little spread. Choice items (. . .) are extremely difficult to find, especially when old. Sometimes, they reach astounding prices, even in Holland'.[25] To his mind, Chinese lacquer 'has no appeal [for the experts]'. In 1748, in another preface of a sales catalogue, Gersaint gives the reasons: the old has a 'hardness comparable to that of metal' and lasts infinitely, the new is tender and fragile (quoted by Wolvesperges,1998). Watin, one of the great Parisian glazers, explains it in turn in his *Art du peintre, doreur, vernisseur* . . . (1773): Chinese could not master the secret of producing the glaze as transparent as water. At the far end of the century, the depreciation of the Chinese lacquer remains vivid; a selling catalogue of 1791 underlines that the Chinese glaze 'draws on a rather unpleasant yellow' (Wolvesperges, 1998).

8.5 Conclusion

Differences in quality concerned all objects and all matters. This is why it is difficult to distinguish between old, second-hand, recent and new pieces of furniture in the inventories of haberdashers and cabinetmakers. Prices offer little help because, as with clothing, re-fashioned furniture and old rings and watches could be more expensive than new ones (Roche, 1989: 340). Second hand did not necessarily mean that goods were of lower quality or little value, to be bought only by less wealthy people (Coquery, 2004: 84–86). Conversely, novelty did not necessarily mean scarce and expensive goods for elites. New and old mingled: luxury retailers linked second hand with curiosity, quality and

25 Preface of the knight de la Roque's catalogue, 1745, 95, quoted in Wolvesperges, 1998 and by Glorieux, 2002: 274 ('Le lacq est encore une sorte de curiosité peu connue et par conséquent aussi peu générale. Les morceaux de choix sont (. . .) extrêmement rares à trouver, particulièrement quand ils sont anciens. Ils sont quelquefois portés à des prix qui étonnent, même en Hollande').

fashion. Furniture, jewels, crockery and garments could all acquire value when old. This trend started in the eighteenth century and has endured ever since.

At the heart of the retailing circuit, between production and consumption, shopkeepers represent the kingpin of a flourishing market where genuine and fake, new and old, fashion and second-hand items mingled: intended for mixed customers. Thanks to the diversity of their merchandise, there was unprecedented development of the market which, in turn, was linked to a blurring of social boundaries. In this way, shopkeepers were key players in the diffusion of new goods and in the emergence of a new culture of consumption.

BIBLIOGRAPHY

Primary Sources

Unpublished sources

Archives de Paris (Arch. de Paris), D5B6/3451, account book of the upholsterer and mirror cutter Law: *M. de Trémouville owes for furniture supplied to his flat, located place de Louis-XV*, 1st October 1786; D5B6/3066, account book of the upholsterer and mirror cutter Law, 1782.

Archives Nationales (A.N.), T166, invoice heading from Sassary, years 1780; T186, invoice heading from Bertrand, 1783; T220/5-7, invoice heading from Langlois, 1761.

Published sources

Almanach du Dauphin, ou Tablettes royales du vrai mérite des artistes célèbres, et d'indication générale des principaux Marchands, Banquiers, Négocians, Artistes et Fabricans des Six Corps, Arts et Métiers *de la Ville et Fauxbourgs de Paris, et autres Villes commerçantes du Royaume, etc.* (1777) Paris.

Diderot, D. and d'Alembert, J. Le Rond (1966) *Encyclopédie, ou Dictionnaire raisonné des sciences, des arts et des métiers*, Stuttgart [Bad Cannstatt, Friedrich Frommann Verlag, (facsimile of the 1st edition 1751–1780)].

Molière (1962) '*Le Bourgeois gentilhomme*', *Théâtre complet*, Lausanne [1670].

Notices des dix premières années de l'Almanach sous verre des associés, rue du Petit-Pont, à Paris. Contenant les découvertes, inventions, ou expériences nouvellement faites dans les sciences, les arts, les métiers, l'industrie, etc. etc., (1778-an IX; quotation in the text: 1779) Paris.

Thomas, M. (1770) *Almanach des marchands, négocians et commerçans de la France et du reste de l'Europe*, Paris.

Literature

Braudel, F. (1979) *Civilisation matérielle, économie et capitalisme, XVe-XVIIIe siècle*, t.2: *Les jeux de l'échange*, Paris.

Berg, M. (1999) 'New commodities, luxuries and their consumers in eighteenth-century England', Berg, M. en Clifford, H. (eds.), *Consumers and luxury. Consumer culture in Europe 1650–1850*, Manchester, 63–85.

Berg, M. (2003) 'Asian luxuries and the making of the European consumer revolution', Berg, M. and Eger, E. (eds.), *Luxury in the eighteenth century. Debates, desires and delectable goods*, Basingstoke, 228–244.

Berg, M. (2004) 'In pursuit of luxury: global history and British consumer goods in the eighteenth century', *Past & Present*, 182, 85–141.

Berg, M. (2005) *Luxury and pleasure in eighteenth-century Britain*, Oxford.

Berg, M. and Clifford, H. (eds.), Consumers and luxury. Consumer culture in Europe 1650–1850, Manchester, 63–85.

Bergeron, L. (1975) 'Paris dans l'organisation des échanges intérieurs français à la fin du XVIIIe siècle', *Aires et structures du commerce Français au XVIIIe siècle. Colloque national de l'association française des historiens économistes, 4–6 octobre 1973*, Lyon, 237–263.

Chapman, S.D. and Chassagne, S. (1981) *European textile printers in the eighteenth century. A study of Peel and Oberkampf*, London.

Chassagne, S. (1991) *Le coton et ses patrons, France, 1760–1840*, Paris.

Clifford, H. (1999a) 'A commerce with things: the value of precious metalwork in Early Modern England', Berg, M. and Clifford, H. (eds.) *Consumers and luxury. Consumer culture in Europe 1650–1850*, Manchester, 147–168.

Clifford, H. (1999b) 'Concepts of invention, identity and imitation in the London and Provincial metal-working trades, 1750–1800', *Journal of Design History*, 12/3, 241–255.

Coquery, N. (1998) *L'hôtel aristocratique. Le marché du luxe à Paris au XVIIIe siècle*, Paris, 93–105.

Coquery, N. (2004) 'The language of success: Marketing and distributing semi-luxury goods in eighteenth-century Paris', *Journal of Design History*, 17, 71–89.

Coquery, N. (2006) 'Fashion, business, diffusion: an upholsterer's shop in eighteenth-century Paris', Goomand, D. and Norberg, K. (eds.) *Furnishing the eighteenth century: what furniture can tell us about the European and American past*, New York, 63–77.

Craske, M. (1999) 'Plan and control: design and the competitive spirit in early and mid-eighteenth-century England', *Journal of Design History*, 12, 187–216.

De Vries, J. (1997) 'Between purchasing power and the world of goods: understanding the household economy in Early Modern Europe', Brewer, J. and Porter, R. (eds.), *Consumption and the world of goods*, London, 85–132.

Fairchilds, C. (1993) 'The production and marketing of populuxe goods in eighteenth-century Paris', Brewer, J. and Porter, R. (eds.), *Consumption and the world of goods*, London, 228–248.

Ferrieres, M. (2004) *Le bien des pauvres. La consommation populaire en Avignon, 1600–1800*, Seyssel.

Feyel, G. (1995) 'Négoce et presse provinciale en France au XVIIIe siècle: méthodes et perspectives de recherches', Angiolini, F. and Roche, D. (eds.), *Cultures et formations négociantes dans l'Europe moderne*, Paris, 438–511.

Fine, B. and Leopold, E. (1990) 'Consumerism and the Industrial Revolution', *Social History*, 15/2, 151–179.

Fox, R. and Turner, A. (eds.) (1998) *Luxury trades and consumerism in Ancien Régime Paris. Studies in the history of the skilled workforce*, Aldershot.

Fowler, C. (1998) 'Changes in provincial retail practice during the eighteenth century, with particular reference to central-southern England', *Business History*, 40/4, 37–54.

Glorieux, G. (2002) *À l'Enseigne de Gersaint. Edme-François Gersaint, marchand d'art sur le pont Notre-Dame (1694–1750)*, Seyssel.

Hilaire-Pérez, L. (2000) *L'invention technique au siècle des Lumières*, Paris.

Lemire, B. (1990) 'The theft of clothes and popular consumerism in Early Modern England', *Journal of Social History*, 24, 255–276.

Medick, H. (1982) 'Plebeian Culture in the Transition to Capitalism', Samuel, R. and Jones, G.S. (eds.) *Culture, ideology and politics: essays for Eric Hobsbawm*, London, 84–112.

Pardailhe-Galabrun, A. (1988) *La Naissance de l'intime*, Paris.
Roche, D. (1981) *Le Peuple de Paris, essai sur la culture populaire au XVIIIe siècle*, Paris.
Roche, D. (1989) *La culture des apparences. Une histoire du vêtement XVIIe–XVIIIe siècle*, Paris.
Roche, D. (1997) *Histoire des choses banales. Naissance de la consommation XVIIe–XIXe siècle*, Paris.
Sarrazin, V. (1997) *Les almanachs parisiens au XVIIIe siècle : production, commerce, culture*, Université Paris I PhD, typed copy.
Styles, J. (1994) 'Clothing the North: The Supply of Non-élite Clothing in the Eigtheenth-Century North of England', *Textile History*, 25/2, 139–166.
Styles, J. (1996) 'Clothes and non-elite in the north of England 1660–1800', Bottin, J. and Pellegrin, N. (eds.) *Échanges et cultures textiles dans l'Europe pré-industrielle. Actes du colloque de Rouen, 17–19 mai 1993*, *Revue du Nord*, 12, 295–308.
Styles, J. (2000) 'Product innovation in early modern London', *Past & Present*, 168, 132–140.
Styles, J. (2003) 'Custom or Consumption? Plebeian Fashion in Eighteenth-Century England', Berg, M. and Eger, E. (eds.), *Luxury in the Eighteenth Century. Debates, desires and delectable goods*, Basingstoke, 103–115.
Verley, P. (1997) *L'échelle du monde. Essai sur l'industrialisation de l'Occident*, Paris.
Weatherill, L. (1988) *Consumer Behaviour and Material Culture in Britain 1660–1760*, London.
Wolvesperges, T. (1998) *Le mobilier parisien en laque au XVIIIe siècle*, Université Paris IV PhD. (The thesis was published under the title: *Le meuble français en laque au XVIIIe siècle*, Brussels and Paris, 2000).

CHAPTER 9

In and Out of Fashion? Advertising Novel and Second-Hand Goods in Georgian England

Jon Stobart – University of Northampton, United Kingdom

9.1 Introduction

Historians of consumption have placed great emphasis on the growing importance of fashion as a stimulus to demand in eighteenth-century England. For McKendrick (1982: 11), the 'hypnotic effects of fashion' were central to processes of social emulation and class competition: it was part of conspicuous consumption (see Veblen, 1912), designed to underline wealth and augment social standing. In doing so, fashion built on notions of taste and distinction – not, perhaps the 'difficult' consumption that we associate with Bourdieu's (1984) theorisation, but a means of codifying goods as elite, rare and discriminating. This involved the bundling of certain goods and attributes into particular combinations of social practices which allowed elites to distinguish themselves not merely in terms of their wealth or their ownership of key goods, but in how these formed part of their broader lifestyle. Indeed, Simmel (1971) defines fashion precisely in these terms: the coding of objects in order to claim membership of particular (elite) groups.

According to Berg, this coding built on three key aspects of fashion. First were notions of taste and the sensuality of goods. She argues that it was the 'sensual arousal' of fashion goods – how they felt, looked and tasted – that attracted all social groups, 'inducing people to forgo necessities in order to obtain them' (Berg, 2005: 250). Second was the idea of novelty or newness. Citing Scitovsky, Berg suggests that the pursuit of novelty is intrinsically pleasurable since it stimulates arousal by providing variety, complexity and surprise. And, of course, fashion is all about novelty: the constant renewal and reinvention of the familiar in a way that challenged the status quo, both of material culture and social order. Third was the ability to assimilate new goods into established genres. Fashionable goods were presented as part of practical groupings (for example, within a porcelain dinner service), linked with particular practices (the association of vases with travel) or associated with other fashionable goods (as part of fashionable interiors).

Fashion is thus central to our understanding of changing patterns of consumption and the rise of consumerism. It was the engine that drove consumption, but was also its guiding ethos. Yet the idea of fashion – with its connotations of tasteful, new, 'networked' goods – brought with it the corollary that other goods would be out of fashion. What became of goods that were left behind as fashion moved on? Many 'unfashionable' goods, especially furniture and household items, were retained of part of the established fabric of the house: a reflection of the investment made and their continued utility. Nenadic argues that few of the middling sorts had the money or inclination to follow fashions in furniture, with the result that many houses were a mixture of old and newer items (Nenadic, 1994. See also Edwards, 2005). Vickery, meanwhile, notes how even the gentry were involved in recycling clothing. Such reuse could both reflect emotional attachment to goods – the reworking of a favourite dress as a work-bag – and imbue them with a different set of symbolic meanings (Vickery, 1993: 282). Alternatively, goods deemed unfashionable or undesirable (as well as those no longer needed) could be sold, exchanged, given away or simply discarded. The fate of goods disposed of in these ways was varied. Servants might retain clothing given by their employers; old furniture might be broken up and the wood reused, and there was a thriving rag trade. Yet many unwanted goods entered the second-hand market. This is often portrayed as a distinct circuit of exchange: one which gave poorer sections of society the opportunity to engage in 'fashionable' consumption and to own goods which were, more or less, fashionable (see Lemire, 1991).

Fashion and second-hand can thus be seen as effective antonyms: symbolically, socially and economically. The two tiers of consumer society theorised by Lemire (1991: 61–63) were divided by financial barriers, social distinctions and geography. But such divisions can be too easily overplayed. They were linked through common cultural values (including the importance of fashion and the exercise of discernment: Lemire, 1991; Wall, 1997) and the flow of goods from the upper to the lower tier. Moreover, they were also connected by the activities of individual buyers and sellers, both of whom could be intimately engaged in first-hand and second-hand circuits of exchange (Nenadic, 1994; Edwards, 2005: 38–74; Stobart, 2006; Ponsonby, 2007: 31–39 and 85–93).

This inter-connection between fashionable and second-hand consumption was reflected in and affected through the advertisements placed in provincial newspapers. As a medium for transmitting knowledge and information, these had grown steadily, if somewhat uncertainly in individual cases, from the early eighteenth century (Walker, 1973). Advertisements were a feature of most newspapers from the outset, but they grew increasingly numerous and varied in the provincial press from the 1740s. Initially, notices for books and patent medicines were predominant, but by the 1760s there was an equally large number of advertisements being placed by local tradesmen and professionals (Ferdinand, 1993: 398). Gauging the character and number of readers enjoyed by particular newspapers is extremely difficult, but Ferdinand estimates that a typical provincial newspaper, the *Salisbury Journal*, had a circulation of perhaps 1,500 in the 1740s, rising to 2,500 by the 1760s and 4,000 in 1780. Given that many copies would have read by more than one individual (especially true for those held in coffee houses or circulating libraries), the actual readership was probably more like 10,000 in the mid 1700s and many more than this by the end of the century. Significantly, most readers were drawn from amongst the gentry and the middling sorts: precisely those groups who would be most engaged in the growing consumerism of the age. This makes analysis of these advertisements doubly significant. At one level, these were the consumers who were expected (not least by those advertising) to buy the goods being offered, implying at least some overlap in the markets for fashionable and second hand goods. At another, by bringing together new and used on the page of the newspaper, the advertisements constructed a virtual landscape of consumption (see Stobart, Hann and Morgan, 2007: 185–187) which encompassed and encouraged engagement in both circuits.

It is newspaper advertisements, then, that form the focus of this chapter. In it, I draw on a sample of over 300 advertisements for shops and sales from a range of provincial newspapers published between the 1740s and the 1790s in towns of various sizes across the Midlands and north-west England. More particularly, then, the towns were chosen to reflect a range of different types of urban community: large county towns with wide hinterlands (Worcester and Chester); smaller and county towns with more restricted spheres of influence (Northampton); large commercial towns (Liverpool), and growing manufacturing centres (Blackburn). They were thus intended to be broadly representative of provincial England and provincial consumption. Not all the advertisements contained in the newspapers are included here; those for leisure activities, real estate, livestock, patent medicines and ships' cargoes have been omitted to provide a sharp focus on consumer goods. These data collected are used to address two key issues. The first is how advertisements sought to sell both fashionable and used items. Here, I focus on the language used, the associations drawn and, more generally, on the attractions highlighted as particular selling points. The second is the way in which first and second-hand circuits were brought together on the page of the newspaper, in the minds of its readers, and in the business practices of certain advertisers.

9.2 Selling Fashion: Sensuality, Novelty and Ensembles

Newspaper advertisements frequently played on notions of taste, fashion and novelty. Whilst implicit in many advertisements, around 15 per cent made direct reference to fashion or the 'genteel' nature of the goods or services being offered – a figure which appears to have peaked in the 1770s, but remained fairly constant through the second half of the eighteenth century (Table 9.1.). As noted earlier, fashion was most important, and changed most rapidly, in personal clothing. It is unsurprising then that mercers, drapers, milliners and hairdressers were prominent amongst those advertising fashion and newness. Thus, for example, Mrs Coppell informed her friends that she had 'just purchased a very genteel assortment of goods in the MILLINERY WAY, of the newest taste', and Sebastian Finglass noted that he made 'all sorts of stays after the newest and neatest fashion' (*Gore's Liverpool Advertiser*, 1 June 1770, 27 April 1770). However, fashion penetrated all forms of material culture: Slater and Murray offered carriages 'in the neatest and most fashionable manner', whilst Dutton and Diggles announced the opening of their new shop in Temple Bar, Liverpool, with the assurance that they had added 'a fresh and genteel assortment of Ironmongery and Hardware' (*Gore's Liverpool Advertiser*, 27 April 1770, 14 September 1770).

Sentiments such as these link closely to Berg's (2005: 249–257) tripartite definition of fashion. Indeed, some advertisements emphasised sensuality as a selling point. This was most obvious with consumables like tea, coffee and wines, but such concerns permeated a wide variety of advertisements. The Northampton nursery and seedsman Mr North, waxed lyrical about his celery plants. He stressed their shape, colour and taste, claiming that they 'grow to an enormous size (. . .) comes very upright and close (. . .) blanches very white, and fine flavoured' (*Northampton Mercury*, 31 January 1780). At the other end of the spectrum, the fashion in later eighteenth-century England for highly polished mahogany furniture was reflected in the advertisements of cabinet makers and upholsterers (see Pryke, 1989: 56; Edwards, 2005: 96), but so too were other aspects of the visual impact of furnishings. Samuel Nicholson, for example, trumpeted his 'entirely new and superb assemblage of printed Furniture' (*Chester Chronicle*, 18 March 1806). With textiles, the feel, colour and design of the cloth were important. In February 1770, the Liverpool drapers Orton and Co. announced that they had 'already laid in for the spring, great variety of the new colours, and those of the first quality'. Around the same time in Coventry, William Cart advertised a variety of flowered, striped and plain cloths; 'silks and satins [in] all colours'; 'Silk and cotton hats of the newest fashion' and a 'great variety of drest caps, in the newest taste' (*Gore's Liverpool Advertiser*, 9 February 1770; *Jopson's Coventry Mercury*, 15 June 1767). In such advertisements, the emphasis on fashion was underpinned by suggestions of how the cloth would appeal to both the eye and the skin.

Other advertisers emphasised fashion as novelty and newness, playing on the need to keep up to date with changing trends, often seen as central to the growing consumerism of the eighteenth-century (McKendrick et al, 1982; McCracken, 1988; Berg, 2005). Mr Pickersgill, a Liverpool mercer, announced that he had just acquired a 'very large and fresh supply of every article both of the millinery and haberdashery goods calculated for the spring trade' (*Gore's Liverpool Advertiser*, 20 April 1770). A few weeks earlier P. Prichard had advertised that: 'he has just come down from London with as great a variety of the different new patterns calculated for the spring, as the earliness of the season would admit of, and will make a point of furnishing himself, by all the weekly conveyances, with such others, and those of the most elegant fancy, that are now making for the approaching months' (*Gore's Advertiser*, 23 February 1770).

Here, Prichard was emphasising the rapid turnover in fashion; the position of London as a key point of supply, and his own status as a gatekeeper to the world of fashionable material culture. The importance of London as a signifier of quality and fashion was a leitmotif of many advertisements, especially from the 1770s when over 10 per cent made explicit mention of the metropolis (Table 9.1.). As with Prichard, it was most often cited as the source of goods, but it also formed a guarantor of workmanship and knowledge of material culture. For example, J. Meller, a Knutsford upholsterer, announced that he 'had the Advantage of being for some Time in some of the most capital Shops in London' and had 'acquired sufficient Share of Knowledge in the various Parts of his

TABLE 9.1. Selected themes appearing in newspaper advertisements, 1742–94

	1740s		1770s		1780s/90s		Total	
Subject of advertisement	No.	%	No.	%	No.	%	No.	%
Reputation of trader	6	10.2	33	20.4	10	9.9	49	15.2
Addressing friends / the public	4	6.8	42	25.8	31	30.7	71	22.6
Fashion / taste	7	11.9	28	17.2	13	12.9	48	14.9
London	2	3.4	18	11.0	12	11.9	32	9.9
Second-hand goods	8	13.6	24	14.7	19	18.8	51	15.8
Total adverts	59		163		101		323	

SOURCE: *Adams Weekly Courant*, 1780; *Blackburn Mail*, 1793–94; *Gore's Liverpool Advertiser*, 1770; *Northampton Mercury* 1743–44, 1780; *Worcester Journal*, 1742–52.

Business as to render him capable of executing any Part of it with Skill and Exactness' (*Adams Weekly Courant*, 23 May 1775). Similarly, the Northampton hairdresser, Mr Lockett, noted that he had 'lately been in London to furnish himself with the most fashionable Mode of Dressing now in Practice, by which Means, he hopes to give Satisfaction to those who please to favour him with their future Commands' (*Northampton Mercury*, 22 May 1780). Such connections made shopkeepers like Prichard, Meller and Lockett arbiters of taste within provincial society: London fashions reached the middling sorts of the English provinces through, and were thus in part meditated by, such tradesmen (see Edwards, 2005: 38–74; Ponsonby, 2007: 26–31). In linking products and places, newspaper advertisements were thus important in linking fashion as an idea and an ideal to the practical means of making and keeping oneself fashionable (Cox and Dannehl, 2007: 109–111).

Advertisements also sought to fit these new and novel goods into established genres. Reference to spring fashions linked goods together as ensembles as well as stressing their newness and fashionability. Goods were also brought together as sets in the advertisements placed by dealers in furniture and household goods: hence Nicholson's emphasis of the assemblage of furniture he had available (see also Pryke, 1989: 53–56). More explicitly, Thomas Bromilow offered 'small and complete sets of China', whilst M. Campione advertised his 'large collection of STATUES, modelled from the Antiques of Italy', suggesting that they would be 'the greatest ornaments for halls, parlours, staircases, book-cases, dining-rooms, chimney-pieces, summer houses, &c.' (*Gore's Liverpool Advertiser*, 20 April 1770, 2 November 1770). These were fashionable goods which would link into and augment existing sets of goods in the homes of polite consumers. Furthermore, their association with Italy and with travel (more specifically, the Grand Tour), linked them with fashionable leisure practices – a point underlined by Campione's offer of a 'large collection of Roman and English copper and silver coins' (see Earl, 1986; Bianchi, 1999: 74–75; Berg, 2005: 251–252).

9.3 Selling Second Hand: Value, Quality and Kudos

Alongside advertisements for fashionable goods, eighteenth-century newspapers carried numerous notices for second-hand tableware, furniture, books, carriages and clothing. All in, nearly 16 per cent of advertisements in the sample were for second-hand goods, a figure which rose in the final decades of the eighteenth century (Table 9.1.). Of these, around three-quarters were for auctions, mostly of household goods but occasionally of books, pictures or other art. These were generally placed by professional auctioneers or booksellers. The remaining advertisements were for carriages being sold either privately or by coach-makers, or announced the services offered by second-hand dealers (for example, *Gore's Liverpool Advertiser*, 15 June 1770). The absence of advertisements for second-hand clothes probably reflects the market for such goods amongst the poorer sections of society who were unlikely to be reading newspapers. Conversely, the presence of so many notices offering a wide range of used household goods confirms the broad market for such items amongst the middle ranks of society (Nenadic, 1994; Mitchell, 1999; Stobart, 2006, Ponsonby, 2007: 85–93). This impression is reinforced by the ways in which these second-hand goods were being promoted in the provincial press.

Despite the relative cost of new and used goods, price was seldom mentioned as a selling point, except when the stock-in-trade of a bankrupt was being sold-off quickly to recover money for creditors. That said, it is clear that the expectation of obtaining good quality items at low cost was central to the success of auctions of household goods, just as it is today (see Gregson and Crewe, 2003: 9–13, 75–84 and 98–103). This motivation surfaced occasionally in the advertisements, as when Edward Cox, announcing a furniture auction, stressed that 'the Public, who are desirous of purchasing cheap Lots, are desired to attend in good Time, as the Lots are many, and must all be sold in one Day' (*Northampton Mercury*, 31 January 1780). Clearly, it was expected that bargain hunters would be out in force.

More often, however, emphasis was placed on the variety and quality of wares available. Sometimes, particular stress was laid on the fact that the goods being sold were well-made or of a recognised type or fashionable material – qualities which Nenadic argues were valued amongst consumers of the middling sort when purchasing furniture (Nenadic, 1994: 132–133. See also Ponsonby, 2007: 89–91). Thus, the sale of the possessions of the bankrupt Elliot Elmes included a 'particularly fine-toned Harpsichord', and 'almost a complete set of Queen's Ware'; whilst the household goods of the late Rev. Russell were advertised as 'genuine', and included mahogany tables and chairs, 'good carpets' and 'many valuable prints elegantly framed and glazed'. Significantly, the auctioneer added that 'the Goods are all new' (*Gore's Liverpool Advertiser*, 8 June 1770; *Adams Weekly Courant*, 23 May 1775). Three related imperatives appear as significant marketing points in such advertisements. One was the need to reassure the public about the quality of the goods being offered (they were 'as new'); a second was the importance of the provenance of the goods (and thus their 'genuine' nature); a third was the idea that they constituted good value for money – a 'bargain'.

These sentiments were brought together in the elegantly phrased advertisement for the auction of William Walton's household and garden furniture. After a lengthy list of goods which emphasised the quality of the wares ('fine seasoned Goose Coat Feather-Beds', 'a most delicate Mahogany Bureau', and 'the best set of Brewing vessels ever offered for sale by Wm Cart'), the notice concluded by asserting that: 'There are no Scraps or Scrapings of Time, to be met with in this House – most of the Articles are new – Beauty and Art are so happily blended in the principal Pieces, that, it is hoped, Criticism will lose her Sting on the Day of Viewing and give an assenting Nod on the Day of Sale' (*Northampton Mercury*, 3 January 1780).

Assurances of quality and good value were important in advertisements for other sorts of second-hand goods. Carriages were described as being 'nearly carved, and warranted firm and good', 'little used', or 'very little the worse for wear' (*Worcester Journal*, 18 May 1744; *Northampton Mercury*, 6 June 1743; *Berrow's Worcester Journal*, 24 September 1772). Sometimes, these general assurances of quality and road-worthiness were underlined by details of their upholstery and appearance, as with the advertisement for 'A Handsome coach, lined with Crimson Velvet' (*Northampton Mercury*, 6 March 1744). As with new goods, visual qualities were clearly significant.

Books could be marketed in a variety of ways. Some advertisements stressed the number and range available, playing on the fact that second-hand was often the only way to obtain desirable volumes (Mitchell, 1999; Ramsay, 2001). A notice appearing in the Liverpool press announced the auction of 'a LARGE and VALUABLE COLLECTION of BOOKS, In most *Languages, Arts and Sciences*, Also great Variety of Maps, Prints, German Flutes, Pocket Instruments and Letter Cases, Paper Books, &c.' (*Gore's Liverpool Advertiser*, 8 December 1770). This was clearly being promoted as a big event for the book-buying public since catalogues were available from five of the most prominent booksellers in the town. That said, such grand sales were by no means unusual occurrences (Ramsay, 2001). At a similar time, the *Worcester Journal* carried an advertisement for 'a large and valuable collection of several thousand volumes of the most useful English books (. . .) maps, pictures perspective views, letter cases, pocket books, etc, etc' (*Worcester Journal*, 17 September 1772. See also *Worcester Journal*, 30 July 1772). However, an addendum to the advertisement stressed another attraction of the books being auctioned: they were 'all new and neatly bound, gilt and lettered'. This emphasis of the visual qualities of books reflected their function as decorative and display items: the social status marked by the ownership of such volumes was as much in their appearance as their content. Indeed, for the elite, the bindings often formed a significant element of the cost of acquiring books, whether new or second hand. Many of the bills presented to the fifth Lord Leigh of Stoneleigh Abbey in Warwickshire by his London booksellers made mention of the cost of morocco or Russian leather bindings (see Stobart, 2008).

Such practical and aesthetic concerns were sometimes overlain with others of a less tangible kind. The identity of the previous owner of goods appears to have been important to some buyers, in part as a reassurance of their provenance, but also because it could add kudos to the goods and enhance the cultural capital of the purchaser. Wall argues that sales at the London auction houses produced the 'possibility for *anyone* of buy a piece of the Great, to import the world of another into one's own' (Wall, 1997: 14. See also Smith, 1989; Stobart, 2006: 233). Provincial auctioneers rarely had the chance to sell off the goods of aristocrats or notable public figures – these were largely the preserve of Christie's and Sotheby's in London – but they were careful to note the rank as well as the name of the person whose goods were being sold. Thus, Charles Gore advertised 'That a Parcel of Table Linen, Plate, China and Glasses; Belonging to the Estate of *Richard Eccleston*, Gentleman, deceased, Will be sold by Auction' (*Gore's Liverpool Advertiser*, 14 December 1770). The effect could be further heightened by identifying the seat of the ex-owner and even holding the auction in situ. As Ponsonby argues, this allowed middling sort consumers to view household furnishings in an opulent setting and to consume vicariously as well as practically (Ponsonby, 2007: 90). Such imperatives are clear from the notice placed by Mr Cock for an auction of 'The Entire Household Furniture' to be held 'at Warkworth, the seat of the late William Holman, esquire deceased, nr Banbury' (*Northampton Mercury*, 24 June 1745). The scale of the event is apparent from the three days given over to pre-sale viewing and the fact that catalogues were available in Banbury, Oxford, Northampton and even London. As well as catering for a healthy bit of voyeurism and social climbing, advertisements such as these played on the desire of certain consumers to express difference (Nenadic, 1994: 133; Edwards, 2005: 84–88). They sold 'distinction' as well as goods.

9.4 Selling Fashion *and* Second Hand?

The emphasis on the personal associations held by previously-owned goods parallels that placed on new goods produced by prominent designers or manufacturers. Both were portrayed as more desirable because they added to the cultural capital of the owner by allowing them to mark their taste and discernment. But this was not the only or even the most prominent way in which the promotion of new and used goods came together. Many advertisements for second-hand goods placed emphasis on their fashionable or tasteful qualities. Although some have argued that fashion was less important to the middling sort when buying furniture, especially beyond the public rooms of the house (Vickery, 1993: 289; Nenadic, 1994: 132–3; Ponsonby, 2007: 89–91), auctioneers often took care to highlight fashionable mahogany pieces and styles. The sale of William Walton's effects, for example, included 'modern' bedsteads, and 'Oval, Oblong, Pembroke, Claw and Card Tables', all in mahogany. Tableware was subject to more frequent changes of fashion, but, as with Elmes' set of Queensware, it could still be sold second hand as modern and desirable; whilst silver plate was often explicitly described as being 'fashionable' (*Northampton Mercury*, 3 January 1780; *Gore's Liverpool Advertiser*, 8 June 1770; *Adams Weekly Courant*, 23 May 1775).

It was carriages, however, that were most often promoted in terms of their fashionability. This is, perhaps, unsurprising given their prominence in the public street and the very bold statement of wealth that they made. Yet the vehicle itself accounted for only a part of the costs involved in turning out an elegant equipage – much more might be spent on painting, lacquering and upholstering, refurbishments which could help to render an older vehicle new and fashionable (see Blondé, 2001: 500). Nonetheless, advertisers frequently highlighted the intrinsically fashionable quality of the carriage. Thus, in Liverpool, Thomas Fleetwood advertised a four wheel chaise 'made in genteel taste and in a particular manner', whilst the Northampton press carried a notice for a 'Compleat and Fashionable Landau' (*Williamson's Liverpool Advertiser and Mercantile*, 11 June 1756; *Northampton Mercury*, 6 June 1743). To an extent, of course, stressing the fashionable nature of the vehicle might reflect a certain amount of exaggeration on the part of the seller, but much the same could be said for advertisements stressing the fashionability of new goods. In both cases, the consumer was, to an extent at least, reliant upon the shopkeeper, auctioneer or coach-maker to act as an arbiter of fashion. Moreover, the fact that second-hand as well as new goods could be plausibly promoted as fashionable (regardless of whether this was strictly true) is revealing of consumers' perceptions of what constituted fashion and how rapidly fashion might change across a range of different goods.

The selling of new and used goods was also brought together physically, on the pages of provincial newspapers. Advertisements for mercers, toy sellers and china dealers were set alongside those for auctions, second-hand carriages and furniture brokers, creating a montage of images and ideas of consumption (Stobart, Hann and Morgan, 2007: 186–187). This juxta-positioning of new and used at once reflected and informed the realities of eighteenth-century consumption, where consumers moved easily between first- and second-hand circuits of exchange. China or furniture, for example, might be bought new, from a specialist dealer, or second hand at an auction (Edwards, 2005: 44–50, 71–74; Stobart, 2006: 229, 239; Ponsonby, 2007: 33–38, 85–93). Moreover, the visual and perceptual collage of advertisements formed a representation of consumer space: they mirrored the shop fronts and street signs with their plethora of competing imagery, and represented the mixing of premises along the street. Reading the advertisements thus offered a virtual tour of the retail spaces of the town: one which highlighted the options available to the consumer.

This mixing of new and used sometimes took place within single advertisements and individual businesses. Some metropolitan tailors offered part-exchange on old clothes, one advertising that: 'Gentlemen having Cloaths to dispose of, from Mis-fitting or Alteration in Fashion, he takes those back, allowing more than is generally allowed' (quoted in Lemire, 1991: 69). Others ran rather different schemes, Mr Warburton of Little Marlborough Street, London, announcing that: 'Any Gentleman, choosing to contract by the Year, may be furnished with Four Suits per Year, of the best superfine cloth, at 14L 10s, or with Three Suits for 12L. First Suit to be paid for at the Delivery and every other Suit to be paid for at the separate Times when the Cloaths are delivered; and the Whole to be returned at the Conclusion of the Year from the Delivery of the First Suit' (Shakespeare Birthplace Trust Record Office, DR18/5/3137). Clearly this tailor had a ready market for good quality suits that were barely one year old, presumably to be found amongst London's huge market for ready-made clothes (Lemire, 1991).

Whilst the newspapers sampled here failed to reveal similar advertisements in provincial England, it seems likely that such practices were widespread. Certainly, other tradesmen offered to buy used goods in part exchange for new. In Worcester, John Eades advertised his skills as a goldsmith and jeweller, noted that he had a 'collection of Fine China', and concluded by announcing that 'He gives the best price for old gold, silver or second hand plate' (*Worcester Journal*, 23 August 1750). Similarly, two coach-makers appeared on the same page a Liverpool newspaper advertising that they 'purchase or exchange second hand or new carriages of any sort' (*Gore's Liverpool Advertiser*, 27 April 1770). On occasions, traders might mix the sort of goods that they bought and sold, most famously with china dealers offering to change 'all sorts of fine china for left-off Cloaths' (quoted in Lemire, 1991: 67).

It is in the businesses and advertisements of furniture dealers, upholsterers and cabinet makers that the mixing of old and new is most evident (see Edwards, 2005). In Shrewsbury in 1794, the cabinet and chair maker Richard France advertised his intention to 'open a Repository for second-hand Cabinet and Upholstery Furniture' and offered to buy or part exchange unwanted furniture, allowing 'much more than the common Valuation' (quoted in Ponsonby, 2007, 87). Moreover, as Ponsonby argues, such businesses were not catering primarily for the lower orders. The fact that they advertised in newspapers suggests an appeal to consumers of the middling sort, as do the list of stock bought and sold by such tradesmen, and their use of specialist auction rooms rather than inns. In this light, the advertisement of Hunt and Co., upholsterers operating on one of the main streets in Northampton, is revealing. They announced that they: 'Buy, Sell, or Exchange for New, all Kinds of HOUSEHOLD FURNITURES: Such as Four-post Bedsteads; Moreen, Manchester, and Check Furnitures; Tent ditto, in the newest Taste; seasoned Feather-Beds, Blankets, Quilts, Counterpanes, and Carpets; Cabinet and Chair Work in general; all Sorts of Looking Glasses, in rich carved, gilt or Mahogany Frames; with a Variety of other Articles. By Desire of their Friends, they have opened a Repository and

Auction-Room (. . .) where Gentlemen, Tradesmen and Others may send their Goods, without the Inconveniency of having Sales at their own Houses' (*Northampton Mercury*, 1 May 1780). It is not clear whether this list of tasteful and fashionable furniture, fit for any polite and respectable household, is a real inventory of stock or examples of the kind of thing that Hunt and Co. were interested in buying and would thus be able to offer second hand. However, they were clearly mixing new and used goods, and promoting all as desirable and respectable. That they were seen by consumers in much the same light is apparent from the purchasing practices of even quite wealthy individuals, including the Lancashire gentleman, Nicholas Blundell and the Norfolk Parson Woodeforde, who both bought a wide range of new and used furniture from auctions, house sales and cabinet makers (Edwards, 2005: 71–73).

9.5 Conclusion

First- and second-hand markets are all too readily seen as being distinct from one another: catering for different consumers, occupying different economic and spatial domains, and responding to different cultural imperatives and motivations. Yet it is apparent that any separation between the two was effective only at the extremes of the social scale, and that distinctions were blurred by the mixing of new and used goods both in retailers' advertisements and showrooms, and in the perceptions and homes of consumers of the middling sort. Many newspaper advertisements played on notions of taste, fashion and novelty to promote goods and retailers, but a greater number aimed to encourage the consumption of second-hand goods by emphasising their quality, kudos and even fashionability. In terms of used goods, this further challenges the notion that consumers were forced into second-hand circuits by financial necessity. The very fact that newspapers – predominantly read by the middling sorts and the gentry – carried such advertisements underlines the existence of a buoyant market for used goods amongst these relatively wealthy groups. Cost was clearly a concern for many consumers, but was probably far less important to the middling sorts than were other concerns. Principal amongst these were pragmatic considerations – the simple availability of many desirable and useful goods, especially at auctions and house sales. Layered onto these was the desire to indulge in 'clever' consumption and secure a bargain, and, in some cases at least, to trade on the associations of certain used goods to create difference via the construction of 'another reality' (Smith, 1989: 129. See also Wall, 1997: 3, 14, 20; Stobart, 2006: 233, 236).

More generally, the importance and nature of second-hand consumption, and the ways in which used goods were marketed in newspaper advertisements, questions the position of fashion as the paramount concern in consumption. The presence of a large market for used goods of all kinds suggests that, through the second half of the eighteenth century at least, other concerns motivated consumers. The wording of the advertisements surveyed here indicates that utility, quality and value were also important considerations. The significance of this is potentially profound: if fashion was not of over-riding importance to most consumers, but merely one consideration to be weighed with – or perhaps against – others, then the logic of emulative consumption is further undermined. Of course, it is dangerous to read too much into the promotional material of those trying to sell goods. We need to balance such analysis with studies of the practices and motivations of individual consumers. However, it is equally apparent that more serious consideration of the second-hand market is needed in our theorising of consumption and consumerism in the eighteenth century.

BIBLIOGRAPHY

Primary Sources

Unpublished sources

Shakespeare Birthplace Trust Record Office, DR18/5/3137 Leigh Family Bills and Receipts

Published sources

Adams Weekly Courant, 1775, 1780
Berrow's Worcester Journal, 1772
Blackburn Mail, 1793–94
Chester Chronicle, 1806
Gore's Liverpool Advertiser, 1770
Jopson's Coventry Mercury, 1767
Northampton Mercury, 1743–44, 1780
Williamson's Liverpool Advertiser and Mercantile, 1756
Worcester Journal, 1742–52

Literature

Berg, M. (2005) *Luxury and pleasure in eighteenth-century Britain*, Oxford.
Bianchi, M. (1998) 'A taste for novelty and novel tastes: the role of human agency in consumption', Bianchi, M. (ed.) *The active consumer: Novelty and surprise in human choice*, London.
Blondé, B. (2001) 'Indicatoren van het luxeverbruik? Paardenbezit en conspicuous consumption te Antwerpen (zeventiende-achttiende eeuw)', *Bijdragen tot de geschiedenis*, 84, 4, 497–512.
Bourdieu, P. (1984) *Distinction. A social critique of the judgement of taste*, Cambridge.
Cox, N. and Dannehl, K. (2007) *Perceptions of retailing in Early Modern England*, Aldershot.
Earl, P. (1986) *Lifestyle economics: consumer behaviour in a turbulent world*, New York.
Edwards, C. (2005) *Turning houses into homes. A history of the retailing and consumption of domestic furnishings*, Aldershot.
Ferdinand, C. (1993) 'Selling it to the provinces: news and commerce round eighteenth-century Salisbury', Brewer, J. and Porter, R. (eds.), *Consumption and the world of goods*, London.
Gregson, N. and Crewe, L. (2003) *Second-hand cultures*, London.
Lemire, B. (1991) *Fashion's favourite: the cotton trade and the consumer in Britain, 1660–1800*, Oxford.
McCracken, G. (1988) *Culture and consumption. New approaches*, Bloomington.
McKendrick, N. (1982) 'The consumer revolution of eighteenth-century England', McKendrick, N., Brewer, J. and Plumb, J.H. (eds.), *The birth of a consumer society*, London.
Mitchell, I. (1999) 'The book trades in Cheshire, 1680–1830', *Transactions, Lancashire and Cheshire Antiquarian Society*, 95, 23–38.
Nenadic, S. (1994) 'Middle-rank consumer and domestic culture in Edinburgh and Glasgow, 1720–1840', *Past & Present*, 145, 122–156.
Ponsonby, M. (2007) *Stories from home. English domestic interiors, 1750–1850*, Aldershot.

Pryke, S. (1989) 'A study of the Edinburgh furnishing trade taken from contemporary press notices, 1708–1790', *Regional Furniture*, III, 52–67.

Ramsay, N. (2001) 'English book collectors and the salerooms in the eighteenth century', Myers, R., Harris, M. and Maudelbrote, G. (eds.), *Under the hammer: Book Auctions since the seventeenth century*, Newcastle, Delaware.

Simmel, G. (1971) *On individuality and social forms*, Chicago.

Smith, C. (1989) *Auctions: The social construction of value*, London.

Stobart, J. (2006) 'Clothes, cabinets and carriages: second-hand dealing in eighteenth-century England', in Blondé, B., Stabel, P., Stobart, J. and Van Damme, I. (eds.), *Buyers and Sellers: Retail circuits and practices in Medieval and Early Modern Europe*, Turnhout.

Stobart, J. (2008) 'Gentlemen and shopkeepers: supplying the country house in eighteenth-century England', paper presented at the *European Social Science History Conference*, Lisbon, February 2008.

Stobart, J., Hann, A. and Morgan, V. (2007) *Spaces of consumption: shopping and leisure in the English town, 1680–1830*, London.

Veblen, T. (1912) *The Theory of the Leisure Class: an Economic Study of Institutions*, Basingstoke.

Vickery, A. (1993) 'Women and the world of goods: a Lancashire consumer and her possessions, 1751–81', Brewer, J. and Porter, R. (eds.), *Consumption and the world of goods*, London.

Walker, R.B. (1973) 'Advertising in London newspapers, 1650–1750', *Business History*, xvi, 112–30.

Wall, C. (1997) 'The English auction: narratives of dismantlings', *Eighteenth-Century Studies*, 31, 1–25.

CHAPTER 10

Supply of Shopkeepers in Besançon in the First Part of the Nineteenth Century: Novelties between 'Old' and 'New'

Marie Gillet[1] – University of Franche-Comté, France

10.1 Introduction

At the dawn of the industrial era, the retail trade was undoubtedly central to the process of diffusion of a material culture corresponding to the needs and desires of an incipient 'consumer society' (McKendrick, Brewer and Plumb, 1982; Brewer and Porter, 1993). Consumption was driven by a range of factors, including: the growth of the working population (0.6 per cent per annum increase between 1806 and 1840); urbanization; the improvement of thoroughfares and consequently of trade between urban and rural environments; rising standards of living (one per cent per annum growth in GNP per capita between 1815 and 1840); falling prices of consumer goods; and the arrival onto the market of a growing range and quantity of novelties (Barjot, Chaline, Encreve, 1995: 94–95; Roche, 1989 and 1997). It is in this new context that tradesmen sought to meet the demands of customers which swung between a domestic economy mainly concerned with the acquisition of basic goods (because it was limited by weak purchasing power) and a culture of appearances dominated by luxury, opulence and ostentatious desires. As in other provincial towns, the small shopkeepers of early nineteenth-century Besançon had to satisfy a heterogeneous population whose needs, tastes and choices reflected social, cultural and political differences as well as widely differing lifestyles. To this end, they sought to diversify their supply, often mixing new and second hand.

Until the early nineteenth century, the majority of retailers sold their goods at fairs and markets or by peddling: places and methods of exchanges which, despite their ancient nature, still took an active part in the circulation of new goods and the diffusion of fashions in the provinces, especially in the countryside (Margairaz, 1997). Only important cities had permanent shops: 'Generally speaking these shops are either related to artisanal activities of production, or either kinds of bazaars where one sells everything' (Verley, 1997: 275).[2] Besançon, a regional capital, had a commercial population corresponding to this description: small craftsmen rubbing shoulders with merchants selling any kinds of products (drapers and grocers, for instance), as well as specialised retailers (hatters, wig makers, milliners, and so on) who promoted the latest

1 I would like to thank Madame Agnès Daumas for having corrected the English translation of this article.

2 'En général ces boutiques sont soit liées à des activités artisanales de production, soit sont des sortes de bazars où l'on vend un peu de tout'.

Parisian fripperies. In addition, although usually associated with itinerant merchants and hawkers, the second-hand trade was not exclusive to them: fixed shops, established in the middle of the city, also sold both necessities and novelties second hand – a trade which has not been widely recognised outside the clothing trade (Charpy, 2002: 125–150; Lemire, 2005: 29–47; Roche, 1989).

Connected to France under Louis XIV, Besançon, a county town of the Franche-Comté region, is a medium-size town located in north-eastern France, halfway between Strasbourg and Lyon. Encircled by the River Doubs and by seven hill-forts and overlooked by the citadel built by Vauban, this town gained strategic military significance in the eighteenth century. By the end of the century, Besançon was established as the regional capital and had a population of 25,000 inhabitants (in 1794) and an economy stimulated by the foundation of charity and spinning workshops, as well as the establishment of a clock-making factory. The latter signalled the beginning of a significant specialised industry in the town (one that had originally been brought in by Swiss immigrants). Yet, unlike other regional towns (where Protestantism dominated), the economy of Besançon was based largely on service sector activity characterised by retailing. This makes it the ideal subject of a study into the multiplicity and diversity of provincial retailing and shops.

This chapter focuses on the ways in which the retail trade of Besançon adapted to changing patterns of demand. In particular, it will focus on the development of the trade in luxury goods, millineries and second-hand objects. What were the products comprising the luxury and semi-luxury trade? What was the importance of the latter? What was the impact of Parisian fashions on the supply of Besançon tradesmen? What products were available second-hand? What was the relative prevalence of old/used goods and new/novel goods on the Besançon market? These questions can be addressed via analysis of the post-mortem inventories of tradesmen who died during the first half of the nineteenth century. These inventories contain detailed descriptions of their stock-in-trade. In spite of certain obvious gaps (they do not, for example, inform us about the date of acquisition of a product or its source), inventories provide a wealth of information about the goods stocked by retailers (including price, quantity, size, form, material, colour and quality) and, in some cases, even give the final use and destination of an object (linen to produce mattresses, sheets for trousers and so on). In addition, local and regional newspapers are replete with commercial advertisements and opinions: information on the arrival of new products in store, those objects which were 'en vogue' or the latest technical innovations available. Such data provide a better understanding of the diversity of products in circulation, the passing and renewal of fashions, and the practices of tradesmen as well as – to a certain extent – those of consumers.

In what follows, I will initially describe the situation of retail in Besançon in the first half of the nineteenth century in order to capture, as well as possible, the commercial practices of retailers and the choices of consumers. The chapter then turns to the question of the availability and diffusion of new products of various kinds (luxuries, semi-luxuries, millineries and current consumer goods). Lastly, I will focus on the plurality of supply: the means used by tradesmen to attract customers with their wide-ranging choices, tastes, desires and financial means, as well as on the variety of second-hand articles present on the Besançon market.

10.2 The State of Trade in Besançon in the First Half of the Nineteenth Century

During the periods of the Consulat and First Empire, Besançon's economic recovery was aided by the restoration of order after revolutionary tumults and by its proximity with Switzerland, with which most of its trade was carried out (*Annuaire du Doubs de 1804*).[3] Indeed, in spite of the run-down state of its roads and the scarcity of money (a problem exacerbated by the absence of credit organisations), its commercial activity was strengthened by the establishment of six fairs in 1807 (instead of four) in addition to the three already existing twice-weekly markets (Strehmel, 2006). These attracted many consumers from neighbouring boroughs and villages. Furthermore, its geographical situation – which placed it at the centre of a commercial axis formed by two great urban centres (Basle and Strasbourg) whilst moving it away from military operations – ensured a certain prosperity to the local trade.

However, this growth was short-lived: it became a victim of the continental blockade and the weakening of control by centralised authorities. From 1811, the effects of smuggling were felt in the drapery and hosiery trades and in the clock-making industry. Moreover, because of a shortage of cash, small shopkeepers saw the value of their stock depreciate and their financial standing degrade, leading some to bankruptcy. Thus, during the first eight months of 1811, thirteen bankruptcies were declared involving individuals in the wholesale as well as retail trade. Indeed, no trade was spared: grocers, iron merchants, second-hand clothes dealers, caterers, linen merchants, hatters, tobacconists and wallpaper merchants give up their businesses. The most famous tradesmen of the city also found themselves in difficult situations: 'such is the case of the house Pochet, one of the richest and best-supplied in Besançon, which is in bankruptcy at the end of August 1811. 'It made very large deals with the richest bankers of Paris and Lyon and even with foreign tradesmen" (Fohlen, 1982: 288).[4] The establishment of a town octroi tax collected on drinks, foods, fuels, fodders and materials, coupled with poor weather that caused significant damage to corn harvests, contributed to a rise in prices and particularly to the cost of bread. The standard of living of the population deteriorated considerably and people had to cope with a period of shortages in 1816–1817. Louis Bretillot offers a rather dour description of the commercial state of the city at this time: 'around 1820, the trade known as grocery did not exist in a manner of speaking. Retail trade, extremely circumscribed in its operations of purchase and sale, was carried out in a rather restricted number of shops and stores which, except for some rare exceptions, were concentrated in the rue Battant, the

---

3 'En général, le commerce du département du Doubs se réduit au commerce d'importation et d'exportation avec la Suisse. (. . .) Pour l'importation, il consistoit en toiles de coton blanches et peintes, en mousseline, draperies, bonneterie et horlogerie. (. . .) Le commerce d'exportation consiste principalement dans les fers blancs, fers en barre, martinets, cercles, tôles, clouteries, fils de fer, fonte en gueuses et sablerie; dans les vins, les cuirs tannés, les peaux chamoisées, les porcs et quelques autres productions' – 'Generally speaking, the trade of the department of Doubs is no more than an export and import trade with Switzerland. (. . .) Imports consist of white and painted cotton fabrics, of muslin, draperies, hosiery and clock making. (. . .) The export trade consists mainly of tinplate iron, bars iron, tilt hammers, circles, sheet metal, nail industry, iron wires, cast iron and sand industry; of wines, tanned leathers, towed skins, pigs and some other productions', 152.

4 'Tel est le cas de la maison Pochet, une des plus riches et des mieux assorties de Besançon, en faillite à la fin d'août 1811. "Elle faisait de très grosses affaires avec les plus riches banquiers de Paris et de Lyon et même avec des commerçants étrangers"', Baverel 76, f. 19 (27 août 1811), BMEC, Besançon, quoted in Fohlen, 1982: 288.

Grande Rue from the bridge to the Granvelle palais, and in the rue des Granges from the market place to the rue Saint-Paul' (Bretillot, 1878: 102).[5] The poor state of the retail trade was alarming and a Besançon newspaper, *Les Tablettes franc-comtoises*, devoted an article to the causes of the decline in retailing in large provincial towns (*Les Tablettes franc-comtoises*, n 36, 27 july 1828: 143). Using Dijon as an example, it explained how the ruin of the retail trade was a consequence, firstly, of consumers' habit of buying goods (on credit) in Paris which local merchants could provide at a better price, and secondly of the illegal trade practices by stall-keepers: selling without the authorisation of the commercial court.

Nevertheless, after these economic setbacks, the situation improved, not least because of the growth of the watch and clock industry: the production of watches doubled in seven years (from 30,000 watches in 1821 to 62,000 in 1828) and offered a broad range of goods with varied prices 'from a 15F robust watch to a more than 400F engraved gold watch' (Defrasne, 1990: 67).[6] Moreover, thanks to improvements in transport and in particular of waterways, with the construction of the 'canal du Rhône au Rhin' completed in 1832, Besançon became a commercial place which exerted a growing domination in the area. The population saw a multitude of goods arriving by boat, including rice, sugar, soaps, cotton, madder, cloths, leathers, oil and wine. New shops stocked like those in Paris appeared in the middle of the city (for example, *A la Frileuse* located at 27, Grande Rue) and attracted an increasingly abundant clientele: 'Seeing that the city gradually became a warehouse from which the hinterland could be supplied, the retail trade recognised that it had to take advantage of this circumstance to increase the number of customers. Spacious and elegant stores were set up, doubling at least the number of those previously opened. There, not only goods that were necessary or useful to various ways of living, but all objects the possession of which flatters taste and gives life charm and variety, were offered to consumers from within and out of town. Success followed suit. Customers were numerous, and it is for the specialists of the profession a matter of astonishment that the great commerce successively opened with this kind of business, found enough purchasers, and that retailers could obtain remuneration and great benefit from their work' (Bretillot, 1878: 108).[7]

In 1843, out of 35,000 inhabitants in Besançon, 1,860 were licensed traders, including bankers, industrialists, warehouses specialising in textiles, wines, groceries, hardwares, colonial products and flour, and a large number of small shopkeepers: an average of one licensed trader for every 18.8 inhabitants. In Paris, the average ratio was 13.2 inhabitants per recorded licence, suggesting a commercial framework rather more

5 'Vers 1820, le commerce dit de gros n'existait pour ainsi dire pas. Le commerce de détail, fort circonscrit dans ses opérations d'achat et de vente, s'exerçait dans un nombre assez restreint de boutiques et de magasins qui, sauf quelques rares exceptions, étaient concentrés dans la rue Battant, dans la Grande-Rue depuis le pont au palais Granvelle, et dans la rue des Granges depuis la place du marché à la rue Saint-Paul'.

6 'Depuis l'oignon robuste à 15 F jusqu'à la montre d'or gravée à plus de 400 F'. The currency used throughout this article is the franc (represented by the franc sign F).

7 'Voyant que la ville devenait petit à petit un entrepôt où les contrées voisines trouvaient à s'approvisionner, le commerce de détail jugea qu'il devait mettre à profit cette circonstance pour augmenter le nombre de ses acheteurs. Des magasins spacieux, établis avec élégance, doublèrent au moins le nombre de ceux précédemment ouverts. Là, non-seulement les choses nécessaires ou utiles à la vie, mais tous ces objets si divers dont la possession flatte le goût et jette dans l'existence du charme et de la variété, furent offerts aux consommateurs du dedans et du dehors. Le succès répondit à ces nouveaux essais. Les clients ne manquèrent pas, et c'est pour les hommes du métier un sujet d'étonnement que les très nombreux débits successivement ouverts à ce genre d'affaires trouvent assez d'acheteurs, pour que les débitants puissent obtenir une rémunération de leur travail et des bénéfices suffisants'.

dense than that in Besançon (Gaillard, 1997: 458, see table 4n and 5n).[8] By 1849 the *Annuaire du Doubs* registered approximately 653 retailers for 39,949 inhabitants, that is to say an average of approximately 61 inhabitants per tradesman. The best represented sectors are those of food (45.3 per cent) with amongst other things 78 grocers, 55 bakers and 55 butchers or pork butchers; textile (20.2 per cent) with 33 cloth merchants, 32 tailors and 24 haberdashers, and household goods (11.9 per cent) with 19 tinkers, 17 locksmiths and 11 ironmongers. Many craftsmen also belonged in the retail sector since they gave citizens the opportunity to meet their need for staples as well as for luxuries and semi-luxuries (see Table 10.1.).

Before 1830, the Besançon tradesmen were not very specialised and many of them were referred to their inventories as 'merchants'. Like haberdashers, these were men who 'dealt in everything', '*vendent de tout*': they provided the population with foodstuffs as well as items necessary to daily life (candles, crockery, clothing, tools and so on) and thus served primarily the demands of an 'economy of need' (Roche, 1989: 269). However, there were also a considerable number of specialised tradesmen (38.5 per cent of our sample). These were men such as the milliner Jeanne Louise Gilmert (post-mortem inventory, 1813) and the hatter Jean François Boillot (post-mortem inventory, 1801) who provided consumers with a broader choice. According to the inventories, it would seem that second-hand goods formed a large part of the tradesmen's stock. In this way, they were catering to the needs of a middle class whose means did not always allow them to acquire new articles, but they were also part of the circulation of goods discarded by the higher classes which afforded them insights into the consumption imperatives of these primary consumers. This type of trade continued until after 1830 despite the considerably widened supply of tradesmen who, thanks to the improvement of transport and its growing speed, were increasingly able to offer goods in a wider choice of styles, prices and qualities.

10.3 Diffusion and Availability of New Consumer Goods

As principal actors in the circulation of goods, retailers were quick to adopt a range of techniques to attract consumers. Advertisements, window displays, offering the latest goods or the cheapest prices: all were used to draw in customers, facilitate the flow of stock and increase profits. Faced with a demanding population with varied needs, tastes and choices, Besançon retailers were forced to adapt their supply and regularly renew their stock in order to keep up with successive changes in fashion. Torn between tradition and modernity, did the commercial system of this provincial city allow retailers to satisfy consumers in search of novelties? Did it cater for the demands of privileged customers, and adapt itself to the influence of Parisian fashions?

Luxury and Half-Luxury Products: a Quiet but Real Presence – Luxury products – whose quality, scarcity and cost made them beyond the reach of most of the population – were available in very limited quantities in Besançon shops. They included products made in

8 See Tables 4n 'Comparison of licence numbers on both banks' (in 1852, 61,055 are recorded on the right bank and 14,354 on the left bank) and 5n 'Inhabitants number in old districts' (in 1851, 750,221 inhabitants are recorded on the right bank and 243,396 are recorded on the left).

TABLE 10.1. Distribution of small trade professions by branch of activity according to the *Annuaire du Doubs de 1849*

Fields	Professions	Number	%
Food	64 innkeepers 9 caterers 1 liquor merchants 78 grocers 5 flour merchants 55 bakers 27 butchers 28 pork butchers 3 chocolate makers 11 confectioners 12 pastry cooks 2 food sellers 1 wine merchant	296	45.3
Textile and accessories	2 ribbon merchants 33 cloth merchants 4 hosiers 24 haberdashers 9 thread, fibre, cotton and wood merchants 7 linen merchants 1 maker of corsets 32 tailors 10 milliners 1 fur merchants 3 umbrellas makers 6 second-hand clothes dealers	132	20.2
Clock industry / Jewellery	7 jewellers 5 merchants of clock industry supplies 1 pendulum merchant 12 clock and watch makers	25	3.8
Interior decoration	4 upholsterers 11 cabinet makers 2 dealers in engravings	17	2.6
Beauty	4 perfumers	4	0.6
Novelties	6 merchants of new products	6	0.9
Health	10 pharmacists 3 herbalists	13	2.0
Household goods	11 ironmongers 19 tinmen 1 lamp maker 9 stove makers 4 dye merchants 3 crystal merchants 7 crockery merchants 4 rope makers 17 locksmiths 1 stationers 2 coppersmiths	78	11.9

Materials	5 iron merchants 10 firewood merchants 12 timber merchants 2 rice merchants 3 lime merchants 4 gypsum merchants 11 coal merchants	47	7.2
Leather	2 leather merchants 2 saddlers 11 harness makers	15	2.4
Miscellaneous	13 blacksmiths 7 booksellers	20	3.1
		653	100

Source: *Annuaire du Doubs de 1849*, Archives départementales du Doubs, PER. 878

precious metals (hall-marked gold and silver, for instance) and those resulting from complicated and highly skilled craftsmanship (including clocks and watches, the making of which involved technical expertise but were products of an 'artist's work') (*L'Impartial*, 18 January 1835). Their high value made them accessible only to a small number of elite consumers who, it might be argued, thought more about the social significance of the goods than their economic value. Moreover, the status of such goods as 'luxuries' was subjectively defined since it depended on both the consumer's point of view and the social hierarchy of the object itself. The goods considered here as luxury products met the demand of a small-town bourgeoisie whose tastes, value judgements and incomes, of course, were somewhat different from those of the Parisian bourgeoisie. These items were viewed as luxurious (or at least belonging to the lower range of luxury) in Besançon, but belong to the semi-luxury category on the Parisian market. Semi-luxury products, meanwhile, might be seen as including objects with a lower value, made with less precious raw materials and which needed less skill and time to produce. They were aimed at consumers concerned with distinguishing themselves, but who, in contrast to the clientele of luxury products, were more price conscious.

Luxuries especially were present only in very limited quantities in the inventories, especially if we look beyond clocks and watches. Indeed, among the shops studied here, such objects were present in only four (8.3 per cent), two of which were clock-makers. As Table 10.2. shows, these men carried very different qualities and quantities of goods. Thus, Louis Simon Perron offered his customers a range of unique watches or a small number of similar pieces (post-mortem inventory, 1835). These included a regulator representing '*la Cour des astres*' (stars' Court) in a mahogany case worth 250F and a gold repeater watch with a value of 200F – significant sums at a time when the average daily wage for a labourer was just 2.06F (Chevallier, 1887: 42).

TABLE 10.2. Quantities and values (in francs) of models suggested by Louis Simon Perron (1835) and Xavier Simon Lacroix (1823), clock making merchants in Besançon, according to their post-mortem inventory

Louis Simon PERRON (1835)			Xavier Simon Thomas LACROIX (1823)		
Quantity	Articles	Total value (Francs)	Quantity	Articles	Total value (Francs)
	Articles with higher values			*Articles with higher values*	
1	regulator representing '*La Cour des astres*' (stars' Court), in a mahogany case	250	1	gold repeater watch	230
1	simple regulator, in a mahogany case	250	33	gold repeater watches	5024
1	gold watch '*à la Lépine*'	200	6	simple gold watches	503
1	gold repeater watch	200	41	simple gold watches	3300
1	marine watch, in a silver box	200	24	simple gold watches	1765
1	watch '*à la Lépine*', with 3 carsets and 2 keys	200	3	simple gold watches	480
	Articles with lower values			*Articles with lower values*	
1	small clock with its box	50	42	silver watches	714
1	watch in a silver box	40	42	pinchbeck watches	714
1	enamelled gold watch, for women	30	21	pinchbeck watches	336
2	silver '*savonnette*' watches	24	35	pinchbeck watches	576
30	silver watches	300	13	pinchbeck watches	261
5	silver watches	25	13	pinchbeck watches	252
16	pinchbeck watches	48	21	silver and pinchbeck watches	288
Total quantity of articles available: 108			*Total quantity of articles available: 1644*		

SOURCE: Post-mortem inventories of Louis Simon Perron and Xavier Simon Thomas Lacroix, clock making merchants, Archives départementales du Doubs, classification marks 3E19-75 and 3E28-20.

The majority of stocks held by Perron were valued at over 30F; but this did not prevent him from providing lower cost articles such as pinchbeck watches which, at 3F each, were accessible to many workmen. In contrast, Xavier Simon Thomas Lacroix stocked a much greater number of watches, mostly at lower (if still considerable) prices: 33 gold repeater watches were valued at 5,024F or 152F apiece, whilst 41 simple gold watches were 80.5F each (post-mortem inventory, 1823). Significantly, his cheaper watches were far more numerous. A total of 198 pinchbeck and silver watches were in stock, valued at 13.7F apiece. Paradoxically, though, it is Perron who offered the least expensive articles along with the most expensive ones. Moreover, whilst he provided his customers with a wide range of goods (watches, seals, pendulums, regulators and musical boxes) and different styles and ornamentation (with repetition, music, columns, '*à la Lépine*', alarms, subject, simple, marine, and so on), Lacroix was apparently content with presenting only one type of object, a watch, and this in only a few varied models.

Other tradesmen provided some luxury products. Amongst them was Claude Joseph Augustin Billot, a jeweller, whose stock included a set of jewellery made up with diamonds for 1,100F; another with pearls and diamonds worth 850F; a gold chain worth 330F, and a silver censer for 120F (post-mortem inventory, 1832). Another was the tailor Charles Antoine Blanche (post-mortem inventory, 1836), who had fine cloths costing from 15F to 19F per metre – considerably more than the printed calico and cottons worth 1F to 3F per metre sold in 1812 by the milliner Marguerite Peaulier (post-mortem inventory, 1812) or the wide variety of textiles offered forty years later by the cloth merchant Nicolas Sebastien Muess (post-mortem inventory, 1875) which were valued at an average of 6.4F per metre.

These rare and expensive products were accompanied by others made with new materials whose quality and value were less high. Imitating non-easily accessible types of goods, semi-luxury articles attracted consumers thanks to their innovative or whimsical qualities and tradesman did not shrink from presenting them along with more costly objects. Indeed, among the stock of the tradesmen discussed above, we see a huge variety of goods. Perron, for example, offered his customers gold, silver and bronze goods as well as pinchbeck watches, and gilded or silver-plated copper pendulums. Billot, meanwhile, sold a vast range of gold or solid silver jewellery: some adorned with precious stones (diamonds, rubies, emeralds and sapphires), others with fine stones (amethysts, topazes, aquamarines, tourmalines, garnets, agates, cornalines and turquoises). However, he also had gold plated, silver plated and silver gilt jewellery containing fake pearls and stones which together accounted for approximately 12 per cent of his stock. In terms of necklaces, he offered items valued at just 45F for one adorned with faked pearls, and up to 700F for another set with nine diamonds. This range of luxury and semi-luxury goods extended beyond jewellery and watches: there were fine brass sieves at 7F a piece (whereas a wooden sieve cost just 0.65F), a pair of gilded copper torches at 45F, a silver plated teapot at 35F, a silver plated soup tureen at 40F, and a silver plated copper Blessed Sacrament worth 15F.

The arrival of new techniques and new chemical and metallurgical processes which made it possible to imitate perfectly the beauty and richness of luxurious objects had considerable impact on some local manufacturers. Indeed, in 1845, the *Annuaire du Doubs* pointed out the presence of foreign competition which, thanks to the use of new cheaper materials alloy, made its way into the Besançon watch-making industry: 'One can quickly understand all the advantages in favour of foreign competition which result from this combination; it can, with impunity, imbue its products with all the value of gold replaced by platinum and the value of silver replaced by nickel' (*Annuaire du Doubs de 1845*: 223).[9] This example perfectly illustrates the competition between semi-luxury products resulting from industrial productions and a traditional

9 'On comprend bien vite tout l'avantage qui résulte de cette combinaison en faveur de la concurrence étrangère; elle peut baisser impunément ses produits de toute la valeur de l'or remplacé par le platine et de la valeur de l'argent que remplace le nickel'.

manufacture related to craft industry and based on valuable materials (Daumas and Ferrière le Vayer, 2007).

The textile sector also saw the quantity and the variety of its products increase with the arrival of new industrial goods. Consumers were attracted by mixed silk fabrics instead of fine silk, tulle instead of lace, and moleskin instead of leather. This multitude of goods did not seem to hinder the Besançon cloth trade, which relied on high quality materials and manufactures to make up losses due to stocks being devalued through rapid changes in fashion: 'These causes [multiplicity and variety of products] which will never have limits are all the more dangerous as far as the retail trade in small towns is concerned. If the multiplicity of fabrics disturbs the harmony which would be necessary to their distribution, and we must say that it cannot be any different for these thousand creations of fashion which a season sees appearing then disappearing, we must also note that it is not the same as far as numerous goods, frivolous but more primarily useful to consumption, are concerned. This goes mainly for plain woollen fabrics from the factories of the North and the South. They remain stable in their price, which must be undoubtedly be attributed to the scarcity of raw materials' (*Annuaire du Doubs de 1845*: 224).[10]

The *Annuaire du Doubs de 1845* underlines in this way that the new practices related to successive and altering fashions proved dangerous for tradesmen of small cities who could thrive only as long as they offered a steadier and more uniform supply. This is why their preference was for the plainer fabrics of the North and the South rather than novelties from Elbeuf and Sedan. Here we are dealing with the traditional conceptions of trade which retailers must overcome if they want to cater for a new demand and adapt themselves to an increasingly varied supply.

The Impact of Fashion on Product Selling – These new industrial techniques, the use of new materials and the lowering of costs made it possible to offer goods which had been exclusive to a privileged social class: to buyers who, in pursuit of social distinction, were increasingly willing to play the game of keeping up appearances. The abundance of goods and the growing imperative to follow fashion, brought the local market under the influence of Paris, the capital of fashion and unrivalled model for provincial cities. Daniel Roche underlines the effect that Paris had on the provincial clothing during the eighteenth century, arguing that, in Versailles and Auxerre, 'the evolution of textiles was a sensitive matter; the succession of colours and the diversification of garments followed the same rhythm as in Paris (...). In Limoges, linen, new textiles and colours appeared with a delay of fifty years, a gap which was wider in Brittany. In Besançon, the same gap can be found for men's wear, but was closing up for

10 'Ces causes [multiplicité et variété des produits] qui n'auront jamais de limites sont plus particulièrement dangereuses au commerce de détail des petites localités. Si la multiplicité des tissus dérange l'harmonie qui serait nécessaire à leur écoulement, et l'on doit dire qu'il ne peut en être autrement pour ces mille créations de la mode qu'une saison voit éclore puis tomber, on doit constater aussi qu'il n'en est pas de même de beaucoup de marchandises moins légères, mais plus essentiellement utiles à la consommation. Ce sont particulièrement les tissus unis de laine des fabriques du Nord et du Midi. Ils se tiennent fermes dans leur prix, ce qu'il faut attribuer sans doute à la rareté de la matière première'.

women's wear: linen was within the reach of almost everybody by the mid-eighteenth century' (Roche, 1997: 232).[11]

This observation was made about personal goods and assessed the penetration of fashion in households; it does not mean that tradesmen were unable to offer their customers the opportunity to follow fashion. However, if such a gap existed in demand, it is likely to have been present on the supply side as well – a trend which persisted through the eighteenth century and into the nineteenth century. Indeed, Besançon was a small and somewhat sleepy town, where habits changed slowly: if fashions from Paris arrived late on the market of Besançon during the eighteenth century, there is little to suggest that this situation would have changed much in the early nineteenth century.

Newspapers were the chief medium by which information concerning fashionable products (and particularly clothing) was diffused through provincial France. At the end of the eighteenth century, the Besançon newspaper *La Trompette*, at the request of its readers, began publishing regular articles on the latest trends in Parisian clothing: 'Always politics, a young woman said nonchalantly as she was reading our last issue. Cheer up smart ladies, here is an article for you; but do not leave it for more than 24 hours on your dressing-table, otherwise you might become old fashioned, and our elegant women might well believe you to be a ghost' (*La Trompette*, 29 ventose year VIII: 590–91).[12]

This type of article – published until the closure of the newspaper in 1800 – testifies to the importance which the female public of Besançon attached to fashion and the way in which high society women were dressed. Other newspapers kept their readers informed about the latest innovations and technical patents in Paris, such as that of Thilorier who invented 'a new way of burning fuels, through which smoke or odorous vapour is consumed by fire' (*Journal du département du Doubs*, 3 vendémiaire 1800: 162).[13] However, Parisian supremacy on the provinces was not unchallenged. A chronicler from *Les Tablettes franc-comtoises* denounced it in the following terms: 'The influence of Paris on certain minds is such that they do not find anything beautiful, good or to their taste except what comes from Paris. What their country produces draws from them only disdain and scorn, it is Provincial, which says everything (. . .). It is not just the dull fashion magazines with their caricatures – to them only perfect models of elegance and grace – which Paris bestows upon us for money, while [at the same time] laughing with us (. . .). What comes from Paris is therefore not a banal passport, [but] a title of blind confidence. Perhaps we judge things better in the provinces than in Paris, because we are less inveigled by the example, we are more fundamentally attached to things than to appearances, our mind is more at rest, more thoughtful, more independent because we are less concerned with the

---

11 'L'évolution des textiles est sensible; le progrès des couleurs et la diversification des objets portés suivent le même rythme qu'à Paris (. . .). A Limoges, le linge, les nouveaux textiles, les couleurs apparaissent avec un retard de cinquante ans, décalage qui est accentué en Bretagne. A Besançon, même décalage pour le vêtement masculin, mais décrochage pour le vestiaire féminin: le linge est pratiquement gagné par tous à la mi-XVIIIe siècle'.

12 'Toujours de la politique, disait nonchalamment une jeune femme en lisant notre dernier numéro. Consolez-vous belle dame, voici un article pour vous; mais ne le gardez pas plus de 24 heures sur votre toilette, autrement vous risqueriez d'adopter une vieille mode, et nos élégantes pourraient fort bien vous pendre pour une revenante'.

13 'Une nouvelle manière de faire brûler les combustibles, au moyen de laquelle, toute fumée ou vapeur odorante est consumée par le feu'.

multitude of objects, and less open to errors of imagination, and we judge there as we feel' (*Les Tablettes franc-comtoises*, 15 July 1827: 138).[14]

Only Paris held the secret to 'good taste', and the rhythm of fashions it imposed on the rest of France was set in contra-distinction to the more stable and less futile tastes of the province. And yet this traditionalism, though firmly rooted in small cities, could not resist the Parisian influence and new patterns of demand.

In the light of this craze for fashion, small shopkeepers tried to offer as many new products as possible to keep up with the rhythm of Parisian trends. During the first decade of the nineteenth century, various fashionable items began to appear amongst the stock of some merchants: cotton from the Indies, lawn, taffeta, Siamese, printed calico, crepe, nankeen, embroidered and plain muslin, percale, organdie, flannel, dimity from Orleans, cloth from Basel and velvet appear in the fabric stock of the cloth merchant Jean Claude Duret (post-mortem inventory, 1804); silk shoelaces and purses, buttons with small round bells, silk and leather gloves, silk tights and handkerchiefs, laces, ribbons, gold and silver braids, and braids from Rouen can be found amongst other things in the stock of the haberdasher Pierre Célestin Clerce (post-mortem inventory of his wife Jeanne Thérèse Pras, 1810). However, the novelties sold by haberdashers and specialised merchants did not form a large part of the market for cloth. Thus, when a merchant came from Paris, the Besançon newspapers always carried advertisements announcing his arrival and the wide choice of objects he was selling: 'Mr Pasquier, merchant of Paris, has arrived in town with a great assortment of porcelain, crystal, vases with gilded flowers, hardware, fancy-goods, all kinds of boxes, shoulder-straps, garters, bracelets, all kinds of jewellery, all perfectly gilded, *reticule*,[15] dimity, nankeen, silk, cloths and an infinity of objects the details of which would be too long' (*Feuille d'affiches – judiciaires et commerciales. Annonces et avis divers du département du Doubs*, 24 July 1808: 8).[16]

Later, the selling of 'articles de Paris' was mainly the work of milliners, who accounted for 10.8 per cent of retailers between 1810 and 1850. A long list of accessories of any kind are available from their shops, including beauty accessories, artificial flowers, feathers, trimmings, stationery, cosmetics, perfumery, health preparations, shoes, clothing accessories, clothing, fabrics, jewellery and toys (see Table 10.3.).

Shawls appeared for the first time in our sample in 1813, in the shop of the milliner Jeanne Louise Gilmert (post-mortem inventory, 1813), amongst whose stock were seven shawls worth a total of 28 F. Another novelty appearing on the Besançon market in 1824 were opera and theatre costumes (post-mortem inventory, 1824). There were costumes for the Savoyard, Russian farmers, gleanor, parish priests, Chinamen, page-boys, marquis, knights

---

14 'L'influence de Paris sur certains esprits est telle, qu'ils ne trouvent rien de beau, rien de bon, rien de leur goût que ce qui vient de Paris. Ce que produit leur pays n'attire de leur part que dédain et mépris, c'est la Province, cela dit tout (...). Il n'est pas jusqu'au plat journal des modes, avec ses caricatures, dont Paris nous gratifie pour notre argent en se moquant de nous, qui ne leur semble des modèles parfait d'élégance et de grâce (...). Cela vient de Paris, n'est donc pas un passe-port banal, un titre à une aveugle confiance. Peut-être même juge-t-on mieux des choses dans la province qu'à Paris, parce qu'on est moins entraîné par l'exemple, qu'on s'y attache plus au fond des choses qu'aux apparences, que l'esprit y est plus en repos, plus réfléchi, plus indépendant parce qu'on est moins préoccupé par la multitude des objets, et moins exposé aux erreurs de l'imagination, et qu'on y juge comme on sent'.

15 A kind of handbag used during the Directory by women and called '*ridicule*' in french by distorsion.

16 'Le sieur Pasquier, marchand de Paris, est arrivé en cette ville avec un grand assortiment de porcelaines, cristaux, vases à fleurs dorés, quincaillerie, tabletterie, cartonnage de tout genre, bretelles, jarretières, brasselets élastiques, bijouterie de toute espèce, le tout parfaitement doré, ridicule, basins, nankins, soie, draps et une infinité d'objets dont le détail seroit trop long'.

TABLE 10.3. Examples of the items available in shops of milliners between 1810 and 1835 (according to post-mortem inventories)

Categories	Objets	Categories	Objets
Beauty accessories	Powder boxes, mirrors, brushes, combs to hold buns, toothbrushes, beard-brushes, shaving straps, curling papers, toothpicks	**Clothing accessories**	Shoes, fans, gloves, mittens, stockings, brimless caps, hats, voiles, peaked caps, collars, silk scarves, garters, skullcaps, headscarves, shawls, bags, purses, handkerchiefs, detachable collars, cravats, belts, headbands
Cosmetics	Perfumed powder, lipsticks, antique oil, cream for eyebrows, cucumber cream, sorrel cream, bars of soap	**Fabrics**	Velvet, satin, crepe, tulle, muslin, lace, silk, coarse linen from Naples, taffeta, lawn, cambric, blonde lace, fancy fabrics, levant cottons, cambric, gauze
Perfumery	Scented water, lavender water, essences, eau de Cologne, Hungarian Queen water	**Jewellery**	Glass necklaces, copper rings, bracelets, ear-rings, crosses, watches, diadem
Health preparations	Creams, opiates	**Writing supplies**	Pencil pots, pencils, inkstands, notebooks
Trimmings	Ribbons, threads, braids, piping, dress sets, chenilles, pompons, gold braids, '*padous*',[17] buttons, laces, spurs, small round bells, strings, '*comètes*',[18] favours, bows	**Toys/Games**	Dolls, miniatures, set of skittles, cup-and-ball, dominos
Trimmings accessories	Needles, pins, needles holders, scissors, workbags, thimbles, hooks	**Miscellaneous**	Snuffboxes, fashion drawings
Clothing	Waist petticoats, dresses, short-sleeved shirts, corsets, theatre costumes, pinafores, disguises		

SOURCE: Post-mortem inventories, 3E19-19 to 3E19-56 and 3E28-1 to 3E28-61, Archives départementales du Doubs.

and mummies, and others for characters from *Comedia dell'arte* ('Punchinello', 'Harlequin' and 'Pierrot'), the *Barber of Seville* (including Figaro), light operas, and tales such as 'Little Red Riding Hood'. These various costumes are accompanied by masks (made with paper-board, wax or a kind of gauze called in French '*marli*') and false noses of various kinds. In addition, in 1843, the shop of the hatter Jules Gustave Bochud contained a variety of cloth hats specifically identified as 'fashionable' (post-mortem inventory, 1843).

In order to inform the population of Besançon of a new arrival or a single deposit of goods, retailers frequently placed advertisements in the local press. Diversity, exclusiveness and low prices were the main arguments used to attract customers. For instance, a wholesaler

17 French name for ribbons made of silk waste.
18 French name for tight ribbons made with a lot of finish.

called Beuque, informed his fellow citizens 'that he has just received superb crockery known as '*cailloutage*'[19] perfectly imitating porcelain, preferable to English crockery because of its whiteness and its price' and offered cheaper alternatives to English products (*La Trompette*, 29 messidor year VIII: 880).[20] At Moutrille's shop, 'shawls, silks and all novelties for dresses are sold at astonishingly low prices' (*Le Franc-comtois*, 6 April 1844),[21] whilst Lablanche was the only retailer in town stocking 'the analeptic chocolate made by the Laurent company' of Paris (*Le Petit Album franc-comtois*, 18 December 1825: 470).[22] The manager of the *Au Bon Pasteur* shop, meanwhile, 'is pleased to inform with the public that he has just received a new set of sophisticated clothes from the wholesalers in Paris' and promises 'elegance, high quality [and] good value in all clothing offered for sale' (*Feuille d'affiche – judiciaires et commerciales. Annonces et avis divers du département du Doubs*, 11 November 1849).[23]

The influence of Parisian fashions was such that the availability of a new article was announced by tradesmen as a special event: 'Cretenet, who is already known to the public, has the honour to inform them that he has just returned from the factory with a wide choice of fabrics of the best quality, as well as a great choice of novelties for waistcoats and trousers made in 24 hours, guaranteed very well tailored, of recent fashion, and to the taste of the person ordering them' (*La Gazette de Franche-Comté*, 12 May 1832).[24] At the same time, he announced that he had brought a tailor from Paris for the occasion and guaranteed a very high standard of work, on a level 'with the latest fashion, and with all the grace from and elegance of the best workshops of the capital' (*La Gazette de Franche-Comté*, 12 May 1832).[25] In this way, retailers were quick to play on the variety of goods available and even offered extra services in order to attract customers and encourage them to buy.

10.4 Diversity and Plurality of the Supply: between 'New' and 'Old'

Taking part in the diffusion of novelties at the local and regional level, traditional merchants relied mainly on the plurality of supply to attract consumers from different social classes. Variations in quality, style, materials and price were used by shopkeepers to direct their sometimes vast choice of products towards customers with highly differentiated tastes. Novelties, second-hand and cheap articles were all part of the stock-in-trade of merchants who tended to push back the limits of their traditional market.

A Broad Range of Qualities and Values – When dealing with the inventory of goods in a shop, most notaries tried to give the most accurate account of the stock position.[26] The

19 French name for a high-quality crockery.

20 'Qu'il vient de recevoir de la superbe faïence dite cailloutage imitant parfaitement la porcelaine, préférable à la faïence anglaise tant par sa blancheur que par son prix'.

21 'Les châles, soieries et toutes nouveautés pour robes s'y vendent à des prix étonnants par leur modicité'.

22 'Le chocolat analeptique de la société Laurent'.

23 'A l'honneur de faire part au public qu'il vient de recevoir un nouvel assortiment d'habillements perfectionnés de leurs maisons de gros à Paris: élégance, solidité, bon marché pour tous les vêtements qui sont mis en vente'.

24 'Cretenet, qui est déjà connu du public, a l'honneur de le prévenir, qu'il vient d'arriver tout récemment de la fabrique, avec un grand assortiment de draps dans les belles qualités, ainsi que d'un grand choix de nouveautés pour gilets et pantalons dans 24 heures, garantis très bien conditionnés, à la dernière mode, et au gré de la personne qui les aura commandés'.

25 'Au dernier genre, avec toute la grâce et l'élégance dont sont susceptibles ceux tirés des meilleurs ateliers de la capitale'.

26 It is unfortunately not the case for all notaries; some gave an overall enumeration without giving any details on quality, use, source, style or even quantity.

numerous adjectives used to describe shop goods enable us to understand the valuations given and to be aware of the variety of stock, particularly in terms of quality. Thus, we have descriptions of goods as *fine*, *extrafine* and even *superfine* (a 'term especially employed in trade to mean a higher degree of fineness in things of comparable nature');[27] *good*, *new*, *solid*, *first choice* or *stamped* are counter-posed with *false*, *ordinary*, *common*, *simple* and *second choice*. It is therefore significant that, in the terms used by the notaries, superlatives appear less often than adjectives suggesting poor quality. Indeed, the former were used to emphasise the quality of a product considered to be excellent; objects judged as simply good were not designated with any particular qualifier. Thus, if fine muslin had a higher value than plain muslin, this does not necessarily mean the latter was of less acceptable quality.[28]

These designations were used in all shops, whatever their speciality: *common* fans, *common* combs, *fine* muslin and *fine* sheets filled the shelves of milliners, whilst small *common* hats for children, *extrafine* fabric hats, *ordinary* semi-hair hats, and *false* and gilded supplies were present in hatters shops. In grocers' shops there was *common* or *fine* mustard, chocolate of *good quality*, *ordinary* jams, honey of *good* and *less good* quality, and prunes of *first quality*. The supply of new products was thus structured by the opposition between expensive articles of particularly high quality and ordinary, common or cheap articles.

The variety of products is endless and each shopkeeper appears to have stocked subtly different ranges or qualities of goods. In the case of grocers, for example, one offered a narrow range of ordinary goods for everyday use: coffee at 2F per kilo, chicory, sugar, oil at 1F per kilo, soap, cotton of various colours and qualities ranging in value from 1F to 10F per kilo, spices, vinegar and wood from India (post-mortem inventory, Claude Antoine Humbert, 1822). Another stocked a greater variety and higher quality goods: coffee from Santo Domingo at 4F per kilo, peppers from Jamaica at 3.5F per kilo; different varieties of sugar packaged in bars, lumps and as powder, aniseed, almonds, green and pearled tea at 15F per kilo; nutmeg, cloves, hazel nuts, honey, chocolate, preserves, pastilles, lozenges, ginger, biscuits, pears with brandy, sugared almonds, marshmallow, various essences and scented water, and olive oil at 2.5F per kilo (post-mortem inventory, Claude Philippe Riduet, 1822). Milliners, meanwhile, ranged from one offering a great choice of combs (to hold buns, called 'Cinderella', plated, to make tufts, made of horn and so on) (post-mortem inventory, Jeanne Louise Gilmert, 1813) to another who sold only plain combs at 0.2F per piece, preferring to focus on a wider range of toys and miniatures (dolls, dominos, busts, bodies and shoes for dolls, toy drums, cup-and-ball toys, skittles, games, bows and arrows, small chests of drawer, bedsteads, secretaries and dolls houses) (post-mortem inventory, Thérèse Parisot, 1824).

Like Aubourg, the jeweller studied by Natacha Coquery in Paris at the end of the eighteenth century (Coquery, 2006 and 2004: 71–89), Billot, a Besançon jeweller (post-mortem inventory, Claude Joséphine Etreyer, 1832) had a range of products of various prices and qualities, and a range of precious materials: new gold at 2.88F per gram, old gold

27 'Terme surtout employé dans le commerce pour signifier un degré supérieur de finesse dans des choses de même nature', definition from the dictionnary, *Trésor de la langue française* available on *http://atilf.atilf.fr*.

28 Fine muslin was 4 F a metre and light muslin 3 F a metre, both available at the shop of the milliner, Jeanne Louise Gilmert's.

at 2.35F per gram, new hallmarked silver at 0.26F per gram, other new silver at 0.23F per gram, old silver at 0.20F per gram and false garnets at 0.58F per piece. Whilst the value of these different metals varied relatively little, finished products were offered at very different prices, including torches from 4F to 40F a pair and snuffboxes from 8F to 84F each. This illustrates how semi-luxuries elided into products for daily use. In the same way, Marie Claude Clocher, a merchant in coopers' wares, offered wooden pails costing between 0.9F for a reject bucket and 12F for one made of oak (post-mortem inventory, 1831). To all this we must add an endless variety of styles and ornamentation which were the stamp of each tradesman. The jeweller Billot offered his customers a range of articles of high value: he stocked shanks, '*étincelles*'[29] (costing up to 30F each), pendant ear-rings (up to 39F a pair), bracelets, necklaces (700F), chains (330F), rings (230F), plain ear-rings, sets of jewellery, crosses, medals, plaques, snuffboxes, and a range of silverware decorated with precious or fake stones, pearls, roses, or embellished with fluting, chasing, engraving or enamelling. In contrast, another jeweller, Jean Philibert Guerre, targeted consumers whose tastes were altogether more modest: snuffboxes at 2F a piece, gold rings at 3.80F, earrings at 6F a pair and gold crosses at 4.8F (post-mortem inventory, Catherine Rouillot, 1822).

If new products were characterized by their value and their quality, they were placed in opposition to second-hand goods which were generally indicated by the terms *bad* and *worn*. Items such as *odd* shoes, *worn out* tablecloths, *broken* toys for children, *old* flowers, *old* straw hats, *threadbare* glazed hats, *old reject* hats and *spoiled* mustard sat side by side with brand new articles on the shelves of the shops. This coexistence gives an insight into the place held by second-hand or poor quality products in the stock of tradesmen. The constant renewal of fashions made it difficult for retailers to match the supply and turnover of their stocks with demand for novelties. However, outdated or unfashionable items could also satisfy a clientele anxious to acquire goods which were previously beyond their means.

Prevalence of Second-Hand Products: a Market Adapted to the Population of Besançon – The sale of second-hand products involved the majority of tradesmen in Besançon, with 60 per cent of retailers in our sample selling *old* or *worn* products, and most activity sectors. In addition to second-hand clothes dealers, who specialised in selling used goods, haberdashers, grocers, cloth merchants, milliners, hatters, ironmongers and jewellers all stocked second-hand articles in larger or smaller quantities. According to P. Verley, 'most shops did not sell new manufactured goods, but second-hand ones. This second market did not constitute a barrier to the consumption of new products, but perhaps paradoxically supported it by organising a social circulation of goods' (Verley, 1997: 276).[30]

Perhaps the most important sector concerned with second-hand selling was the cloth trade, especially before 1830 when new clothing was mainly the business of dress-makers, tailors and other craftsmen. To second-hand clothes dealers we must add merchants of all kinds who saw a means of broadening their customer base and gaining a larger

29 French name for gold threads made to catch the light and used for military or liturgical clothes.

30 'Une grande partie des boutiques ne vend pas des produits manufacturés neufs, mais de l'occasion. Ce second marché ne constitue pas un frein à la consommation de produits neufs, mais la favorise peut-être paradoxalement en organisant une circulation sociale des merchandises'.

Table 10.4. New and second-hand goods available in the shops of Jean Pierre Gurgey, wig-maker and Claude François Cugnon, haberdasher

		Jean Pierre Gurgey	Claude François Cugnon
New	**Quantity**	109	70.5
	Part in %	24.4	68.8
	Value (in Francs)	183	18.55
	Part in %	40.7	36.7
Second-hand	**Quantity**	337	32
	Part in %	75.6	31.2
	Value (in Francs)	267	32
	Part in %	59.3	63.3

Source: Post-mortem inventories of Jean Pierre Gurgey, wig maker (1802) and of Jeanne Marie Duret, merchant of fabrics' wife (1803), Archives départementales du Doubs, 3E19-27 and 3E19-29.

share of the market. These included men such as the wig-maker Jean Pierre Gurgey (post-mortem inventory, 1802) and the haberdasher Claude François Cugnon (post-mortem inventory, Jeanne Marie Duret, 1803). The former stocked second-hand goods, which accounted for 75.6 per cent of the total number of articles in his store but only 59.3 per cent of the overall value. Conversely, for the latter, they accounted for 31.2 per cent of items, but for 63.3 per cent of overall value (see Table 10.4.). Whilst the total value of the recycled goods in both shops was about the same, they were far more numerous in the wig-maker's shop than in the mercer's. Yet the second-hand textiles were of much greater value. Moreover, the two retailers targeted different markets: one offered men's wear (an old blue suit at 2F, a bad jacket and an old waistcoat at 2F each or old shoes at 2F a pair), whilst the other aimed mostly at women (shirts for women at 1F a piece or old underskirts at 2F). Conversely, second-hand clothes dealers sometimes dealt in new clothing: Antoine Boutroud, for example, included in his stock of clothing a grey great coat made of *kalmuk*[31] at 15F (post-mortem inventory, 1800).

The presence of second-hand products on the Besançon market aimed to satisfy, on one hand, middleclass consumers anxious to reduce their daily expenses so as to treat themselves to luxuries and, on the other hand, the lower classes who wished to provide for their basic needs as cheaply as possible. Thus, in the same shop, *old* braids and shoulder straps to *be burned* estimated at 9.6F per 100 grams sit side by side with *new* braids at 22.5F 100 grams; *old* hats at 0.75F a piece on sale along with Flemish hats at 8F a piece; *old* goose feathers at 1.75F per kilo sit close to fine downs at 9.3F a kilo; and a small square stove without its marble, old and broken sold at 20F found next to earthenware stoves at 120F a piece. The list of comparisons is endless.

The participation of permanent tradesmen in the second-hand market is also characterised by their capacity to retouch outdated objects and give them a new lease on life. Thus, the hatter Jules Gustave Bochud offered several dozen *remade* hats at 4F a piece and the metalworker Joseph Despoir used cheap reclaimed materials (*old* iron at 0.25F per kilo, *old*

31 Unteased wool cloth.

lead at 0.8F per kilo and *old* copper at 1.4F per kilo) to manufacture a range of objects, including candlesticks, taps, lamps, lanterns, bells and firedogs (post-mortem inventory, 1840). The newspaper *La Trompette* even encouraged its readers to retain objects which appeared out of fashion by repeating: 'You are not fashionable any more, smart ladies; do not throw your clothes away, you may find them useful' (*La Trompette*, 6 germinal year VIII: 606).[32] The suggestion was that they might be re-decorated to make them fashionable again – a practice which was long established in terms of hats.

Moreover, second-hand objects were not always sold through shop-keeping retailers: this point is apparent from the local press, in which we find many commercial advertisements concerning voluntary sales, sales by authority of justice (auction sales and public sales) and sales at the Pawnshop. Voluntary sales were carried out by private individuals who wished to dispose of one or more goods. All sorts of objects (pieces of furniture, books, food products, wood, animals, tools, pianos and so on) of varying quality thus came onto the market without going through the hands of retailers: 'Voluntary sale of furniture: comprises several boat-shaped bedsteads, and others; bedside tables; mahogany writing desks and chests of drawers, and other woods; cupboards, tables, iron and earthenware stoves, astral lamps, guns, watches, various utensils for ovens, gardening, wheels and tools; cherry tree and oak boards and panelling, tanks, casks rimmed with wood and iron; firewood, wine of the harvest of 1823, saddles and harnessing (. . .)' (*Le Petit Album franc-comtois*, 30 January 1825: 60).[33] As shown by the advertisement above, this type of sale allowed the circulation of goods formerly in the hands of a privileged population (mahogany furniture, guns or specialised pieces of furniture for living or bed-rooms, silverware, mirrors, books, engravings, rifles, porcelain, linens and so on) (*Le Petit Album franc-comtois*, 17 April 1825) to the lower classes and thus contributed to the diffusion of a middle-class model of consumption.[34]

10.5 Conclusion

Shopkeepers, whether specialised or not, relied for their success on the diversity of their stock (the multiplicity of models and styles, and the range of prices and qualities); the emphasis on novelty and fashion over second hand and old products, and the advertisements they placed in the local press. Be they new or old, luxury or basic, the goods offered for sale were aimed at a socially differentiated customer base whose needs, financial means and tastes varied widely. In a city the size of Besançon, where elites were few, the luxury market was inevitably small. Nonetheless, it was real. Moreover, the circulation of semi-luxury products eased the penetration of cheaper but good quality products into a wider circle of customers. Therefore, *objets d'art* rubbed shoulders with

32 'Vous n'êtes plus à la mode, belles dames; ne jettez cependant pas vos chiffons au feu, vous en tirerez encore quelque parti'.

33 'Vente volontaire de mobilier: il se compose de plusieurs bois de lits à bateau, et autres; tables de nuit; bonheur-du-jour et commode en acajou, et en autre bois; crédence; armoires, tables, bureau, poêles en fonte et faïence, lampe astrale, pistolets, montres, différents ustensiles de four, de jardinage, de tour et de menuiserie; planches et lambris en cerisier, en sorbier, en chêne, cuvier, futailles cerclées en bois et en fer; bois de chauffage, vin de la récolte de 1823, selles et harnachements'.

34 Sales by authority of justice (including post-mortem sales and of those in accordance with a commercial activity transfer) required the prior agreement of the commercial Court.

mass produced and standardised goods – a juxta-positioning most evident in the clock and watch trade.

In addition, strongly influenced by Parisian fashions, Besançon was opened to novelty, partly by tradesmen coming from the capital to sell their latest products; partly by frequent advertisements in the local press announcing the arrival of new and fashionable goods; and partly by the interest shown by consumers reading specialised (fashion) newspapers. However, the circulation of novelties came up against the traditionalism of some tradesmen and the press, which made their penetration of local markets slower than in big cities and of course in Paris.

Far from being unstructured, the second-hand trade was perfectly integrated into the commercial landscape of Besançon in the first half of the nineteenth century. Moreover, whilst it is often linked to the clothing sector, it concerned all fields of consumption, including food, materials, jewellery and furniture. Second-hand goods, which were traditionally sold mostly by hawkers, were found on the shelves of shop-keeping retailers, not least because they saw in such goods a means to attract new consumers and to widen their customer base. In addition, the circulation of these goods contributed to the circulation of novelties beyond the wealthy elite: customers with more restricted purchasing power saw the second-hand trade as a means of acquiring goods which would otherwise be quite out of their reach.

Bibliography

Primary Sources

Unpublished sources

Post-mortem inventories, Archives départementales du Doubs (ADD), Besançon:

Blanche, Charles Antoine, tailor, 1836, classification mark 3^{E}28-44.

Bochud, Jules Gustave, hatter, 1843, 3^{E}19-94.

Boutroud, Antoine, secondhand clothes dealer, 1800, 3^{E}19-19.

Boillot, Jean François, hatter, 1801, 3^{E}31-7

Clocher, Marie Claude, merchant in boissellery, 1831, 3^{E}28-35.

Despoir, Joseph, founder mechanic, 1840, 3^{E}19-88.

Duret, Jean Claude, fabrics merchant, 1804, 3^{E}19-33.

Duret, Jeanne Marie, wife of Claude François Cugnon, haberdasher, 1803, 3^{E}19-29.

Estreyer, Claudine Joséphine, wife of Claude Joseph Augustin Billot, jeweller, 1832, 3^{E}28,36.

Gilmert, Jeanne Louise, milliner, 1813, 3^{E}28-9.

Gurgey, Jean Pierre, wig maker, 1802, 3^{E}19-27.

Humbert, Claude Antoine, grocer, 1822, 3^{E}19-56.

Lacroix, Xavier Simon Thomas, clock making merchant, 1823, 3^{E}28-20.

Muess, Nicolas Sébastien, fabrics wholesaler, 1875, 3^{E}19-158.

Parisot, Thérèse, milliner, 1824, 3^{E}28-21.

Peaulier, Marguerite, milliner, 1812, 3^{E}28-8.

Perron, Louis Simon, clock making merchant, 1835, 3^{E}19-75.

Pras, Jeanne Thérèse, wife of Pierre Célestin Clerce, haberdasher, 1810, 3^{E}28-6.

Riduet, Claude Philippe, grocer, 1822, 3^{E}28-19.

Rouillot, Catherine, wife of Jean Philibert Guerre, jeweller, 1822, 3^{E}19-56.

Published sources

Annuaire du Doubs de 1804, ADD, PER. 878.
Annuaire du Doubs de 1845, ADD, PER.875.
Annuaire du Doubs de 1849, ADD, PER. 878.
Bretillot, L. (1878) 'L'industrie et le commerce à Besançon depuis 1820', *Académie des Sciences, Belles-lettres et Arts de Besançon, années 1876–1877*, Besançon, 102–116.
Chevalier, E. (reproduction of the edition of 1887) *Les salaires au XIXe siècle*, Paris, available in microfiche on the website *www.gallica.bnf.fr*
Feuille d'affiches – judiciaires et commerciales. Annonces et avis divers du département du Doubs, n35, 24 july 1808, Bibliothèque municipale d'Etude et de Conservation (BMEC), Besançon, PER.C. 6210, stock of Franche-Comté.
Feuille d'affiches – judiciaires et commerciales. Annonces et avis divers du département du Doubs, n45, 11 november 1849, BMEC, Besançon, PER.C. 6210, stock of Franche-Comté.
Journal du département du Doubs, n20, 3 vendémiaire 1800, BMEC, Besançon, PER.C.6206, stock of Franche-Comté.
L'Impartial, 18 january 1835, BMEC, Besançon, classification mark 8290–8313.
La Gazette de Franche-Comté, n80, 12 may 1832, BMEC, Besançon, classification mark 12455.
La Trompette, n74, 29 ventose year VIII, BMEC, Besançon, PER.C.6206, stock of Franche-Comté.
La Trompette, n76, 6 germinal year VIII, p. 606, BMEC, Besançon, PER.C.6206, stock of Franche-Comté.
La Trompette, n110, 29 messidor year VIII, BMEC, Besançon, PER.C.6206, stock of Franche-Comté.
Le Franc-comtois, 6 april 1844, BMEC, Besançon, classification mark 7574–7579.
Le Petit Album franc-comtois, 30 january 1825, BMEC, Besançon, PER.C.6200.
Le Petit Album franc-comtois, 17 april 1825, BMEC, Besançon, PER.C.6200.
Le Petit Album franc-comtois, 18 december 1825, BMEC, Besançon, PER.C.6200.
Les Tablettes franc-comtoises, n34, 15 july 1827, BMEC, Besançon, PER.C 2181.
Les Tablettes franc-comtoises, n36, 27 july 1828, BMEC, Besançon, PER. C 2181.

Literature

Barjot, D., Chaline, J.-P. and Encreve, A. (1995) *La France au XIXe siècle, 1814–1914*, Paris.
Berg, M. and Clifford, H. (1999) *Consumers and luxury. Consumer culture in Europe, 1650–1850*, Manchester.
Berg, M. and Eger, E. (2003) *Luxury in the 18th century. Debates, desires and delectable goods*, Basingstoke and New York.
Braudel, F. and Labrousse, E. (1976) *Histoire économique et sociale de la France, 1789–1880*, t. 3, Paris.
Brewer, J. and Porter, R. (1993) *Consumption and the world of goods*, London and New York.
Charpy, M. (2002) 'Formes et échelles du commerce d'occasion au XIXe siècle. L'exemple du vêtement à Paris', *Revue d'histoire du XIXe siècle*, 24 Varia, 125–150.
Coquery, N. (2000) *La boutique et la ville. Commerces, commerçants, espaces et clientèles, XVIe–XXe siècle*, Tours.
Coquery, N. (2006) *La boutique à Paris au XVIIIe siècle*, thesis for the achievement of the authorization to advise doctoral students and oversee research, supervised by Dominique Margairaz, Université de Paris I-Panthéon-Sorbonne.
Coquery, N. (2004) 'The language of success: marketing and distributing semi-luxury goods in eigtheenth-century Paris', *Journal of Design History*, 17/1, Special Issue: Disseminating design: the French connection, 71–89.

Daumas, J.-C. and Ferriere Le Vayer, M. de (2007) 'Les métamorphoses du luxe vues d'Europe', *Entreprises et Histoire*, 6–16.
Defrasne, J. (1990) *Histoire d'une ville: Besançon le temps retrouvé*, Besançon.
Fohlen, C. (1982) *Histoire de Besançon: de la conquête française à nos jours*, Besançon.
Fontaine, L. (1984) *Le voyage et la mémoire. Colporteurs de l'Oisans au XIXe siècle*, Lyon.
Fontaine, L. (1993) *Histoire du colportage en Europe, XVe–XIXe siècle*, Paris.
Gaillard, J. (1997) *Paris, la ville (1852–1870)*, Paris.
Lemire, B. (1991) 'Peddling fashion: salesmen, pawnbrokers, taylors, thieves and the second-hand clothes trade in England, c. 1700–1800', *Textile History*, 22/1, 67–82.
Lemire, B. (1998) 'Consumerism in preindustrial and early industrial England: the trade in second-hand clothes, *The Journal of British Studies*, 27/1, 1–24.
Lemire, B. (2005) 'Shifting currency: the culture and economy of the second hand trade in England, c. 1600–1850', Palmer, A. and Clark, H. (eds.), *Old clothes, new looks, second hand fashion*, Oxford and New-York, 29–47.
Lipovestky, G. (1987) *L'empire de l'éphémère. La mode et son destin dans les sociétés modernes*, Paris.
Margairaz, D. (1997) *Foires et marchés dans la France préindustrielle*, Paris.
McKendrick, N., Brewer, J. and Plumb, J.H. (1982) *The birth of a consumer society, The commercialization of eighteenth-century England*, London.
Marseille, J. (1999) *Le luxe en France, du siècle des 'Lumières' à nos jours*, Paris.
Ormen-Corpet, C. (2000) *Modes, XIXe–XXe siècles*, Paris.
Palmer, A. and Clark, H. (2005) *Old clothes, new looks: second hand fashion*, Oxford and New York.
Perrot, P. (1995) *Le luxe: une richesse entre faste et confort, XVIIIe–XIXe siècle*, Paris.
Roche, D. (1989) *La culture des apparences. Une histoire du vêtement, XVIIe–XVIIIe siècle*, Paris.
Roche, D. (1997) *Histoire des choses banales, naissance de la consommation, XVIIe–XIXe siècle*, Paris.
Simmel, G. (1957) 'Fashion', *The American Journal of sociology*, 62, 541–549.
Stearns, P.N. (2001) *Consumerism in world history. The global transformation of desire*, London and New York.
Strehmel, B. (2006) *Les foires et les marchés dans le Doubs au XIXe siècle*, Term paper for the achievement of the second year of History Master supervised by Jean-Claude Daumas, Université de Franche-Comté.
Verley, P. (1997) *L'échelle du monde. Essai sur l'industrialisation de l'Occident*, Paris.
Weber, E. (1983) *La fin des terroirs. La modernisation de la France rurale, 1870–1914*, Paris.

PART IV

AUCTIONING

CHAPTER 11

Changing Geographies and the Rise of the Modern Auction. Transformations on the Second-Hand Markets of Eighteenth-Century Antwerp

Dries Lyna[1] – University of Antwerp, Centre for Urban History, Belgium

11.1 Introduction

Ever since Neil McKendrick's pioneering article appeared just over twenty-five years ago, historians have vividly discussed the concept of eighteenth-century consumerism (McKendrick, 1982). Research in recent decades has demonstrated convincingly that the consumer and ownership patterns of citizens throughout Europe witnessed a remarkable shift from durable to fashionable consuming between 1700 and 1800, with ever quickening and shortening fashion cycles. The credo of the contemporary consumer seems to have been 'Out with the old and in with the new' (Campbell, 2001). Ever more specialized shops and boutiques *à la mode* fostered this idea and offered customers myriad novelties on a regular basis. Clever entrepreneurs, equipped with an arsenal of marketing techniques, perpetuated this wave of consumption.

Many historians tend to characterize the eighteenth century as the first 'age of consumerism', yet in recent years researchers have established important nuances to this hypothesis. One influential line of thinking highlights continuity with traditional forms of distribution and downplays the modernity of certain marketing techniques (Cox, 2000; Van Damme, 2007). Retailers, rather than inventing new ways of attracting customers, adapted and transformed existing methods. Whether advertising indeed 'whipped up demand for knick-knacks, curios, and the disposable', as Porter claimed, remains debatable (Lyna and Van Damme, 2009). Other contributions to our understanding of eighteenth-century consumerism stress the importance of second-hand consumption for the early modern citizen, an area that researchers often neglect (except Woodward, 1985 and numerous articles on reused clothing). Recycling products and materials was a vital mechanism for the urban society in the period 1500–1700, and even in the eighteenth century old objects unmistakeably played a part (Fontaine, 2008). Yet the strong connections between markets for old and new, and ways in which they encroached upon another, have hardly been investigated. In this article we wish to demonstrate how changing consumer preferences after 1750 had a profound impact on the Antwerp second-hand markets. More in particular,

1 Dries Lyna is Research Fellow of the Fund for Scientific Research – Flanders (FWO-Flanders). I would like to thank Bruno Blondé and Ilja Van Damme for their comments on an earlier version of this text.

we will focus on the emergence of new auction houses in Antwerp. We will show that the current handling of antiquarian objects dates back to the late eighteenth century, and that a strong desire for social and geographical distinction propelled the rise of the modern auction.

To tackle these research questions, we have two types of contemporary promotional prints at our disposal: newspaper advertisements and auction catalogues. From the end of the seventeenth century onwards, local retailers promoted their business in the *Gazette van Antwerpen*, which appeared twice a week on Tuesdays and Fridays. Similar to evolutions in England, France and the Dutch Republic (Walker, 1975; Ferdinand, 1993; Todd, 1989; Feyel, 2000; Broersma, 2002: 40), the average number of advertisements in the *Gazette* rose remarkably throughout the eighteenth century: from less than one per edition in 1703 to over fifteen nearly ninety years later. A growing commercial strife among Antwerp retailers partly explains this remarkable growth of commercial announcements, although the revival of the Antwerp economy and demography after 1770 also influenced this evolution. Among all retailers, especially second-hand dealers employed vividly the Antwerp newspaper. This strengthens our use of these sources. Four sample years (1730, 1750, 1770 and 1790), some 3500 announcements in total, will allow for a thorough quantitative and qualitative scrutiny of the commercial advertisements on the second-hand markets (also see Lyna and Van Damme, forthcoming).

The first appearance of a printed auction catalogue in the Low Countries dates back to the late sixteenth century, but it was not until the eighteenth century (and especially after 1760) that editions were dispersed on a large scale and used in a progressively more commercialized second-hand market for luxury objects. Published several weeks before the auction, these booklets informed potential customers about the objects for sale, often with lengthy descriptions. Our corpus contains all 61 preserved catalogues of Antwerp art auctions in the period 1741–1794, with a bias towards the high end of the market. In addition, some Brussels art auction catalogues are used in a comparative approach. Regarding public sales of books, we rely on published material which covers large parts of the eighteenth century (Delsaerdt and Vanysacker, 1997; Remeysen, 1947).

Although it remains debatable if these promotional prints indeed were true reflections or rather idealistic representations of contemporary commercial reality, it is exactly in this tension field that the true value of these sources is hidden. Advertisements and catalogues offer us an exceptional view on how local dealers in second-hand goods portrayed themselves and their merchandise towards their potential clientele; they offer us crucial inside information on how the organizers of public sales coped with the growing desire for newness in eighteenth-century Antwerp.

11.2 Second-Hand Markets in Early Modern Antwerp

As with numerous early modern cities, trade in second-hand objects was essential for the economy in the city by the river Scheldt. Since the late Middle Ages trade in second-hand goods was dominated by the corporation of the *oudekleerkopers* (second-hand cloth dealers): besides trading old garments, the guild dealt in all sorts of used products (Deceulaer, 2001). Their organization was characterised by strong social divergences, as it included both poor peddlers and rich dealers. Many of these well-off *oudekleerkopers* were the so-called sworn criers and appraisers, an elite group with the exclusive right to auction and appraise a wide array of second-hand objects ranging from firewood, real estate, and land to old clothes, pots and pans, and used luxury products. Especially the criers held an important position in the Antwerp society. They were crucial as public servants in organizing household sales of fellow citizens, auctioning plain utensils alongside luxury objects.[2]

The universe of Antwerp's second-hand trade evolved around the *Vrijdagmarkt* (Friday Market), a public square designed in the sixteenth century specifically as the hub of corporate dealing in used objects.[3] At this place, sworn criers of the second-hand cloth dealers ran their daily businesses and organized estate sales, often in open air. Occasionally auctions were held *in situ* (in the houses of the deceased or bankrupted), especially if the estate was too large or too costly to move to the Friday Market. From the sixteenth century onwards, lower types of second-hand dealers were progressively excluded from this square. The few houses at the Friday Market were reserved for sworn criers. The further an *oudekleerkoper* lived from this second-hand business district, the lower his social and financial standing. During the seventeenth century, city and corporate officials alike sought to civilize the Friday Market and filed various ordinances, such as a ban to sell rags at the square from 1655 onwards. But especially the disorderly public sales of the criers were subject to legislation: a specific sequence for selling was mandated so that criers and customers could understand each other; sellers were forbidden to insult customers or use aggressive salesmanship; and sales could no longer pursue after midnight. Apparently dishonest criers frequently employed the falling darkness to con ignorant citizens. The numerous repetitions of these regulations indicate that civilizing the core of second-hand trade was not an easy job (Van Damme, 2006: 208–210).

Nevertheless, throughout the seventeenth century the Friday Market attracted citizens from all walks of life, and rich and poor citizens visited the shops and auctions to fulfil various recycling needs. The dealer Mathijs Musson frequented the square during the 1650s to supply himself with old paintings and other artwork. Dealer Willem Forchondt was also active at the Friday market: in March 1673 he bought a set of paintings, copper plates to make prints, and furniture to export abroad (Deijnckens, 1988: 43–44). Between 1665 and 1670 Elisabeth Moretus, a wealthy niece of the famous Antwerp printer, often sold used clothes to a second-hand cloth dealer at the Friday Market (De Staelen, 2002: 139). Other *oudekleerkopers* bought their stocks of second-hand merchandise at the public auctions and resold them in their own shops.[4] Trade in second-hand objects formed an important aspect of Antwerp society. Consumption of second-hand objects was not

2 There were a few other institutions that held the right to organize public sales in specific circumstances, but their overall influence on the second-hand markets was limited, compared to the *oudekleerkopers*. Craftsmen also had the right to auction off their merchandise, but only if they had produced it themselves (Van Damme, 2007: 63–102).

3 Gilbert van Schoonbeke urbanized this part of the city in mid-sixteenth century. The corporation of second-hand cloth dealers took the opportunity and requested the city council to move their public sales to this new location. Up until that time, the second-hand trade was scattered throughout the arterial roads of the old city, often causing trouble and traffic congestion (Soly, 1977: 183–184).

4 'Want degene die voorbert houden doen dit van goederen de welcke sij t' sij in publicke vercoopingen ofte andersins hebben ingekocht'. City Archive Antwerp (SAA), *Gilden en Ambachten* (*GA*), nr. 4293, Lawsuit of the deans of the corporation of second-hand cloth dealers against Joannes van Lemens (September sixteenth 1744). Thanks to Ilja Van Damme for guiding me to this document.

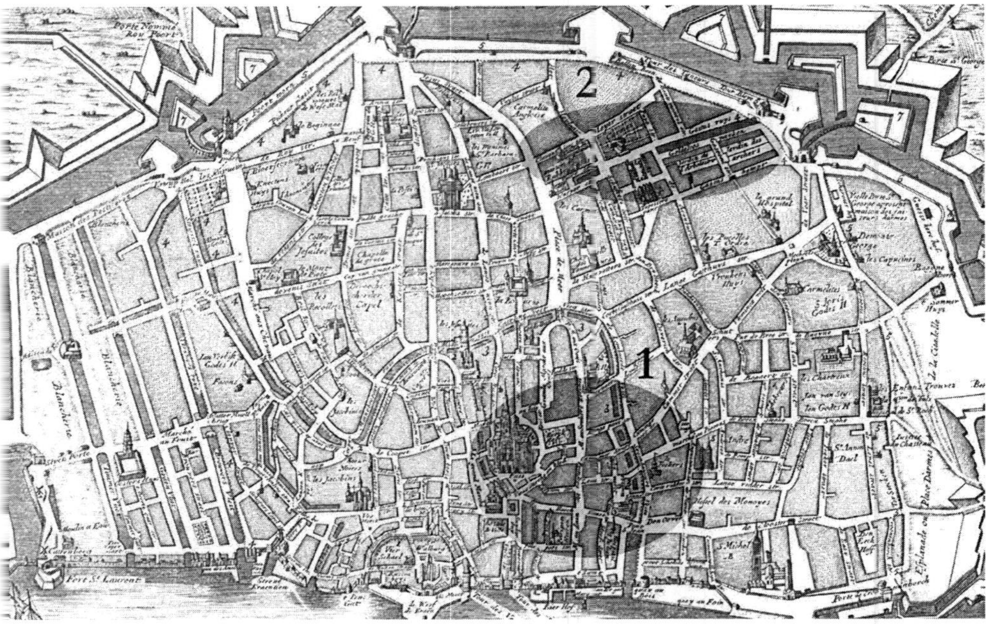

MAP 11.1A. A map of early eighteenth-century Antwerp. *Plan de la Ville et Citadelle d'Anvers* by J.C. Deur, published by P. Mortier, Amsterdam, 1706

SOURCE: Private collection.

perceived as inferior, as in the second half of the seventeenth century people from all social strata shopped regularly at the Friday Market.[5]

In the eighteenth century the consumption patterns of Antwerp citizens underwent remarkable transformations, albeit on a more modest scale than in major cities like Paris, London, and Amsterdam (Blondé, 2002). Exotic and foreign products like coffee, chocolate, porcelain, and Indian cotton were imported from overseas. The use of cheaper raw materials and lower production costs yielded less durable but low-priced products. Antwerp citizens happily engaged in conspicuous consumption of these new and fashionable goods, stimulating evolution towards quickening fashion cycles, greater variability, and ever-widening product choice. The advent of the 'age of consumerism' affected not only the rich and wealthy: throughout the eighteenth century the demand for these new products trickled down the social hierarchy.

As a result of these mutual reinforcing evolutions, the second-hand markets were increasingly overwhelmed by inferior objects whose recyclable value had plunged considerably (Blondé, 2002; Blondé and Van Damme, 2007). Indirect evidence appears to support this hypothesis: for example, the value of pawns in the Antwerp *Berg van Barmhartigheid* dropped from an average of 9 to 10 guilders in the seventeenth century to below 6 guilders a century later (Van Damme, 2007: 251). The sworn criers of the Friday Market surely

5 Antwerp was no exception in this perspective: in early seventeenth-century Amsterdam all social strata of society participated in the second-hand sales of the *Weeskamer* (Montias, 2002), as was the case in *almoneda*-auctions in Spain during the sixteenth- and seventeenth centuries (Alvarez, 2007).

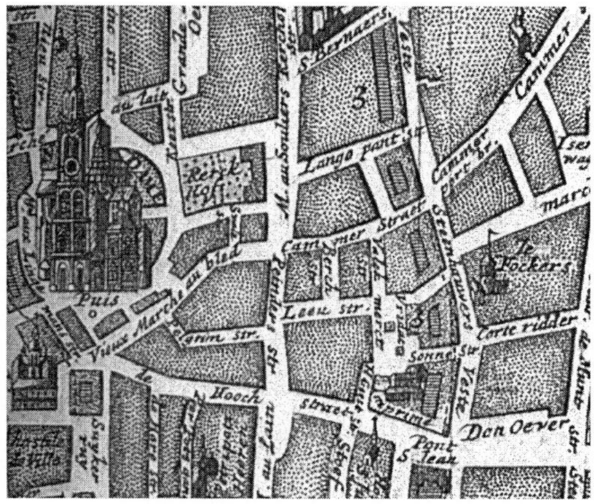

Map 11.1b. The *Vridac Merct* or Friday Market (left of *le Fockers* or Fuggers-tower), detail from map 11.1a

Source: Private collection.

suffered in their pockets, as their wages were a percentage of the value of the auctioned objects. Signs of internal frictions and growing competition between criers confirm that corporation of the *oudekleerkopers* faced increasing social and economic setbacks during the eighteenth century (Lyna, forthcoming).

Yet, perhaps paradoxically, the local *Gazette van Antwerpen* reveals a spectacular rise in the number of advertised public sales of fine consumer goods: from barely six auctions per year in 1705 to almost three a week eighty-five years later (Table 11.1.). This growth partially reflects criers' increasing willingness to promote their merchandise, incited by stiffening competition (Lyna and Van Damme, 2009). But the marked rise of advertised public sales tells only part of the story, and probably an overly optimistic one, since the recyclable value of products in the growing numbers of auctions surely dropped considerably. More evidence regarding actual prices of second-hand goods is needed to fully understand the faith of the second-hand trade. Antwerp markets for old objects were nevertheless confronted with major evolutions during the eighteenth century: changes in

Table 11.1. Newspaper advertisements for public sales containing luxury objects in eighteenth-century Antwerp (repetitions included)

	Advertised public sales of amongst others luxury objects (books, artwork, furniture, . .)	Total number of advertisements
1705	6	29
1730	11	247
1750	19	524
1770	77	1159
1790	147	1613

Source: *Gazette van Antwerpen.*

consumer mentalities spurred processes of segmentation and differentiation on the second-hand markets, whereby the distinctive notion of 'space' would prove essential.

11.3 Segmentation and a Changing Geography

The growing consumerism in the course of the eighteenth century was paralleled by change in the mindset towards second-hand objects. Although commercial recycling had always been an integral part of the early modern society, used objects were increasingly perceived as inferior to new ones. Even the word 'old' acquired negative connotation, while its antipodes 'new' and especially 'modern' became key elements in marketing discourse: their sudden appearance in dozens of Antwerp newspaper advertisements from the 1750s onwards should be understood in this way. Even sworn criers would paradoxically promote their second-hand merchandise using this fashionable terminology (Lyna and Van Damme, forthcoming).

The creation of this (somewhat artificial) gap between old and new brought remarkable evolution to second-hand markets: in the growing mass of inferior household goods several product categories were dealt with differently. The concept of 'old' in terms of 'used' and 'worn' did not apply to certain second-hand objects: used paintings, books, and jewellery were esteemed as more valuable than clothing, pots, and pans. The stigma of 'old', fatal for many consumables, even became vital for certain second-hand luxury objects: their age and provenance contributed significantly to their perceived importance.

This change in mentality had significant consequences, especially in the handling of art and books on the used-products markets. During the eighteenth century numerous collections of such luxury products were sold at separate auctions rather than as integral parts of estate sales, as had been customary in the second half of the seventeenth century. The growing numbers of advertisements and auction catalogues for specialized sales in Antwerp indicate that these collections of deceased citizens were increasingly put to sale (Table 11.2.) (Lyna and Vermeylen, forthcoming).[6]

This product-related segmentation of second-hand markets was accompanied by important spatial differentiation (Table 11.3.). Further scrutiny of the advertised auctions according to sale location reveals an interesting geographical pattern: throughout the eighteenth century the traditional *loci* of second-hand selling (Friday Market and houses of mourning) were overtaken by new salesrooms across town. The Painters Hall, on the first floor of Antwerp's stock exchange (*Borse*), was an important location for art auctions in the early decades of the century, yet it nearly disappears from the records after 1750.

Nevertheless the houses of mourning remained important: not surprisingly, since it was easier and cheaper to sell large estates *in situ*. Also the Friday Market did not vanish as a site for second-hand trade, but its character altered: public sales at the Friday Market continued offering worthwhile objects to customers, albeit as parts of larger estates, often without a printed catalogue. The high-end luxury sales with printed auction catalogues moved to

6 Between 1730 and 1790 the number of advertisements for specialized auctions (books, artwork, jewellery, . . .) in the *Gazette van Antwerpen* rose from 7 to 35 per year. Announcements in the same paper for public sales of amongst others books doubled in only several decades time: 44 in the decade 1755–64 and 89 in 1775–84 (Delsaerdt and Vanysacker, 1997).

TABLE 11.2. Preserved art and book auction catalogues of specialized public sales in eighteenth-century Antwerp

	Catalogues art	Catalogues book
1715–24	0	0
1725–34	0	2
1735–44	3	2
1745–54	2	1
1755–64	6	3
1765–74	21	8
1775–84	16	32
1785–94	17	60

SOURCE: Unpublished database and Remeysen, 1947.

TABLE 11.3. Advertisements for public sales containing luxury objects in eighteenth-century Antwerp, spatial differentiation (repetitions included)

	Houses of mourning	Friday Market	Borse	Meir	Jonge Voet-bogenhof	Oude Voet-bogenhof	Kolveniers-hof	Rest	Unknown	Total
1730	6	1	3	1	0	0	0	0	0	11
1750	7	1	4	0	1	2	0	4	0	19
1770	24	15	1	3	0	17	13	4	0	77
1790	61	25	0	11	10	18	2	18	2	147

SOURCE: *Gazette van Antwerpen*.

other locations, and the Friday Market, like its protagonists the second-hand cloth dealers, lost its privileged position in the late eighteenth-century Antwerp second-hand trade.

Not only 'average' luxury sales moved to other salesrooms across Antwerp; newspaper advertisements indicate that the new type of specialized auctions were particularly susceptible to this reallocation (Tables 11.4. and 11.5.).[7] The Jonge and Oude Voetbogenhof, two important examples in this regard, were the eponymous meeting rooms of the respective guilds, and were adjacent to the fields where they held shooting practices. Although the properties were next to each other, the premises had separate entrances. The Oude Voetbogenhof site was far more popular for holding auctions than its counterpart next-door, particularly for book sales: nearly a third of all Antwerp book sales in the period 1750–1800 were in the Oude Voetbogenhof (Delsaerdt and Vanysacker, 1997). Besides auctions, other social activities like theatre plays, concerts and carnival festivities took place in this hall.[8]

7 The high figures for the Meir and the 'rest' category can be ascribed to two types of auctions that occurred there. Firstly, carriages and horses, popular items of conspicuous consumption in eighteenth-century Antwerp, were sold exclusively on the Meir (Blondé, 2001a). Secondly, the pawnshop of the *Berg van Barmhartigheid* began advertising monthly liquidation of non-relieved pledges only in 1790, which explains the rise of the 'Rest' category in the last sample year.

8 SAA, *GA*, nr. 4632: Ouden Voetboog Resolutie Boeck 1661–1792, 1770–1772.

TABLE 11.4. Advertisements for unique specialized sales of luxury products in Antwerp (1730 + 1750), spatial and product-related differentiation (repetitions not included)

	Houses of mourning	Friday Market	Borse	Jonge Voet-bogenhof	Oude Voet-bogenhof	Kolveniers-hof	Meir	Rest	Total
Books	4	0	0	0	0	0	0	1	5
Artwork (paintings, prints, drawings and sculptures)	1	1	3	1	0	0	0	1	7
Musical instruments and scores	0	1	0	0	0	0	0	0	1
Furniture	0	0	2	0	0	0	0	0	2
Tapestry	0	0	2	0	0	0	0	0	2
Total	5	2	7	1	0	0	0	2	17

SOURCE: *Gazette van Antwerpen*.

TABLE 11.5. Advertisements for unique specialized sales of luxury products in Antwerp (1770 + 1790), spatial and product-related differentiation (repetitions not included)

	Houses of mourning	Friday Market	Borse	Jonge Voet-bogenhof	Oude Voet-bogenhof	Kolveniers-hof	Meir	Rest	Total
Books	5	2	0	1	14	1	0	1	24
Artwork (paintings, prints, drawings and sculptures)	3	4	0	0	2	3	0	1	13
Musical instruments and scores	0	3	0	0	0	0	0		3
Furniture	0	1	0	0	1	0	0	1	3
Jewellery, coins, silverware	3	2	0	0	1	1	0	1	8
Carriages	0	0	0	0	0	0	11	0	11
Total	11	12	0	1	18	5	11	4	62

SOURCE: *Gazette van Antwerpen*.

The salesroom in the Kolveniershof was initially a reception hall for the Kolveniers guild, built in the 1630s next to the field where the guild had its training grounds. With a monumental mantel piece, marble columns, a great chandelier, and numerous paintings and sculptures, it was surely a beautiful room. In 1738 a fire destroyed the wooden roof and the building's façade, but miraculously spared the hall itself

(De Poorter and Huvenne, 1981). After the repair works the Kolveniershof became a popular venue for cultural events, including musical concerts, puppet shows, performances of tightrope walkers, waxwork exhibitions and auctions. From the late 1780s so-called *redoutes* were held there: at these balls the local high society could meet, dance, and gamble until the early morning hours.[9] The Oude Voetbogen- and Kolveniershof thus assumed major prominence within the Antwerp cultural scene after 1750; only the renowned theatre of the nearby *Tapissierspand* was more influential (Luypaers, 2001).

11.4 Between Corporation and Specialization

The eighteenth-century mentality shift towards old objects clearly foreshadowed massive alterations in traditional ways of selling used products. Increasing product segmentation and geographic shift of luxury sales were highly visible results. But these were hardly the only consequences: several other mutual reinforcing events would permanently transform the second-hand markets.

The previously described evolutions supported the next step in the professionalization of the second-hand trade, since the movement away from traditional sale locations in Antwerp was accompanied by slow change of power (Lyna, forthcoming). The sworn criers gradually lost control over the high-end sales to professional art and book dealers. Their main handicap was inability to specialize on specific product groups. Indeed, their all-round experience in dealing with wide arrays of consumer products was crucial in their seventeenth-century success but became a critical impediment in the changing markets of the eighteenth century. Dealers handling luxury objects like books or artwork on a daily basis held an obvious information advantage and other leads over the criers. They were also able to stay far more attuned to the changing market than were the criers. This led to a new structure of second hand selling, whereby the role of corporate criers was limited to the actual hammering of the objects. All other aspects of the auction fell to specialized dealers, who became directors of sale. In late eighteenth-century advertisements and catalogues this distinction was semantically underpinned: from 1783 onwards numerous sworn criers, in their advertising for forthcoming book sales, mentioned that the auction was under their 'supervision', thus differentiating between their corporate roles as crier and functions as directors of the sales (Delsaerdt and Vanysacker, 1997). These examples clearly indicate changing functions and the construction of new hierarchies. An anonymous Brussels sale catalogue of 1793 unambiguously states that the art sale was held by sworn criers Suys and Anoul but was under the supervision of dealer J.A. Rombaut (KMSKB, 11/11/1793).

The change from corporate to dealer-controlled auctions was a steady (not sudden) process with long periods of transitions and hybrid solutions. A remarkable intermediary

9 Since 1686 all organizers of Antwerp spectacles had to pay a tax to the city's almoners, who recorded these incomes under the heading 'Foreign spectacles'. Although their accounts are far from complete and a lot of activities probably escaped their control, these documents nevertheless offer us a nice view of the blooming Antwerp cultural life (see Openbaar Centrum voor Maatschappelijk Welzijn-Archief Antwerpen (OCMW-AA), *Oud archief* (OA), Kamer der Huisarmen, 967 and 968).

was the Antwerp printer and book dealer Guillielmus Josephus Bincken (?–1815), son of the influential printer Hubertus. The young Bincken did not appear to have intention to follow his father's footsteps: as a sworn crier of the corporation of second-hand cloth dealers he advertised his first public sale in 1778.[10] However, he would soon begin to focus on book sales. Although corporate rulings normally forbade such practice, he acquired the title of master printer and bookseller in 1787 and was granted a royal print patent in the same year (Voet, 1952: 341). The reputation of his father, dean of the Guild of Saint Luke in 1782, likely influenced this abnormal situation, as the Guild's *Liggeren* does not mention Guillielmus Josephus serving apprenticeship. The apparent ease in obtaining another title of master and the absence of corporate reaction confirms the idea that Antwerp's second-hand cloth dealers were facing serious loss of control. Yet Bincken was unconcerned, as his unique combination of professions allowed him to control all aspects of the book auction: henceforth he alone could draw up, print and sell the catalogue, place the advertisements, hammer off the books, and arrange the post-auction financial settlements. In 1790, for example, he advertised seven public sales in the local newspaper; six were specialized book auctions and all included catalogues available only in Bincken's bookshop. Five of the book auctions took place in the Oude Voetbogenhof, again emphasizing its role as the new hub for Antwerp's second-hand book trade (SBA, *GvA*, 19/2, 4/5, 11/5, 4/6, 22/6 and 16/7/1790). Underscoring his commercial creativity and cleverness, Bincken even used an announcement for his book sale to promote new literature stocked in his bookshop; this was quite an unusual method (SBA, *GvA*, 4/5/1790). Another remarkable intermediate was the book dealer Jean Francois de Bock, who followed a somewhat inversed trajectory: he began in 1775 as a printer of book auction catalogues, and advertised sales under his own supervision from 1779. Although De Bock organised many book sales in late eighteenth-century Antwerp, he seemed not to specialize in any specific product group and location, instead holding auctions throughout town for various products.[11] Between 1778 and 1795 De Bock and Bincken were involved in almost a third of all book sales and dominated the market for book auctions.[12]

The situation for art auctions is less clear, but there are indications that *connaisseur-marchands* took over the second-hand art trade during the eighteenth century. Unlike their colleagues in book auctions, art dealers were less eager to step into the limelight, although reasons for this are not yet clear. Promotional prints for high-end art sales articulate this reluctance to step forward: the prints bulge with information about the sales, yet lack the fundamental element of the organizer's name.[13] Virtually all other announcements for public sales refer to the sworn crier responsible for the sale's organisation. But in other

10 An earlier mention of the same name in 1766 probably refers to someone else, since the next public book sale that state his name only appears twelve years later, after which this person regularly advertised (see Delsaerdt and Vanysacker, 1997: 33).

11 Between 1775 and 1779 he was the printer of four catalogues: because these were all anonymous sales without an organizer's name in the Oude Voetbogenhof, there is a possibility that De Bock already had control over these auctions as director of sale, but did not advertise as such. In 1790 he organized a total of six auctions, often in team with other criers. Only one of these was a specialized book sale, notably in the Kolveniershof.

12 To be precise: they were involved in 116 of a total of 362 advertised auctions that contained amongst others books in Antwerp between 1778 and 1795, or 32 percent.

13 Of the 61 preserved auction catalogues for Antwerp art sales, only three mention the organizers, all of them sworn criers of the *oudekleerkopers*. Contemporary Brussels' art dealers in a comparable setting however were less prudent to advertise overtly in the local newspaper and distribute catalogues with their own name prominently on the title page, not bringing up possible corporate interference (see Lyna, forthcoming).

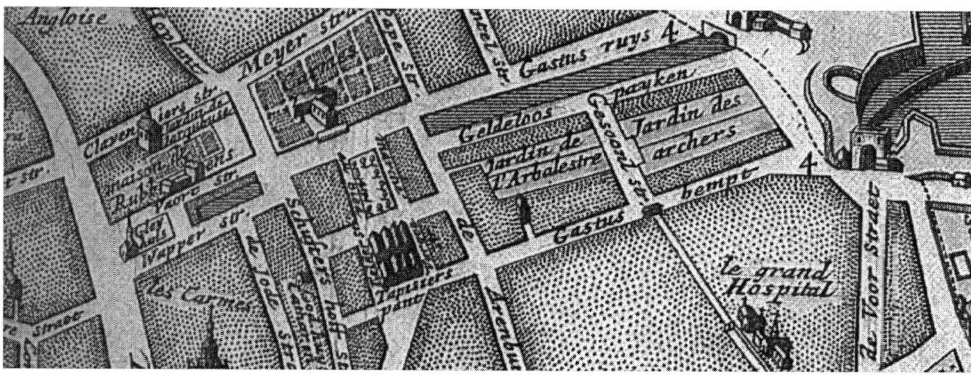

Map 11.1c. The Kolveniershof or *Jardin de L'Arqubuse* (left) and the Jonge & Oude Voetbogenhof or *Jardin de L'Arbalestre* (centre right), detail from map 11.1a

Source: Private collection.

advertisements, such as for quack doctors or book sellers, the name, often printed in italics or capitals, appears to be among the most important constituents of the commercial discourse. From about 1770 many Antwerp book auctions display similar shortage of organizers' names, often when the sale was held at one of the modern locations like the Oude Voetbogen or the Kolveniershof. Several hypotheses can be formulated for why Antwerp dealers did not use names to promote their sales. For this article one particular explanation seems valuable: if the organizer's name was absent in promotional prints addressed to potential customers, this can only mean that other mentioned characteristics mediated trust and reputation. The luxury goods for sale varied constantly and advertisements, due to space limitations, often gave only dry, short lists, omitting persuasive features. The only constant element was the auction's location. This was often one of the new salesrooms, which suggests that a sale's location functioned as a sort of warranty of quality. For Antwerp, the geographical move of luxury auctions from the old city to the outskirts of town thus brought another type of guarantee, one that was no longer linked to the name of the sworn crier but to the salesroom. This is reminiscent of similar evolutions in late eighteenth-century London and Paris, where Christie's and Sotheby's, as the new auction rooms of Paillet and Lebrun, became actual brand names (Wall, 1997; and Guichard in this volume).

11.5 The Birth of the Modern Auction: a Conclusion

Whatever the exact agents of change in Antwerp's evolving second-hand markets, one thing is clear: the geographical reallocation and product specialization indicated emergence of a new type of auction. Parallel with the move to the Kolveniers- and Oude Voetbogenhof in the 1760s and 1770s, new commercial practices came into use. These customs focused on creation of a highly specific auction culture that evolved around the sale catalogue as innovative tool. The catalogue formed the nucleus of change especially for art auctions: from the 1760s onwards art sale catalogues displayed a remarkable shift from simply listing informative descriptions to providing elaborate narratives on the artwork. These booklets were exceptionally notable in the increasingly sophisticated terminology

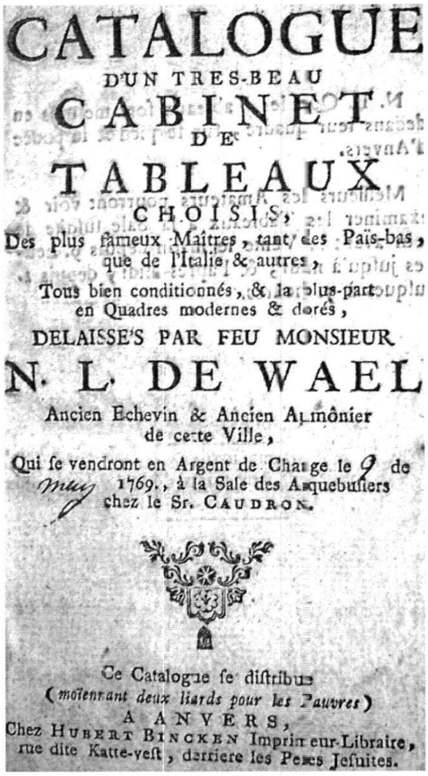

CATALOGUE
D'UN TRES-BEAU
CABINET
DE
TABLEAUX,
CHOISIS,
Des plus fameux Maîtres, tant des Païs-bas, que de l'Italie & autres,
Tous bien conditionnés, & la plus-part en Quadres modernes & dorés,
DELAISSE'S PAR FEU MONSIEUR
N. L. DE WAEL
Ancien Echevin & Ancien Almônier de cette Ville,
Qui se vendront en Argent de Change le 9 de May 1769., à la Sale des Arquebusiers chez le Sr. Caudron.

Ce Catalogue se distribue (moïennant deux liards pour les Pauvres)
A ANVERS,
Chez Hubert Bincken Imprimeur-Libraire, rue dite Katte-vest, derriere les Peres Jesuites.

Figure 11.1. Example of an Antwerp auction catalogue (Title page of the De Wael-sale, Kolveniershof, 9 May 1769)

Source: Royal Museum of Fine Arts Antwerp.

used to describe a painting's colour, expression, composition, and drawing, often ascribing a work to a certain artist. Construction of such a repertory of rhetoric and the development of attributive skills foreshadowed the birth of art history as a scientific discipline nearly a century later (Von Stockhausen, 2005).

Besides the purely economic dimension of reselling old objects, the Antwerp art auction also acquired a cultural dimension: the catalogues increasingly promoted a separate sale culture, one with a particular etiquette. The mercantile language of the Friday Market was abandoned for more exalted discourse of marked aristocratic influences, not surprisingly in French, the cultural *lingua franca* of the eighteenth century. Politeness and honesty were cardinal in this paradigm: the authors of art auction catalogues sought to convince customers of the offered quality, but they never did so in an intrusive or direct manner. Judging product excellence was the client's privilege and not the auctioneer's. Although contemporaries sometimes criticised the exaggerated language, the centrality of the catalogues' discourse in the formation of a new auction culture should not be underestimated. From this perspective it is unsurprising that the Kolveniershof, a cultural breeding ground of exceptional importance in late eighteenth-century Antwerp, emerged as the venue for this new type of art auction.

The up-and-coming art and book dealers clearly wished to discard old sales methods and manners, but more importantly they sought to attract a different audience. Their combined efforts convey much about their perceived clientele: separate sales of collectables, held in semi-cultural meeting halls and within in a lofty atmosphere, would especially attract well-off collectors and dealers who wished to trade luxury products in honest fashion. An initial survey of high-end art auction catalogues indicates that these attempts produced quick results. The contrast with the melting pot of the late seventeenth-century Friday Market sales is glaring: gone were the second-hand cloth dealers, street vendors, and other representatives of the urban lower and middle classes. The limited information on the buyer's market indicates a rather restricted core group of well-off art lovers and dealers (and an occasional foreign collector). The auction system as market form and emergence of the printed auction catalogue greatly supported the ongoing internationalisation of the art trade. In the last decades of the eighteenth century Antwerp auction catalogues even began announcing measures for facilitating participation of foreigners. They also refer explicitly to the practice of buying via local agents for foreign art lovers unable to attend an auction.[14]

In their creation of a new type of auction and a search for another audience, the endeavours of art and book dealers closely resembled changes in the eighteenth-century leisure culture of Antwerp's high society. The driving force behind these transformations was the growing need of the local elite to distinguish themselves from the lower strata, not only in social and economic terms but most overtly in geographical terms. During the eighteenth century the Antwerp privileged increasingly pursued spatial segregation in daily life and in leisure. Such segregation included leaving the old city centre to inhabit spacious houses in the outskirts of town, abandoning crowded market squares to shop in small boutiques, and turning away from popular plays at the Great Market to indulge in new French theatre at the Tapissierspand. This quest for distinction had a strong spatial characteristic, shifting from the old city centre to the arterial roads and the town periphery (Blondé, 2001a: 510; Blondé, 2001b). The new auctioneers propagated the same idea of differentiation by redistributing the luxury second-hand trade from the traditional Friday Market to the Kolveniers- or Oude Voetbogenhof and, more importantly, by simultaneously transforming the auction from a purely economic transaction to a dignified cultural event, hereby following earlier Dutch and French, in particular the Parisian dealer Gersaint (McClellan, 1996; De Marchi and Van Miegroet, 2006). Their approach proved fruitful, and a small group of local well-off collectors found appeal in the lofty language and auction atmosphere, especially as a site where they could meet and deal with kindred spirits. There were no official restrictions to participate in these luxury auctions, although numerous informal thresholds prevented random consumers and passerbys from joining the bidding.[15] Unlike the public sales on the square of the Friday

14 The following Antwerp catalogues advertised measures to attract 'étrangers': the Delvigne-sale, (24/7/1780), Knijff-sale (18/7/1785), Proli-sale (18/7/1785), M.J.F. Beschey (21/8/1787) and an anonymous sale (30/8/1788), of which catalogues can be found in the library of the Royal Museum of Fine Arts Antwerp (KMSKA) and the City Library Antwerp (SBA). Regarding the buying from a distance and the use of local agents: 'Du moins qu'ils daigneront y envoyer leurs Commissionaires afin d'y effectuer leurs ordres' (SBA, Catalogue anonymous sale, Antwerp, 30/8/1788) and 'les Amateurs qui ne pourront se trouver en personne à cette vente' (KMSKB, Catalogue anonymous sale, Brussels, 11/11/1793).

15 For the first decades of the nineteenth century however there are signals of restrictions to participate in Antwerp art auctions, such as paid entrance tickets and obtaining a catalogue as entrance permit.

Market, these auctions had a notably private character. And although their impact on late eighteenth-century Antwerp society in general was perhaps limited, the continuing information flow and transport revolution ensured a steady supply of curious customers from nearby cities and abroad. The modern international auction, arising from the ruins of the declining second-hand markets, had seen daylight.

Bibliography

Primary Sources

Unpublished sources

Openbaar Centrum voor Maatschappelijk Welzijn-Archief Antwerpen (OCMW-AA), *Oud archief* (OA), Kamer der Huisarmen, 967 and 968.

Stadsarchief Antwerpen (SAA), *Gilden en Ambachten (GA)*, 4293, Lawsuit of the deans of the corporation of second-hand cloth dealers against Joannes van Lemens (September sixteenth 1744).

Stadsarchief Antwerpen (SAA), *Gilden en Ambachten (GA)*, 4632, Ouden Voetboog Resolutie Boeck 1661–1792, 1770–1772.

Unpublished database of Antwerp and Brussels' art auction catalogues (1716–1794).

Published sources

Bibliotheek van het Koninklijk Museum voor Schone Kunsten, Antwerpen (KMSKA), Catalogue Delvigne, Antwerp (24/7/1780), Catalogue Knijff, Antwerp (18/7/1785), Catalogue Proli, Antwerp (18/7/1785) and Catalogue M.J.F. Beschey, Antwerp (21/8/1787).

Bibliotheek van het Koninklijk Museum voor Schone Kunsten, Brussel (KMSKB), Catalogue anonymous sale, Brussels (11/11/1793).

Bibliothèque Nationale Paris (BNP), *Cabinet des Estampes (CDE)*, Catalogue Pierre Snijers, Antwerp (22/8/1752) and Catalogue Wouters, Brussels (1/4/1794).

Stadsbibliotheek Antwerpen (SBA), Catalogue anonymous sale, Antwerp (30/8/1788); *Gazette van Antwerpen (GvA)*, 1730, 1750, 1770 and 1790.

Literature

Alvarez, M.-T. (2007) 'The Almoneda: the second-hand art market in Spain', Warren, J. and Turpin, A. (eds.), *Auctions, Agents and Dealers. The Mechanisms of the Art Market 1660–1830*, Oxford, 33–39.

Blondé, B. (2001a) 'Indicatoren van het luxeverbruik? Paardenbezit en conspicuous consumption te Antwerpen (zeventiende-achttiende eeuw)', *Bijdragen tot de Geschiedenis*, 84, 4, 497–512.

Blondé, B. (2001b) *Cultural transfers in European cities. The social importance of changing consumption patterns, urban manners and the use of space in Antwerp, sixteenth-eighteenth centuries* (unpublished paper, European Science Foundation, Ghent, May 10th and 11th 2001).

Blondé, B. (2002) 'Tableware and changing consumer patterns. Dynamics of material culture in Antwerp, seventeenth-eighteenth centuries', Veeckman, J. (ed.), *Majolica and Glass. From Italy to Antwerp and beyond. The transfer of technology in the sixteenth-early seventeenth century*, Antwerp, 295–311.

Blondé, B. (2006) 'Cities in decline and the dawn of a consumer society: Antwerp in the seventeenth-eighteenth centuries', Blondé, B. et al (eds.), *Retailers and consumer changes in Early Modern Europe. England, France, Italy and the Low Countries*, Tours, 37–52.

Blondé, B. and Van Damme, I. (2007) 'Een crisis als uitdaging? Kleinhandelsevoluties en verbruiksveranderingen te Antwerpen (ca. 1648-ca. 1748)' *Tijdschrift voor Sociale en Economische Geschiedenis*, 4, 61–88.

Broersma, M. (2002) *Beschaafde vooruitgang. De wereld van de Leeuwarder Courant 1752–2002*, Leeuwarden.

Campbell, C. (2001) 'The desire for the new. Its nature and social location as presented in theories of fashion and modern consumerism', Miller, D. (ed.), *Consumption. Critical concepts in the social sciences*, vol. 1, London/New York, 246–261.

Cox, N. (2000) *The complete tradesman. A study of retailing, 1550–1820*, Aldershot.

Deceulaer, H. (2001) *Pluriforme patronen en een verschillende snit. Sociaal-economische, institutionele en culturele transformaties in de kledingsector in Antwerpen, Brussel en Gent, 1585–1800*, Antwerp.

Deijnckens, L. (1988) *De kunsthandel in Antwerpen in de zeventiende eeuw* (unpublished MA thesis), Leuven.

Delsaerdt, P. and Vanysacker, D. (1997) 'Repertorium van Antwerpse boekenveilingen 1750–1800', *De Gulden Passer*, 75, 5–119.

De Marchi, N. and Van Miegroet, H. (2006) 'Transforming the Paris Art Market, 1718–1750', De Marchi, N. and Van Miegroet, H. (eds.), *Mapping markets for paintings in Europe and the New World, 1450–1750*, Turnhout, 391–402.

De Poorter, N. and Huvenne, P. (1981) 'Het kolveniershof te Antwerpen', *Feestbundel bij de opening van het Kolveniershof en het Rubenianum*, Antwerp, 25–45.

De Staelen, C. (2002) *Levenswijze en consumptiepatroon van een Antwerpse weduwe. Het huishoudjournaal van Elisabeth Moretus (1664–1675)* (unpublished MA thesis), Ghent.

Ferdinand, C.Y. (1993) 'Selling it to the provinces: news and commerce round eighteenth-century Salisbury', Brewer, J. and Porter, R. (eds.), *Consumption and the world of goods*, London/New York, 393–411.

Feyel, G. (2000) *L'annonce et la nouvelle: la presse d'information en France sous l'Ancien Régime (1630–1788)*, Oxford.

Fontaine, L. (ed.) (2008) *Alternative exchanges. Second-hand circulation from the sixteenth century to today*, Oxford/New York.

Luypaers, C. (2001) *'Le goût pour les spectacles est tellement devenu à la mode'. Spektakelcultuur in het achttiende-eeuwse Antwerpen* (unpublished MA thesis), Leuven.

Lyna, D. (forthcoming) 'Somewhere between old and new. Selling second-hand artwork in eighteenth-century Antwerp', Van Damme, I. and Stobart, J., (eds.), *Modernity & second-hand trade, 1680–1900.*

Lyna, D. and Van Damme, I. (2009) 'A strategy of seduction? The role of commercial advertisements in the eighteenth-century retailing business of Antwerp', *Business History*, 51, 100–120.

Lyna, D. and Vermeylen, F. (forthcoming) 'Hammering Rubens. Art auctions in Antwerp during the seventeenth and eighteenth centuries', Vermeylen, F., Vlieghe, H. and Lyna, D. (eds.), *Art auctions and dealers. The dissemination of Netherlandish art during the Ancien Régime.*

McClellan, A. (1996) 'Watteau's Dealer: Gersaint and the Marketing of Art', *Art Bulletin*, 78, 439–453.

McKendrick, N. (1982) 'The consumer revolution in eighteenth-century England', McKendrick, N. et al (eds.), *The birth of a consumer society. The commercialization of eighteenth-century England*, London, 9–33.

Montias, M. (2002) *Art at auction in seventeenth century Amsterdam*, Amsterdam.

Remeysen, J. (1947) *Bibliografie van de Antwerpse boekenveilingen, 1652–1947*, Antwerp.

Soly, H. (1977) *Urbanisme en kapitalisme te Antwerpen in de 16de eeuw. De stedebouwkundige en industriële ondernemingen van Gilbert van Schoonbeke*, Brussels.

Todd, C. (1989) 'French advertising in the eighteenth century', *Studies on Voltaire and the eighteenth century*, 266, 513–547.

Van Damme, I. (2006) 'Changing consumer preferences and evolutions in retailing. Buying and selling consumer durables in Antwerp (c. 1648-c 1748)', Blondé, B., Stabel, P., Stobart, J. and Van Damme, I. (eds.), *Buyers and sellers. Retail circuits and practices in Medieval and Early Modern Europe*, Turnhout, 199–223.

Van Damme, I. (2007) *Verleiden en verkopen. Antwerpse kleinhandelaars en hun klanten in tijden van crisis (ca. 1648-ca. 1748)*, Amsterdam.

Voet, L. (1952) 'Boeken en drukkers', *Antwerpen in de XVIIde eeuw. Instellingen-economie-cultuur*, Antwerp, 314–347.

Von Stockhausen, T. (2005) 'Formen des ordnens: auktionskataloge des 18. jahrhunderts als beginn der modernen kunstgeschichte', Bertsch, M. and Grave, J. (eds.), *Räume der kunst. Blicke auf Goethes sammlungen*, Göttingen, 89–101.

Walker, R.B. (1975) 'Advertising in London newspapers 1650-1750', *Business History*, 15, 112–130.

Wall, C. (1997) 'The English Auction: Narratives of Dismantlings', *Eighteenth-Century Studies*, 31, 1–25.

Woodward, D. (1985) "Swords into ploughshares': Recycling in Pre-industrial England', *Economic history review*, 38, 175–191.

CHAPTER 12

The Indispensable Market: Auctions in Sweden in the Eighteenth and Nineteenth Centuries

Kristina Lilja, Sofia Murhem, Göran Ulväng – Uppsala University, Sweden

12.1 Introduction

Today, the auction is usually either an exclusive venue for wealthy collectors or a popular event during the summer where people go bargain hunting. Seldom is it part of regular consumption. In this chapter, we argue that this was very different during the eighteenth and nineteenth centuries. Auctions were regular market places providing all social groups with a plethora of objects: from real estate to foods stuffs. Using a unique source, namely, the Swedish auction records which encompass hundreds of thousands of goods sold by auction, we assess what was bought at the auctions and by whom.

The auction was probably one of the most important sources for second-hand consumption, a subject which has gained increasing attention during the past few years. Resent research has shown that during the eighteenth and nineteenth centuries second-hand consumption was an important source for accessing goods as well as realising possible assets. We know that second-hand retailing took place in a variety of ways, including peddling, pawn-broking, markets and auctions. Nevertheless, the size, scope and function of second-hand retailing are to a great extent unknown, mainly due to lack of good sources. The Swedish material, however, makes it possible to gain new knowledge about the apparently large and widespread second-hand retail. Through the auction records, we can shed new light on consumption in general and second-hand consumption in particular, allowing us to challenge the established picture of the development of consumption. This chapter deals with the second-hand retail of goods at Swedish auctions during the eighteenth and nineteenth centuries.

12.2 Second-Hand Consumption in the Eighteenth and Nineteenth Centuries

The industrial revolution caused economic growth but not an immediate general increase in real wages. According to Pomerantz, consumption in general in Europe remained more or less stable in the first half of the nineteenth century (Pomerantz, 2000: 117–122). Given that Sweden industrialised relatively late, it is unsurprising that it was not until the second half of the nineteenth century that real wages increased in Sweden – a position reflected in Britain, Germany and France (Trentmann, 2004: 381). Nevertheless, there is evidence of change in the composition of consumption parallel to the industrial revolution. De Vries points to the fact that probate inventories show an increased proportion of durable and novel goods, despite more or less static real wages. He denotes this change the 'industrious revolution', emphasising an altered demand for new commodities produced outside the household – a new consumption made possible through the reallocation of resources within the household (De Vries, 1993: 107, 177). This demand was found not only among the very well off but also among the middle class and the poorer sections of society. Maxine Berg calls it a 'rapidly growing and socially diversified demand which provided the basis for the sale of goods as commodities rather than as personal creations' (Berg, 2002: 3). A transformation of the composition of demand in the direction of more durable goods was certainly possible without there being any increase in overall consumption, as claimed by Pomerantz. However, it is also possible that consumption estimates based on production and import figures have underestimated the real level of consumption, as they do not include second-hand consumption.

As this chapter will show, second-hand consumption was considerable during the eighteenth and nineteenth centuries. Growth in the demand for more durable goods, which Ahlberger (1996) has shown was also seen in Sweden, would also have affected the second-hand market since such goods were precisely those suitable for recycling. If domestic production and imports could not satisfy the demand for such goods at a price level that customers, especially middle and lower rank customers, could afford, then second-hand consumption would become an attractive alternative. Stena Nenadic's study of Scottish auctions held following deaths and bankruptcies shows that, before 1800, middle-rank consumers used auctions as means of buying furniture and household goods, which were of high use-value but of low status-value. The lack of skilled craftsmen made high quality furniture rare and difficult to obtain, and thus it was often recycled among middle-rank consumers. However, after 1800 the middle ranks had other means of accessing suitable goods and working people took over the auctions (Nenadic, 1994: 130–134). Beverly Lemire (1988, 1991, 1997 and 2005) claims that a second-hand market for clothes emerged in England during the eighteenth century. As the value of clothes was relative stable, they could be used for cash by those in temporary economic difficulties, thus enabling other consumption. The seller received cash, whilst the buyer could consume clothes at an affordable price. Hence, the market for clothes was much larger than what is evident if we look only at the market for new items, allowing people with limited means to be part of consumerism. Focusing on the second-hand market in Venice between 1450 and 1700, Allerston (1996, 1998 and 2000) maintains that access to second-hand circuits meant that consumers could use clothing as economic security and that consumption, in the case of marriages, has been overestimated, as goods could be bought second hand. In all, second-hand retail meant that both the circulation and supply, of goods improved considerably during the eighteenth century. Lemire (1988) argues that the scale of second-hand retail in clothes and its duration was connected with industrialisation: when new and fashionable clothes became affordable for the lower classes, the demand for second-hand clothes diminished, as it did in London during the 1870s, due partly to the now reasonably priced English muslin.

We might thus conclude that second-hand retail is dependent on offering something lacking in 'regular' or first-hand circuits of exchange. Such advantages have to be enough to outweigh the possible disadvantages of buying and selling second-hand goods. Such disadvantages might, in the case of auctions, be that items were less accessible compared to buying in shops, that they were less fashionable, in worse condition or of unknown provenance. In the case of Scotland before 1800, the lack of skilled craftsmen made quality such an advantage, but price was usually the compensating factor. But when an object is a collector's item, its value to the collector, rather than its price, is the reason for purchase on the second-hand market. The vast majority of auctions discussed here were not for collectors, however. Instead, they were market-places for goods intended for daily use. Auctions for collectibles and antiquities were rare in Sweden until the late nineteenth century.

12.3 Auctions: a Market-Place for Second-Hand Goods

As a means of second-hand consumption, the auction was popular in Sweden during the eighteenth and nineteenth centuries. There was an auction house or an auctioneer in most Swedish towns from the eighteenth century onwards and local auctioneers were active in the surrounding countryside. The oldest known regulated auction in Sweden dates from 1639, when Uppsala University inaugurated an establishment for auctioning goods (Almén, 1897: 130). In the following decades, auctions and the terms for auctioning goods were regulated in Swedish law. It was most likely in 1664 that the first book auction was held in Stockholm. A catalogue was printed of a collection of books owned by the court counsellor and director Henrik de Moucherons. The terms of the auction were printed not only in Swedish but also in Dutch and Latin (Lundell, 1974: 14).

From a comparatively extensive regulation of auction chambers in 1674, it is clear that the main motives for auctions were either voluntary, such as a need for cash, or forced, by bankruptcy for example. The auction was a marketplace for selling goods in general. When needed, the auction could be used to quickly transform goods into cash and make it possible to pay debts by selling consumer durables. The auction chamber decree seems to have influenced how auctions were organised in other parts of the country (Lundell, 1974: 24–30). Swedish auction houses were given privileges to act as monopolists in a given city. This was disputed several times in Stockholm, when competitors tried to challenge the monopoly by holding auctions just outside the city walls. This caused the King to declare in 1772 that the privileges of the Stockholm Auction House (*Stockholms Auktionsverk)* were extended to include these areas as well. Other towns were entitled to enforce monopolies on auctions within the town walls, but auctions held outside the city walls were in general not restricted.

As monopolists, the auction houses held sales that dealt with everything from real estate to the most humble items. Auctions were held whenever there was a need: in some places several days a month. The items sold at the auctions reflect local business structures as well as economic conditions, with farm equipment, animals and grain being more common at countryside auctions. In cities, we often find merchants' goods at auctions, either in the form of unneeded stock or the results of bankruptcy. This is unsurprising as the laws restricted trade and commerce to the cities until the middle of the nineteenth century (Magnusson, 1996: 244). In the very largest cities, auctions were bigger than those held in the countryside, both in terms of the number of lots sold and their total value.

There were various kinds of auctions. Some were voluntary; others were held to sell off the estate of the deceased. As mentioned above, auctions were also used as a means of realising cash in cases of bankruptcy, in which case, goods might be new or second hand.

Figure 12.1. Sellers queuing outside the Stockholm Auction House in 1868 with items they wish to sell

Source: G. Broling in *Ny Illustrerad Tidning*, 1868.

After the main sale it was usual for people to sell a few items, so as to get cash or get rid of surplus items. In addition, there were special auctions for real estate and leases. Most post-mortem auctions were held in the house of the deceased, whilst large bankruptcy auctions were usually held on the premises of the firm in question. Public or regular auctions were held in public buildings or in the auction house's own rooms. Such auctions became an increasingly common phenomenon in nineteenth-century towns, whilst house auctions remained popular in the countryside. Auctions held regularly in the same place eased public access, not least because the size of public buildings and auction rooms meant that more people could be accommodated than was possible in most private houses. Stocks, bonds and lottery tickets were also sold at auctions in the late nineteenth century. However, this was a dying practise. As society became more monetarised, the Stockholm Exchange of Bonds was established in 1861 on the initiative of the Stockholm Chamber of Commerce. The buying and selling of shares was then transferred to its own special marketplace which began operating in 1863 (Algott, 1963: 6–16).

In Stockholm, auctions were held twice a week – on Mondays and Thursdays – until 1858, when the number of auctions per week was increased to four or even six during the busiest periods: normally the spring and autumn. Until the end of the nineteenth century, an auction house servant rang a bell at 8 o'clock in the morning to call the public. Just before the auction began, the bell was again rung and the auction declared open. The goods – or in the case of real estate or stocks, documents concerning them – were displayed to the public on the day or days before the actual auction (Lundell, 1974: 51 and 63–64). During the nineteenth century, auctions were also announced by advertisements in papers and on posters. The inspector on duty, who announced the auction and the terms of payment, supervised Stockholm auctions. Immediately after the auction, the notary had to sign the protocol and the inspector established its accuracy. The auctioneer earned a fee on the sale which varied between 1.5 and 3 per cent, depending on the goods for sale. In addition there was a buyer's premium for every lot sold (Lundell, 1974: 64–65).

In the Swedish archives, we can gain access to information on the second-hand consumption of all social groups and all kinds of goods. Whilst other research concerning auctions, little as there is, has been confined to published action catalogues, and thus limited to valuable assets, we can study urban and rural auctions with goods ranging from valuable art, weapons and furniture, to food, clothes, household goods and even once, notably, a manure heap.

Most studies of consumption in both Sweden and in the rest of Europe are based on inventories. This means that not only do we lack knowledge of consumption by poor people, and in many countries of women's consumption, but also that we know little about consumption during the life cycle, as we only know what people had left when they died. Consumption of less durable goods may therefore be underestimated and we may see changes in consumption only after some time, as there is an inevitable if variable time lag between a good being acquired and its appearance in a probate inventory. This chapter explores second-hand consumption in Sweden as shown in the records of two auction houses: those in Stockholm (*Stockholms Auktionsverk*) and Enköping (*Enköpings Auktionsverk*). The former was situated in the capital of Sweden and the latter in a small country town, about 81 kilometres west of Stockholm. We also use material from country house auctions in the vicinity of Enköping.

All Swedish auction houses were obliged to preserve their records (Lundell, 1974: 24–29 and 40–51), which today offer a remarkably rich source of information on second-hand consumption in Sweden. At the auction, the buyer seldom paid cash. Instead they were given credit, usually until the end of the business year (the first of November), meaning that the period of time before the buyer actually had to pay could extend to several months. Because of the system of giving credit, buyers were also noted in the auction records, often with their title. Moreover, the records clearly state that the bidder was the actual buyer: when there was bidding by proxy, both the proxy and the real buyer were noted. The same was true for the sellers: the titles given were usually occupational or, for women, denoted marital status. If a person's title is missing, it is possible to trace them in the clerical survey books kept at this time by the church. The auction records thus form tables, showing buyer, seller, item and price. The reason for the auction (for example, bankruptcy) was also written down, as were commissions for the auctioneer, the name of the notary, and the cost of advertising and so on.

12.4 Auctions in Stockholm and Enköping

Consumption has been one of the most researched areas in economic history. Yet the notion of a consumer society has been increasingly questioned in recent years and to some extent replaced by greater emphasis on the ways in which groups have used consumption to create a desired socio-cultural identity (Smith, 2002). In this context, discussion has often centred on the ways in which groups position themselves against each other, as well as how they interact within the group and create a mutual cultural and social language, thus constructing their identity (see for instance Douglas and Isherwood, 1996). To this should be added the development of the economy: not only did the eighteenth and nineteenth centuries witness the creation of industrial modernity, but the increased wealth also encouraged a democratisation of demand (Berg, 1999).

The Stockholm Auction House was founded in 1674 and held auctions with items ranging from royal sales of estates to the most humble objects. This reflected the size and importance of Stockholm within Swedish society and economy: its 1780 population (of about 75,000) had doubled by 1870, much of the growth being due to high levels of in-migration. During the period studied here, a large proportion of Swedish foreign trade emanated from Stockholm, which in turn meant that a considerable part of the production of the surrounding regions ended up in the city, either for re-selling abroad or to provide for the growing population. The dynamics of the city's business life was such as to make it known as the capital of Swedish industrialism (Ericson, 2001: 63, 100 and 104). Enköping, whose Auction House was founded in 1720, was a very different place: during the eighteenth and nineteenth centuries, it was a small rural and agrarian town. In the beginning of the eighteenth century, Enköping had about 500 inhabitants, and one hundred years later the population was about twice that. The nineteenth century witnessed a marked expansion of the town and, by the end of the century, there were about 4,000 inhabitants. Yet farming remained an important part of the town's economy. Like all Swedish towns at that time, Enköping was the regional centre for the surrounding countryside: its merchants were responsible for trade and the manufacturing of goods and services for both the town and its hinterland (Kjellberg, 1905: 498–508).

Due to the vast extent of the records, two years were selected. In 1781, 183 auctions were organised by the Stockholm Auction House; in 1760 there were 12 auctions at the Enköping Auction House. In 1870, 365 auctions were held in Stockholm and again 12 auctions in Enköping. In order the produce manageable and comparable figures for the two Houses, we have sampled the auctions held by the Stockholm Auction House, taking the records of a single notary in May and October of both 1781 and 1870. The data for Stockholm are thus based on 12 auctions in 1781 and 13 auctions in 1870 – approximately 5 percent of the auctions held these two years. All auctions held by Enköping Auction House in 1760 and 1870 are included.

A large number of lots were sold at the auctions, some consisting of a single item, others of several objects together, meaning that the number of goods sold at a given auction could easily exceed the number of lots. In 1781, about 31,000 lots were auctioned in Stockholm; this figure which had doubled by 1870. In Enköping, 1,029 lots were auctioneered in 1760, and 1,956 in 1870. In many instances the quality of the goods was sometimes stated: silver and gold items were described and their weights given, and clothes, especially more expensive items, were described by colour and style. When Christina Orre, the daughter of a wealthy burgher in Enköping, died in 1760, all her belongings were sold at an auction. These included a green striped skirt, a blue-and-white striped linen cloth cardigan, a blue striped apron, a dotted linen cloth cardigan, white and red wool socks, and a black satin skirt. The master mason Erik Söderblom of Enköping left after his death a blue broadcloth coat, a yellow-brown coat, a sheepskin coat, and a black broadcloth shirt – all to be sold at an auction the same year.

12.5 Sellers at the Auctions

We find persons from all social categories in the auction records as both buyers and sellers, including counts and countesses, mayors, merchants, carpenters, workers and servants. We have divided them into four status/occupational groups: *persons of rank* (officers and landed proprietors or gentry); *burghers and civil servants* (merchants, craftsmen and civil servants living in the city); *peasants* (people living in the countryside with their own or leased land), and *landless*, (people without property). There are also people we have not yet been able to identify: some without a title and others who paid cash. These people have been classified as *others*, although most likely they were landless.

The four groups are far from homogeneous, of course, but roughly divide the actors according to status and wealth. The first group, the persons of rank, is the highest in status and in most cases also the wealthiest. Burghers and civil servants equate with Nenadic's middle-rank consumers and increased in both numbers and wealth from the eighteenth century onwards, sometimes rising to join the titled: successful merchants were knighted and rich craftsmen bought country houses. In general, though, they were reasonably and increasingly well-off, often owning their own property in the city. The peasants were lower in status, but were in certain instances as wealthy as burghers. They differed in that they did not live in the city and were to a larger extent self-supporting. The last group, the landless, were the poorest. At the start of the study period they were often without their own household, but later in the nineteenth century most had their own home, albeit a poor one.

Sellers were a relatively homogeneous group, with *Burgers and civil servants* totally dominating at the auctions in Stockholm and Enköping, (Table 12.1.). Those in the former had a slightly more diverse range of sellers: the *landless* category already comprising 17 per cent of the sellers in the eighteenth century; this figure rose to 20 per cent a hundred years later. In Enköping, burghers and civil servants dominated as sellers throughout the eighteenth and nineteenth centuries, but peasants and the landless increased their share as a result of growing economic wealth in the lower levels of society. This is more obvious if we include the 'others' group, which most likely consisted of landless people. Also the numbers of lots increased, showing that the auctions grew in size in the nineteenth century.

Both men and women were active at auctions. This may seem surprising, given that Swedish women during this period were under the guardianship of their husbands or fathers, unless they were widows, in which case they were considered to be of age, both financially and legally. Despite this, women made up 17 per cent of the sellers in Stockholm in 1781 and 31 per cent in Enköping in 1760. Virtually all women who sold goods were *burghers*. In 1870, 42 per cent of the sellers in Stockholm were women, while in Enköping women accounted for 14 per cent. The reason the high percentage of women sellers was maintained in Stockholm was probably because women in the larger cities, in comparison to women in the countryside, managed their own households and were financially active (Magnusson, 1996: 340). The reason women sellers became less common in the town of Enköping can be explained by the fact that burghers in general became less frequent sellers and that women of lower social orders seldom owned objects of such value that they could

Table 12.1. Sellers at auctions organised by Enköping Auction House and Stockholm Auction House, per cent

	Stockholm 1781	Enköping 1760	Stockholm 1870	Enköping 1870
Persons of rank	5	0	1	1
Burghers and civil servants	75	100	59	77
Peasants	0	0	0	6
Landless	17	0	20	2
Others	3	0	20	14
Total	100	100	100	100
Number	41	14	58	33

Source: Stockholm Auction House in 1781 and 1870 and also from Enköping Auction House in 1760 and 1870.

be sold at an auction. Estates of deceased women of prosperity were more likely to be sold in larger cities, where better prices could be reached.

12.6 Buyers at the Auctions

The auction was an important source of affordable goods for the population of the capital. As a consequence, a large number of people visited the auctions and bidding was lively. In 1781, 355 people bought one or more items at the auctions studied here, a figure that rose to 740 by 1870 (Table 12.2.). Enköping had only about 500 inhabitants in 1760, yet as many as 287 people visited auctions and bought objects, meaning that the majority of households in the town were buying goods at auction. Many of them were regulars who visited several auctions and bought several lots. By 1870, out of Enköping's total population of 1,000, 634 different people bought objects at one or more auctions. As the majorities of the inhabitants had limited means and had to find affordable items to buy, the auction remained an important marketplace.

Burghers and civil servants were the dominating category of buyers, but *peasants* and the *landless* also bought items at auctions in Stockholm and Enköping (Table 12.2.). The latter groups became more common as buyers in the nineteenth century. Economic growth made it possible for the wealthier to buy new goods, whilst economic growth also meant that those previously too poor to buy any or only very few items now could afford more goods (albeit second-hand goods). Of course, because the landless bought less valuable goods, the burgers' purchases still remained higher in their overall value.

For a comparatively large proportion of buyers at the auctions in Stockholm titles were not given and we have not been able to accurately identify them from church records. Hence there is a large number of *others* in Table 12.2. From the family names, we have assumed for 1781 that most of those without a title were burghers, but this is not yet confirmed. Probably, most of the *others* in 1870 were labourers, *landless*, rather than *persons of rank* or *burghers and civil servants* who in general would have used their titles by this date. In Enköping, several of those who visited the auctions came from the

TABLE 12.2. Buyers at auctions organised by Enköping Auction House and Stockholm Auction House, per cent

	Stockholm 1781	Enköping 1760	Stockholm 1870	Enköping 1870
Persons of rank	7	1	1	0
Burghers and civil servants	49	90	42	49
Peasants	0	6	0	23
Landless	2	1	27	21
Others	42	2	30	7
Total	100	100	100	100
Number	355	287	740	634

SOURCE: Stockholm Auction House in 1781 and 1870 and also from Enköping Auction House in 1760 and 1870.

surrounding countryside, a phenomenon which seems to have increased during the nineteenth century. The growth of the town's population and increasing trade had made Enköping more of a regional commercial centre by that time.

Auction goods were not always used goods. Sometimes merchants used the auction as another form of selling new or unused goods. This meant that merchants played an important part as sellers and buyers, not least because auctions were used for selling stock from one merchant to another. In Stockholm, the auction gradually turned from private sales to business sales in the nineteenth century, while they retained their private character in Enköping. In Enköping, merchants were comparatively rare at the auctions. Most items were sold and/or bought by private individuals for private use. Increasingly in nineteenth-century Stockholm, the typical auction seller was not a private person but a wholesaler or merchant using the auction to pass on goods difficult to sell in the 'regular' way or as a means of increasing business liquidity. The auction records include notes on objects that were returned to the seller when the asking price was not met. Two thirds of such lots were offered by wholesalers or merchants. Merchants also passed on goods to one another. This is also reflected in the higher value of Stockholm lots compared to those of Enköping. For instance, merchant Nylander bought 10 bottles of sherry from merchant Hjerta at an auction in Stockholm in 1870. His interest in wine and spirits was shared by another Stockholm merchant, Otterdahl, who among other items bought 462 bottles of brandy from city broker Pauli. Merchant Liepa was more interested in buying plants. The same year, he bought 5 Seville orange trees, 100 pot plants and 4 myrtles, among other plants auctioned by gardener Blomberg at a house auction. Altogether, the auctions in Stockholm in the late nineteenth century were more of a marketplace for merchants and wholesalers, buying and selling both new and used goods, than one for consumers.

Women often visited auctions and made up 17 per cent of buyers in Stockholm in 1781 and 27 per cent in Enköping in 1760. One hundred years later, about one in four buyers at the auctions in both Enköping and Stockholm were women. In many cases, the same women attended several auctions, most often when the sellers were also women.

A clear example is the fashion dealer Mathilda Carlsson, who visited four sales at the Stockholm Auction House during March 1870, buying twelve lots mostly of household items. Almost all the lots that she bought were sold by women. The presence of such women in the auction records suggests that, although they had a legal position that theoretically would hamper them in acting as economic agents, in practise they could act at least with a limited independence. There are also several examples when both husband and wife attended and bought goods at the same auction. For instance, Mrs Boman, the wife of a Stockholm clothes broker, attended several auctions in Stockholm in 1781 accompanied by her husband. She bought furniture, including a chest of drawers and a bed, and textiles such as curtains and bed clothes; her husband bought metal household goods such as a pewter coffee pot and a brass lamp. Similarly, Mrs Mattsson appears to have attended auctions that her husband, a trader, was unable to attend. She went to six auctions in 1870 and bought 43 lots. Her husband visited only the auction with goods from gardener Blomberg. Mrs Mattson bought textiles, household goods, clothes and some furniture, but she also bought a firearm and some tools. Most of the lots bought by Mrs Boman and Mrs Mattson are good examples of the kind of objects generally bought by women at auctions. It is clear from the records that the value of the goods bought by women was considerably lower than those bought by men. Thus, whilst women bought just below half of the lots sold in Stockholm in 1870, the total value of their purchases was barely one-fifth of the value of those bought by the men.

Women entrepreneurs used the auctions as well. For instance, the clothes broker Helena Åkerberg visited three of the thirteen sampled auctions in 1870. She bought twelve lots, mostly clothes. The seamstress Fredrika Westerberg bought eight lots, all consisting of clothes. It is likely that the clothes these two women bought were for resale, either as they were or after alterations.

12.7 Goods Sold on the Auctions

To analyse the kinds of items being bought and sold, we have divided the auction goods into a number of broad categories: *Foodstuffs and liquor, farming and outdoor equipment, construction materials, animals, furniture, textiles, household (metal), household (pottery/china), household (other), books, weapons, clothes (under), clothes (outer) and other*. Unsurprisingly, the greater size and more complex social structure of Stockholm is reflected in the goods sold. In the late eighteenth century, the percentage of *furniture* and *clothing* sold in the Stockholm auctions was much greater than that in Enköping: one half compared with one-third (Figures 12.2. and 12.3.). Instead, more *foodstuffs* and *liquor* were sold in Enköping. Not surprisingly *farming and other outdoor equipment, construction materials and animals* were more common in Enköping in the eighteenth century, as were *household utensils*. The large number of goods found in the category *other* is because there are many objects that we have been unable to identify with certainty – a problem which is most severe for Enköping in 1760. We can assume that most of these were *household utensils* of different kinds, *farming and other outdoor equipment* and *construction materials*.

The single largest category of goods sold at the auctions in both Stockholm and Enköping in both the eighteenth and nineteenth century were *household utensils*

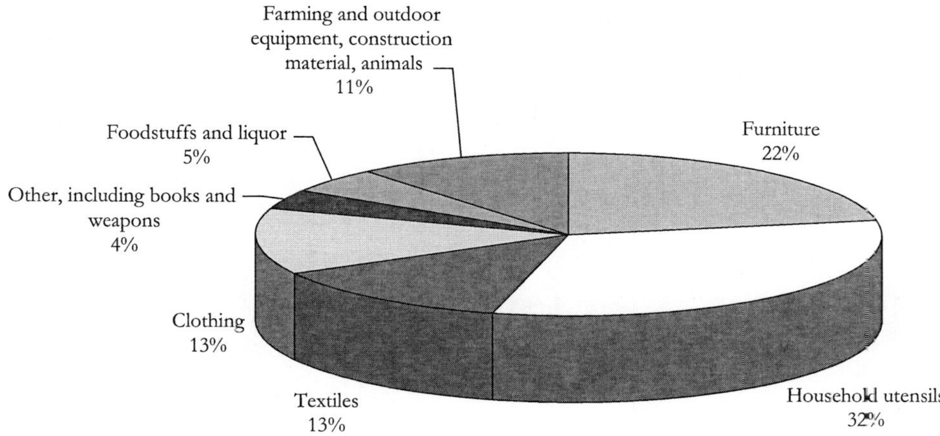

FIGURE 12.2. Categories of Goods Sold at the Stockholm Auction House 1781, per cent

SOURCE: Auction records from Stockholm Auction House in 1781.

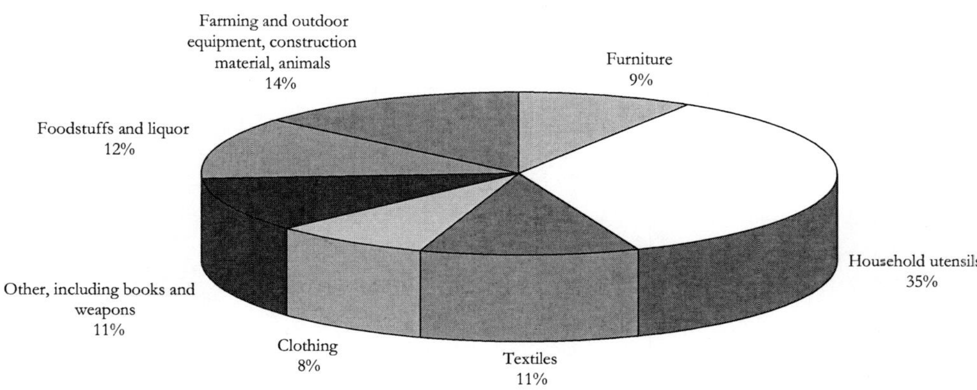

FIGURE 12.3. Categories of Goods Sold at the Enköping Auction House 1760, per cent

SOURCE: Auction records from Enköping Auction House 1760.

(see Figures 12.2.–12.5.). However, this apparent stability is misleading because, as we shall see later, their quality could vary considerably. More obvious changes arose from the growing tendency for professional ironmongers to use the auctions as means of distributing their goods, As a result, *farming and outdoor equipment, construction materials and animals* increased their percentage of the sold goods (compare Figures 12.2. and 12.4.). Moreover, the growth of Stockholm and its housing stock (Ericson, 2001: 63–72) is reflected in the large amount of *construction material* sold at the auctions. Apart from this, merchants bought mainly *foodstuffs and liquor* in late nineteenth-century Stockholm. In contrast, the category *clothing* decreased considerably – a result of the increased supply of clothes in the city's growing number of shops, much as Lemire (1997) has argued. Fashion may also

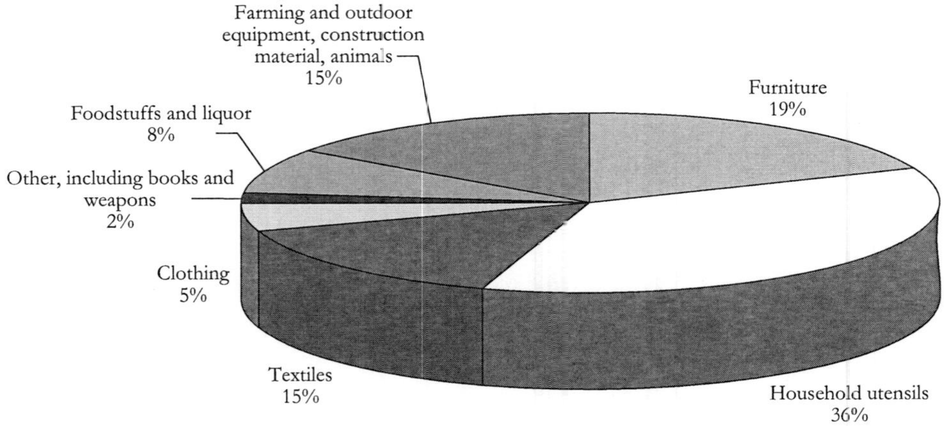

FIGURE 12.4. Categories of Goods Sold at the Stockholm Auction House 1870, per cent

SOURCE: Auction records from Stockholm Auction House in 1870.

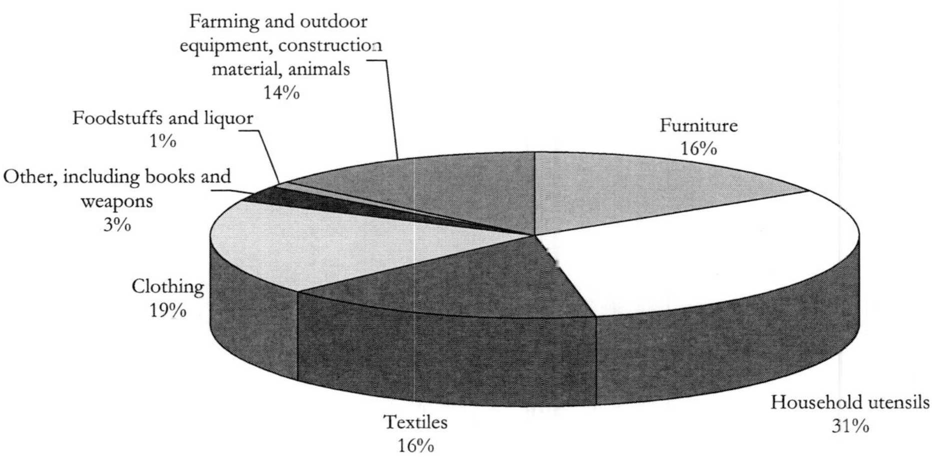

FIGURE 12.5. Categories of Goods Sold at the Enköping Auction House 1870, per cent

SOURCE: Auction records from Enköping Auction House 1870.

have been more important in the capital than in country towns and we can also assume the consumer society was more developed in Stockholm.

As in Stockholm, *farming and outdoor equipment, construction materials and animals* still made up a considerable proportion of auction lots bought in Enköping in 1870 (Figure 12.5.). A significant change, compared to the eighteenth century, is that *clothing* was increasingly important – a trend much more apparent here than in Stockholm. Also, *textiles* and *furniture* were increasingly important. Taken together, these three categories made up half of all lots sold in late nineteenth-century Enköping. This is probably due to the fact that more buyers and sellers belonged to the categories *peasant* and *landless* and that the increased presence of these groups changed the auction into a marketplace with goods that were more desirable to them. When these groups gained more purchasing power, they demanded better used clothes, furniture and textiles with which to adorn themselves and their homes. Most likely, prices were higher on consumer items in the smaller towns than in Stockholm, making the auction an affordable alternative to fixed shops.

Not only did the type of items sold at the auctions in Stockholm and Enköping differ; so too did their quality. *Household goods* of metal totally dominated in Stockholm in the eighteenth century, whilst in Enköping *household utensils* made from wood were as common as those made of metal. More silver, gold, copper and brass objects were sold in Stockholm, reflecting the larger size and wealth of the city's households, and the popularity of silver as a means of storing wealth – especially in the eighteenth century. Although the lots in Stockholm were bigger and more valuable, the number of lots of pottery and china sold in Enköping was larger. Thus, whilst entire sets of china were sold in Stockholm; auction lots in Enköping might consist of a single or a few plates. The *furniture* sold in Stockholm was also much more valuable: gilded mirrors, chests of drawers veneered with walnut, chandeliers and other such treasured objects. When *clothes* were sold in Stockholm, it was usually in the form of entire wardrobes made from silk and other expensive materials. In contrast, underwear and less expensive *clothes* were common in Enköping. Indeed, well into the nineteenth century, the majority of items bought consisted of items most households considered as affordable alternatives to new objects. Antique objects or collectables were not sold in small town auctions to any larger extent, but in Stockholm, special auctions with art and collectable objects were held. Such auctions mostly attracted people of means.

12.8 Circulation of Goods

Not only burghers, but also the nobility and gentry sold possessions at sales, especially during the eighteenth century. Partly, this was a result of the fact that, on average, estates and manor houses remained in their owners' hands for only 10–15 years in Sweden during the eighteenth and nineteenth centuries. With military officers, for example, the house went with the commission; when an officer's commission ended, he had to move. Also, financial difficulties were common and goods had to be sold to obtain money. However, sales were held even on estates and manors that were entailed, usually at the time of the owner's death, to raise money. For all these reasons, goods often moved between homes. Moreover, during the eighteenth and nineteenth centuries, wealth tended to accumulate amongst the nobility and gentry as a class – if not always on an individual level – with the result that the amount of furniture doubled in Swedish manor houses between 1740 and 1860 (Ulväng, 2004:147). This further added to the circulation of furniture, with auctions remaining an important venue for the nobility and gentry to both buy and sell goods.

The sales by nobles were not only important for people of the same class wishing to acquire a certain object, but also for the lower classes. Auction records from sales by nobles in 1765 and 1820 at Höja Manor outside Enköping show that farmers, peasants and the landless bought half of the objects in question. They bought mostly linen, china and curtains, but also furniture (see also Nenadic, 1994). The more expensive items usually went to the nobility and gentry.

In 1765, the 24 year-old owner of Höja Manor, count Carl Gustaf Spens, had just returned from his studies at Uppsala University to claim his estate. He promptly held a sale to dispose of unfashionable furniture and other items. The count was a wealthy man and did not particularly need the money, but he used the auction as a means to clear out old furniture and make room for new. For example, at the auction a pair of late-baroque guerdons, which had been bought by the count's grandfather whilst modernising the manor house in the 1720s, was sold to a neighbouring farmer, Jan Ersson. At the same sale, two china soup bowls were sold to a landless man, Lars Larsson. Clearly, those of more modest means could buy luxury or semi-luxury items at reasonable prises. They could utilize their increased wealth, compared to fifty years earlier, and adorn their houses and cottages with objects that previously had belonged to wealthier classes. Sixty years later, the count went bankrupt. At the resulting auction, lieutenant Tersmeden of Hässle Manor, who came from a family of wealthy ironmasters, bought a tablecloth and 24 napkins which used to be stored in the linen cupboard situated conveniently next to the dining-room at Höja. The count's family also bought some items. His brother, also called Carl Gustaf Spens, purchased objects from the dining room, including a fruit bowl and a cream jug, for his manor in the south of Sweden.

12.9 Conclusions

The Swedish auctions in the eighteenth and nineteenth centuries were a marketplace for the consumption of goods for everyday use, rather than collectibles. That the auctions formed an important and integral part of consumption processes is evident from the ways in which the local business structure was reflected in the goods being sold. The considerable volume of second-hand consumption revealed in the auction accounts indicates that general estimates of the growth of consumption in the eighteenth and nineteenth centuries should be revised upwards. Of course, not all goods sold at auctions were second hand. Auctions were also important for wholesalers buying and selling to each other and as a means of selling unused stock direct to consumers. This again points to higher levels of consumption than hitherto estimated.

The number of auctions increased during the period 1770–1870 as did the number of items for sale. However, as the population also grew, the number of items per inhabitant remained approximately constant. In the larger city of Stockholm, auctions formed an arena for precious goods, whilst, for a long time, those in small towns such as Enköping were more important as a source of household goods: items that the inhabitants might have found it difficult to otherwise afford. Evidently, demand for goods changed during the period. In addition, general wealth increased, making it possible for more people and new groups of people to buy a more and greater range of goods. However, even in the late eighteenth century, when real wages were still more or less static, landless labourers were active consumers, suggesting that household priorities had changed even if wages did not increase. During the nineteenth century, the landless appear as sellers as well. They were now a group who not only consumed but also disposed of unwanted items, not least because more of them had their own households. The housing pattern for servants also changed, with a growing tendency for servants to move out of the master's house and set up home in their own quarters. The increasing sale of furniture was thus both a result of growing wealth, and thereby larger homes, and the fact that more people had their own rooms or houses. Better furniture could also serve as a means for people to position themselves closer to the upper classes and more distant from the lower. As Smith (2002) argues, it also served to distinguish them as a separate social group.

Burghers were the dominant group until the middle of the nineteenth century, when their patronage of auctions began to diminish. Evidently, the pattern of consumption then changed. Industrialisation had meant cheaper prices, making new goods more affordable. This can be related to Lemire's discussion of the market for second-hand clothes, which diminished when cheap new ready-made garments became available. Second-hand clothes were then exported instead (Lemire, 2005). This is because second-hand goods were an alternative to more expensive new items. When cheap new goods were available, they were usually viewed as higher status and more fashionable – a finding that is in line with Nenadic's findings, albeit that quality as well as price was important in Scotland (Nenadic, 1994). The result of these changes was that the burghers had an incentive to buy their goods in shops rather than at auctions.

In some instances, new goods clearly put an end to the market for second-hand items. The demand evidently changed during the period to novelties. As in England (if a little later), clothes disappeared from the auctions in Stockholm, but they remained important in smaller towns. Compared to countries which industrialised earlier, the shift from burgher or middle-rank consumer dominance at the auction was later in Sweden. Farming and outdoor equipment increased at the auctions until the beginning of the nineteenth century, but diminished afterwards. However, the value of these items increased suggesting that more expensive farming and outdoor equipment remained attractive on the second-hand market, whilst cheaper items were replaced with new ones. As De Vries argues, household consumption was transferred to less durable goods: pewter and wooden household goods diminished in value, as the newly fashionable china replaced them to an increasing extent (De Vries, 1993). Silver, which was used for saving during the eighteenth century, seems to have lost its role as a 'piggy bank' in the nineteenth century.

Interestingly, the auction was an arena for consumption, especially during the nineteenth century, for many groups in society. The records show that many individuals were present and bought items. Previous research has spoken of a democratisation of demand, but we may also speak of a democratisation of the public sphere of consumption: in this case, the sales room. Women were eager visitors to auctions and were active both as sellers and as buyers. They bought textiles, whilst men bought farming and outdoor equipment, indicating different areas of responsibility within the household. Particularly in nineteenth-century Stockholm, it is apparent that the auctions were increasingly an arena not only for private consumers but also for merchants selling their goods to private individuals or other merchants. It is thus reasonable to assume that the auctions were important markets, as well as meeting places, in the local community and thus played an important part in the local economy.

The auction encouraged the circulation of goods and social status. Objects retained their social value if bought by an individual from the same social standing as the seller. Whilst objects bought by lower social groups depreciated in value in the eyes of the wealthier, they gained a new social value within the group of the buyer, perhaps serving to bolster the individual's social standing. The public auction was, in itself, a manifestation of social status and wealth, within and between groups.

BIBLIOGRAPHY

Primary Sources

Unpublished sources

Höja Godsarkiv (Höja Manor Archive)

Auktionsprotokoll (auction records) 1765 and 1820.

Bouppteckningar (inventories) 1737 and 1816.

Stockholms Stadsarkiv

Register till mantalsböcker 1800–1875. CD-record (2003), Stockholms stadsarkiv.

Stockholms auktionsverk (Stockholm Auction House): Auktionsprotokoll (auction records) 1781 and 1870.

Uppsala Landsarkiv

Enköping auktionsverk (Enköping Auction House): Auktionsprotokoll (auction records) 1760 and 1870.

Enköpings församlingar. Husförhörslängder. 1896–1900, volume 33–35; 1900, volume 1–6.

Literature

Ahlberger, C. (1996) *Konsumtionsrevolutionen*, Göteborg.

Algott, S. (1963) 'Bidrag till Stockholms fondbörs historia' *Stockholms fondbörs 100 år*. Stockholm.

Allerston, P. (1996) *The market in second-hand clothes and furnishings in Venice, c. 1500-c. 1650*, Florence.

Allerston, P. (1998) 'Wedding finery in sixteenth-century Venice', Dean, T. and Lowe, K. J. P. (eds.), *Marriage in Italy, 1300–1650*, Cambridge.

Allerston, P. (2000) 'Clothing and early modern Venetian society', *Continuity and Change*, 15:3, 367–390.

Almén, T. (1897) *Om auktion: såsom medel att åvägabringa aftal*, Uppsala.

Berg, M. (1999) 'New commodities, luxuries and their consumers in eighteenth-century England', Berg, M. and Clifford, H. (eds.), *Consumers and luxury*, Manchester.

Berg, M. (2002) 'From imitation to invention: creating commodities in eighteenth-century Britain', *Economic History Review*, 55:1, 1–30.

De Vries, J. (1993) 'Between purchasing power and the world of goods: understanding the household economy in early modern Europe', Brewer, J. and Porter, R. (eds.), *Consumption and the world of goods*, London.

Douglas, M. and Isherwood, B. (1996) *The world of goods*, London.

Ericson, L. (2001) *Stockholms historia under 750 år*, Lund.

Kjellberg, C. M. (1905) 'Upplands städer. Uppland', *Skildring af land och folk*, Uppsala.

Lemire, B. (1988) 'Consumerism in pre-industrial and early industrial England: the trade in second-hand clothes', *The Journal of British Studies*, 27:1, 1–24.

Lemire, B. (1991) *Fashion's favourite: the cotton trade and the consumer in Britain, 1660–1800*, Oxford.

Lemire, B. (1997) *Dress, culture and commerce. The English clothing trade before the factory, 1660–1800*, Basingstoke.

Lemire, B. (2005) 'Shifting currency. The culture and economy of the second hand trade in England, c. 1600–1850', Palmer, A. and Clark, H. (eds.), *Old clothes, new looks. Second hand fashion*, Oxford.

Lundell, Å. (1974) *Auktionsverket i Stockholm*, Stockholm.

Magnusson, L. (1996) *Sveriges ekonomiska historia*, Stockholm.

Nenadic, S. (1994) 'Middle-rank consumers and domestic culture in Edinburgh and Glasgow 1720–1840', *Past & Present*, 145, 122–156.

Pomerantz, K. (2000) *The great divergence: China, Europe, and the making of the modern world economy*, Princeton.

Smith, W. D. (2002) *Consumption and the making of respectability 1600–1800*, London.

Trentmann, F. (2004) 'Beyond consumerism: new historical perspectives on consumption', *Journal of Contemporary History*, 39:3, 373–401.

Ulväng, G. (2004) *Hus och gård i förändring. Uppländska herrgårdar, boställen och bondgårdar under 1700- och 1800-talens agrara revolution (Building and property in a State of change. Manor estates, vicarages and farms in Uppland during the aparian revolution of the 18th and 19th centuries)*, Hedemora.

CHAPTER 13

From Social Event to Urban Spectacle: Art Auctions in Late Eighteenth-Century Paris

Charlotte Guichard[1] – Centre National de la Recherche Scientifique, IRHIS (Lille-3), France

13.1 Introduction

In eighteenth-century Paris, auctions became central institutions in the emerging art market. Whereas they remained rare and irregular events before 1730, their number grew steadily in the second half of the century, reaching up to fifty a year in the 1780s (Bailey, 2002: 16). Recent research in social art history has shown the importance of auctions in the circulation of works of art, the professionalisation of art dealers, and the history of taste in France (Duverger, 1967; Pomian, 1987: 163–194; Fredericksen and Perronet, 1998; Preti-Hamard and Sénéchal, 2005). This chapter aims to study Parisian art auctions and salesrooms from a cultural and social perspective in order to address the question of the art public.

As new institutions in the Parisian art market, auctions participated in the consumption and commodification of art and culture, and in the birth of a public space for art (Brewer and Bermingham, 1995). But they were also social spaces where distinctive communities displayed their emulative taste and participated in the new 'orgy of spending' (Campbell, 1987: 20; McKendrick, Brewer and Plumb, 1982: 10). Indeed, auctions are different to other economic institutions in that they establish socially accepted definitions of value and provenance, rather than straight economic value: they constitute 'rites of passage for the items that pass through them, in which a new social identity is established for the item. Such identities entail not only price but ownership and often category-grading status' (Smith, 1989: 48). In eighteenth-century Paris, art auctions were therefore places where prestigious works of art circulated but also where reputations were established. As such, they allowed for the display of new social identities and for the transmutations of values. In particular, they provided a public arena for the emergence and the display of a new social figure, that of the *amateur*. Although they were open to the public, auctions still maintained some social boundaries amongst its attendees. Potential buyers, who presented themselves and were being presented as *amateurs* in sale catalogues, were put to the test during the competitive process of bidding. Auctions were social arenas in which individual reputations were established, or ruined, by artistic consumption turned spectacle. In this respect, the 1770s appeared as a turning point: a few prominent auctions of highly priced artworks began to be reported in a press which became increasingly fascinated by the

1 This article was translated into English by Ariane Fennetaux.

growing number of paintings sold and the extravagant amounts of money at stake. Art auctions now participated in the culture of urban leisure and played a key part in the rise of Paris as a cultural and artistic capital. To house these events, a new space was invented at the end of the eighteenth century: the *hôtel des ventes*. With architecture inspired by theatres, the *hôtel des ventes* turned the social event of sales into an urban spectacle.

13.2 A New Social Figure: the *Amateur* and Auction Communities

In the middle of the eighteenth century, Parisian auctions still took place in a variety of undifferentiated locations. Edme-François Gersaint (1694–1750) – the art dealer who introduced ascending price, open-outcry auctions from Holland in the 1730s – organized public sales in his shop on the Pont Notre-Dame, in the Couvent des Grands-Augustins, whose large rooms were convenient for auctions, and in the homes of deceased whose collections he sold (Glorieux, 2002: 349; De Marchi and Van Miegroet, 2006). Indeed, many art auctions continued to be held at the homes of the collectors, especially in the case of prestigious collections: in 1776, the auction of Louis-François de Bourbon, prince de Conti, took place in the Palais du Temple, while that of Paul Randon de Boisset, a wealthy farmer general, was held in his townhouse located in the rue Neuve des Capucines, next to the Place Vendôme.

The first attempts to have a space specifically dedicated to art auctions were made by the art dealer Alexandre-Joseph Paillet (1743–1814). In 1775 he bought the hôtel d'Aligre: situated in the rue Saint-Honoré, this townhouse already had connections to the world of art, as the Salons of the *Corporation des Maîtres Peintres et Sculpteurs*, known as the *Académie de Saint-Luc*, had been held there in the years 1762 and 1764 (Guiffrey, 1872). In 1778 Paillet moved to the former hôtel Bullion, parts of which he bought for 180,000 *livres*.[2] The transaction concerned a three-storey building looking onto the rue Plâtrière (Edwards, 1996: 22). The ground floor was composed of seven rooms where public sales were held, a new room being fitted on the ground floor to house art auctions. This is how it was described in 1791: 'there are several rooms on the ground floor: the sale of paintings is usually held in the biggest of those whose light comes from the ceiling. Amateur concerts, assemblies and Masonic gatherings are also held there' (Dulaure, 1791: 73).[3] The atmosphere of the salesroom is neatly captured by the painting of Pierre-Antoine Demachy (1723–1807) (see Figure 13.1.).

The painting represents the exhibition of the paintings before the sale. On the right-hand side, an art dealer conducts the sale, assisted by two *huissiers-priseurs*. Since the 1681 regulation, reasserted in 1758, the *huissiers-priseurs* of the *Châtelet de Paris* enjoyed a monopoly over the valuation and auction of any movable property. The art dealer, often trained as a guild artist, acted as an expert and wrote the sale catalogues, while the corporation of the *huissiers priseurs* – then called *commissaires priseurs* – gave the auction its legal format. The composition of the painting illustrates the relative confusion created by the

2 The *livre tournois* was the French monetary unit until 1795.

3 'Cet Hôtel intéresse aujourd'hui par les ventes qui s'y font presque journellement de meubles précieux, de bijoux, de livres provenant de quelques bibliothèques particulières, et de tableaux rares, souvent du plus grand prix. Il y a plusieurs salles au rez-de-chaussée; celle des tableaux se fait, pour l'ordinaire, dans la plus grande, qui est éclairée par le plafond. On donne aussi, dans cette même salle, des concerts d'amateurs, des bals et fêtes maçonniques'.

FIGURE 13.1. Pierre-Antoine Demachy, *An art auction in Paris (thought to be the hôtel Bullion)*, c. 1785
SOURCE: Paris, Musée Carnavalet © Roger Viollet.

absence of architectural arrangements for the sale. Only the light coming from the overhead windows and the candelabras around the room distinguished the area where the auction was held. The painting stresses the difficulty of seeing canvases: the crowd is gathered haphazardly despite some makeshift arrangements to try and improve visibility and overall spatial organisation. Some chairs are provided to people of quality – recognisable from their portly figures, their wigs and their rich clothes – while some members of the audience stand on stepladders to get above the rest of the crowd. The room has no specific architectural feature fitted to its use as an auction room. On the contrary, the painter insists on the prevailing confusion: only the contrasting use of light and darkness allows the highly dramatic rendering of the auction.

Although not necessarily completely realistic, this painting suggests that the auction took place in front of an audience composed of a nondescript crowd and of a select community of buyers, recognisable by their proximity to the paintings, their attitudes and their social rank. Similarly, sale catalogues distinguished a select community of readers whom they called *amateurs*: 'the precious, albeit large circle of *amateurs* for whom we are writing is almost entirely composed of various enlightened persons and artists or distinguished dealers whose knowledge of art never fails them' (Paillet and Miliotti,1785). The term *amateur* is not to be understood as a large and somewhat vague equivalent of art lover. Like the *virtuoso* in late seventeenth-century London (Houghton, 1942), it referred to a specific figure in the Parisian artistic space of the eighteenth century, defined by connoisseurship (knowledge) and social status (distinguished), and distinct from the larger public (Guichard, forthcoming). This social figure was first theorised in 1748 in a conference held in the *Académie royale de peinture* by the count of Caylus (1692–1765), who proposed it as a norm of collective taste. *Amateurs honoraires* in the *Académie royale de peinture* were chosen among the social elite – in particular aristocrats, financiers, and members of government – and were expected to support the French school of painting. Initially, this normative definition was formulated in the Academy, but it contributed to shaping a social figure which was defined by its conflation of artistic sociability, social distinction and good taste. In art auctions, buyers presented themselves and were presented as *amateurs*. As members of the social elite, they were able to spend the large amounts of money necessary to acquire prestigious paintings, but this name *amateurs* enabled them to display their good taste and not only their economic capacity to bid and buy. Associated with the traditional values of the aristocracy, artistic sociability and connoisseurship, the community of *amateurs* introduced a social hierarchy inside the public of buyers and promoted legitimate exercises of good taste and of artistic consumption.

Sale catalogues were sent to potential buyers by art dealers whose job it was to bring sellers and buyers together (Bessy, 2003). *Amateurs* known by the dealer or who had made themselves known to him were often sent these catalogues free of charge: 'We beg *Amateurs* to send their exact addresses, carriage paid, so that we may send them the catalogues as soon as they are published' (Anon., 1783a).[4] In his diary, Jean-Georges Wille (1715–1805), a member of the *Académie royale de peinture et de sculpture*, confirmed the select distribution of catalogues when he mentions the sale of his collection of engravings '[M. Basan] composed and printed the catalogue for the whole thing which was given to *amateurs* and connoisseurs' (Wille, 1857: 107).[5] Faced with growing demand linked to the increasing success of public sales, the art dealer Paillet decided in 1783 that the people outside this select network of *amateurs* or those wishing to have several copies would, henceforth, have to pay for them (Anon., 1783b). Catalogues themselves were clearly meant for two different audiences. On the one hand they were sold to a large public, the wide circle of idle observers; on the other hand, they were handed out freely to the select circle of renowned *amateurs* who belonged to the social or professional network of the dealer. This part of the audience was linked by mutual recognition and acquaintance, as evidenced by the frequent use of partial anonymity in the advertisements for sales. The name of the collector was often not published openly and the sale remained anonymous, but some elements suggest that one part of the audience saw through the façade of anonymity. Indeed, this is the only way one can interpret the following quote, taken from a sale catalogue: 'saying from now on that such painting is part of the collection of M. le duc de Ch . . . , will be clear enough to persuade the most fastidious and most enlightened *Amateur* to try and have it in his [collection]' (Le Brun, 1787b: 3).[6] Meaningless to lay readers, this sentence can only be understood if, despite the declared anonymity, possibly governed by etiquette, *amateurs* attending the sale, who had their own information networks, could identify the duc

4 'Nous prions les Amateurs de nous faire passer leur adresse juste, franc de port, afin de leur faire parvenir les Catalogues lorsqu'ils paraîtront'.

5 '[M. Basan] a composé et fait imprimer le catalogue du tout, qui a été distribué aux amateurs et connoisseurs'.

6 'dire à l'avenir que tel tableau a fait partie de la Collection de M. le Duc de Ch . . ., ce sera l'annoncer suffisamment pour décider l'Amateur le plus difficile et le plus éclairé à en orner la sienne'.

Louis-Antoine de Rohan-Chabot (1733–1807). Thus, there was clearly a two-tier process of publication: the catalogue remained anonymous for a large audience, whereas it was identified as referring to an individual by the community of *amateurs* who thereby also recognized themselves as people in the know. Wilhelm von Wolzogen, a German traveller, who frequented the artistic circles of the capital when staying in Paris between 1788 and 1791, summed up the way in which auctions were advertised: 'a *catalogue raisonné* is drafted, distributed free of charge to 3-400 people, sold to the rest. An advertisement is then published in the *Petites Affiches*' (Wolzogen, 1998: 146). This illustrates the same opposition between a select circle who read the catalogue and potentially bought the paintings and a wider public notified of the sale by billboards in the streets. The archives concerning the auction of the collection of the prince de Conti in 1776 enable us to form an idea of the spread and circulation of billboards and catalogues: 400 billboards were put up across Paris and over 800 catalogues were handed out. Circulation was therefore rather large, even if these figures need to be considered with caution, since the auction of the prince de Conti was one of the biggest in the century, generating 1,125,000 *livres* (Pomian, 1992: 22). This sale profited from unprecedented advertising, and the catalogues and billboards published for the occasion must therefore have been particularly numerous.

Despite the fact they were public, auctions themselves largely remained characterised by sociability and by their roles in making and unmaking social reputations. As such they were very different from the *Salons du Louvre*, whose public was much more varied and which have been seen as one of the sites of the formation of 'the public sphere' (Habermas, 1962: 50–51). As we have already noted, the auction was targeted at both the public and the *amateurs*. Whilst the former were generally portrayed as marginal to the events of the auction – little more than a passive audience – the latter were placed close to the works being offered for sale. Yet the community of *amateurs* was recognizable thanks to a series of features besides their dress or their physical proximity to works of art. Some attributes helped to distinguish them: for example, the possession of lorgnettes, such as that lost during the sale of the prince de Conti. Its owner placed an advertisement in the *Annonces, Affiches et Avis divers* in May 1777: 'on April 29th, at the auction of the paintings of HSH Mgr the Prince de Conty, a green, finely grained LORGNETTE by *Dollond* was lost. A 12 livres reward will be given to whoever will bring it back to M. *Thirson*, rue Jacob, opposite La Charité'.[7] Manipulating and taking notes in catalogues were also clues that enabled mutual recognition and signalled their common belonging to the world of taste (Smith, 1989: 68). Catalogues were a scholarly tool for expertise, pleasure and fantasy. Some *amateurs* collected them. The copious quantity of annotated sale catalogues to be found in today's archives – bearing the price fetched by works, the name of the bidder who acquired them and even sometimes a brief summary of the sale itself – shows the key role of individuals appropriating print culture in self-fashioning practices aimed at establishing their social identities.

The auction was a space and a time of self-promotion based on wealth, connoisseurship and good taste. In the salesroom, 'auction communities' were created: as the work of art was being put to the test by the auction, a self-recognising community

7 'Le 29 Avril, on a perdu à la vente des Tableaux de S.A.S. Mgr. le Prince de Conty, au Temple, une LORGNETTE de *Dollond*, verte & à petits grains. On promet 12 livres à celui qui la rapportera à M. *Thiron*, rue Jacob, vis-à-vis la Charité'.

emerged out of the process of mutual assessment and challenge entailed by competitive bidding (Smith, 1989; Baudrillard, 1972: 135). It defined itself as a community composed of the privileged few. The recurring use of the phrase 'Messieurs les *Amateurs*' which was used to refer to them in catalogues, had, in the social and political context of the *Ancien Régime*, a specific meaning: it was used to refer to a community of individuals united by their belonging to an institution marked by strong political, intellectual or social prestige ('Messieurs du Parlement' or 'Messieurs de l'Académie' for example). The phrase implemented social distinction. Bidding was thus both a form of entertainment and a means of social recognition. And, as they started being regularly chronicled in the press, auctions also became privileged sites enabling moralists and satirists to capture the follies and excesses of their times.

13.3 From Social Event to Spectacle: the Auction and the Press

The number of masterpieces exhibited in auctions and the extravagant sums at stake fascinated contemporaries. The 1770s appeared as a turning point in this respect as auctions multiplied and created huge profits. Three exceptional public auctions were held in 1776. On 14th November, François Mettra, a regular attendee at auctions as he was King Frederick II of Prussia's intermediary in charge of his artistic acquisitions in France, wrote in the *Correspondance secrète, politique et littéraire* that: 'M. Randon de Boisset is dead. He was one of our millionaires, the owner of the most richly endowed cabinet in the whole kingdom (. . .) Here are some terrible temptations for *amateurs*, three major collections for sale: that of the late prince de Conti, that of M. Blondel de Gagny and that of M. Randon'.[8] Thus, three collections of paintings and curiosities belonging to people coming from the nobility, the court administration and the world of finance were sold at auction in the same year. For each, the total profits topped one million livres due to the outstanding quality of the works being offered for sale.

The exhibition of masterpieces played an important role in the reputation of auctions and in their profits. Some circulated frequently between the different private collections and appeared repeatedly in auctions. Two works then attributed to Rembrandt, *Philosopher with an Open Book* and *Philosopher in Meditation* (now in the Louvre), were sold in 1776 at the auction of Paul Randon de Boisset. They had already been on the art market several times since they had been part of the 1760 comte de Vence's auction and had also been mentioned as part of the private sale of the marquis de Voyer d'Argenson. In 1772, they featured in the sale catalogue of the duc de Choiseul, former *ministre des Affaires étrangères* of Louis XVI, where they were sold for 14,000 *livres*. In 1776, Randon de Boisset sold them for 10,900 livres to the comte de Vaudreuil, a wealthy courtier, who himself sold them in 1784 to the Royal collection. These two paintings were part of the purchases commissioned by the comte d'Angiviller, Louis XVI's *Directeur général des Bâtiments du Roi*, when putting together the collection of the future Museum. This was the end of the

8 'M. Randon de Boisset est mort. C'était un de nos millionnaires, possesseur du plus riche cabinet du Royaume. Le public verra du moins ses tableaux qu'il tenait renfermés. Voilà de terribles tentations pour les amateurs, trois grandes collections à vendre, celle de feu le Prince de Conti, de M. Blondel de Gagny and de M. Randon'.

'social life' of these two paintings as they have since been in the collection of the *Musée du Louvre* (Appadurai, 1986). Yet, before being acquired for the Museum, they had gone through the hands of no fewer than six different owners in the space of twenty-five years. Old master paintings thus moved frequently between collections whose owners obviously sought the aesthetic pleasure derived from owning these paintings, while they also represented for them an economic investment bringing a profit as well as a means to publicly establish their reputations as *amateurs*. This pair of paintings by Rembrandt indeed came with a rare pedigree: they served to guarantee the reputation of the collections in which they were kept which, in turn, added to their value.

With the increased circulation of works, the press started to become more and more interested in auctions. At the end of the century, they were seen as places of urban entertainment and luxury. Thus periodicals not only published advertisements for auctions, but also turned them into a new form of urban spectacle. Periodicals gave auctions prime treatment, thereby testifying to the unprecedented importance of the phenomenon in the series of social events that constituted the Paris season. Admittedly, a few big auctions had previously had some impact on the world of *amateurs*, but these had been talked about relatively little and had not really featured in the press. In contrast, the three auctions held in 1776 were reported in all newspapers, where they were presented as entertaining events. The *Mercure de France* advertised them and described their catalogues in great detail according to a well-tried advertising technique that had already been used by the dealer Gersaint. Meanwhile, the *Journal de Paris* published detailed chronicles of the auctions in which an anonymous artist quoted the prices fetched by the works and compared the quality of the various collections that were being auctioned. He thus wrote on 8th March 1777: 'the paintings of the late HSH Prince de Conti have lately appeared for auction. Artists and *amateurs* have noticed with pleasure the different impressions produced on the audience by this rich collection and that of M. de Boisset by M. de Boisset's. Before either was known, the few people who had seen the paintings of the latter, raved about them with transports of admiration'.[9] Now chronicles took the shape of a moral tale on the world of art lovers. From social events, auctions became spectacles that enabled moralists to capture the follies of the time. On 18th March 1777, the columnist of the *Journal de Paris* cast an amused look at those new social practices and criticised the social dynamics of auctions, based on the appearance of a new artistic jargon, the display of reputations and petty individual vanities: 'I cannot leave, Sirs, the sale of M. de Boisset's collection and I take almost as much pleasure in what I hear there as in the masterpieces which are daily exhibited to the curiosity of the public. Lately, considerable art collections have been dismantled and renewed enthusiasm for painting has seized all *amateurs* or those who pretend to be. People would be ashamed now not to know the various schools of painting, and it is the most delightful thing to hear young men who often have only thought about *dessus-de-porte* or women who know nothing but the varnished decorations of their boudoirs, utter with pretension the words '*ragouts*', '*flouflou*', 'good effect', 'bold stroke', 'rich

9 'On a vu ces jours derniers les Tableaux de feu S.A.S. Mgr le Prince de Conti. Les Artistes & Amateurs ont remarqué avec plaisir l'impression différente qu'ont produit sur le Public cette riche Collection & le Cabinet de M. de Boisset. Avant que l'un & l'autre fussent connus, le peu de gens qui avoient vu les tableaux de ce dernier, en parlaient avec des transports d'admiration'.

composition' etc. etc. (. . .) a buyer's pride makes him sacrifice extravagant sums of money to satisfy himself and give himself the air in public of being a *dilettante*'.[10]

The metaphor of theatre and performance became a common trope in the representation of auctions. In 1786 an art dealer and auctioneer, Claude-François Joullain, introduced his guidebook for *amateurs* by a long description of the Parisian world of art. Auctions were described in great detail and their drama was highlighted: 'The fact that sales attract a great many people is not to be wondered at: they constitute an entertaining spectacle by the sheer variety and the value of the objects that are presented; they draw people's attention as they offer the most delightful picture of the rivalry among *amateurs*, between *amateurs* and dealers, between dealers and artists, between dealers and fellow dealers. The man drawn by curiosity to attend an auction is always surprised to see the same object being met alternately by the warmest exhilaration and cold indifference, and see sluggish bidding *sol* by *sol* followed by the rapid bidding of whole *pistoles* and hundreds of *livres*. He is fascinated by the look of hesitation on the face of the *amateur* which accompanies the latter's most enthusiastic taste for a piece and his wish that the auction slowed down. He smiles at the composed look of the dealer who pretends to lose interest in an object he is dying to possess and who only acts thus so as to push the *amateur* to make a decision' (Joullain, 1786: 124–125).[11] The passage foregrounds the dramatic quality of auctions: under the calm façade of a purely economic transaction, the warmest desire for possession can be felt and fiery passions rage. Joullain compares 'the look of hesitation on the face of the *amateur*' and the 'composed look of the dealer' to the pantomimes of actors.

13.4 Auction Rooms in Paris: Inventing the *hôtel des ventes*

In the 1770s, the growing popularity of auctions required a more formal space for them. The *hôtel des ventes* was invented by Jean-Baptiste Lebrun (1748–1813), Paillet's main competitor and Élisabeth Vigée-Lebrun's husband: trained as a guild painter, he was the most prominent art dealer at the turn of the century (Bailey, 1984: 32–46). The competition between art dealers to attract wealthy and aristocratic clients made the need for a purpose-fitted room more pressing. In London, James Christie had already founded an auction house, and had opened his 'Great Auction Room' in 1768 near Pall Mall

10 'Je ne quitte point, MM., la vente de M. de Boisset, & je m'amuse presqu'autant des propos que j'entends, que des chef-d'œuvres qu'on expose tous les jours à la curiosité du Public. Depuis quelque temps, voilà des collections considérables de tableaux qui se vendent en détail, & il en a résulté un redoublement de passion pour la Peinture, qui s'est emparé de tous les Amateurs ou de ceux qui prétendent l'être. On rougirait maintenant de ne pas connaître les différentes Ecoles, & c'est la chose la plus plaisante que de voir des jeunes gens qui souvent n'ont pensé qu'à des dessus-de-porte, ou des femmes qui ne connaissent que le vernis de leurs boudoirs, prononcer avec prétention les termes de ragoûts, flouflou, bon effet, fini précieux, touche vigoureuse, composition riche, &c &c (. . .) l'amour propre d'un acheteur lui fait sacrifier des sommes considérables pour se contenter, & se donner en public la réputation d'un dilettante'.

11 'Il ne faut pas s'étonner si les ventes attirent une grande affluence de monde; elles font spectacle par la variété et le mérite des objets qui les composent ; elles excitent l'attention, en ce qu'elles offrent le tableau le plus piquant de la rivalité des amateurs entre eux, des amateurs contre les marchands, des marchands avec les artistes, des marchands avec leurs confrères. L'homme que la simple curiosité attire à une vente, est toujours surpris de voir succéder en un instant sur un même objet, la chaleur à l'indifférence, la lenteur des enchères sol à sol à la marche rapide des pistoles, des centaines de livres. Il se plaît à contempler sur le visage de l'amateur cette indécision qui accompagne visiblement son goût le plus décidé, le désir qu'il aurait que l'on prolongeât l'intervalle des enchères. Il sourit de la figure composée du marchand qui feint à chaque instant d'abandonner un objet qu'il brûle d'avoir en sa possession, et qui n'agit ainsi que pour presser de plus en plus l'amateur à se déterminer'.

(Wall, 1997). Ten years later, in 1778, Jean-Baptiste Lebrun bought the hôtel de Lubert for 200,000 *livres* and undertook construction work on a site he bought between the rue de Cléry and the rue du Gros-Chênet. On the rue du Gros-Chênet, the building housed the workshop of his wife, Élisabeth Vigée-Lebrun, as well as a neo-classical gallery. 28 metres long and 12 metres high, it was decorated by Ionic columns, featured overhead natural lighting, and could be used to exhibit paintings and sculptures (Gallet, 1960: 275–284; Talenti, 1999: 101–108). On the rue de Cléry, the new auction room was inaugurated in 1787: 'we have always considered the necessity of having a place fitted to receive people who, not content with only visiting workshops and the shops of art dealers, like attending auctions where paintings which appeal to their taste and their curiosity are being sold. We have also noticed that *Amateurs* sometimes wanting to sell their collections at the same time, often could not do so because such a venue was always booked and other venues did not provide good enough lighting nor were they as commodious as they might have wanted' (Le Brun, 1787a: 3–4).[12] Jean-Baptiste Lebrun understood that auctions had turned into spectacles and that they had to take place in venues that had good lighting, good display potential, sufficient storage, and were readily available. Choosing the appropriate location was also part of a wider strategy to attract clients of means (Quemin, 1994: 52–71): his auction room had been built, he added, in 'one of the most beautiful areas of Paris'. It was located in the centre of Paris, in the vicinity of the Faubourg Saint-Honoré and the Louvre, as were other hôtels where auctions were occasionally organized: the hôtel d'Aligre was located on rue Saint-Honoré, the hôtel de Louvois was situated in the rue de Richelieu, and the hôtel de Bullion was on rue Plâtrière (see Map 13.1.).

Lebrun's salesroom in the rue de Cléry inaugurated a new type of space; one that was solely devoted to auctions. It duly became a famous landmark in the Parisian art world. That the room created quite a stir at the time is shown by the many contemporary commentaries. In April 1787, the *Journal de Paris* gave a long description of the saleroom, insisting upon its architectural novelty and its public use in the formation of taste: 'M. Le Brun has just had work done in the former hôtel de Lubert on the rue de Clery to build a room dedicated to public auctions of paintings and other artistic productions. We all know it is not easy, especially for young people, to be introduced into private collections. It is only when masterpieces are sold and change owners that the public can admire them. But we believe that this room will make it up to students and *amateurs* before the great treasures owned by His Highness are permanently and constantly displayed in the superb royal museum – the latter being open to the public, these treasures will then really be called national'.[13] The auction room offered to the public admiration of paintings traditionally

12 'Nous avons toujours pensé au choix d'un emplacement disposé pour recevoir les personnes, qui, non contentes de visiter les ateliers des Artistes, & les magasins des Marchands, aiment encore à suivre aux ventes les tableaux qui sollicitent leur goût en piquant leur curiosité. Nous avons aussi, d'ailleurs, remarqué que les Amateurs voulant quelquefois se défaire de leurs collections dans la même saison, & à la même époque; ils ne pouvaient satisfaire leur désir parce que telle salle était toujours retenue d'avance, & que telle autre ne leur offrait pas un jour aussi beau & un local aussi commode qu'ils auraient souhaité'.

13 'M. Le Brun vient de faire construire à l'ancien hôtel de Lubert, rue de Cléry, une Salle propre aux ventes publiques de tableaux & autres productions des arts... On sait qu'il n'est pas aisé aux jeunes gens surtout, de se procurer l'entrée des cabinets des particuliers, ce n'est pour ainsi dire que lorsque les chefs-d'œuvre changent de possesseurs que le public peut en jouir, or nous croyons que cette salle pourra servir en quelque sorte de dédommagement aux élèves & aux amateurs, jusqu'à ce que le superbe muséum du roi étale un dépôt permanent & constant des grandes richesses que Sa Majesté possède en ce genre, & qui, par l'entrée donnée au public pour en jouir rendra ces richesses vraiment nationales'.

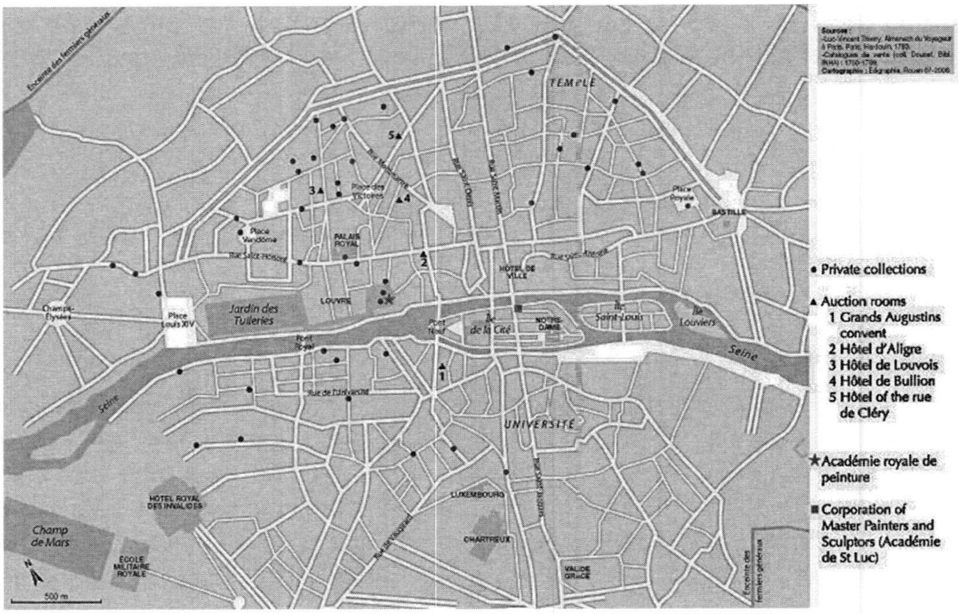

MAP 13.1. *Hôtels des ventes* in Paris at the end of the eighteenth century

housed in private collections, and thus could compensate for the absence of a national museum (Poulot, 1997).

Wilhelm von Wolzogen described the architecture of the room in 1788: 'from time to time [Le Brun] organizes auctions. To this purpose, he had a house fitted-up next to his with a room which provides very good overhead lighting for the paintings. The walls are like the sides of a pyramid and the whole room can be compared to a truncated pyramid with the ground as its base' (Wolzogen, 1998: 48).[14] The drawings made in pen and ink by the architect Raymond enables us to form a better idea of the layout of the room (Figures 13.2. and 13.3.).

The architecture of the room shows the careful attention paid to improved lighting and overall visibility for paintings thanks to the tiered seating arrangement and the light that flooded into the room through the large openings in the roof. The architecture was very similar to that of theatres. In the centre, the platform was like a stage concentrating people's gazes whilst the works were visible from all sides thanks to the seats forming two amphitheatres above the central platform. Under the platform and behind the scenes, cupboards and storage spaces provided room to store works and could act like wings in a theatre. As in a theatre, boxes in the dress circle were set apart from the *parterre* which was more democratic (Ravel, 1999; Frantz and d'Oria, 1999). Lebrun's auction room thus combined all the elements required to stage a dramatic and entertaining spectacle: that of competitive bidding. Paintings, *amateurs* and art dealers were the actors on the stage; the plot being enacted was that of the collective construction of the value of a work of art,

14 'De temps en temps, [Le Brun] arrange des ventes. À cette fin, il a fait apprêter une maison à côté de la sienne, avec une salle qui, d'en haut, éclaire très bien les tableaux. Les murs sont des faces de pyramides, et l'ensemble de la salle une pyramide tronquée dont le plancher est la base'.

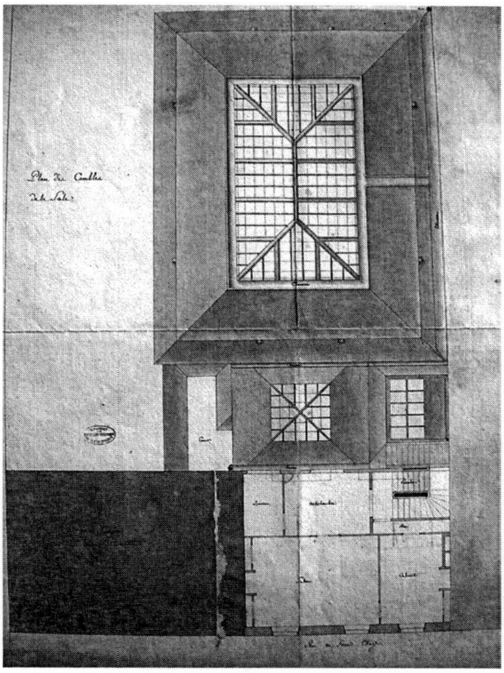

FIGURE 13.2. Raymond, plan of Lebrun's auction room, pen and ink

SOURCE: National Archives, Paris.

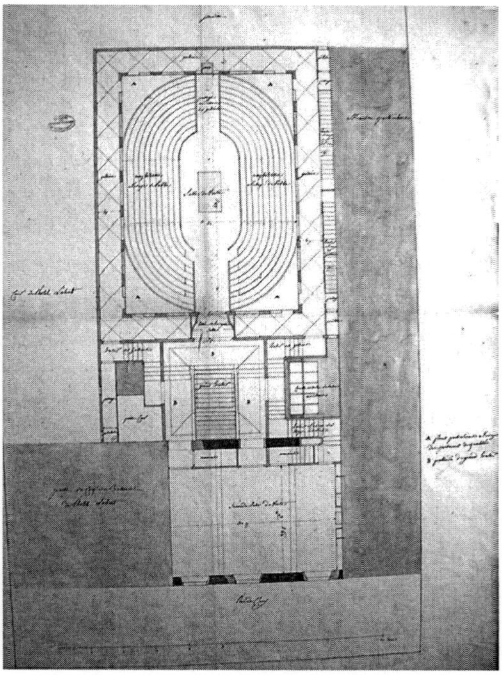

FIGURE 13.3. Raymond, Cross section of the auction room

SOURCE: National Archives, Paris.

whilst the final sale brought the auction to a climactic denouement. In the centre of the room stood a platform where objects could be exhibited and, on the sides, seats were arranged in two semi-circular tiers – marked B – that were made 'for the public'.[15] In the corners, seats – marked A – were reserved 'more particularly for people of quality', as specified by the architect himself on the plan.[16] This spatial distinction inside the audience shows that social hierarchy and the prescriptive exercise of taste – coming from the *Académie royale* and associated to the figure of the *amateur* – continued to prevail at the eve of the French Revolution, even in the new venues dedicated to art consumption. This is confirmed by a booklet published in June 1789, when Lebrun's auction room housed the *Exposition de la Jeunesse* and therefore replaced the open-air fairs held on the place Dauphine on the day of the *Fête-Dieu* (Crow, 1985; Berger, 1999). The author is enthusiastic and confirms that this venue continued to promote the community of *amateurs*, absent from the public place but gathered in this new auction room: 'the certainty of being assessed by the right sort of company, by *amateurs* who used to be scared off by the confusion of a public square, will encourage young artists in their work'.[17] The

15 'à l'usage du Public'.

16 'plus particulièrement à l'usage des personnes de qualité'.

17 'La certitude d'être jugé par la bonne compagnie, par les amateurs qu'éloignait autrefois le désordre d'une place publique, entretiendra le courage des jeunes artistes', Corpus Deloynes, t. 16, pièce 408: 'Exposition des tableaux, desseins &c des élèves et amateurs de la peinture depuis le jeudi 18 jusqu'au dimanche 21 juin 1789', 20.

new venue quickly became used for a variety of events at a time when new urban entertainments developed. It served as a meeting place for the Society of Agriculture and as a venue for concerts during the Revolution and then under the *Directoire*.

13.5 Conclusions

As early as the end of the eighteenth century, art auctions took a full part in representations of the city. The formal invention of the *hôtel des ventes*, by the art dealer Jean-Baptiste Lebrun, helped to transform the social dynamic of auctions into a new kind of urban spectacle. With its theatrical disposition, the *hôtel des ventes* allowed the display of social identities – not least as it improved the exhibition of works of art on sale, thanks to the new attention paid to the stage and the overhead lighting. As new institutions in the public art market, auctions re-inscribed social boundaries, and staged social hierarchies and collective identities built on artistic consumption. A test for the value of works of art, auctions also drew on and reinforced the social status of its participants. Advertised in the press and open to all, auctions were still dedicated to specific communities, linked by acquaintance and self-recognition. As Brian Cowan has stated for art auctions in late Stuart England: 'Far from promoting a unified arts "public", this shared enthusiasm for the arts resulted to form an intensely competitive disunity' (Cowan, 1998: 163). *Amateurs* provided a moral, social and political ethos 'for the development of an aesthetic that would continually renew itself through its resistance to more popular mass forms of culture. The *cordon sanitaire* drawn between high art and other forms of art and entertainment marked a line which commerce was not permitted to cross' (Brewer and Bermingham, 1995: 5). The importance of the *amateur* and of connoisseur ideals in art auctions thus demonstrate the tension in eighteenth-century Paris between the opening of the art market to the public sphere and the permanence of forms of sociability associated with the academy, aristocratic values and a prescriptive exercise of taste. This elitist dimension of art auctions in Paris was particularly strong in the few prestigious sales we studied. Of course, recent scholarship has shown the importance of the circulation of less costly paintings, yet the figure of the *amateur* and the language of connoisseurship, used by expert-dealers in highly priced sales, contributed to legitimize auctions as a new sales mechanism in the art world. This tension weakened in the nineteenth century with the loss of influence of the *Académie royale de peinture* after the French Revolution and the birth of the 'dealer-critic system' (White and White, 1992). In 1852, the opening of the hôtel Drouot marked the advent of the *hôtel des ventes* as the emblem of the Parisian art world: a showcase of the city as an artistic capital (Benjamin, 1989).

BIBLIOGRAPHY

Primary Sources

Published sources

Anon. (1783a) *Catalogue d'une petite collection d'estampes en feuilles et en recueils, provenans du cabinet de M****, Paris.

Anon. (1783b) *Catalogue des tableaux, dessins, marbres, bronzes . . . du Cabinet de M**** [Blondel d'Azincourt], Paris.

Dulaure, J.A. (1791) *Nouvelle description des curiosités de Paris*, Paris.

Guiffrey, J.-J. (1872) *Livrets des expositions de l'Académie de Saint-Luc à Paris pendant les années 1751, 1752, 1753, 1756, 1762, 1764 et 1774*, Paris.

Joullain, C.-F. (1786) *Réflexions sur la peinture et la gravure, accompagnées d'une courte dissertation sur le commerce de la curiosité, et les ventes en général; ouvrage utile aux amateurs, aux artistes et aux marchands*, Paris.

Le Brun, J.B. (1787a) *Catalogue de tableaux capitaux et d'objets rares et curieux . . . provenant des cabinets de M. le chevalier Lambert & M.* [Porail], Paris.

Le Brun, J.B. (1787b) *Catalogue d'une précieuse collection de tableaux et d'objets rares et curieux . . . provenant du Cabinet de M. le Duc de Ch**** [Chabot], Paris.

Paillet, A.J. and Miliotti, A. (1785) *Catalogue de tableaux des trois écoles, Dessins sous verre & en Feuilles . . . du cabinet de M. de S. M.* [Saint Morys], Paris.

Wille, J.-G. (1857) *Mémoires et Journal de Jean-Georges Wille, Graveur du Roi*, Duplessis, G. (ed.), 2 vols., Paris, 1857.

Wolzogen, W. von (1998) *Journal de voyage à Paris (1788–1791) suivi du Journal Politique (1793) et de la correspondance diplomatique (1793)*, Lille.

Literature

Appadurai, A. (ed.) (1986) *The social life of things: commodities in cultural perspective*, Cambridge, 1986.

Bailey, C. (1984) 'Lebrun et le commerce d'art pendant le Blocus continental', *Revue de l'Art*, 63, 35–46.

Bailey, C. (2002) *Patriotic taste. Collecting modern art in pre-revolutionary Paris*, New Haven and London.

Baudrillard, J. (1972) *Pour une critique de l'économie politique du signe*, Paris.

Benjamin, W. (1989) *Paris, capitale du XIXe siècle. Le livre des passages*, Paris.

Berger, R.W. (1999) *Public access to art in Paris. A documentary history from the Middle Ages to 1800*, Pennsylvania.

Bessy, C. (2003) 'L'organisation des ventes publiques. Publication, qualification et espaces de circulation des objets', Stanziani, A. (ed.), *La Qualité des produits en France (XVIIIe–XXe siècles)*, Paris, 177–194.

Brewer, J. and Bermingham, A. (eds.) (1995) *The consumption of culture, 1600–1800: image, object, text*, London, Berkeley and Los Angeles.

Campbell, C. (1987) *The romantic ethic and the spirit of modern consumerism*, Oxford.

Cowan, B. (1998) 'Arenas of connoisseurship: auctioning art in later Stuart England', North, M. and Ormrod, D. (eds.), *Art Markets in Europe, 1400–1800*, Aldershot, 153–166.

Cowan, B. (2006) 'Art and connoisseurship in the auction market of later seventeenth-century London', De Marchi, N. and Van Miegroet, H. J. (eds.), *Mapping markets of paintings in Europe, 1450–1750*, Turnhout, 263–284.

Crow T. (1985) *Painting and public life in eighteenth-century Paris*, Yale and London.

De Marchi, N. and Van Miegroet, H. J. (2006) 'Transforming the Paris art market, 1718–1750', De Marchi, N. and Van Miegroet, H.J. (eds.), *Mapping markets of paintings in Europe, 1450–1750*, Turnhout, 383–404.

Duverger, E. (1967) 'Réflexions sur le commerce d'art au XVIIIe siècle', *Stil und Überlieferung in der Kunst des Abendlandes*, Berlin, 65–88.

Edwards, J. (1996) *Alexandre-Joseph Paillet: expert et marchand de tableaux à la fin du XVIIIe siècle*, Paris.

Frantz, P. and d'Oria, M.S. (1999) *Le Siècle des théâtres. Salles et scènes en France, 1748–1807*, Paris.
Fredericksen, B. and Perronet, B. (eds.) (1998) *Répertoire des tableaux vendus en France au XIXe siècle*, Los Angeles, 2 vols.
Gallet, M. (1960) 'La Maison de Mme Vigée-Lebrun, rue du Gros-Chemin', *Gazette des Beaux-Arts*, LVI, November, 275–284.
Glorieux, G. (2002) *À l'enseigne de Gersaint. Edme-François Gersaint, Marchand d'art sur le pont Notre-Dame*, Seyssel.
Guichard, C. (forthcoming) *Les amateurs d'art à Paris au XVIIIe siècle*, Seyssel.
Habermas, J. (1962) *L'Espace public. Archéologie de la publicité comme dimension constitutive de la société bourgeoise*, Paris.
Houghton, W. (1942) 'The English Virtuoso in the Seventeenth Century', *Journal of the History of Ideas*, III-1, 51–73 and III-2, 190–219.
McKendrick, N., Brewer, J. and Plumb, J.H. (1982) *The birth of a consumer society*, London.
Mongrédien, J. (1986) *La musique en France des Lumières au Romantisme*, Paris.
Pomian, K. (1987) *Collectionneurs, amateurs et curieux. Paris-Venise: XVIe-XVIIIe siècle*, Paris.
Pomian, K. (1992) 'L'art entre le musée et le marché', Bertrand-Dorléac, L. (ed.) *Le Commerce de l'art de la Renaissance à nos jours*, Besançon, 9–33.
Poulot, D. (1997) *Musée, nation, patrimoine, 1789–1815*, Paris.
Preti-Hamard, M. and Sénéchal, P. (ed.) (2005) *Collections et marché de l' art en France 1789–1848*, Rennes.
Quemin, A. (1994) 'L'espace des objets. Expertises et enchères à Drouot-Nord', *Genèse*, 17, 52–71.
Ravel, J. (1999) *The Contested Parterre. Public Theater and French Political Culture (1680–1791)*, Cornell.
Smith, C. (1989) *Auctions: the social construction of value*, London.
Talenti, S. (1999) 'Des hôtels aux immeubles', Szambien, W. and Talenti, S. (eds.), *Le Sentier Bonne-Nouvelle de l'architecture à la mode*, Paris, 101–108.
Wall, C. (1997) 'The English Auction: Narratives of Dismantlings', *Eighteenth-Century Studies*, 31:1, 1–25.
White, H.C. and White, C.A. (1992) *Canvases and careers: Institutional change in the French painting world*, Chicago.

CHAPTER 14

The Auction House and its Surroundings: the Trade in Antiques and Second-Hand Items in Paris during the Nineteenth Century

Manuel Charpy – University of Tours, CEHVI, France

14.1 Introduction

The vast quantity of inventories, drawn up following bankruptcies and deaths, documents little-known Parisian homes during the second half of the nineteenth century. Although public buildings favoured glass and iron, bourgeois homes were filled with knick-knacks and curios of different origins and periods. These interiors mirrored the city, to which led local and international routes. At their crossroads lay the auction house, as the *Journal Illustré* reminded its readers in 1866, reporting that 'everybody gathered there: buyers and sellers filled the place from whence was cleared off the great shambles that one calls Paris.'

The aim of this chapter is to show how the Parisian bourgeoisie, by the means of auction sales, fostered a new material and urban culture which was characterized in part by its passion for antiques (Rosselin and Julien, 2005). In regular or special sales, the range of items passing through the auction house of the Hôtel Drouot and its subsidiaries was considerable and eclectic: wines and spirits, coal, paintings, art items, curios, trinkets, antiques, furniture and tapestries. As early as 1830, and even more so after 1858 when the new saleroom was built, the place crowded with bourgeoisie, *amateurs*, antique dealers and interior decorators. The paths of Hôtel Drouot customers and auction goods revealed a new geography which was heterogeneous in its contents, mixing urban, imaginary and rustic dimensions. In the auction house, the desire for social distinction and the lure for imitation were aroused and a new conception of time and space took form: indeed, Drouot constituted the best place to observe the making of a new urban material culture.

14.2 The Quest for Time: Family Narratives and History

During the nineteenth century, whilst the department stores (with their luxury and semi-luxury industrial products) and the fixed-price stores experienced a well-known success story, the trade of antiques also flourished. Drouot and the antique dealers certainly benefited from a prosperous economy under the July Monarchy and again under the Second Empire, but between 1830 and 1850 they experienced a major commercial change as a new cultural trend emerged: the commerce in items from the past. As ancient times came into fashion and the aristocracy rejected industrial products, antiques offered a convenient way for their buyers to become part of history. By redecorating their brand new houses with remains from the past, the bourgeoisie found a way to acquire some nobleness and hide their recent social ascent. Coming from distant prehistoric times, the Renaissance or the eighteenth century, these items told stories that fulfilled the bourgeois picturesque and romantic imagination.

The novelty did not lie in the taste for vanished forms, but in that of authenticity: for items preserved from adulteration. The anxious Musset wrote in 1836: 'The apartments of the wealthy are cabinets of curios; the antique, the gothic, the taste for the Renaissance and the Louis XIII period, are all mixed together (...) so that we only thrive on wreckage, as if the end of the world were near' (Musset, 1838: 105–107). Half a century later, Paul Ginisty recorded the advent of this obsession: 'what a strangely modern cult, of which the altars [we]re boudoirs, in which higgledy-piggledy spread a pleasant and shimmering jumble of very old things (...). It is not in the past we have faith, it is in 'old-fashionedness', acquired at great expense!'. Anything made a collection: 'Posters, locks, walking sticks, murderers' autographs and skulls', as long as it was old (Ginisty, 1888: Preface). In 1843, the transformation of Du Sommerard's collection into the Museum of Cluny represented a decisive turning point; thereafter, the tiniest sign of the past, any prosaic or domestic item became an interesting witness of vanished times and found its way into the homes of the bourgeoisie.

From 1840 until the beginning of the twentieth century, the auction house was directly in the middle of this obsession. Since the eighteenth century, very different goods had been sold by auction: horses and old master paintings were traded this way, in addition to the various second-hand items that bankruptcies and judiciary sales dispersed. By the 1840s, however, the antique became the main trade, first in value and, later in the century, in quantity as well. In the 1858 building of the auctioneers' company, furniture, paintings, prints, tapestries, curios, art bibelots and trinkets met the desires of the bourgeoisie and the aristocracy who gathered there, for the place guaranteed the provenance of the items sold. In telling the items' stories in the catalogues and the salerooms, and in revealing their previous owners' names and the travels they had experienced, auctioneers fostered models for imaginary novels. Through the auction house and its antique dealers the bourgeoisie had a chance to acquire history – in the shape of the belongings of aristocratic families – and to experience in their apartments its ability to install a kind of vertigo.

Like the painter who sought local colour, the *amateur* looked for the unique in an industrial world where 'one f[ou]nd everywhere the same Lyons fabrics, the same fitted carpets, (...) the same bronzes produced by ten thousand copies, the same dazzling white bare ceilings' (Texier, 1852: 197). By contrast, the items gleaned at Drouot protected one against the accusation of bad taste and the perils of the industrial commonplace.

In nineteenth-century Paris, Drouot was the place where the early signs of numerous revivals were first felt. The craze for the neo-gothic, for instance, was consecrated there in the 1830s, as pieces of gothic architecture, religious and everyday items from the Middle Ages, in addition to garments and accessories which completed the wardrobes, were sold to a new generation who had developed a passion for the romantic and national styles (Caron, 1991). In the same way, the second half of the century favoured the Louis XV and Louis XVI styles. At the close of the century, the passion for Japanese and Chinese objects developed, thanks to Drouot Hotel (*Le Cabinet*, 2004). The auction house recorded the smallest fashion change and fostered it; there, old-fashioned and obsolete items were disposed of by the elite and, by the same means, the less wealthy had the opportunity to acquire rare things. During the 1840s, the Count of Mackau, *pair de France*, regularly sold and purchased large amounts of art curios at Drouot. Forty years later, the retired civil servant Dujardin sold parts of his collections of books and trinkets in order to purchase furniture to decorate his newly bought flat (Arch. Nat., AB/XIX/3496, Dujardin). At the end of the century, the writer and paleographer Eugène Aubry-Vitet went at least once a week to Hôtel Drouot to dispose of pieces of the very large antiques collection he had acquired during his lifetime (Arch. Nat., 572/AP/22, Aubry-Vitet). Meanwhile, Doctor Richelot sold a large number of Renaissance items to replace them with new ones and thus completed his collection in his mansion in Rocher Street (Arch. Nat., AB/XIX/4226, dossier nr. 1, Richelot).

In 1866, Victor Cochinat wrote about the auction house. He declared that: 'The love of change, the taste for novelty, the inconstancy of fashion, the desire for well-being, and the craze for luxury, are the common suppliers of this grand bazaar. Nearly all the furniture made in our most elegant cabinetmakers' workshops; all the hangings, the draperies, the fine fabrics from our most famous upholsterers; all the statues, statuettes, groups and oils that desert the studios of our best artists, will end up there, in that land of auctioneers' (*Le Journal Illustré*, 1866: 8). The auction house, which offered the possibility of buying and selling, let its clientele follow the trends and develop a passion for new collections. Moreover, the department stores, which created shorter fashion cycles, fed the Drouot's sales with new luxury items, more or less out of date.[1] In this way, bourgeois could find in Drouot old as well as new items.

For the old and the new, the auctioneers of the Hôtel Drouot proved to be essential middlemen. They offered individual customers a way to purchase old family paintings and, if required – as the merchant Mr. Asse did in the 1850s – to touch up the background to make it match with the family history (Arch. Dép. Paris, 2AZ/14). This is why antiques dealers and interiors decorators were useful auxiliaries: as they added patina, covered or fitted the furniture purchased at Drouot in order to redecorate the Paris apartments, they connected the public sales to the private interiors. As early as 1840, these artisans customised Renaissance chairs with springs and padding, and seventeenth-century Dutch chandeliers were fitted with gas burners. Around 1900, Doctor Richelot had 'electric chandeliers' made out of eighteenth-century faience and bits of Renaissance furniture: a triumph of antiques which covered the utmost modernity.[2]

The quest for the past could not be separated from the quest for authenticity which lay at the heart of collecting practices. Indeed, the fear of fakeness, which affected every nineteenth-century *amateur*, was highly justified. In the late 1860s, the journalist and dandy Nestor Roqueplan noticed that, at every turn, one ran into 'French history made out of wood, glass or porcelain'. 'Unless', the author wondered, 'one is to suppose that a France existed underground or in the air, where all monarchy's furniture would be stocked, (. . .) is it possible that all modern France could have been so entirely refurnished with items inherited from our forefathers in less than ten years (. . .)? The fact is that second-hand items are a tremendous industry' (Roqueplan, 1869: 167–168). In the manner of books of

1 See 'Warrants' and 'Soldes', série Actualité, BHVP.

2 As for Beaulieu, trader of 'curiosities, art ojects, restoration and furniture copies', Arch. Nat., AB/XIX/4226, dossier nr. 1.

savoir-faire aimed at the new bourgeoisie, handbooks – for example, those by Eudel (1884) and Bayard (1914) – helped the innocent to avoid buying forgeries. Fraud allegedly ran from slight reshaping down to complete copies. According to the 'Clunisian' method, an eighteenth-century 'console' became a table and an armchair a bench; the industry of the Faubourg Saint-Antoine was famous for recreating antique-like steel and wood by use of nitric acid, which ate into the wood epidermis, and permanganate, which tinted it. According to Eudel, in one of these antique furniture workshops, the wood was mechanically worm-eaten before it was assembled. From 1860 until the end of the century, the destruction of dwellings due to 'Haussmannian' works supplied the fake industry with used wood. Even prestigious collections held fraudulent items. Indeed Thiers' donation in 1881, in which fraud was patent, was quite embarrassing for the administrators of the Louvre. In 1912, the careful *amateur* Marcelle Tinayre noted that 'There [we]re some extremely costly living rooms that ha[d been] furnished with forgeries or copies' (Tinayre, 1912: 93–96). Early on, in order to avoid the swindle that was thought to be an urban invention, Parisians ventured further away, but soon the antiques craze created a new fake industry even there. Since not even a trip to the provinces guaranteed against fraud, Drouot was thought to be the only safe haven.

Auctioneers were state officers under the jurisdiction of the *Tribunal de Commerce* (Court of Trade), which gave them licence to practice. Dressed in black robes like judges, joined by bailiffs dressed in the *Ancien Régime* fashion, and armed with an ivory hammer from the 1830s, they ran the auction sales in the manner of a legal trial (Guyot and Raffalovitch, 1900–1901: '*Commissaires-priseurs*'). Their expertise was thus not just staged; it was also highlighted by an increasing number of experts, usually antique dealers, most of whom were appointed by the auctioneers themselves. Figures like Charles Manheim and Paul Féral dominated the second half of the century.[3] Involved in valuations and the writing of catalogues, they had authority in a world where fraud threatened society's credit. Thanks to such experts, the bourgeoisie, equipped with binoculars or magnifying glasses, could safely act like connoisseurs. Yet auctions did not, by themselves, prevent fraud; rather, they prevented its most devastating effects: indeed, insomuch as bids continued to rise, any forgery was collectively consented to, thus protecting the individual buyer from subsequent ridicule.

A number of publications constructed Drouot as a place of expertise. The *Journal des Commissaires-Priseurs*, launched in Paris in 1843, announced the forthcoming sales, commented on them and published their results. In this way, these publications created a public valuation. In 1858, as the building of the new Hôtel Drouot reached an end, the creation of the *Journal des Amateurs d'objets d'art et de Curiosité*, under the control of auctioneers and experts, strengthened the new sphere of information and expertise.

14.3 The Stock Market for Art and Emotions: the Fabric of Taste

In the auction house, built in 1833 on Place de la Bourse by the Chamber of Auctioneers, one could find paintings and curios, but also more and more collections of antique furniture. In the Hôtel des Jeûneurs, initially created for luxury items, 'boxes packed with

3 They were involved in a large number of auction sales, for instance those of auctioneer Pillet, Arch. Dép. Paris, D4E3/23 à 85, de 1850 à 1899.

jewels support[ed] scattered armour (. . .), artful clocks hid (. . .) less artistic paintings, mountains of old books [we]re covered with incomplete sets of old porcelain. (. . .) Its four shops [we]re full of enough curios to fill three to four provincial museums' (Texier, 1853: Chapter LXVII). The trade took off once the Grand Hôtel had been built in Drouot Street. The guides recommended it to travellers who wished to catch a glimpse of the *mode Parisienne*. In 1863, the *Guide Joanne* reported that: 'The attraction of exhibitions where can be seen nice paintings and furniture [and] all kinds of curios, the lively show that characterises the auctions, [and] the hope of making a good bargain demonstrate that the auction house is not only a bazaar busy with buyers, but also a continuous show for the idle rich.' The art and society press advertised and reported on the sales, revealing the buyers' names and their expenses.

The reputation of the auction house rested on its central urban location and on the way in which the building was organized. Advertisements emphasized that the house could be seen as a world in itself, in which each floor reflected the social strata: bourgeoisie, wealthy *amateur* collectors, antique dealers and upholsterers, *marchandes à la toilette* and travelling pedlars. Inside, items and clients were even more carefully separated from 1860s-1870s onwards: hygienist concerns encouraged the spatial separation of old items and real antiques, the latter thus being protected from the shady second-hand deals on the ground floor where 'it smell[ed of] an indescribable mixture of army barrack, hospital and omnibus office'. Everything was different on the first floor: 'one c[ould] mix with the elite of intellectual Parisian society and high-ranking foreigners. The remaining splendours of the burnt-down *Palais d'été* ha[d] passed through these rooms, as did the most famous collections (. . .) of statuettes, paintings, medals, weapons, prints, pottery, faiences, the finest and most rare furniture, (. . .) everything on which time had born the mark of curiosity and immortality'.[4] A journalist from *L'Illustration* gave the same description twenty years later: 'Do not think the composition of the public is the same in the different rooms. (. . .) It is easy to notice that on the ground floor, the crowd does not have the same background as that on the first floor, where [elite society from] Faubourg Saint-Germain and Faubourg Saint-Honoré fraternized with merchants in their shared love of curios and trinkets' (*L'Illustration*, 1898). The carefully maintained segregation of different types of customers and goods enabled the second-hand and antique trades to co-exist and strengthened the social success of Drouot.

Along with the success of the auction house grew the lure for new trading practices mainly characterised by their staged and Romantic qualities – most notably in the practice of bargaining in the manner of Orientals bazaars which were at times organised in department stores. Indeed, in the absence of production costs and set prices, the selling of items did not comply with any economic rationality.

In 1883, when Jules Claretie described the Hôtel as the '*Bourse de l'art et du bric-à-brac*' (Stock Market for Art and Bric-à-Brac) (Eudel, 1883: XVI), he highlighted that, inside Drouot, individual and private passions were collectively indulged and the mechanisms of imitation and distinction clearly displayed. A display of fine taste, crucial in 'the scale of sensory values' where the social and the cultural meet, was decisive in shaping purchasing practices (Corbin, 1990: 24). The final price paid for an item

4 See the entry '*Hôtel des ventes*' in *Le Grand Dictionnaire Universel du XIXe siècle* of Pierre Larousse. This description is commonplace: see Rochefort (1883); and Champfleury (1867).

FIGURE 14.1. View of Hôtel Drouot

SOURCE: Engraving from *L'Illustration*, 5 mars 1898, 184. Private collection M. Charpy.

gave a clear indication – more sensitive than elsewhere – of whether it was truly fashionable or not (Smith, 1989: 162–184). The fact that this price was fixed collectively and publicly gave the Drouot a dramatic touch. Furthermore, dealers and buyers went to Drouot to find pomp and fame. The room was set like a theatre stage: a platform, red velvet seats for the audience, carefully set gas, and, after 1880, electric light. A more solemn setting replaced the fine mess of eighteenth-century auction rooms. There, like at the theatre, romantic dramas were put on: wealth was dissolved or perhaps revealed by a sumptuous purchase. The romantic character of the place did not escape journalists or writers: let us remember how Madame Dambreuse and Frederic had felt first dread and then delight when they attended the auction sale of Madame Arnoux's furniture, carpets and trinkets (Flaubert, 1910: 591). On a lesser scale, the lower middle class also experienced the auction excitement.

Drouot was a place where reputations could be made: anyone organizing or putting up for sale a collection was given a publicity that no interior decorator could afford. Posters, luxury catalogues, chronicles in the society press, and annual chronicles helped *amateurs* and collectors acquire notoriety. After 1840, one can find many examples of how some collectors transformed their private passion into a public and urban action, and thus consecrated their character of patient and wise *amateur* (Guyot and Raffalovitch, 1900–1901: '*Collection*'). Whilst their utmost achievement lay in donating to a museum (Sauvageot, for instance, gave his antique faience collection to the Louvre in 1856), Drouot offered the opportunity to act as a real collector, whether prestigious or modest.

Another reason why the bourgeoisie flocked to Drouot was because it afforded free access to and handling of goods. The exhibition sessions offered a convenient way to learn good taste, in much the same way as going to a museum. Indeed, they were so important as a means by which the bourgeoisie might learn how to appreciate and 'sense' antiques that Octave Uzanne called Drouot the '*musée des Arts décoratifs*' (Eudel, 1888: Preface). *Paris Guide* agreed, reporting that: 'It is a museum, it is a library, it is a place where the display cabinets are incessantly garnished and emptied' (Burty, 1867: 949). In contrast with antique shops, items were labelled and, in addition to the catalogues, experts and auctioneers were present to give advice. In the manner of a social visit, one was allowed to touch the furniture of a room or an apartment. Indeed, the auction house invited its customers to safely stroll and make discoveries of their own.

Certain sales particularly attracted the bourgeoisie, as they formed models of fine taste and originality. This was the case when the goods of famous collectors were being sold. For instance, the crowd was so large at James Rothschild's sale that additional buildings had to be built for the occasion (Arch. Dép. Paris, D42E/3/25, Me Bedel). But numerous other examples could be mentioned: in the 1840s and 1850, the sales of de Pourtalès-Gorgier, de Ponthon d'Amécourt or, at the end of the century, de Spitzer. These sales symbolically meant privileged access to a collector's intimacy and therefore allowed those attending the sales to become part of a distinct society. Even *amateurs* and diplomats from London and Vienna ferreted about at the sales, often with a view to finding rarities dating back to the *Grand Siècle*. Wealthy and mobile customers, they also organised many auction sales themselves and helped therefore to diffuse the practice. American citizens, for want of history, also rushed to Drouot and to the provinces, fostering new interest in hitherto neglected items.

After 1840, one can distinguish those who were acknowledged by the bourgeoisie as 'legislators of fine taste', and, in first and foremost, the *bohèmes*. Romantic writers and painters who travelled around the 'old France' – that is, the provinces – invented a picturesque style which formed the basis for a growing enthusiasm for items from the past. The bourgeoisie of the second half of the century had its own herald: Victor Hugo. The defender of historical monuments and inventor of the Notre Dame became infatuated with romantic old items as early as 1830. 'He ha[d] been the very first', as Mirecourt recalled, 'to have us feel again the taste of beautiful historical furniture'. His apartment on *Place Royale*, was full of antiques: 'Dining room walls hung with *haute-lice* tapestry and full of antique chests (...) a splendid collection of old weapons that looked like it had been in use for the past twenty centuries (...) a red standard with golden embroidery, captured in 1830 from the Kasbah of Alger', a few old Sèvres pieces, and, star attraction to that historical travel, 'an arched stained-glass window' (Mirecourt, 1869: 16–20). Hugo acknowledged the crucial role of Drouot in this commerce: in 1852, he put his furniture on sale there, because of his 'leave' as it was advertised in the catalogue, and the bourgeoisie hurried to have a look at the famous writer's belongings.[5]

The *Bohèmes*, particularly painters, often fostered new trends by means of the auction house, as they frequently went there in order to refurnish their homes with antiques that gave them local colour and to inspire their historical paintings. Indeed,

5 *Catalogue d'un mobilier vendu pour cause de départ de M. Victor Hugo*, August 1852, Paris, Mannheim.

Figures 14.2–14.4. Auctions' bills, 1856, 1867, 1868

Source: Archives Départementales de Paris, D42E3.

the bourgeoisie was fascinated by the studios of painters whose artistically composed jumbles were easily viewed as models. Among them, Giraud's '*quartier Beaujon*' was quite remarkable: 'skeletons, bones and unusual musical instruments, strange daggers and weapons, harnesses, stirrups, saddles of all kinds' and all times met a real success among the 'elegant society' (Texier, 1852: 197). Chroniclers of society described thoroughly these mysterious and surprising interiors (for instance Gueullette, 1864). In 1887 Eudel concluded his '*chroniques de Drouot*' with descriptions of a few artists' studios – Bernier, Gérôme, Bouguereau, Detaille and his stuffed animals or Constant with his 'lovely *moucharabiehs*'[6] – and thus emphasised the connection between Drouot and the artists. When he described the home of Carolus Duran, whose first name was in itself a mark of the past, Eudel observed that 'hanging from the ceiling, a large eighteenth-century vase made of shiny copper [wa]s used as a chandelier' and everywhere one could see '*Chiraz* snatched from nomads' tents, and threadbare *Kourdistans*'. Twice a week, his studio – a few blocks away from Drouot – was packed with the bourgeois who had come to see items, some of which had just been purchased at Drouot (Eudel, 1888: 414). A sign of their role in fashion-making was the fact that the sales of artists' belongings, either on their own command or after their deaths, were always a great success. In the 1830s auctions were regularly held in private studios; yet once the new Hôtel Drouot had been built, spectacular sales were organised there instead. In 1859, society massed at Willems' sale to contemplate and buy 'art objects, antique furniture of Henri II's and Louis XIII's times, weapons, armour, tapestries, crockery, stain glass windows and old master paintings'. In 1860, Nestor Roqueplan, the brother of the painter Camille Roqueplan, summed up the new trend by noting that: 'all of a sudden, a generation of artists, inspired by literary revelations, had started a quest for remains from the past. Sculpted wood panels, bas-relief fragments, old brocade, ancient damask, anything they had come across in a pub, a farm, at the hearth of a cottage, had been hauled to decorate their studios (. . .). But that craze had seized every class (. . .). Items that had only been the subject of a study in the eyes of painters became part of the common furniture' (Roqueplan, 1869: 161–165). By 1880, 'stuffed lions', collections of 'oriental weapons', 'coleopterans' and 'Egyptian items' were successfully auctioned: evidence of a well-settled trend.[7]

By the middle of the century, another social group ruled over fashion-making: the *demi-mondaines*. During the 1840s, everyone hurried to the auctions that originated from their frequent financial misfortunes.[8] For instance, in February 1847, a bourgeoisie female crowd went to Mademoiselle Duplessis' home, on Madeleine Boulevard. Auctioneer Ridel presented there 'an elegant and rich set of furniture, made of marquetry, rose wood, carved woods and purple wood, curios, Sèvres and Sax's crockery, handsome bronzes, rich fireplace decorating, chests and caskets, trinkets of *Petit Dunkerque*, paintings, pastels, sketches and

6 A grid made with many turned pieces of wood, generally from Morocco.

7 See the auction sale of the painter Brisot de Warville (8° V 36/30688) 'Objets d'art et de curiosité, faïences anciennes, grès, verrerie, objets de vitrine, orfèvrerie, bijoux, bronzes de Mène, de Rosa Bonheur, de Barbedienne, cuivres du XVIe siècle, étains, armes orientales, instrument de musique, meubles anciens, tapisseries du XVIIe et XVIIIe siècle, ustensiles d'atelier garnissant l'atelier de feu M.Brisot de Warville, artiste peintre'; or that of 'Meubles et curiosités' of painter Pelouse (April 1893, Arch. Dép. Paris, D11E3).

8 Arch. Préf. de police, série BB1. Between 1856 and the 1870's, the police kept watch on *demi-mondaines*. More than six hundreds individual cases remain, retracing their movements and describing their apartments' furniture – taken as a sign of their lovers' wealth. For further information, see Larchey (1870) and Zola (1880).

FIGURE 14.5. Antique dealers' advertisements, 1890s

SOURCE: Advertisements published in *Le répertoire annuaire général des collectionneurs de la France et l'étranger* of Ris-Paquot (1892) and in *L'Annuaire de la curiosité et des Beaux-Arts* (1914). Private collection M. Charpy.

books'.[9] The novelist Dumas was there and used the auction sale as the opening scene of *La Dame aux Camélias* (Dumas, 1848: Chapter 1). Visitors, both male and female, gathered there because, '[if] there was indeed something high society ladies wanted to see: (. . .) it was those women's insides'. Auctioneers' archives and different auction catalogues of *demi-mondaines*' furniture confirm the craze of the bourgeoisie for those Romantic items. In 1865, for example, when Cora Pearl moved into her new apartment, 'every fashionable and elegant lady [was] invited to visit'.[10] Ten years later at Drouot, people fought for Miss Blackfort's furniture (Arch. Préf. de police, BB1, Blackfort). Paying attention to new trends and high society's auctions, Eudel reported the successful auction of 'a sumptuous set of furniture that garnished a magnificent mansion on Pereire Boulevard' which had belonged to Gabrielle-Elluini-Abel, a kept actress (Eudel, 1883: 161). By the end of the century, whilst the attraction of *demi-mondaines* faded away, the tragediennes' auction sales were still

9 Catalogue published by the auctioneer Ridel in February 1847 after the decease of Mademoiselle Plessis – her real name- it is kept at the Bibliothèque National de France.
10 Arch. Préf. de police, BB1, 1865, 'Cruch Emma dite Cora-Pearl, rue de Ponthieu'.

successful.[11] Indeed, the study of Drouot sales reveals a major change: after the disappearance of the royal court in 1830, the bourgeoisie found its fashion models amongst its social fringes (Martin-Fugier, 1990: 67–70).

14.4 Drouot, the City and its Peripheries: Geographies of the Antique Trade

The fashion for antiques left its mark on the city. Outside the apartments where furniture, tapestry, prints and stain-glass windows accumulated, antiques were also to be seen in the windows of shopping arcades, boulevards and fashionable districts. As early as the 1830s, the second-hand trade was pushed away to poorer wards or suburban areas. Up to that date, the French word *antiquaire* meant archaeologist, in particular those working in the provinces, whilst *brocanteurs* were second-hand dealers; from then on, *antiquaire* referred to antiquaries. The second important change occurred between 1850 and 1870, when second-hand and antique trades were distinguished, as the former became more specialised. The location of antiquarian shops changed accordingly: they concentrated in the IXth *arrondissement* and on the banks opposite the Louvre. There, noted Roqueplan, antiquaries were doing very well: 'horses and carriages stop[ped] at the[ir] entrance on Quai Voltaire' and 'well-mannered ladies, talking about Middle Ages (. . .) Renaissance and Rococo purchase[d] a gothic stall or a panel by Jean Goujon at high prices' (Roqueplan, 1869: 163). Trade directories of that period confirm that antiquaries concentrated on the south bank and on the boulevards, and it was in these areas where *amateurs* of art and antique items strolled.[12]

Antiquaries also settled in the new streets of the fashionable districts, where the fresh white walls in the new homes of the bourgeoisie who had just moved in invited antique furnishings. In those shops, Occidental and Oriental antiques, including 'late fifteenth-century gothic marquetry chests decorated with rosettes, sixteenth-century oak credence, late sixteenth-century oak caskets with caryatid ornaments, fifteenth-century ceiling panels' advertised the transformation of Haussmann mansions into Renaissance homes.[13] At the same time, *brocanteurs* settled near the industrial district of Faubourg Saint-Antoine. There, hopeful *amateurs* went to secure a bargain in shops which sold bric-a-brac, jumbling up 'two globes, an Italian marquetry chest, a sketch by Tiepolo without a frame, a golden Louis XV-style pendulum', some worm-eaten furniture and tapestry pieces.[14]

The trade in antiques, scattered across the boulevards and the riverside, had its own headquarters: the auction house. In its rooms, *amateur* collectors and merchants mixed with antiquaries and interior decorators. The success of the furniture auctions grew around 1830 because of the craze for antique. As early as 1833, the Chamber of Auctioneers had a

11 See the catalogue 'Livres, autographes, gravures, dessins, tableaux, meubles et curiosités provenant de Mademoiselle George, tragedienne, (. . .) et dont la vente aura lieu à Drouot salle n°8', Paris, Baugé (M. et L.), January 1903.

12 See Fournel, 1858: 261–263. Beside Bottin-Didot's directory, see *Le répertoire annuaire général des collectionneurs de la France et de l'étranger*, published by Ris-Paquot in 1892 and *L'Annuaire de la curiosité, des Beaux-Arts et de la Bibliothèque* by Campbell.

13 Arch. Dép. Paris, Bankruptcy of Mademoiselle Lagleize, 'Marchande d'Antiquités, 12 bd Malesherbes', D11U3 /937, dossier nr. 6938, 1879. She worked with auctioneer Oudard and the famous antiquaries Oppenheim and Bing. See also 'Inventaire de James Duhamel, antiquaire, cité Gaillard', D11U3/1175 dossier nr. 17120, 1885.

14 Arch. Dép. Paris, Boursier, 'brocanteuse-antiquaire', 57 boulevard Beaumarchais, D11U3/1778 nr. 4848, 1899.

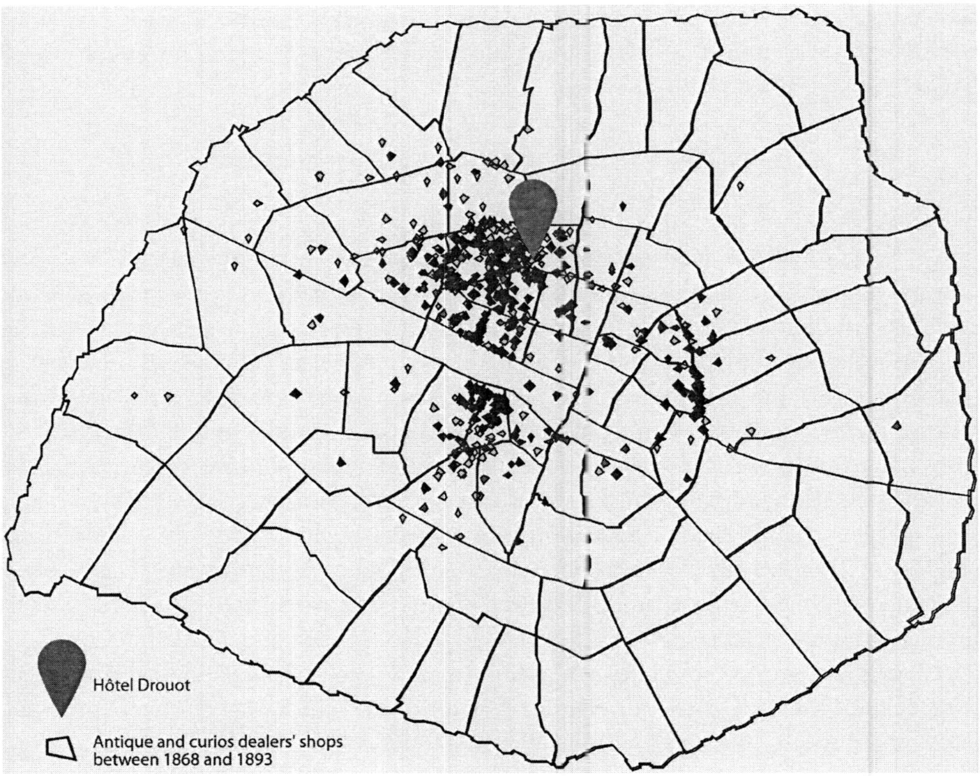

Map 14.1. Antique's geography. Hotel Drouot and curios and antiques dealers' shops between 1868 and 1893

Source: Data from *Annuaires Bottin-Didot* (1868, 1876 and 1893) and *Le répertoire annuaire général des collectionneurs de la France et l'étranger* (1892). Plotting by M. Charpy.

house built on Place de la Bourse. There one could find not only paintings and curios, but also more and more collections of historical items, curios, furniture and tapestries, even if that trade suffered from competition with Hôtel des Jeûneurs (Texier, 1853: Chapitre LXVII). The antique trade grew further once the auctioneers moved into Drouot Street, where they gathered all their auction salerooms in one place. Located just behind the Opéra, in one of the areas that was being completely reshaped, not far from the Louvre and the artists' quarter, the new auction house was opened in 1858. And, of course, it benefited from its very convenient location. The Hôtel Drouot was not just a building: at a local level, it organised the trade of antiques; at a district level, it formed the locus of antique dealers and upholsterers, attracted by supply convenience and customers. On a city scale, the influence of Hôtel Drouot continued growing during the second half of the century. Its large number of subsidiaries, up to six, in addition to advertising posters, provided Drouot with much notoriety all over the city.

Meanwhile, the *amateurs*-collectors desirous of finding rare items had to travel off the beaten track. The less brave hired antiquaries to travel around the country, whilst the more adventurous travelled in person beyond the city walls. In the nineteenth century, there was a notion that the provinces were somehow older than Paris. Accordingly, trespassing

Paris' enclosure meant the breaking into another spatio-temporal dimension (Corbin, 1992). From this idea a trade originated, according to which the provinces became Paris' attic. Outside the city centre at the core of modernity, the *faubourgs* and outer suburbs were thought to be exploratory lands of another age. As provincial people were imagined as lying beyond the capital's craze for antiques, a Parisian might be able to achieve the best bargains or, at least, find items preserved from the dawn of time still in use.

From 1830 onwards, the *brocanteurs* visited castles, churches and suburban chapels in order to collect items that would be sold to the antiquaries or to Drouot. Rémonencq, a *brocanteur* in Balzac's *Cousin Pons*, went '*chiner* in the suburbs of Paris': in a technical sense, *chiner*, which means to seek and collect worn-out items, is derived from the word *s'échiner*, meaning to work to death (Balzac, 1848: Chapter XXIX). It originally had connections with the suburbs, but, at the end of the century and following the craze for exotic items, it had become synonymous with looking for Chinese objects. Just outside Paris, second-hand dealers, who had been driven from the city, had found refuge in the *non aedificandi* areas like Montreuil, Clignancourt, Vanves, and Kremlin-Bicétre: they attracted a few *amateurs* expecting to dig up authentic curios that had ended up in those picturesque places. Further away, thanks to trains and later cars, the whole suburban area became an exploratory playground. At the end of the century, Madeleine, an enlightened bourgeoise – the main character of a novel by Marcelle Tinayre – recounted a curios-seeking session: 'We started from the fine shops on the riverside where arty merchants [and] erudite archaeologists looked like Institute applicants. And we finished the tour in bric-a-brac stores in Plaisance, in dark and stinking shops (. . .) no matter the spiders and the dust, no matter the stench in the shops (. . .). I got back that feverish feeling that I love, the pleasure of chasing around and discovering, the feeling that passionate collectors prefer to any other feeling (. . .). So much money expended for such lovely old things!' (Tinayre, 1912: 92).

Gradually, interest in the suburbs extended into the provinces. Whereas the second-hand dealer in *Cousin Pons* went beyond the city walls to *chiner*, Romantic novelists, looking for local colour, travelled the roads of the country to collect 'the ruins of old France' (Parsis-Barubé, 2008, 271–292). Local places, as Thierry Gasnier has argued, had become 'territories of the particularities' (Gasnier, 1997: 3423). Against the industrialised city stood a representation of an ageless and picturesque France: a rustic and soothing destination to which fled those affected by modern and corrupting city life. Learned societies of antiquaries paved the way for archaeology, as they fostered the trade of antiques. Fascinated with aristocratic castles as much as peasants' homes, the bourgeois brought souvenirs back from trips to the country and the past. As fraud threatened even at Drouot, many a person attended auction sales in the provinces – Lisieux, Rouen or Dijon – with the hope of finding items untouched by Parisian fashions or trade. In its quest for authenticity, the Paris bourgeoisie went so far as getting away from sales altogether and instead visited castles, churches and farms which formed museums of the past.

Parisians on holiday in the spas of Normandy and Brittany ventured to villages in order to glean antiques whose discovery and purchase involved, in themselves, imperishable remembrances. The road between Paris and Rouen became a pilgrimage for those seeking antiques. Flaubert, who set the narrative of his *Bouvard et Pécuchet* in Normandy in 1860, had his two main characters enjoy that experience. Ecstatic about a mail coat or a stoup shaped like a druid pot, the two Parisians discovered a soup tureen, a 'family item' that 'inspire[d] them with the taste for faiences and which formed a new subject of study and travel into the countryside' at a time when 'the high society was looking for old Rouen dishes' (Flaubert, 1881).

Drouot sales recorded this trend: items from the provincial aristocracy – hunting trophies, saddles, armour and faiences bearing the coat of arms of a family – were successfully auctioned. Drouot was also the place where provincial architectural monuments were sold in parts. The Renaissance Montal castle, in Haut Quercy, for instance, was stripped of its 'main sculptures', of its 'inner courtyard and of several large chimneys'. They were sold on the Clichy Boulevard and at Drouot (Eudel, 1882: Introduction).

The quest for the picturesque included the most commonplace things: bread bins, Normandy cupboards, yokes and other farming tools. 'The antiquary-traveller and the erudite tourist', Roqueplan wrote in 1869, 'roam farms and villages, go inside peasants' homes, always preoccupied with the Middle Ages and the Renaissance, and buy chests from Brittany or Normandy credences that they consider precious inheritances and proudly bring back to Paris' (Roqueplan, 1869: 167–168).

This fashion fostered a prosperous industry in Paris because, in antiquaries' shops, a common sideboard from Normandy was priced as much as a Louis XVI furniture. Indeed, 'with a hard scrubbing brush [artisans] soften[ed] selected sharp angles (…); they [made] up ancient filth with a mix of water and mud (…). These simple fakes, made up in the Batignoles quarter, c[ould] be found everywhere in the spas of Normandy or Brittany, and particularly in farms. (. . .) Peasants [we]re essential to the supply of authenticity and the picturesque' (Eudel, 1884: 132 and Warnod, 1914). In people's minds, provincial dealers and peasants ignored the value of their belongings and would therefore never cheat. Marcelle Tinayre, once she had denounced the Paris fraud, could write that: 'above all, I like old country dealers in love with their curios (. . .). In their shops nothing is cheap but nothing is fake' (Tinayre, 1912: 93).

It was very tempting for the curious and the *amateur* to go further back in time and experience the excitement of prehistoric times. In the ploughed fields, the amateurs looked for the Gallo-Romans and prehistoric fragments that ended up on the shelves of Parisian apartments. Émile Bayard, *inspecteur* (controller) for the Fine Arts, also noted that 'one has managed to copy the slightest deteriorations from the most distant times' (Bayard, 1914: 66), on items that were to be found at Drouot.

In addition to the trade of provincial curios, the quest for authenticity lay also in exotic items. This trade was not new in the middle of nineteenth century, but until 1850 these crafts were more often taken apart, reassembled and imitated than acquired in their original form. Yet the *chineurs* were only interested in authenticity. To rescue puzzled *amateurs*, historians were required. What was to be chosen among the wave of new objects coming to Paris from across the globe: Slavonic tunics or pottery; items from Algeria or Maghreb that were appreciated as early as 1830; poisoned spears, shields, animal skins or statuettes that came from Saint-Louis of Senegal; war clothing shipped from Tonkin; pre-Colombian terracotta from a time when America ignored everything about Europe? Whilst going beyond the city walls was like moving back in time, trespassing the western European borders abolished chronology. Antiquaries and experts like Manheim organised great auctions sales of 'antiques from all over the world' from the late 1850s onwards.

Pieces from Greek statues and Roman bronzes were well located inside Drouot. For around one hundred francs, Parisians could purchase a piece of humanity's history. Egyptian antiques sales drew also large crowds, even though quite a number of mummies came from the Grand-Montrouge suburb (Bayard, 1914: 66). After 1860, Constantinople was the place to find antique weapons such as Bulgarian sabres and Albanian guns. Yet Turkish gunsmiths, as Eudel reported, made antique weapons from all over the world 'in the open air': weapons 'that Westerners hung like trophies up their walls' and that were sold by any antiquary or at Drouot (Eudel, 1884: 347). Pre-Colombian items were also very popular after 1860 – a trade fostered by the French campaign to Mexico (Eugène Boban, 1878; Rivial (2001), 351–362 and Bibliothèque Nationale de France, NAF 21476–21479).[15] Between 1880 and 1900, it was the 'heavily decorated porcelains and faiences, art bronzes and furniture from Japan, China or Tonkin, cloisonné-enamel, antique wooden sculpture originated from a pagoda, ironwood furniture, folding screens, luxury tapestry, fabrics, sets of clothes, ivories, lacquers, weapons, music instruments' that drew the masses to Drouot.[16]

Every fashion, even from remote places, was celebrated at Drouot. Paris *amateurs* considered the world, from the closest suburbs to the Far East, as a vast bazaar. Yet the attraction of authenticity encouraged fraud at an industrial scale, as the desire for *couleur locale* led the way to a massive delocalisation of the objects in an 'utopian game of space' supported by the migration of images (Marin, 1973). From a Parisian point of view, the world was like a large tank full of narratives and signs from the past; the auction house was its antechamber.

14.5 Conclusion

The new material culture, mainly defined by the circulation of signs in space, can be thus analysed by tracing items and *amateurs* and collectors in apartments, shops, at Drouot and on their journeys within and outside the city. Right in the middle, the auction house structured a new geography, both real and imaginary, by which the nineteenth-century bourgeoisie had a conversation with the past. It was a place for society, where the artisans of taste – artists, *demi-mondaines* and foreigners – were on show, prices set and new trends celebrated, and was thus central to the making of Parisian bourgeois taste. Beyond the Drouot building, many newspapers and reviews diffused information about items, prices and this passion for curios and authenticity, making, in this way, a new field of fashion and expertise, essential for a bourgeoisie who looked for cultural models. In a world where social rises were new and fast, objects from the past reassured and consolidated the new bourgeoisie. Running away from industry and urbanity, the Parisian bourgeoisie withdrew to its apartments but also into the past. The Hôtel-Drouot gave the opportunity to answer to that twofold desire, offering some necessarily authentic, highly picturesque and romantic pieces of history.

15 In Paris, Eugène Boban contributed to spread around that new trend with his 'Comptoir d'archéologie préhistorique' and his various catalogues. See Rivial (2001), 351–362, and above all his archives (Bibliothèque Nationale de France, NAF 21476–21479).

16 See for example the sale of 'collection de M. Tanaka le jeudi 26 février 1891, commissaire-priseur Me Coulon', Paris, Bloche, 1891.

Bibliography

Primary Sources

Unpublished sources

Archives Nationales [Arch. Nat.], AB/XIX/3496, Accounts Family Dujardin et Bernard.
Arch. Nat. 572/AP/22, comptes d'Aubry-Vitet, années 1890–1910.
Arch. Nat. AB/XIX/4226, dossier n°1, 1883–1914. Archives privées du Docteur Richelot
Archives Départementales de Paris [Arch. Dép. Paris], 2AZ/14, Comptabilité du marchand de couleurs Asse.
Arch. Dép. Paris, D4E3/23–85, from 1850 to 1899, Me Pillet.
Arch. Dép. Paris, D42E/3/25, Me Bedel.
Arch. Dép. Paris, D11U3 /937, file nr. 6938, 1879. Bankruptcy of Mademoiselle Lagleize, 'Marchande d'Antiquités, 12 bd Malesherbes'.
Arch. Dép. Paris, D11U3/1175 file nr. 17120, 1885, 'Inventaire de James Duhamel, antiquaire, cité Gaillard'.
Arch. Dép. Paris, D111E3, April 1893, 'Meubles et curiosités' of painter Pelouse.
Arch. Préf. de Police, BB1, about demi-mondaines between 1856 and 1875; see, in particular Miss Blackfort's file.
Bibliothèque des Arts décoratifs, Collection Maciet. *Le cabinet des merveilles de Monsieur Maciet*, Paris, 2004.
Bibliothèque historique de la Ville de Paris [BHVP], 'Warrants' and 'Soldes', série Actualité.
Bibliothèque Nationale de France, département des manuscripts, NAF 21476–21479, 'archives privées de Eugène Boban, antiquaire'.

Published sources

Auction catalogues:
Catalogue des livres, autographes, gravures, dessins, tableaux, meubles et curiosités provenant de Mademoiselle George, tragédienne, (...) et dont la vente aura lieu Hôtel Drouot, salle nr. 8, le samedi 31 janvier 1903, Paris, 1903.
Objets d'art et de curiosité, faïences anciennes, grès, verrerie, objets de vitrine, orfèvrerie, bijoux, bronzes de Mène, de Rosa Bonheur, de Barbedienne, cuivres du XVIe siècle, étains, armes orientales, instrument de musique, meubles anciens, tapisseries du XVIIe et XVIIIe siècle, ustensiles d'atelier garnissant l'atelier de feu M. Brissot de Warville, artiste peintre, Paris, 1875.
Catalogue d'un mobilier vendu pour cause de départ de M. Victor Hugo, August 1852, Paris, Mannheim, 1852.
Collection de M. Tanaka le jeudi 26 février 1891, commissaire-priseur Me Coulon, Paris, 1891.
Balzac, H. de (1848) *Le cousin Pons*, Paris.
Bayard, É. (1914) *L'art de reconnaître les fraudes*, Paris.
Boban E. (1878), *Catalogue du Comptoir d'archéologie préhistorique, Eugène Boban, antiquaire, 35 rue du Sommerard, près le musée de Cluny*, Paris.
Collection Maciet. *Le cabinet des merveilles de Monsieur Maciet*,à la Bibliothèque des Arts décoratifs, 2004.
Burty, P. (1867) 'L'Hôtel des ventes et le commerce des tableaux', *Paris-Guide*, Paris.
Champfleury, (1867) *L'Hôtel des commissaires-priseurs*, Paris.
Cochinat V., 'L'Hôtel Drouot', *Le Journal Illustré*, n° 116, 29 avril au 6 mai 1866, 7–8.
Dumas, A. (1848) *La dame aux camélias*, Paris.
Eudel, P. (1882) *L'hôtel Drouot en 1881*, Paris.

Eudel, P. (1884) *Le truquage: les contrefaçons dévoilées*, Paris.
Eudel, P. (1888) *L'hôtel Drouot et la curiosité en 1886–1887*, Paris.
Flaubert, G. (1881) *Bouvard et Pécuchet*, Paris.
Flaubert, G. (1910 [1869]) *L'Éducation sentimentale, œuvres complètes*, Paris.
Fournel, V. (1858) *Ce qu'on voit dans les rues de Paris*, Paris.
Ginisty, P. (1888) *Le dieu bibelot*, Paris.
Gueullette, Ch. (1864) *Les ateliers de peinture en 1864, visite aux artistes*, Paris.
Guyot, Y. and Raffalovitch, A. (1900–1901) *Dictionnaire du commerce de l'industrie et de la Banque*, Paris.
Larchey, L. (1870) 'Comptes d'un budget parisien, toilette et mobilier d'une élégante de 1869', *Documents pour servir à l'histoire de nos mœurs*, Paris.
Larousse P., '*Hôtel des ventes*' in *Le Grand Dictionnaire Universel du XIXe siècle*, 1873.
Mirecourt, E. de (1869) *Victor Hugo*, Paris.
Montheuil, A. (1898) 'L'hôtel des ventes', *L'Illustration*, 5 mars 1898, 180–188.
Musset, A. de (1938[1836]) *La confession d'un enfant du siècle, in Œuvres en prose*, Paris.
Rochefort, H. (1883) *Les petits mystères de l'hôtel des ventes*, Paris.
Roqueplan, N. (1869) *La vie Parisienne. Regain*, Paris.
Texier Ed. (1852–1853), 'L' Hôtel des ventes et le timbre' and 'Les Habitations modernes', in *Tableau de Paris*, Paris.
Tinayre, M. (1912) *Madeleine au miroir, Journal d'une femme*, Paris.
Warnod, A. (1914) *La brocante et les petits marchés de Paris*, Paris.
Zola, E. (1880) *Nana*, Paris.

Literature

Benjamin, W. (1986) *Paris capitale du XIXe siècle. Le livre des passages*, Paris.
Bernhardt, S. (2000 [1907]), *Ma double vie*, Paris.
Caron, J.-C. (1991) *Générations romantiques: les étudiants de Paris et le Quartier latin, 1814–1851*, Paris.
Corbin, A. (1990) 'Histoire et anthropologie sensorielle', *Anthropologie et sociétés*, 14, 13–24.
Corbin, A. (1992) 'Paris-province', Nora, P. (ed.), *Les lieux de mémoire. Les France: conflits et partages*, Paris, 777–823.
Gasnier, T. (1997) 'Le local', *Lieux de Mémoires*, vl. 3, Paris.
Guichard, Ch. (2005) *Les amateurs d'art à Paris dans la seconde moitié du XVIIIe siècle*, thèse sous la direction de Dominique Poulot, Paris-I Panthéon-Sorbonne.
Marin, L. (1973) *Utopiques jeux d'espaces*, Paris.
Martin-Fugier, A. (1990) *La vie élégante ou la formation du tout-Paris, 1815–1848*, Paris.
Parsis-Barubé, O. (2004) 'Bouvard, Terninck et Pécuchet. Des formes de l'amateurisme et du statut d'expert dans la pratique archéologique au XIXe siècle', *Regards sur l'histoire du Nord-Pas-de-Calais*, Artois Presses Université, 65–85.
Parsis-Barubé, O. (2008) 'Le discours sur l'apparence des populations autochtones dans le processus d'invention de la couleur locale par les voyageurs français du premier XIXe siècle', Paresys I., *Paraî tre et apparences du Moyen Âge à nos jours*, Lille, 271–292.
Rivial, P. (2001) 'Eugène Boban ou les aventures d'un antiquaire au pays des américanistes', *Journal de la Société des Américanistes*, 87, 351–362.
Pomian, K. and Laurens, A.-F. (1992) *L'anticomanie: la collection d'antiquités aux XVIIIe et XIXe siècles*, Paris.
Pomian, K. (1996) *Collectionneurs, amateurs et curieux, Paris, Venise: XVIe-XVIIIe siècle*, Paris.
Rosselin, C. and Julien, M.-P. (2005) *La culture matérielle*, Paris.
Smith, Ch. (1989) *Auctions: the Social Construction of Values*, New York.